PRAISE FOR *ON TO CHICAGO*

James Rogan's novel is a political classic. Not only does he deal with one of the most interesting "what ifs" in history, but also he presents a fascinating and accurate account of the tumultuous 1968 campaign of the presidency. Five stars!

—JULIE NIXON EISENHOWER AND DAVID EISENHOWER, BESTSELLING AUTHORS OF *PAT NIXON* AND *EISENHOWER AT WAR: 1943-1945*

For me, reading On to Chicago brought back a very painful memory, yet in the pain I also found a healing when thinking about how it could have turned out differently. Jim Rogan brings Bobby Kennedy and the other presidential candidates from 1968 back to life, and he balances their political throat-cutting and caring sides so we can know them. Best of all, this story gave me a look into a future that was taken from us 50 years ago. I'm not much of a bookworm, but in my humble opinion this is worth the read. Thanks to Mr. Rogan for opening this door to what might have been.

—JUAN ROMERO, THE TEENAGE HOTEL BUSBOY WEARING THE WHITE MESS JACKET IN THE ICONIC PHOTOGRAPH OF HIM KNEELING ALONGSIDE AND AIDING SENATOR ROBERT KENNEDY SECONDS AFTER THE BULLETS STRUCK

There are two kinds of writers who tell the story of the 1968 Democratic presidential primary… The first and largest group take the lofty view that the passion for change that briefly swept the country in '68 was an illusion or chimera, and that Nixon was the logical and destined American winner all along. The second, smaller group, contends that the United States was on the brink of momentous change that summer, a feeling that seized upon the candidacies of McCarthy and Kennedy and was on its way to bringing about something very new—when it crashed against the rare coincidence of Bobby's assassination, Gene McCarthy's withdrawal, and the dulling re-appearance of business as usual. But there was that moment, when people all over the country were talking about what was right and wrong in politics on the assumption that things could change, and that we could begin to live up to our basic American values—and that created a very different mood which we have struggled ever since to recapture. Interesting to me that Jim Rogan saw this same thing from the viewpoint of a conservative Republican, while I described it, in Nobody Knows, from (roughly) the Democratic Left. Since then, we've both grown a bit more skeptical. But those of us who were there cannot deny what we felt was happening.

—JEREMY LARNER
1968 CAMPAIGN SPEECHWRITER FOR EUGENE MCCARTHY;
AUTHOR, *NOBODY KNOWS: REFLECTIONS ON THE 1968 MCCARTHY CAMPAIGN*; SCREENWRITER, *THE CANDIDATE*, 1972
OSCAR FOR BEST ORIGINAL SCREENPLAY

I was a teenager when my father ran for president in 1968, and I vividly remember the excitement of being a first-hand eyewitness to history. Jim Rogan has taken one of our nation's most tumultuous and interesting presidential elections and made it even more compelling. Every page makes you wonder how history might have changed with just the slightest twist of fate.

—GEORGE WALLACE, JR.

James Rogan has written a fast-moving account, part-fact, part-fiction, of political events in 1968 based on the premise that Robert Kennedy survived rather than succumbed to Sirhan Sirhan's shooting of him in June of that year. He captures and times and characters well.

—TED VAN DYK,
SENIOR AIDE TO VICE PRESIDENT HUBERT H. HUMPHREY, 1968

What if Bobby Kennedy had survived the assassin's bullet? Jim Rogan's riveting, meticulously researched work imagines the answer to that question in vivid detail—while taking you on a heart-stopping ride through a fascinating-to-contemplate alternative history of the tumultuous 1968 presidential election. This stunningly provocative tour de force puts America on a completely different trajectory, leading to a radically different set of cascading events. You will be spellbound.

—MONICA CROWLEY, PHD,
FOX NEWS CONTRIBUTOR; FORMER AIDE TO RICHARD NIXON

The 1968 Presidential campaign produced far more real-life volatility and heart-pounding suspense than most Americans wanted. On to Chicago moves the excitement needle even higher—portraying Bobby Kennedy as surviving both the actual attempt on his life, and then LBJ's attempt to end his political life. Jim Rogan is a master storyteller with a perfect ear and encyclopedic knowledge of politics that captures the high-level deal-making and breaking of that tense time of crisis. This book kept me up way too late for two nights, and I can't wait to see who they will cast for the major roles in the movie!

—CALIFORNIA GOVERNOR PETE WILSON,
FORMER CAMPAIGN AIDE TO RICHARD NIXON

THE NOTES

BY JAMES ROGAN

"DEAR PRESIDENT TRUMAN"
(*American Heritage*, 1994; *Readers Digest*, 1995)

MY BRUSH WITH HISTORY
(Contributor, 2001)

ROUGH EDGES
My Unlikely Road from Welfare to Washington
(2004)

CATCHING OUR FLAG
Behind the Scenes of a Presidential Impeachment
(2011)

'AND *THEN* I MET...'
Stories of Growing Up, Meeting Famous People, and
Annoying the Hell Out of Them
(2014)

ON TO CHICAGO
Rediscovering Robert F. Kennedy and the Lost Campaign of 1968
(2018)

SHAKING HANDS WITH HISTORY:
My Encounters with the Famous, the Infamous, and the
Once-Famous but Now-Forgotten
(2020)

THE NOTES
A Researcher's Guide to *On to Chicago* and the
1968 Presidential Campaign
(2021)

THE NOTES

A RESEARCHER'S GUIDE TO

ON TO CHICAGO AND THE

1968 PRESIDENTIAL CAMPAIGN

* * *

Compiled and Edited by

James Rogan

SHENANDOAH
PRESS

THE NOTES

Library of Congress Control Number: 2021917183

Hardcover ISBN: 978-1-956033-04-5
Paperback ISBN: 978-1-956033-03-8
ebook ISBN: 978-1-956033-02-1

Book designed by Mark Karis
Printed in the United States of America

For Dana and Claire

CONTENTS

AUTHOR'S INTRODUCTION TO *THE NOTES*

While writing my fourth book, *On to Chicago: Redis-covering Robert F. Kennedy and the Lost Campaign of 1968*, I had no idea that I was inventing a new literary genre.

Released on the 50th anniversary of Kennedy's assassination,[a] *On to Chicago* told the story (through historical fiction) of what likely would have happened in the 1968 presidential election had Bobby Kennedy survived the gunshots that felled him the night that he won the California primary, and then had gone on to finish his campaign.

---

a   June 6, 2018.

During my research and writing, I followed the evidence (an instinct developed from nearly 40 years as a lawyer and judge) and avoided the temptation of creating a finale based on emotion or wishful thinking. As validation for my presentation, the completed work had 1,000 fully sourced endnotes (400 additional pages) appended to a 500-page book.

I never anticipated the problems I had created by taking a fact-based approach to penning historical fiction. When I submitted the final draft for consideration, prospective publishers told me that in their world a book must be either *fiction* or *non-fiction*—there is no middle ground. They remained perplexed by a "historical fiction" book with hundreds of additional pages proving that almost everything portrayed in my work either happened, was based on something that had happened, or would likely have happened. "It's a very compelling book," one told me. "With the 50th anniversary of RFK's death approaching, the story is timely and it's well written. I just don't know how to market it. *It's fiction, but it's not fiction? What do I do with that?*"

"When you write historical fiction," another explained, "you're supposed to pick a period in history, let a couple of famous characters from that era make brief guest appearances in the story to flavor it, but it's supposed to be *fiction*. You've broken all the rules of the genre. I loved the book, but...." He suggested that I delete all the endnotes and just pretend that the book was pure fiction so that it would fit into his industry's template.

Beyond this pushback, an unanticipated legal hurdle popped up. Standard publishing contracts require an author to certify that the manuscript is either "fiction" or "nonfiction." There is no hybrid option available, nor are explanations invited (e.g., *"It's nonfiction— until the protagonist gets shot and survives, and then it morphs into fiction, except that most of the story, even after the shooting, is chiefly fact-based nonfiction."*).

And so it went.

My previous publisher at WND Books, founder Joseph Farah, enjoyed the story so much that he ended these frustrating discussions by accepting the challenge even though WND had never before handled *any* fiction, historical or otherwise. However, his decision to publish came with a caveat: we must exclude the notes from the print version of the book. "I can't publish a second volume filled with a bunch of endnotes," he said. "It's not commercially feasible." As a compromise, WND created a dedicated website with all of the notes posted on the Internet, and we promoted the website in the book's first trade edition.

A year or so later, WND sold off their book publishing enterprise, and the new owner let the dedicated website lapse. To keep the notes available for scholarly use, I uploaded them to my own site (www.jamesrogan.org). That solved the problem for now, but at some point this page will disappear after future technology makes the Internet obsolete (or after I keep my inevitable rendezvous with eternity). Either way, the monumental research that went into compiling, editing, and organizing these notes would be lost if I relied on the worldwide web to preserve them. To ensure that the scholarship behind *On to Chicago* endures, I am publishing the endnotes in this separate volume. As Joseph Farah suggested, it would be folly to expect any financial profit from this project. My only expected "royalty" payment will come from knowing that future researchers and historians might find these notes useful when studying the 1968 election.

This compilation, standing alone, tells the complete saga, albeit in piecemeal fashion, of the candidates and the history of that presidential campaign. One could read *The Notes* and absorb a comprehensive overview of both. However, to enjoy the complete experience, I suggest that you place this volume on a nearby table as you read *On to Chicago*. If you run across a scene or a claim in the novel that you find unbelievable or unlikely, use *The Notes* for confirmation. Look up the corresponding chapter endnote(s) attached to the narrative, and you will see how much of my "historical fiction" mirrored reality. Who knows? A hundred years from now, this book might be a collector's item—if my newly invented genre of *nonfiction fiction* catches on.

Bring along your imagination while reading *On to Chicago* in combination with *The Notes*, and all three will transport you back to the most epic battle in modern political history.

—J.R.

ORANGE COUNTY, CALIFORNIA, 2021

ORIGINAL PREFACE TO

ON TO CHICAGO (2018)

A few quick points before we begin our excursion back to 1968.

First: a present-day reflection. In late summer 2015, at the initial debate of the 2016 Republican presidential candidates, the Fox News network crammed the 17 declared candidates onto two stages. Polls showed that 15 of these would-be presidents registered single-digit or zero in name recognition. Of the two dozen contenders in both parties, even the most energetic of political junkies would have struggled to pick out most of them in a police lineup.

This was not always the case.

The 1968 presidential election was—and remains—spellbinding, because the contestants in that sweepstake were not pygmies: they were titans. No single-digit combatants met on that battlefield. Fifty years later, we still know them: Nixon, Reagan, Johnson, Kennedy, Rockefeller, McCarthy, Humphrey, Wallace, Romney. Most had spent decades on the national scene, and each left their imprint on the major issues of their day.

Although we recognize their names, a dwindling number of us witnessed their epic clash. I was a ten year-old boy in 1968; now I'm over 60, which means that most contemporary readers have no personal memory of the 1968 presidential campaign. To help those latecomers, you will find included brief biographical sketches of the nine major candidates in 1968 (Appendix A), a chronology of the actual 1968 presidential campaign history (Appendix B), and a brief backgrounder on why America fought in Vietnam (Appendix C). The latter is important because, as a trio of historians noted, writing about the 1968 campaign and leaving out the Vietnam War is like explaining Hamlet and leaving out the murdered king.[a]

Second: I exercise my author's prerogative to make a few personal observations about a leading protagonist in this story, Senator Robert F. Kennedy. Growing up in San Francisco in the 1960s in a blue-collar, part-Irish, and all-Roman Catholic family, John and Robert Kennedy were heroes to our generation of immigrant and denominational descendants. We admired them in life and mourned them in death—deeply. I was too young to remember Jack Kennedy's 1960 race, but I was all over Bobby Kennedy's 1968 drive. Although only in the fifth grade, I followed it with the same enthusiasm that other boys my age reserved for the baseball playoffs. That landmark campaign infused me with such an intense interest in history and government that it led to my own eventual career in law and politics.

The excitement of Bobby Kennedy's battle, and then the hor-

---

a   Lewis Chester et al., *An American Melodrama: The Presidential Campaign of 1968* (1969), 21.

rible violence that ended it instantly, left a profound impact on me that never waned. Decades later, during my service as a Republican congressman, I still held Robert Kennedy in awe—a condition that no other conservative House colleague apparently shared. In 1998, Congressman Joseph P. Kennedy III (D-MA) and I cosponsored a bill to name the U.S. Department of Justice building after his late father. Republicans killed the bill in committee. Thirty years after RFK's death, his memory still aroused so much Republican disdain that they would not have named the DOJ outhouse after him. When I tried raising the issue with Speaker Newt Gingrich directly, he cut me off. "That bill is dead—*dead*," he snapped. Later, when my friend Lyn Nofziger (Ronald Reagan's longtime spokesman and adviser) visited my Capitol Hill office, I saw him staring at a large autographed photo of Bobby Kennedy hanging on my wall. Turning to me and looking both confused and disgusted, he asked, "What the hell is *that thing* doing here?"

This leads to my third point: fascination does not cause blindness. Like two other supermen with whom he split the stage in 1968, Robert Kennedy shares a common fate with Lyndon Johnson and Richard Nixon: all three are the subject of countless biographies larded with pseudo-psychological interpretations of what made them tick. Here the comparison ends. With LBJ and Nixon, the pop-culture consensus is that their power-grasping temperaments sprang from sinister motives and deep-seated personal inferiorities. Bobby's biographers usually promote loftier interpretations. For example, Arthur Schlesinger softened for history Bobby's hard-edged and knee-to-the-groin political style: "Because he wanted to get things done, because he was often impatient and combative, because he felt simply and cared deeply, he made his share of mistakes, and enemies. He was a romantic and an idealist."[b]

---

b   At the end of this poetic litany, Schlesinger conceded RFK's other side in the mildest of terms: Bobby could be "prudent, expedient, demanding and ambitious." Arthur M. Schlesinger Jr., *Robert Kennedy and His Times* (1978), xi.

Romance and idealism aside, many of RFK's supporters never knew, or chose to ignore, that Bobby started his political career in the 1950s as one of the lead investigators for Senator Joseph McCarthy, whose last name became (fairly or unfairly) a liberal synonym for reckless and career-destroying witch hunts.[1] After leaving McCarthy's staff, Bobby became chief counsel to the Senate committee investigating labor union racketeering. He dragged in over 1,500 witnesses before the committee in a vendetta to "get" those he perceived as enemies, especially Teamster leader Jimmy Hoffa, an obsession that carried over into his tenure as JFK's U.S. Attorney General. During Bobby's stint at the Justice Department, he supported covert foreign assassinations and coups. He ordered wiretaps on enemies and friends alike, including Dr. Martin Luther King Jr.[2] Bobby knew King cavorted with communists, so he monitored King's associations and activities.[3] Incidentally, these wiretaps disclosed King's many marital infidelities, which FBI agents later used to harass and threaten King. Revisionist histories notwithstanding, Attorney General Robert Kennedy did not champion the cause of Southern civil rights marchers. He viewed them as irritants creating escalating nuisances that threatened his brother's 1964 reelection prospects.[4] Right up to the end of his life, in private conversations he sometimes used vulgarities when talking about blacks and Jews. Just as those of us who venerate Thomas Jefferson, the man who gave voice to freedom's greatest proclamation, must live uncomfortably with the fact that he owned slaves, one would think that the venerators of Robert Kennedy would live uncomfortably with his stark and often disturbing record.[5]

Wrong.

Instead, RFK's biographers overwhelmingly offer a more forgiving explanation: his brother's 1963 assassination *changed* Bobby Kennedy.[6] Dallas supposedly transfigured him from vicious street-fighter into Greek tragedian: deeper, sensitive, selfless. Bobby helped in this rehabilitation by peppering his post-JFK era speeches and interviews with quotations from Camus, Emerson, and Aeschylus. He dined with poets, strikers, and migrant workers. He walked the ghettos. Those perpetuating the RFK myth excuse his calculated backflips on Vietnam.[7] Instead, we discover that he "grew" in his opposition when he saw an unjust war and its aftermath. This renovated RFK meets us in history books as one upon whom fate forced leadership, which he accepted as duty, not for ambition.

The truth: Robert Kennedy, both before and after his brother's death, was a calculating politician who fought dirty, played for keeps, and (when politically expedient) took various sides of an issue to please specific and often conflicting interest groups. Strip Bobby Kennedy of the sentimental hogwash that bathes his memory, and we find that he and his brother had the same cunning ambitions and methods as their non-idealized counterparts. We forgive the martyred Kennedys, but not the graceless LBJ or the sweat-beaded and shifty-eyed Nixon, because the Kennedys had a cultured and smooth veneer when cutting an opponent's throat.

Doubtless Dallas and its aftermath changed Robert Kennedy. All the evidence suggests that Bobby did become more soulful, patient, thoughtful, and empathetic for the underclass, but his darker political side never wandered far. Of Bobby's 1968 opponents—Lyndon Johnson, Hubert Humphrey, Richard Nixon, Nelson Rockefeller, George Wallace, Ronald Reagan, Eugene McCarthy, George Romney—if any were alive today, they would tell you that RFK understood the family business perhaps better than any other member of his clan. When Bobby fought you on the political battlefield, he fought to win, and if that meant leaving your corpse rotting in the dust, tough luck.

A final point: writing a historical novel is easy if the author just makes up the story. My goal was to twist the arc of history with facts. Sometimes I shuffled the timing of statements, persons, and actions to condense the narrative, but I wrote the vast bulk of this account based on actual history. Authors relegate the chapter endnotes to the back of the book because such details interest only researchers and academics. Mine are so extensive and detailed—almost the length of the book itself—that it proved impossible to include them in the print edition (they are included in the e-book version). If you own a print edition and wish to access a complimentary .pdf file containing all 986 fully sourced endnotes, you will find them posted at www. jamesrogan.org. In time, websites will disappear and die (along with their authors). So that the vast research that went into writing *On to Chicago* will not be lost for future historians, the endnotes will be released in a separate print edition entitled *The Notes: A Researcher's Guide to "On to Chicago" and the 1968 Presidential Campaign.*

As you read along in the book, if you run across a story or a scene that you think sounds incredible, impossible, or fictional, if there is an endnote attached to it, then I invite you to review the note. If you skip it, you will miss seeing how much of this account mirrors reality. Many revelations may surprise even the biggest history buffs among you.

With that, let us now journey back in time and see if we might alter what will otherwise remain a brutish crime against a man, a nation, and a cause.

—J.R.

ORANGE COUNTY, CALIFORNIA, JUNE 6, 2018,
ON THE 50TH ANNIVERSARY OF RFK'S ASSASSINATION
WWW.JAMESROGAN.ORG

PART ONE

The Democrats: Prelude to Chicago

PREFACE

[1]   In later years, when a writer asked how Robert F. Kennedy (RFK) justified ever working for Joseph McCarthy, RFK backpedaled on their previously close association. "Well, at the time, I thought there was a serious internal security threat to the United States; I felt at that time that Joe McCarthy seemed to be the only one who was doing anything about it." Then, after a pause, he added feebly, "I was wrong." Arthur M. Schlesinger Jr., *Robert Kennedy and His Times* (Boston: Houghton Mifflin Co., 1978), 106.

One RFK biographer noted that RFK's true dissatisfaction with Joseph McCarthy's Republican-led committee sprang from McCarthy rebuffing Ambassador Joseph P. Kennedy's request that McCarthy name RFK as the committee's chief counsel. Since McCarthy already had filled that slot with Roy Cohn, he named RFK assistant counsel. Almost from the beginning, Cohn and RFK developed a mutual hatred for each other that carried over for the rest of their lives. Despite RFK's later professed "dissatisfaction" with the committee's tactics causing his exit, a contemporaneous FBI report on his departure gave a different reason: RFK "braced Cohn on an administrative matter and brought it to a head by stating it was either he or Roy Cohn. The matter was resolved in Cohn's favor, and Kennedy resigned." Six months after his power struggle with Roy Cohn ended unsuccessfully, RFK returned to the same committee as chief counsel for the opposing party—the Democrats. Cohn recalled later that RFK came back to the committee "not to fight McCarthy; he came back to fight me." Even with the so-called Army-McCarthy hearings underway, which led to Joseph McCarthy's eventual Senate censure, RFK hastened to let McCarthy know of his personal loyalty. RFK tracked down Mary

Driscoll, McCarthy's secretary, in the Senate's beauty salon, and asked her to relay to McCarthy that RFK would do nothing as chief counsel for the Democrats to hurt him. RFK told her, "In fact, I'm going to protect [McCarthy] in every way I can…. But I am really out to get that little son-of-a-bitch Cohn." According to Cohn, Driscoll relayed the message to McCarthy, who called in Cohn and had Driscoll repeat it. See C. David Heymann, *RFK: A Candid Biography of Robert F. Kennedy* (New York: Dutton, 1998), 68-75, 82-83.

Even when Joe McCarthy's career ended in congressional censure and premature death from alcoholism, RFK never apologized for his work as a McCarthy staffer, because he liked McCarthy and considered him a patriot. See Ronald Steel, *In Love with the Night: The American Romance with Robert Kennedy* (New York: Simon & Schuster, 2000), 48.

2   RFK authorized the FBI to wiretap Martin Luther King, Jr.'s telephones, and the FBI later used the compromising tapes between King and his mistresses to blackmail and taunt King until the end of his life. See, e.g., Steel, *In Love with the Night*, 160-161.

3   In 1961, because of Martin Luther King, Jr.'s communist ties, RFK ordered the FBI to begin an intensive investigation of him. In October 1963, RFK ordered wiretaps on King's phones. RFK said he felt King was in "a very vulnerable position because of his association with members of the Communist Party, about whom he had been warned[.]" RFK warned King through a mutual friend that one of King's top lieutenants was a high-level member of the Communist Party and serving secretly on their Executive Board. After the warning, King did nothing about it. RFK raised the issue directly with King, as did JFK: "The President was very firm and strong with him… as we all were." RFK said that King's response to all of this was to laugh it off and make fun of it: "[King's] just got some other side to him…. We never wanted to get very close to [King] because of these contacts and connections that he had, which we felt were damaging to the civil rights movement [and] it also damaged us." When asked if RFK really believed King was under any real influence from his communist aide, RFK answered, "Yes." Robert F. Kennedy interviews with Anthony Lewis (with Burke Marshall present), December 4, 6, and 22, 1964; cited in Edwin O. Guthman and Jeffrey Shulman (eds.), *Robert*

Kennedy in His Own Words: The Unpublished Recollections of the Kennedy Years (New York: Bantam Press, 1988), 139-146.

[4]   As civil rights protests continued throughout the South in the early 1960s, RFK feared a backlash to JFK's 1964 reelection campaign. He tried many times unsuccessfully to get the marchers and activists to back off and let the courts address the issue. The nonviolent protesters rejected those pleas and continued penetrating the Deep South with their demands to end segregation and voter suppression. Too often vicious dogs, swinging nightsticks, fire hoses, church bombings, murders, and mass arrests awaited their arrival. As Attorney General, RFK responded by sending federal marshals to protect protesters in key standoffs, but he did so reluctantly and with great frustration at their presence. JFK and RFK complained constantly about the sit-ins and protesters. "This was not from sympathy for the white segregationists. Rather it was a concern over the impact… on his brother's political fortunes…. Robert Kennedy's task was to do enough for black people to win their support without at the same time losing the votes of white conservatives and Southerners JFK needed to govern and be reelected." Further, "[Robert] Kennedy's sensitivity to racial issues became evident after he sought a political career of his own. Yet during his years as Attorney General he thought that the Freedom Riders were, for the most part, grandstanding troublemakers, and that some black organizations were infiltrated by communists who goaded them to unnecessary confrontations. The Kennedys tried to block the 1963 March on Washington from fear that it would embarrass their administration. When that effort failed they tried to take it over[.]" See Steel, *In Love with the Night*, 159, 162, 163.

RFK argued unsuccessfully with Martin Luther King, Jr. and other civil rights activists to end the civil rights protests in the South. He wanted the activists to focus on registering black voters instead. RFK said King and his followers "rather resented" RFK's plea. "That's not what they wanted to do, and that's not where they were going to focus their attention." After their Birmingham to Montgomery protest, the Freedom Riders decided to bring their protest into Mississippi. RFK did not want to send federal troops into the South to protect the protesters: he knew that would have a terrible political impact on JFK's 1964 reelection plan. RFK grew very frustrated that the Freedom Riders were kicking up a political storm for him. Kennedy felt they had made their point in Alabama, and now needed to "slow down.... They had made their point. What was the purpose of continuing with [their protest]?" RFK claimed that JFK felt the same way: "He was fed up with the Freedom Riders who went down there [to Alabama] when it didn't do any good to go down there." Robert F. Kennedy interviews with Anthony Lewis (with Burke Marshall present), December 4, 6, and 22, 1964, cited in Guthman and Shulman, *Robert Kennedy in His Own Words*, 97-98, 101, 103.

The Kennedys tried without success to have Martin Luther King, Jr. back off his protests and marches. In fact, JFK tried to discourage King from leading the now-famous 1963 "March on Washington" where he delivered his iconic "I Have a Dream" speech, fearing its impact might hurt pending civil rights legislation. Only after organizers refused the president's plea and insisted that the march proceed did the Kennedy Administration work to make it a success. See, e.g., Jonathan Rosenberg and Zachary Karabell, *Kennedy, Johnson, and the Quest for Justice: The Civil Rights Tapes* (New York: WW Norton & Co., 2003), 130.

[5]   Jean Scherrer, a 30-year Los Angeles Police Department veteran who traveled often with RFK, said that behind the scenes RFK's private comments about blacks didn't match his public demeanor. In moments of frustration, RFK called them "coons" and once he griped in frustration, "What do those goddamn niggers want from me?" Scherrer suspected these comments were more "Irish bravado—a kind of suburban prejudice rather than overt racism." Author Truman Capote, RFK's friend as well as his New York neighbor, confirmed this dark trait. Capote said that in private conversations, RFK "often referred to Jews as either 'kikes' or 'yids.' I found it revolting. He was just like his old man." See Heymann, *RFK*, 391. [Author's note: in this book, Heymann incorrectly listed the officer as "Gene" Scherrer.]

[6]   One man who knew RFK well, Senator George McGovern (1922-2012), found RFK changed after Dallas. "I think [RFK] became more thoughtful and perceptive and sensitive after the death of his brother. I think it was time for him to come to terms with himself in a way he hadn't before." See Heymann, *RFK*, 478.

[7]   Throughout most of the 1960s, RFK proved a forceful advocate for U.S. military involvement in Vietnam:

- In 1962, RFK declared boldly, "We are going to win in Vietnam. We will remain here until we do win." See Steel, *In Love with the Night*, 134.

- In late 1964, almost a year after Lyndon B. Johnson (LBJ) became president, RFK stood firmly behind the "Domino Theory" as a justification for the Kennedy-Johnson Vietnam escalation policy. He told an interviewer doing an oral history for the Kennedy Library that America had a strong, overwhelming reason to fight and win the Vietnam War. RFK said it was "quite clear" that a U.S. failure there would cause "the loss of all of Southeast Asia" and undermine areas as far-flung as India, Indonesia, and the Middle East. See Guthman and Shulman, *Robert Kennedy in His Own Words*, 394-395.

- In 1965, RFK claimed withdrawing from Vietnam would demonstrate a repudiation of the commitments made by the last three presidents to the region. A year later, RFK suggested that perhaps the communists should be part of a negotiated settlement in which they would share power in South Vietnam. This shift away from the hardline Domino Theory pleased greatly the small but vocal antiwar protesters that RFK saw as a potential constituency; he also received instant media acclaim anytime he distanced or distinguished himself from LBJ's policies. Testing the waters further, RFK criticized Johnson for his unrelenting bombing of North Vietnam. Rather than receive favorable media attention, this critique brought a sharp rebuke from Secretary of State Dean Rusk, Under Secretary of State George Ball, and National Security Adviser McGeorge Bundy, who called RFK's comments "naïve." What stung the most is that JFK appointed each of these diplomats to their posts, and they continued JFK's Vietnam policies under LBJ. Facing this significant criticism, RFK retreated and, as Adam Walinsky later wrote, he became "gun-shy" in continuing his Vietnam opposition at this point. When the Senate scheduled another vote to repeal the Tonkin Gulf Resolution, Kennedy refused to support it. By late 1966, when a $5 billion appropriations measure to continue funding the Vietnam War came before the Senate, only two senators voted to oppose it, and RFK was not one of them. Later, when RFK saw an unclaimed political base among minorities and youth (where antiwar sentiment was strongest, since their names filled the draft lotteries), he started pushing back more aggressively on U.S.-Vietnam policy. Even then, up to late 1967, RFK still hesitated to break with a war supported by the vast majority of Americans. He also avoided criticizing Johnson too sharply: bizarrely, he still hoped LBJ might select him as his vice presidential nominee in 1968. Only when that door slammed shut did he slide into full-throated opposition to the war. When he finally broke with LBJ over Vietnam, he went all out and attacked both American policy and American morality in Southeast Asia. Hoping to inoculate himself from charges of hypocrisy, he added there was enough blame to go around for Vietnamese policy, "including myself." Although many in the antiwar movement welcomed him (finally) into their fold, his credibility on the subject remained suspect among average voters. Before his breakaway speech, Kennedy topped LBJ in public opinion polls. After he broke with Johnson, his popularity dropped 11 points almost overnight—to 37 percent. What was Kennedy's response to these deflated poll numbers? When the next resolution came before the Senate for unilateral withdrawal from Vietnam, RFK voted against it. Shortly thereafter, he appeared at a New York fundraiser with LBJ and introduced the president in the most glowing of terms, proclaiming, "in 1964 he won the greatest popular victory in modern times, and with our help he will do so again in 1968!" Because of these inconsistencies in RFK's public declarations, biographer Ronald Steel wrote, "Nobody fully trusted [RFK's] motives: Democratic loyalists accused him of splitting the Party to further his ambition; antiwar activists thought him cowardly for not challenging Johnson directly. [¶] For the rest of the year he wobbled back and forth trying to appease the Party regulars who feared that by dividing Democrats he would insure their defeat in the elections. At the same time he tossed out morsels of hope to the dissidents who urged him to run. He commiserated with the antiwar activists, but as long as he saw Johnson as invulnerable, all he would offer the peace dissidents was his sympathy.... Robert Scheer, writing for the leftist journal *Ramparts*, described [RFK as offering] 'the illusion of dissent without its substance.'" See Steel, *In Love with the Night*, 132-133, 136-139.

CHAPTER 1

[1]   RFK as cold, vengeful, fanatical, ruthless: see Schlesinger, *Robert Kennedy and His Times*, xiii.

In his diary entry written a few days after RFK's June 1968 assassination, a grieving Schlesinger wrote that RFK "was supposed to be a hard, ruthless, unfeeling, unyielding, a grudge-bearer, a hater. In fact, he was an exceptionally gentle and considerate man, the most bluntly honest man I have ever encountered in politics, a profoundly idealistic man and an extremely funny man." Arthur M. Schlesinger Jr., *Journals 1952-2000* (New York: Penguin Books, 2007), 292.

A reporter once described RFK as having "all the patience of a vulture, without any of the dripping sentimentality." See Schlesinger Jr., *Robert Kennedy and His Times*, 213.

[2]   Ambassador Joseph P. Kennedy's comment, "Never expect any appreciation from my boys. These kids have had so much done for them by other people that they just assume it's coming to them," was actually made by Ambassador Kennedy to Congressman (later House Speaker) Thomas P. "Tip" O'Neill. In his 1987 memoir, O'Neill recalled how he gave up his delegate slot at the 1956 Democratic National Convention to RFK as a favor to JFK: "I had my first encounter with Bobby in 1956 when, as a Member of Congress, I was in charge of naming four delegates from my district to the Democratic National Convention. I selected three local politicians and kept a fourth spot for myself. [¶] After I made the appointments, Jack [JFK] called and asked me to name Bobby as a delegate. But the positions were already filled, and besides, Bobby didn't even live in my district. [¶] 'I'm sorry, Jack,' I said, 'but I've already notified the delegates.' And I told him who I had picked. [¶] But Jack would not be denied....

'You know, lightning may strike at that convention, and I could end up on the ticket with Stevenson. I'd really like to have my brother on the floor as a delegate so he could work for me.' [¶] 'If you feel that strongly about it,' I said, 'I'll make sure he gets there.' So I took myself off the list and put Bobby on instead.... After the convention, Bobby showed no gratitude for the favor I had done. I once mentioned this to [RFK's father, Joseph P. Kennedy], and I'll never forget what he said: 'Tip, let me tell you something. Never expect any appreciation from my boys. These kids have had so much done for them by other people that they just assume it's coming to them.'" Tip O'Neill and William Novak, *Man of the House* (New York: Random House, 1987), 82-83; see also Heymann, *RFK*, 108.

The 1952 and 1956 Democratic presidential nominee, Adlai E. Stevenson, who served as JFK's U.S. Ambassador to the United Nations, found RFK's inability to maintain civility disturbing. "That young man," Stevenson remarked, "never says please. He never says thank you, he never asks for things, he demands them." Burton Hersh, *Bobby and J. Edgar: The Historic Face-Off Between the Kennedys and J. Edgar Hoover That Transformed America* (New York: Carroll & Graf Publishers, 2007), 6.

[3]   When Ted Sorensen first met RFK, he said he wouldn't have voted for him for anything. "He was militant, aggressive, intolerant, opinionated, somewhat shallow in his convictions." See Ted Sorensen, *Counselor: A Life at the Edge of History* (New York: HarperCollins, 2008), 251.

Another longtime RFK friend, author Arthur M. Schlesinger Jr., wrote that in RFK's early Washington years, he was "a cocky young fellow, opinionated, censorious, rigid, moralistic, prickly, disposed to tell people off and to get into heated arguments." See Guthman and Shulman, *Robert Kennedy in His Own Words*, xiv.

RFK almost dared others to dislike him, and he made it easy for them to do so. Where JFK used charm and seduction, RFK used hostility and aggressiveness. "[H]e got angry easily and held grudges forever[.]" Steel, *In Love with the Night*, 28, 69, 116.

Speaker of the U.S. House of Representatives Tip O'Neill, who succeeded to JFK's House seat in 1952 when JFK won a seat in the U.S. Senate, recalled in his 1987 memoir, "Of all the [Kennedy] brothers, I knew Bobby the least. We weren't friendly, and to be blunt about it, I never really liked him.... To me, he was a self-important upstart and a know-it-all." O'Neill and Novak, *Man of the House*, 83.

[4]   RFK fought bare-knuckled and savagely, and you never wanted him as an enemy. See Theodore H. White, *The Making of the President 1968* (New York: Atheneum, 1969), 152.

[5]   Sorensen's early impression was that RFK was more like his father than like JFK: "In those days, he was a conservative, very close to his father both in ideas and manners, sharing his father's dislike of liberals." See Sorensen, *Counselor*, 251.

During a conversation in the 1990s, Richard Nixon said of JFK's father, "Joe Kennedy was a conservative, and I recall one time during the 1960 campaign we were on a train together, and Joe said, 'Dick, you know if Jack weren't running, I'd be for you.'" See Monica Crowley, *Nixon Off the Record: His Candid Commentaries on People and Politics* (New York: Random House, 1996), 33.

Joseph McCarthy dated two of RFK's sisters, and spent many weekends vacationing with the Kennedys at Hyannis Port and Palm Beach. When RFK's first child, Kathleen, was born in 1951, he chose Joseph McCarthy as her godfather. See Heymann, *RFK*, 69.

In his 1987 memoir, Speaker of the U.S. House of Representatives Tip O'Neill recalled that, on one occasion, RFK's father Joseph P Kennedy "complained to me that [JFK] was too soft: 'You can trample all over him,' he said, 'and the next day he's there for you with loving arms. But Bobby's my boy. When Bobby hates you, you stay hated.'" See O'Neill and Novak, *Man of the House*, 83. See also Steel, *In Love with the Night*, 37, 106; Heymann, *RFK*, 66. In later years, Ambassador Kennedy apparently denied making this statement that RFK was a hater. See Schlesinger Jr., *Robert Kennedy and His Times*, 97.

[6]   To RFK, politics "was the equivalent of war, to be fought to the hilt with no holds barred and no quarter given.... It was this concept of politics which led to the description of Bobby Kennedy as 'a one-man firing squad for [John F. Kennedy].'" See Ralph de Toledano, *R.F.K. The Man Who Would Be President* (New York: G.P. Putnam's Sons, 1967), 134.

When RFK had a job to do for his brother, "[h]e did not care whether or not people liked him along the way." Schlesinger Jr., *Robert Kennedy and His Times*, 96.

[7]   "Jack's death changed Bobby.... I still find him growing and changing." See Sorensen, *Counselor*, 251, 254.

[8]   Advisers Richard Goodwin and Arthur Schlesinger urged RFK to challenge LBJ for the presidency in 1968. Senator Edward "Ted" Kennedy and Ted Sorensen opposed the challenge. Sorensen warned RFK of the difficult task of denying an incumbent president renomination, especially when LBJ and his people controlled the convention. Further, with RFK and Eugene McCarthy running, they would split the peace vote between them, which all but guaranteed LBJ's nomination. Finally, with an RFK-LBJ battle into the late August national convention, it would cement a Democratic Party split that would hand the presidency to the Republicans. Sorensen argued that if RFK ran against his brother's designated successor, the divisive campaign would prove unwinnable. Sorensen also believed RFK had a much clearer path to the presidency if he waited until 1972. See Sorensen, *Counselor*, 454; see also Evan Thomas, *Robert Kennedy: His Life* (New York: Simon & Schuster, 2000, 354; Pierre Salinger, *P.S. A Memoir* (New York: St. Martin's Press, 1995), 189-190; Schlesinger Jr., *Journals*, 268-269.

RFK campaign adviser Fred Dutton warned RFK in a November 1967 memo that running against LBJ in 1968 would be "political suicide." See Thomas, *Robert Kennedy*, 354, 357-358.

[9]   After President Kennedy's assassination, Canada named an unscaled Yukon mountain peak in his honor. In 1965, RFK (with no mountain-climbing experience) joined a group of experienced climbers. They became the first persons to scale Mount Kennedy.

[10]   Despite Senator Edward Kennedy's and adviser Theodore Sorensen's reluctance over RFK running for president in 1968, RFK's wife, Ethel, favored her husband's candidacy. See Schlesinger Jr., *Journals*, 276.

[11]   The long-standing mutual loathing that RFK and LBJ felt for each other is well documented. The dislike between LBJ and RFK was so strong "that it seemed almost as if each had been created for the purpose

of exasperating the other." See Doris Kearns Goodwin, *Lyndon Johnson and the American Dream* (New York: Harper & Row, 1976), 200.

"Both [LBJ and RFK] were powerful, at times overbearing, tyrannical characters who did not treat opponents kindly. They were alley fighters, knee in the groin, below-the-belt punchers, hell-bent on winning at almost any cost. Dirty tricks, intimidation, hard bargains were weapons in their political arsenals they carried into campaigns for high office and for legislative and political gains needed to keep them or, in Bobby's case, Jack there.... But each self-righteously saw the other as less capable of achieving the great ends bringing them together in the same party and in the same administration." Robert Dallek, *Flawed Giant: Lyndon Johnson and His Times 1961-1973* (New York: Oxford University Press, 1998), 35.

The 1952 and 1956 Democratic presidential nominee, Adlai E. Stevenson, described the mutual disdain felt by LBJ and RFK as "savage." See Schlesinger Jr., *Robert Kennedy and His Times*, 203.

In a 1964 series of oral history interviews not released until years after RFK's death, RFK described LBJ as "[v]ery mean. He's a very mean, mean figure." In the same series of interviews, RFK derided LBJ for telling other Kennedy Administration holdover staffers that all the other Kennedys liked him, but RFK hated him. LBJ kept asking the staffers what he could do to get RFK to like him, and said he wanted to have RFK over for a drink or for conversation. To that, RFK responded, "I didn't have any interest, really, in becoming involved with him." In those interviews, RFK also complained that LBJ started getting credit for several things that President Kennedy did—and LBJ wasn't saying enough that JFK was responsible for the accomplishment. See Robert F. Kennedy interviews with John Bartlow Martin, March 1, April 13, April 30, and May 14, 1964, cited in Guthman and Shulman, *Robert Kennedy in His Own Words*, 406-407, 412.

A man who knew both LBJ and RFK, Arthur M. Schlesinger Jr., described their "immiscible" traits. "Robert Kennedy baffled Johnson. Johnson repelled Robert Kennedy." See Schlesinger Jr., *Robert Kennedy and His Times*, 623.

Despite this, LBJ Secretary of Defense Clark Clifford, a rare "Kennedy Man" in LBJ's inner circle, was a credible witness to LBJ's efforts to embrace RFK, only to have his kindness thrown back in his face. Clifford, who also served as JFK's personal attorney, as well as chairman of JFK's Intelligence Advisory Board, said, "President Johnson made every effort after the assassination of President Kennedy to get along with the Kennedy family, and in almost every instance his overtures were rejected, and rejected in a manner that was thoroughly offensive and insulting. I thought the attitude of Robert Kennedy and the other members of the family was inexcusable, and I think President Johnson tried to the best of his ability to get along with RFK. He was gracious and courteous and handled it in statesmanlike fashion, and [RFK] and his followers rejected him at every turn.... [T]hey looked upon President Johnson as a usurper of the job that really belonged to them. Their attitude was exceedingly immature and one of the more unattractive chapters in the life of that particular family." See Heymann, *RFK*, 367-368.

Longtime Washington lobbyist, FDR aide, and Democratic Party insider Thomas "Tommy the Cork" Corcoran traced RFK's hostility toward LBJ to the 1956 presidential campaign. In the autumn of 1955, RFK's father, Ambassador Joseph P. Kennedy, invited Corcoran to lunch in Manhattan. "When Corcoran arrived he was greeted not only by Joe [Kennedy] but also by his twenty-nine year-old son Bobby. The elder Kennedy got right to the point. He wanted Corcoran to carry a message to Lyndon Johnson. He believed that the Texas senator wanted to run for the presidency. If Johnson would publicly announce his candidacy and privately pledge to take Jack Kennedy as his running mate, then Joe promised, 'I have friends who will help finance the ticket.'" Corcoran agreed to pass along the message to LBJ. The following week, Corcoran flew to LBJ's Texas ranch and communicated the offer, which LBJ declined. "Corcoran returned to New York to relay the message to the Kennedys. Corcoran later remembered that young RFK "was infuriated. He believed it was unforgivably discourteous to turn down his father's offer." See David McKean, *Tommy the Cork: Washington's Insider from Roosevelt to Reagan* (South Royalton: Steerforth Press, 2004), 230-231.

CHAPTER 2

[1] RFK and his family lived at apartment number 14-F, 860 United Nations Plaza, New York, from 1964 to 1968.

[2] This particular RFK-Allard Lowenstein argument over whether RFK should challenge LBJ in 1968 is adapted from their February 1968 meeting. See Schlesinger Jr., *Robert Kennedy and His Times*, 840-841.

[3] RFK spoke with Chicago Mayor Richard Daley about his chances against LBJ in 1968. Daley told RFK any 1968 campaign was premature, and that his time would come in 1972. If RFK ran now, Daley warned, he would split the Party. When RFK relayed that excuse to Allard Lowenstein during a January 1968 meeting, Lowenstein exploded, "The people who think that the honor and future of this country are at stake don't give a shit what Mayor Daley and Chairman X and Governor Y think. We're going ahead and we're going to win, and it's a shame you're not with us because you could have been president[.]" See Lewis Chester, Godfrey Hodgson, Bruce Page, *An American Melodrama: The Presidential Campaign of 1968* (New York: Viking Press, 1969), 89.

[4] RFK wore size-nine shoes with high arches added to give him extra height. See Chester, Hodgson, Page, *An American Melodrama*, 335.

RFK had a weak handshake: "It was like a noodle," said campaign aide Stuart Bloch. See Thomas, *Robert Kennedy*, 26.

John Bartlow Martin, a longtime RFK friend and adviser, wrote that by 1968, RFK's once-boyish face was deeply lined and his hair was turning gray. "He really did not look young. He aged more than he should have since his brother's death," Martin said. *Newsweek*'s Evan Thomas wrote that RFK's body was hard from exercise, but varicose veins protruded from his legs, and his wife Ethel counted out a dozen pills each day for him (mostly vitamins). In 1968, at age 42, RFK "was an old man. He had lived a lifetime, really several lifetimes, of hard stress, self-imposed and inflicted by almost constant conflict." See Thomas, *Robert Kennedy*, 383.

On the eve of RFK announcing his presidential candidacy, longtime friend and Senate colleague George McGovern reported that he was "shocked" at how much RFK had aged: his face looked drawn and deeply wrinkled, and "he looked so much older." See Schlesinger Jr., *Robert Kennedy and His Times*, 853.

⁵ RFK liked to end a busy day by eating a big bowl of ice cream and drinking a Heineken beer. See Thomas, *Robert Kennedy*, 21.

⁶ In this RFK-Lowenstein encounter, where Lowenstein again tried to recruit RFK to challenge LBJ, RFK refused. He told Lowenstein that if he ran, people would say he was splitting the Party out of ambition, etc. See Schlesinger Jr., *Robert Kennedy and His Times*, 824-825; see also Chester, Hodgson, Page, *An American Melodrama*, 89.

RFK balked at entering the 1968 campaign because he was "vividly concerned that his entrance into the contest would be attributed to his ruthless ambition, his feuding with LBJ and so on." See Schlesinger Jr., *Journals*, 276-277.

In August 1967, RFK flew to California for a Democratic fundraiser; Lowenstein was on the same flight. Kennedy flew in first class, and Lowenstein flew in coach ("That's the story of my life," Lowenstein joked later). An RFK aide switched seats with Lowenstein so that he and RFK could talk. Lowenstein again lobbied RFK to challenge LBJ. RFK reiterated that he had no interest in the impossible task. See Chester, Hodgson, Page, *An American Melodrama*, 62.

⁷ "Bobby [carried] the conviction that in a crisis… Johnson was a coward." See Jeff Shesol, *Mutual Contempt: Lyndon Johnson, Robert Kennedy, and the Feud that Defined a Decade* (New York: W.W. Norton & Company, 1997), 97-98.

[8]   RFK saying that if he ran for president in 1968, people would say, "I'm just a selfish, ambitious little son-of-a-bitch that can't wait to get his hands on the White House" is adapted from an actual conversation between RFK and Benno Schmidts. See Schlesinger Jr., *Robert Kennedy and His Times*, 840.

CHAPTER 3

[1]   Lowenstein met with General James Gavin, who expressed an interest in running for president in 1968 as an antiwar Republican. See Chester, Hodgson, Page, *An American Melodrama*, 66.

[2]   Lowenstein's meeting with George McGovern to recruit him for a presidential run, McGovern's refusal, McGovern giving Lowenstein names of other potential contenders, and McGovern's later conversation with Eugene McCarthy when McCarthy told him that he might run for president are adapted from actual events. See Schlesinger Jr., *Robert Kennedy and His Times*, 825-826.

In turning down Lowenstein's plea to run for president in 1968, McGovern explained that he had won his Senate race in 1962 by only 597 votes, and he expected a similarly close reelection race in 1968. See Chester, Hodgson, Page, *An American Melodrama*, 67.

[3]   Unlike the Kennedys, Eugene McCarthy was "a small-town boy from the upper Midwest who attended, and later taught at, a Benedictine college and spent the year in between in a monastery.... He had an elegant, original, penetrating wit. Alas, he never turned it on himself." Schlesinger Jr., *Robert Kennedy and His Times*, 828-829.

Eugene McCarthy was one of the most religious men in American political life. See White, *The Making of the President 1968*, 36.

A trio of British reporters covering the Eugene McCarthy campaign in 1968 wrote that McCarthy detested the groundwork of politics and snubbed everyone impartially. When several governors left messages saying they might support his candidacy, he didn't return their calls. After Chicago Mayor Richard Daley agreed to meet and discuss his candidacy,

McCarthy canceled the meeting—twice. United Auto Workers head Walter Reuther showed an interest in McCarthy's campaign. After his manager pressed him, McCarthy called Reuther, who was out. Reuther returned McCarthy's call five times in the next three days. McCarthy never called him back. See Chester, Hodgson, Page, *An American Melodrama*, 413.

A former Eugene McCarthy aide described the senator as "frustrated by the tedium and the rigidity of the Senate routine and he wouldn't play the game. He wouldn't bow to the feudal lords." See Arthur Herzog, *McCarthy for President* (New York: Viking Press, 1969), 59.

In the Senate, Eugene McCarthy's colleagues "regarded him as aloof, indolent, arrogant, and annoying…. They didn't like how he spent so much of his time telling wicked little stories about his distinguished colleagues to reporters…. They thought him a 'truly deeply cynical man, a scoffer." See Chester, Hodgson, Page, *An American Melodrama*, 70.

4   The dialogue in the story between RFK and McGovern is adapted from a discussion between RFK and Arthur Schlesinger as recorded in Schlesinger's journal. McGovern telling RFK that Eugene McCarthy planned to run for president, RFK's unhappy response, and McGovern's impressions are adapted from McGovern's actual recounting of events. See Schlesinger Jr., *Robert Kennedy and His Times*, 826-827.

5   During the 1967-1968 years, Arthur Schlesinger's Washington, D.C., residence was a brick row house at 3132 O Street, N.W.

6   Then-Senator John F. Kennedy purchased Hickory Hill (located at 1147 Chain Bridge Road in McLean, Virginia) from U.S. Supreme Court Justice Robert H. Jackson in 1955. A year later, JFK sold the home to RFK, who lived there until his death. His widow Ethel sold the property in 2009.

7   Eugene McCarthy urged RFK to run for president previously and, after RFK rebuffed him, McCarthy told him that if RFK would not run, McCarthy might. See White, *The Making of the President 1968*, 80; see also Eugene McCarthy, *Up 'Til Now* (New York: Harcourt Brace Jovanovich, 1987), 189.

8   RFK disliked Eugene McCarthy: he thought him lazy, vain, and unfit to be president. See White, *The Making of the President 1968*, 158, 161, 175.

RFK thought McCarthy was undependable, uninvolved, too often absent when needed for a vote, and too cozy with the banking and financial interests. See Schlesinger Jr., *Robert Kennedy and His Times*, 828.

RFK thought McCarthy was vain and envious, and he never forgave him for trying to block JFK's 1960 Democratic presidential nomination by nominating Adlai Stevenson at the convention. See Steel, *In Love with the Night*, 152.

RFK found Eugene McCarthy "pompous, petty, and venal." See Thomas, *Robert Kennedy*, 360.

Eugene McCarthy "was disliked intensely by the Kennedyites. If Bobby Kennedy and Gene McCarthy had been in Sinn Fein together they would have carried their guns in holsters under opposite shoulders—they embodied the ultimate war of the Irish." See Norman Mailer, *Miami and the Siege of Chicago* (New York: Random House, 2016 Trade Paperback Edition), 113.

RFK's assessment that Eugene McCarthy was "lazy" was shared by other Democratic leaders such as McCarthy's home state governor, Minnesota's Orville Freeman. A longtime political associate of McCarthy, Freeman told reporter Drew Pearson (who recorded the conversation in his diary entry of March 28, 1968) that the problem with McCarthy "is that he's lazy. He hasn't put his name on one piece of legislation." Drew Pearson and Peter Hannaford (ed.), *Washington Merry-Go-Round: The Drew Pearson Diaries, 1960-1969* (Lincoln: Potomac Books, 2015), 557-558; see also O'Neill and Novak, *Man of the House*, 201, 202 (McCarthy and O'Neill "had been friends for years, and I respected him, even though he was lazy and a bit of a dreamer. He was also a loner. For a guy who wanted to be president, he never really worked the streets by asking for help from organizational types like me.").

In his diary entry of October 18, 1967, historian Arthur M Schlesinger Jr. (a longtime RFK friend and supporter) wrote that Eugene McCarthy was "a disappointing senator, especially in his laziness[.]" Later, in his March 17, 1968 journal entry, Schlesinger noted that McCarthy "is given to self-pity and bitterness[.]" Schlesinger Jr., *Journals*, 263, 284

[9] RFK's dinner conversation with Schlesinger, including RFK's expression of concern over how Eugene McCarthy's candidacy might affect RFK's possible entry, is adapted from actual events. See Schlesinger Jr., *Robert Kennedy and His Times*, 827.

CHAPTER 4

[1]   Blair Clark (1917-2000), a Harvard classmate and friend of JFK, was a reporter for the *St. Louis Post-Dispatch* before starting the *New Hampshire Sunday News*. He joined CBS News in 1953. After JFK won the presidency, he offered Clark the position of ambassador to Mexico. Clark turned it down and instead became vice president of CBS News in 1961. Later, he worked for the *New York Post* and edited *The Nation* magazine. In 1968, he served as Eugene McCarthy's campaign manager. See Herzog, *McCarthy for President*, 83; see generally, https://en.wikipedia.org/wiki/Blair_Clark.

[2]   JFK promised to support Eugene McCarthy's amendment on a labor bill in the Senate, and then he broke his word. After JFK apologized to him for going back on his promise, McCarthy remembered years later, "I replied that it was all right but took note that I could never accept his more than casual word on a legislative matter again." See McCarthy, *Up 'Til Now*, 132-133.

[3]   In March 1967, in an interview with James Wechsler of the *New York Post*, Eugene McCarthy promoted RFK as the strongest candidate to challenge LBJ for reelection in 1968. See McCarthy, *Up 'Til Now*, 188.

During their 1967 meeting, Eugene McCarthy told Allard Lowenstein he believed that RFK was the one to lead the most effective insurrection against LBJ in the 1968 campaign. See White, *The Making of the President 1968*, 74.

When Lowenstein pleaded with RFK to run, RFK rebuffed him summarily, saying, "Johnson can't be stopped." RFK's full response to Lowenstein is reported in White, *The Making of the President 1968*, 74.

[4]   After urging RFK to run previously, Eugene McCarthy again talked to RFK and told him that if RFK would not run, he would. See White, *The Making of the President 1968*, 80.

Despite Eugene McCarthy's urging, not only had RFK made no move to indicate he would challenge LBJ in 1968, he had actually announced his support for LBJ. As McCarthy later noted, given RFK's repeated public and private assurances he would not run, and because several key RFK advisers had now joined McCarthy's campaign, McCarthy pushed forward, convinced RFK would keep his word. "The evidence was clear to me that [Kennedy] intended to stand by what he had told me. I believed that he would not come into the foray after I had declared and begun my campaign." See McCarthy, *Up 'Til Now*, 188-189.

[5]   By 1968, LBJ kept expanding the war. The last antiwar measure before the Senate, to end U.S. Vietnam involvement, mustered only five votes. Eugene McCarthy concluded that the only way to challenge the war was to challenge LBJ. See McCarthy, *Up 'Til Now*, 184.

[6]   In 1964, after the North Vietnamese allegedly attacked two U.S. destroyers in the Gulf of Tonkin, Congress passed a resolution authorizing the president to use military force to repel armed aggression. Like most of his colleagues, Eugene McCarthy voted for the resolution (only two senators voted nay, and the House of Representatives passed the resolution unanimously). In the coming weeks, LBJ went from defending U.S. personnel to launching an offensive warfare against the communists, citing the resolution as his congressional authorization for continued escalation. To McCarthy, what was presented as an initial holding action had morphed into "a crusade to save all of Southeast Asia[.]" See White, *The Making of the President 1968*, 79.

[7]   In reality, Blair Clark met with Eugene McCarthy at the Blackstone Hotel in Chicago on December 2, 1967, and offered to help the fledgling McCarthy campaign. A week later, on December 10, McCarthy asked Clark to become his general campaign manager. On December 12, McCarthy announced that Clark would manage his campaign. See Eugene J. McCarthy, *The Year of the People* (Garden City: Doubleday and Company, Inc., 1969), 60; Associated Press, "Clark to Head McCarthy

Bid for President," *Fitchburg Sentinel*, December 13, 1967.

Eugene McCarthy's November 30, 1967 press conference "was notably low-key. He began his announcement by not saying that he was a candidate for the presidency but saying, 'I intend to enter the Democratic primaries in four states, Wisconsin, Oregon, California, and Nebraska. The decision with reference to Massachusetts and also New Hampshire will be made within the next two or three weeks.'" David C. Hoeh, *1968 • McCarthy • New Hampshire: "I Hear America Singing"* (Rochester: Lone Oak Press, 1994), 86.

CHAPTER 5

[1]   As Senate majority leader, and later as president, LBJ was a study in perpetual motion. Doris Kearns Goodwin wrote that he dominated Washington as almost no one before him: the Cabinet was *his* Cabinet, the Great Society *his* programs, the Congress *his* instrument. "Johnson seemed to be everywhere—calling for new programs and for action on the old, personally organizing his shifting congressional majorities, signing bills, greeting tourists, settling labor disputes, championing the blacks, constantly on the telephone to publishers, businessmen, astronauts, farm leaders, in a working day that began at seven a.m.... and that ended sometime in the early hours of the next morning." Kearns Goodwin, *Lyndon Johnson and the American Dream*, 158-159, 213, 399-400.

[2]   According to Eugene McCarthy, after LBJ became vice president, he wanted to preside over the weekly Senate Democratic caucus luncheon. McCarthy was one of the few senators to oppose openly this novel move, and mostly on grounds of separation of powers. Soon thereafter, at a D.C. cocktail party, an upset LBJ cornered McCarthy and "pushed his case in harsher and louder tones," causing party guests to back up and withdraw "like the crowd response in a Western in anticipation of a shootout." Rejecting out of hand McCarthy's constitutional and "institutional traditions" argument, Johnson snarled, "I'll take care of you—never fear." McCarthy, *Up 'Til Now*, 140-142.

Eugene McCarthy agreed that he and LBJ had no significant policy differences when LBJ pushed the Great Society welfare expansion programs as an extension of Franklin Roosevelt's New Deal, and when LBJ fast-tracked civil rights legislation. See McCarthy, *Up 'Til Now*, 156-157.

Before he decided to run for president in late 1967, Eugene

McCarthy voted for the Tonkin Gulf Resolution and for various Vietnam War appropriations. "[McCarthy's] antagonism toward [Johnson's] policy in Vietnam, so clearly stated in 1967 and 1968, had [before that time] been vague and periodic." Hubert H. Humphrey, *The Education of a Public Man: My Life and Politics* (New York: Doubleday & Co., Inc., 1976), 376.

3   Jeremy Larner, principal speechwriter for Eugene McCarthy during his 1968 primary campaign, wrote that McCarthy claimed that in 1964 LBJ loyalists back home threatened to find a Senate primary candidate against McCarthy unless he withdrew from vice presidential consideration in favor of Hubert Humphrey. McCarthy withdrew, and then LBJ's chief of staff asked McCarthy to nominate Humphrey. Angry at being manipulated and threatened, at first he refused. Later, he agreed to do it, but McCarthy's irritation with LBJ's treatment of him in 1964 never went away. See Jeremy Larner, *Nobody Knows: Reflections on the McCarthy Campaign of 1968* (New York: Macmillan, 1970), 22-23; see also Walter F. Mondale, *The Good Fight: A Life in Liberal Politics* (New York: Scribner, 2010), 70 (Eugene McCarthy expected to be LBJ's running mate in 1964. When LBJ picked Humphrey instead, McCarthy felt LBJ toyed with him over it.).

In his 1987 memoir, Eugene McCarthy made no claim that LBJ "toyed" with him over the vice-presidential nomination in 1964, nor did he mention any threat of a primary challenge unless he withdrew from vice presidential consideration. McCarthy wrote only that he nominated Humphrey for vice president at the 1964 convention at the request of the White House. See McCarthy, *Up 'Til Now*, 163-164.

4   LBJ's team viewed Eugene McCarthy's presidential candidacy as "'more of a diversion than a serious threat.' He was a one-issue candidate—Vietnam—with little public visibility." See Dallek, *Flawed Giant*, 525.

5   When a reporter asked what kind of president he would be, Eugene McCarthy replied, "Adequate." It was "a charming and obviously honest answer." See Arthur Herzog, *McCarthy for President: The Candidacy That Toppled a President, Pulled a New Generation into Politics, and Moved the Country Toward Peace* (New York: The Viking Press, 1969), 219.

During his early presidential campaign speeches and interviews, Eugene McCarthy wouldn't say he "wanted" to be president; he said he was "willing to serve" if the American people demanded him. See Ben Stavis, *We Were the Campaign: New Hampshire to Chicago for McCarthy* (Boston: Beacon Press, 1969), 132.

Richard Goodwin (a senior campaign staffer for both Eugene McCarthy and RFK) recalled that McCarthy told a reporter, "I didn't say I want to be president. I'm willing to be president." See Richard N. Goodwin, *Remembering America: A Voice from the Sixties* (Boston: Little Brown and Company, 1988), 491.

6 "[LBJ believed] he had given more laws, more houses, more medical services, more loans, and more promises to more people than any other president in history." Kearns Goodwin, *Lyndon Johnson and the American Dream,* x, 340.

7 In the fall of 1967, Postmaster General Lawrence O'Brien presented LBJ with a 44-page reelection memo. After reviewing it, LBJ agreed to meet twice a week with key people to strategize on his 1968 reelection campaign. See Dallek, *Flawed Giant*, 524.

A January 1968 Gallup Poll showed LBJ's popularity rose after a big dip the previous year. LBJ referenced this new 1968 poll and said, "It shows that a majority of the Democrats still approve the job I'm doing, and still approve the conduct of the war." See Horace Busby, *The Thirty-First of March: An Intimate Portrait of Lyndon Johnson's Final Days in Office* (New York: Farrar, Straus and Girioux, 2005), 178.

In December 1967-January 1968, with positive war news from Vietnam, LBJ's favorable poll numbers shot up. During this period, he enjoyed a favorable/unfavorable rating of 48 percent to 39 percent. See Dallek, *Flawed Giant*, 525.

8 Humphrey and Eugene McCarthy first met in the mid-1940s when McCarthy was a college professor and Humphrey was Minneapolis mayor. At the 1952 Democratic National Convention, McCarthy nominated Humphrey as a favorite son candidate for president. In 1960, McCarthy co-chaired Humphrey's presidential race and campaigned for him in Wisconsin and West Virginia against JFK. During the 1960 Democratic

primaries, JFK called and asked to see McCarthy. When they met in JFK's Senate office, JFK demanded that McCarthy tell Humphrey to "lay off in West Virginia or we will unload on him." McCarthy refused to relay the message. Soon after, Franklin D Roosevelt Jr. went to West Virginia on behalf of JFK and suggested Humphrey was a World War II draft dodger. See McCarthy, *Up 'Til Now*, 89-90, 134-136.

During Humphrey's primary campaign against JFK in West Virginia, RFK pressured Franklin D. Roosevelt, Jr.—the namesake of the revered late president—to attack Humphrey as a World War II draft dodger. See Schlesinger Jr., *Robert Kennedy and His Times*, 199-201; Humphrey, *The Education of a Public Man*, 475.

Twenty-five years after JFK's death, Eugene McCarthy wrote that he and JFK never had an ongoing feud or quarrel, despite the claims of many writers and reporters over the years. Further, President Kennedy never showed any signs of lingering resentment over McCarthy's course in the 1960 presidential election. See McCarthy, *Up 'Til Now*, 138, 142-143.

[9] In his 1976 memoir, Humphrey described how he learned Eugene McCarthy planned to challenge LBJ in the 1968 presidential primaries. "[I]n a conversation late in 1967 in the vice president's office.... [McCarthy] told me he intended to enter the primaries, challenging President Johnson. He spoke so casually, as he usually does, that I felt it was just sort of a lark on his part. I asked whether he thought it through carefully, including the difficulties of unseating an incumbent president. He said, in essence, 'Well, I don't have any feeling that I can win, but I don't like the Senate. I've lost interest in it, and I feel very strongly about the war. I guess the best way to show my feelings about it is to go out and enter the primaries.'" Humphrey, *The Education of a Public Man*, 376.

[10] "Gene [McCarthy] disdains whatever peer group he is in. If he was teaching college students, he found most of his colleagues dull. When he was in the House, he grew tired of congressmen. In the Senate, he found few senators or senatorial duties that interested him." McCarthy was "handsome, witty, teacher, poet, Irish mystic, and a clever politician—cleverer for denying it.... Gene is more vain and arrogant than his admirers want to admit[.]" Humphrey, *The Education of a Public Man*, 373, 376.

[11]   "[Eugene McCarthy] bore quiet and long-lasting rancor for Hubert Humphrey[.]" *White, The Making of the President 1968*, 78.

[12]   In dismissing Eugene McCarthy's unkind comments about him, Humphrey said, "I always considered Gene a friend. I still do, knowing he has often ridiculed some of the things I did. But he does that to most people." Humphrey, *The Education of a Public Man*, 375.

A Washington insider who knew both men once speculated on why McCarthy held lingering hostility toward HHH: "Every time McCarthy started to climb the ladder, he found Humphrey's ass staring him in the face." See Larner, *Nobody Knows*, 137.

[13]   LBJ was "like the second husband of a demanding wife: overly sensitive to every nuance, easily angered by real or imaginary slights, trying constantly to erase any memories that might lead to negative comparisons." Humphrey, *The Education of a Public Man*, 288-289.

CHAPTER 6

[1]   Curtis Gans became "a kind of assistant campaign manager" to the Eugene McCarthy campaign. See McCarthy, *The Year of the People*, 60.

"Gans was introduced to national politics in 1967, when he and Allard K. Lowenstein, a kinetic architect of what was then called the New Politics, organized the Coalition for a Democratic Alternative, a group opposed to the war in Vietnam. It evolved into the Dump Johnson movement, with the presidential campaign of Senator Eugene J. McCarthy, a Minnesota Democrat who declared his candidacy on Nov. 30, 1967, as its vehicle." See Sam Roberts, "Curtis Gans, 77, is Dead; Worked to Defeat President Johnson," *New York Times*, March 16, 2015, http://www.nytimes.com/2015/03/17/us/curtis-gans-77-is-dead-worked-to-depose-president-johnson.html

[2]   The Eugene McCarthy for President headquarters on Main Street in Concord, New Hampshire, was a rented electrical supplies warehouse. See Chester, Hodgson, Page, *An American Melodrama*, 88. A vintage 1968 McCarthy campaign brochure listed the actual address as 3 Pleasant Street Extension, Concord, NH. As of this writing (2018), the building still stands on the corner of Main Street and Pleasant Street Extension.

The Concord McCarthy campaign headquarters "was the recently vacated Ralph Pill Electrical Supply Store on Pleasant Street extension.... The store was away from Main Street, and therefore few pedestrians would be passing by.... Inside, to quote Gerry Studds, 'It was in absolutely wretched condition.... There are two to three inches of electrical commotion all over the place. There were wires hanging out of the wall. It looked like a medieval torture chamber, and it was too big. We didn't know what the hell to do with it. There was a full-length basement with an enormous room behind the showroom in the front....' With our first college volunteer, Dennis Donahue, a Dartmouth senior, we began the campaign by sweeping out the mess.... There was no furniture, plenty of wires, and parts of electrical fixtures but few lights. It was dark, dingy, dusty, and dirty. The rent would be more than $100 per month, not including electricity or heat.... The campaign's bank balance was still only $500. The deposit and the first month's rent would draw most of this current cash." Hoeh, *I Hear America Singing*, 144-145.

[3]   With less than four weeks before the primary, volunteers established the New Hampshire McCarthy campaign headquarters in Concord in an old electrical appliance store with holes in the walls and floors. "We shoveled rubbish from a side room, taped extension cords to the ceilings to support light bulbs, and carried pails of water to the basement to serve as fire extinguishers. A large wooden spool that once held heavy wire was set on end to become a table for a borrowed coffee maker. Posters were put up to cover holes in the walls." See Stavis, *We Were the Campaign*, 3.

[4]   A [McCarthy campaign] staff member was essentially anyone who worked during the week.... To be on the staff one only had to come to the office during the week, even part of the week. If he arrived on Thursday, he would know enough about procedures on Friday to supervise people on the weekend, so he was a staff member." Stavis, *We Were the Campaign*, 4.

[5]   RFK's advice to Eugene McCarthy that McCarthy should challenge LBJ in New Hampshire first, not Massachusetts, is adapted from an actual incident. See Chester, Hodgson, Page, *An American Melodrama*, 83.

[6]   After Eugene McCarthy balked at making his first test against LBJ in New Hampshire, manager Blair Clark prepared an extensive memorandum for Eugene McCarthy urging him to file there. Clark argued there was nothing to lose by competing in New Hampshire, since it was a "hawkish" and "conservative" state. Also, Democratic U.S. Senator Thomas McIntyre had said publicly that McCarthy would do no better than 10 percent—between 3,000 and 5,000 votes at most. In the memo he prepared for McCarthy, Clark wrote that with the bar set this low, they would claim victory with anything above that. Clark also pointed

out that McCarthy would enter the race as an underdog, so if he did well, the race might have national repercussions. See Chester, Hodgson, Page, *An American Melodrama,* 85-86.

Eugene McCarthy announced on January 3, 1968, that he would enter the New Hampshire presidential primary. See McCarthy, *The Year of the People,* 66.

[7]   Eugene McCarthy "seemed to pay no attention at all to his campaign. He viewed it as a spontaneous happening, which he should not try to control. He would arbitrarily cancel events on his schedule which had been painstakingly prepared by many people. He would ignore an audience or not make a promised speech." See Stavis, *We Were the Campaign,* 51.

[8]   Once, when the campaign needed a statement from Eugene McCarthy, he was unavailable: he had wandered off to meditate at a monastery. See Stavis, *We Were the Campaign,* 133.

[9]   The vignette of the "bored" Eugene McCarthy abandoning possible supporters and heading for the bar is based on an actual event. Reporters covering McCarthy's 1968 primary campaign wrote of the time McCarthy showed up at a tony New York campaign fundraiser attended by over 100 wealthy supporters. McCarthy arrived, shook three hands, and then, apparently bored, retired to the bar. See Chester, Hodgson, Page, *An American Melodrama,* 82.

McCarthy "was not a mixer. Or if he had ever been a mixer, as he must have been years ago, he had had too much of it since, certainly too much since [the 1968] primaries.... [He] had become, or he had always been, too private a man for the damnable political mechanics of mixing, fixing, shaking the hands, answering the same questions which had already answered themselves by being asked." Mailer, *Miami and the Siege of Chicago,* 97.

[10]   "A visitor to [McCarthy's] New York hotel suite in early January 1968 was surprised to see him ignore attempts of local politicians to see him; they were referred to his assistant while McCarthy went on talking about poetry. He was too tired, he said, to grant a few minutes even to a contributor who had given ten thousand dollars. At fund-raising cocktail

parties he would make the barest genuflection to potential donors, in the belief that they were giving not to him but to a cause, and should expect no special thanks or favors…. He would not give personal thank-yous for support. He would merely congratulate a McCarthy partisan for being in the right place, at the right time, on the right issue." Herzog, *McCarthy for President*, 83-84.

"I knew [Eugene McCarthy] from the House of Representatives, where we had served all through the 1950s before [McCarthy was] elected to the Senate. When the bells rang [summoning House members for a roll call vote], a group of us who all had offices on the same corridor would walk over to the floor of the House…. [We'd] pick up Gene, who would join us if he wasn't writing poetry or reading a book. He was a whimsical fellow who would come over [to vote on legislation] only if he happened to feel like it." O'Neill and Novak, *Man of the House*, 201.

McCarthy "felt he should not have to beg support from those who agreed with him ideologically, and he was often bitterly unhappy with the failure of the liberal politicians to get behind his campaign on their own." Herzog, *McCarthy for President*, 221.

[11] Seymore "Sy" Hersh, later an award-winning investigative reporter and writer, began his career as the press secretary for the 1968 Eugene McCarthy for president campaign.

[12] During the New Hampshire primary, and after booking McCarthy on the nationally televised NBC program *Meet the Press*, his staff almost rebelled when they discovered McCarthy canceled his appearance because he was upset that he wasn't the lead-off interview. See Chester, Hodgson, Page, *An American Melodrama*, 95.

[13] After announcing his challenge to LBJ on November 30, 1967, McCarthy made his first campaign appearance in New Hampshire on January 25, 1968, almost two months later. Between then and the primary on March 12, McCarthy planned only ten campaign days there. After his staff pressured him, he extended the time to 15 days. See Chester, Hodgson, Page, *An American Melodrama*, 88-90.

14 The observations of McCarthy as a presidential candidate that the author attributed to Curtis Gans in this chapter are adapted from various McCarthy campaign staffers who recounted McCarthy's style of campaigning in 1968:

- As McCarthy campaigned, he refused to say he was "running" for president. He'd say he was "willing" to be president. His staff, supporters, and the press saw this semantic as nuanced modesty. But, as McCarthy's campaign speechwriter explained, he meant it: he was only "'willing….' What reporters and others took as modesty or mystery… was really personality itself, in such unfamiliar terms that most people just couldn't believe it…. [McCarthy] was a man of mood who indulged his moods and expected others to indulge them." See Larner, *Nobody Knows*, 30, 31.

- "[McCarthy] was quirky—you could never tell what was principle and what was personal…. [McCarthy] was an appealing candidate—elegant, articulate. He knew the classics and could recite them on the stump. He had great aspirations and great confidence in his talent. But Gene also had a way of fading when it came to the heavy lifting, as if he were tuned out from the expectations of the people around him. He was also something of a lone wolf." See Mondale, *The Good Fight*, 70, 75.

- As a candidate, McCarthy "treated us not as his staff but as the organized segment of the American people demanding his presidency…. Most of the staff did not like this relationship. They wanted to be part of his campaign, not part of a popular demand for him, and expected him to lead, not observe it…. [His] image of integrity and his aloofness from political manipulation were major elements of his appeal…. This style simply was Eugene McCarthy…. Perhaps he was correct in feeling that if the country was not ready for his presidency, it could not be forced to accept him." See Stavis, *We Were the Campaign*, 132, 134.

- McCarthy's approach to campaigning was so detached and nonchalant that reporters began questioning whether he was a serious candidate. See Chester, Hodgson, Page, *An American Melodrama*, 90.

[15] McCarthy's campaign workers "found themselves saddled with a man who seemed to find it difficult to be animated, let alone passionate. Among the insiders, McCarthy's reluctance to muddy his hands with 'nuts-and-bolts' organization... was causing a condition on the verge of despair." See Chester, Hodgson, Page, *An American Melodrama*, 82.

[16] For an in-depth review of Allard Lowenstein's concerns over McCarthy's lethargic campaign, and Lowenstein's secret meetings with RFK to draft "conditions" that Lowenstein wanted McCarthy to accept as a condition of his continued support in the New Hampshire primary, see Chester, Hodgson, Page, *An American Melodrama*, 88-90.

[17] "[An] unexpected boost! On February 10 the entire Bobby Kennedy campaign in New Hampshire closed shop and publicly endorsed Senator McCarthy. This happened immediately after Ted Sorensen went to New Hampshire and presumably discussed the matter with the Kennedy people there. This is the first time any Kennedy group has given public support to McCarthy." Senator Eugene McCarthy for President Headquarters Newsletter I-4, published February 20, 1968 (Author's collection).

CHAPTER 7

¹   According to the LBJ Library, one of LBJ's favorite movies was *Guess Who's Coming to Dinner*, starring Spencer Tracy and Katherine Hepburn. Columbia Pictures premiered the movie on New Year's Day 1968. http:// www.lbjlib.utexas.edu/johnson/archives.hom/FAQs/Favorites/lbjtable.asp

²   This story of LBJ screening a movie for Texas congressmen in early March 1968, and then discussing his reelection prospects with them, is adapted from an actual meeting that happened under different circumstances. On January 31, 1968, LBJ had friends over to the White House for dinner. Later, over cocktails and cigars, he reflected on his upcoming reelection campaign. LBJ sounded relaxed and confident about his prospects in New Hampshire and for the Democratic nomination. See White, *The Making of the President 1968*, 12.

³   After the Tet assault, LBJ's approval rating on Vietnam plummeted to 35 percent, while 50 percent disapproved. Then, after American and South Vietnamese troops routed the communists, LBJ's favorable ratings returned. See Dallek, *Flawed Giant*, 526-527.

Following the Tet offensive, LBJ's overall poll numbers dropped to 36 percent—down 12 points. His approval rating before that, in early January 1968, stood at 48 percent. Kearns Goodwin, *Lyndon Johnson and the American Dream*, 336.

⁴   With only a few weeks to go before the New Hampshire primary, RFK, LBJ, and the Democratic National Committee each commissioned private polls on McCarthy's strength in the conservative state. The results gave no reason to fear the poet-cum-senator: in every poll, McCarthy's

support drifted between 8 percent and 11 percent. See White, *The Making of the President 1968,* 8.

Two weeks before the New Hampshire primary, *Time* magazine's poll showed McCarthy at 11 percent of the vote. See Kearns Goodwin, *Lyndon Johnson and the American Dream,* 338.

By March 4 (one week before the primary), polls showed two-thirds of New Hampshire Democrats supported LBJ, with McCarthy garnering only 11 percent. See Dallek, *Flawed Giant,* 526-527.

[5]   According to the LBJ Library staff, one of LBJ's favorite alcoholic beverages was Cutty Sark. http://www.lbjlib.utexas.edu/johnson/archives.hom/FAQs/Favorites/lbjtable.asp

[6]   Postmaster General Lawrence F. O'Brien, LBJ's 1968 campaign director, wrote that when McCarthy announced his candidacy, it "was not taken seriously by anyone around the president. It was regarded as a joke, an annoyance. At the time, it was Bob Kennedy, not Gene McCarthy, who worried Lyndon Johnson." See Lawrence F. O'Brien, *No Final Victories: A Life in Politics from John F. Kennedy to Watergate* (New York: Doubleday & Company, Inc., 1974), 215.

[7]   Nationally syndicated columnists Roland Evans and Robert Novak predicted that in New Hampshire, McCarthy wasn't facing defeat, he faced annihilation. Further, a recent statewide poll of New Hampshire Democrats showed LBJ beating McCarthy 76 percent to 6 percent. See Dallek, *Flawed Giant,* 526.

[8]   John Roche, president of the Americans for Democratic Action, told LBJ that McCarthy was doing so badly in New Hampshire that he was tempted to float a rumor that McCarthy was actually working for LBJ to dispirit the peace movement. See Dallek, *Flawed Giant,* 525-526.

[9]   LBJ enjoyed support from the entire national Democratic Party establishment, including virtually every elected official in New Hampshire. With RFK not running, LBJ never bothered to file for the New Hampshire primary. After McCarthy declared his candidacy, LBJ's campaign made a tactical decision: rather than ignore McCarthy, the White House allowed

New Hampshire Governor John W. King to mount a write-in campaign for LBJ. See Goodwin, *Remembering America*, 486.

Along with Governor King and Senator McIntyre, all ten of the New Hampshire Democratic Party county chairmen supported LBJ's write-in effort. See McCarthy, *The Year of the People*, 64.

[10]   Governor King ran LBJ's write in campaign in a heavy-handed manner: he tried to force state employees to sign serial-numbered pledge cards for the president. See Stavis, *We Were the Campaign*, 27.

"By the middle of February [1968], [LBJ's] pledge card had become a serious liability. Their hope that the card would serve as a party unifying device without having to face divisive issues had stumbled." McCarthy's campaign sent a letter to each member of the New Hampshire Democratic State Central Committee, stating that "the use of numbered pledge cards—in an effort publicly to commit voters—is unprecedented and indefensible. It constitutes a brand of intimidation and coercion which is an offense to the party rank-and-file. [¶] We are particularly shocked by the open threat of Governor King—namely that New Hampshire Democrats had better stand up and be counted or from now on be counted out. This kind of talk is simply unacceptable[.]" Hoeh, *I Hear America Singing*, 431.

[11]   Governor King sought to impress the White House with the write-in effort for another reason: he hoped to complete his career in public service with a presidential appointment to the federal bench. See Chester, Hodgson, Page, *An American Melodrama*, 94.

[12]   LBJ's monologue about not fearing RFK's entry into the presidential race, and how RFK already alienated major segments of the Democratic Party coalition, is adapted from a variety of sources:

- At a time when RFK was attacking LBJ and his Vietnam policies, RFK spoke at a New York fundraiser in June 1967 and hailed LBJ as a president who has "borne the burdens of the world as few other men have ever borne them." See Chester, Hodgson, Page, *An American Melodrama*, 61.

- In December 1967, less than a week after McCarthy's announcement that he would challenge LBJ, RFK stated in a television interview, "I expect [Johnson] is going to win the nomination and I will support him." See Steel, *In Love with the Night*, 141.

- On January 30, 1968, two months after McCarthy declared his candidacy, and only six weeks before the New Hampshire primary, RFK spoke at a National Press Club breakfast sponsored by the Christian Science Monitor. During his off-the-record remarks to reporters, RFK reiterated that he would not challenge Johnson under any "conceivable circumstances.... My running would automatically elect a Republican by splitting the Democratic Party, and Democratic candidates would be beaten all over the country." At the end of the breakfast, reporters asked if they could quote RFK's remarks. RFK's press secretary, Frank Mankiewicz, insisted that RFK's comment be amended to read that RFK would not challenge LBJ "under any foreseeable circumstances." See White, *The Making of the President 1968*, 9; see also Chester, Hodgson, Page, *An American Melodrama*, 101; McCarthy, *Up 'Til Now*, 188.

- At that same National Press Club breakfast, RFK took a shot at McCarthy, saying a presidential campaign should appeal to the generous spirit of Americans, and "McCarthy is unable to tap that spirit." See Chester, Hodgson, Page, *An American Melodrama*, 106.

- On February 11, 1968, the *New York Times* reported that RFK had pledged his support to LBJ even though RFK had been highly critical of the president's Vietnam policy and some of his domestic policies. See McCarthy, *The Year of the People*, 52.

- RFK's speechwriter and longtime friend, Richard Goodwin, noted that RFK's "dilemma" was in his blasting America's Vietnam war policy as immoral, "[y]et at the same time he responded to questions about his political intentions with the litany of political boilerplate: 'I intend to support President Johnson's reelection in 1968....'" The contradiction between Kennedy's expressed conviction and his political position was too large, too blatant, led many to doubt the sincerity of his conviction, even to question his integrity. And the fiercest criticisms came from his natural constituency—liberals, blacks, the young." Goodwin also noted that RFK's polls numbers began to drop gradually. "His opposition to the war was controversial among the many who supported the administration's policies. His support of Johnson was controversial among those allied with the growing peace movement." See Goodwin, *Remembering America*, 475.

RFK's brother-in-law Sargent Shriver told reporter Drew Pearson in January 1968 that even though RFK stated there were "no foreseeable conditions" under which he would run for president against LBJ, "There is no question that Bobby was considering it…. He had people calling up around the country taking soundings. Frank Mankiewicz, Bobby's press secretary, used to work for me. When someone calls me from Denver saying that Bobby's people have called him to sound him out, you can't get away from the facts." See Pearson and Hannaford, *Washington Merry-Go-Round*, 541.

[13]   To his intimate friend and counselor Horace Busby, LBJ said, "I've got the nomination, too. Somebody may try, but they can't take it away. I've got my votes already." See Busby, *The Thirty-First of March*, 178.

According to Ted Sorensen, there was no doubt LBJ planned to run for reelection in 1968. All the signs were there: LBJ hired pollsters and was organizing in key states. See Sorensen, *Counselor*, 455-456.

The *Washington Post*, on December 15, 1967, quoted an anonymous Johnson Administration official as saying that "everyone in the Administration would campaign against [McCarthy] and that there would be a massive organizational effort by Democratic state officials coordinated through the Democratic National Committee. The plan, the story said, had already been put into effect in New Hampshire, Wisconsin, Nebraska, and California." Further, in January 1968, Democratic National Committee Chairman John Bailey said "[t]he Democratic National Convention is as good as over. It will be Lyndon Johnson's again, and that's that." See McCarthy, *The Year of the People*, 65, 108.

CHAPTER 8

[1]   After the North Vietnamese Tet offensive, McCarthy gave a well-covered policy speech at the Manchester Alpine Club, where he said, "In 1963, we were told that we were winning the war. In 1964, we were told the corner was being turned. In 1965, we were told the enemy was being brought to its knees. In 1966, in 1967, and now again in 1968, we hear the same hollow claims of [progress] and victory. For the fact is that the enemy is bolder than ever, while we must steadily enlarge our own commitment. The Democratic Party in 1964 promised 'no wider war.' Yet the war is getting wider every month. Only a few months ago we were told that 65 percent of the population was secure. Now we know that even the American Embassy is not secure." Chester, Hodgson, Page, *An American Melodrama*, 93.

[2]   Gerry Studds, one of the leaders of McCarthy's New Hampshire effort, said that after Tet, "[f]or the first time, a large portion of the country was capable of being convinced that the government had lied to them." See Chester, Hodgson, Page, *An American Melodrama*, 93.

[3]   With only three weeks before the New Hampshire primary, McCarthy had no formal campaign organization established in the state. Of the brick-and-mortar campaign offices opened there, only three of them had any full-time staff. See Larner, *Nobody Knows*, 35.

[4]   Students traveling to New Hampshire to campaign for McCarthy came from college campuses "as far away as Michigan, Wisconsin, Ohio, and even California." See McCarthy, *The Year of the People*, 69.

[5]   In the closing days of the New Hampshire primary, McCarthy's Concord campaign headquarters "became cluttered with sleeping bags, portable typewriters, textbooks, and term papers in various stages of completion." A record player became a central part of the operation: the volunteers and staff looked forward to the arrival of new inductees into McCarthy's army, because it meant someone would bring some new record albums to play in the headquarters. See Stavis, *We Were the Campaign*, 4.

[6]   "There were no leaders, really, in the campaign. It was a 'Children's Crusade[.]'" Larner, *Nobody Knows*, 52.

[7]   Curtis Gans "carefully selected New York buses to be stopped, on the guess that heavy New York accents and a hard-sell semi-radical approach that might have been learned canvassing in New York would alienate the proud, independent, conservative New Hampshirites.... Part of Gans' plan was to establish the campaign as dignified and polite." See Stavis, *We Were the Campaign*, 17.

Sam Brown (McCarthy's New Hampshire student volunteer coordinator) vetted each volunteer: the "straights" who were clean-cut and presentable did voter outreach and canvassing. The scruffy students with long hair and/or beards were put to work on headquarters operations where they would not have direct voter contact. See Chester, Hodgson, Page, *An American Melodrama*, 97-98.

[8]   "Clean for Gene" meant more than haircuts and shaves: it meant keeping the extracurricular activities of the students from hitting the press and offending the staid New Hampshire voters. "The canvassers, moreover, the core of the campaign, might produce bad press: they might get into fights or get caught smoking pot. A story revealing such behavior could puncture the entire image of the McCarthy Kids. Thus Gans carefully kept the press away from our canvassers frugging at a Manchester party on a Saturday evening." See Stavis, *We Were the Campaign*, 16-17.

[9]   Governor King, leading the write-in campaign for LBJ, stated, "Now is the time for Democrats to stand up and be counted—or be counted out." The McCarthy campaign responded with posters bearing the slogan

"Whatever Happened to the Secret Ballot?" and which depicted the controversial Johnson pledge card. See Chester, Hodgson, Page, *An American Melodrama*, 94-95.

[10] McCarthy said the LBJ pledge cards reminded him of the way they brand cattle in Texas. He viewed it as a test of the independent spirit of New Hampshire, and he hoped the voters would react against such a device. See Chester, Hodgson, Page, *An American Melodrama*, 95.

McCarthy charged that the LBJ pledge cards were part of a "Texas-style branding party" and an "intrusion into a free democratic process not altogether inconsistent with the way the Johnson Administration is operating." See "1968: McCarthy Stuns the President," *New Hampshire Union Leader*, May 3, 2011, http://www.unionleader.com/apps/pbcs.dll/article?AID=/99999999/NEWS0605/110509966.

After McCarthy delivered a campaign speech before a New Hampshire Rotary Club, a local businessman shook his hand and told the candidate he was switching his vote from LBJ to McCarthy. He told McCarthy that he had signed "one of those LBJ pledge cards. But I think I'll write the president—tell him to deduct one card[.]" Hoeh, *I Hear America Singing*, 435-436.

[11] As one member of McCarthy's New Hampshire student army wrote, "If I was willing to stand in the cold, freezing wind and [campaign for McCarthy], it was *my* campaign." Stavis, *We Were the Campaign*, 4.

[12] Blair Clark's "range of acquaintances and friends was wide. Robert Lowell dedicated a book of poems to him." See Chester, Hodgson, Page, *An American Melodrama*, 86.

[13] Regarding poet Robert Lowell's propensity to hang around McCarthy during his campaign, "[n]ot all the McCarthy staffers were persuaded of the advantage of having America's premiere poet permanently built into their political operation. In a campaign not marked for hardness of nose, some people felt that… Lowell distracted McCarthy from the political ordeal before him." Chester, Hodgson, Page, *An American Melodrama*, 338-339.

[14]   RFK continued to vacillate in late 1967 about entering the 1968 presidential campaign. As historian and RFK friend Arthur M. Schlesinger Jr. noted in his diary entry of November 29, 1967, "Bobby says that the only primaries which really matter are New Hampshire and Wisconsin.... He thinks that California comes too late to make any difference.... [He] says that he will have to fish or cut bait within a couple of weeks after the New Hampshire primary. If McCarthy should win in New Hampshire and Wisconsin, I think Bobby might well decide to enter the California primary himself." Schlesinger Jr., *Journals*, 266.

[15]   In early January 1968, Dick Goodwin, Senator Ted Kennedy, Bill vanden Heuvel, and Dave Burke (Ted Kennedy's aide) visited RFK at Hickory Hill to discuss a possible 1968 presidential run. RFK went over his various options before stating, "The support just isn't there. People will think it's a personal vendetta between me and Johnson, not the war. So, I guess I'm not going to do it." As Dick Goodwin later recalled, RFK stared at the floor as if trying to conceal his pain. Later that afternoon, RFK left for Oklahoma and asked Dick Goodwin to drive with him to Dulles Airport. At the airport gate, as they shook hands and parted, Goodwin told RFK that if he wasn't running, Goodwin wanted to go to New Hampshire and help McCarthy. "That'd be helpful," RFK replied. Goodwin interpreted that comment to mean it would be helpful to have a "Kennedy man" inside the McCarthy campaign. See Goodwin, *Remembering America*, 481.

Dick Goodwin met with McCarthy in Washington on February 10, 1968 and volunteered to work on the McCarthy campaign. "He made this offer, of course, because he believed that Senator Kennedy would not be a candidate." See McCarthy, *The Year of the People*, 52.

[16]   RFK's call to Dick Goodwin six days before the New Hampshire primary, where RFK asked Goodwin to relay to McCarthy the message that RFK might enter the presidential campaign is, with the exceptions noted below, adapted from actual events as remembered by Dick Goodwin. See Goodwin, *Remembering America*, 507-509.

- "These kids should be RFK's kids; this army should be RFK's army; RFK is losing them, and when they're gone, they're gone forever" is adapted from an actual conversation between RFK and Joseph Dolan. See Schlesinger Jr., *Robert Kennedy and His Times*, 844.

- Jules Feiffer's "Good Bobby-Bad Bobby" cartoon: see Schlesinger Jr., *Robert Kennedy and His Times*, 835; David Halberstam, *The Unfinished Odyssey of Robert Kennedy* (New York: Random House, 1969), 57.

- While still agonizing over whether he should enter the presidential campaign, RFK spoke at Brooklyn College. Students picketing him held up protest signs: "Bobby Kennedy: Hawk, Dove, or Chicken?" RFK saw the signs and complained about them to his aide, Joseph Dolan, who thought the signs were funny. As he later remembered, RFK "wasn't in a mood to laugh about it." See Schlesinger Jr., *Robert Kennedy and His Times*, 836.

[17] The conversation where Goodwin told McCarthy RFK's response to McCarthy's suggestion that he would serve only one term is adapted from actual events. See Goodwin, *Remembering America*, 507-509; Schlesinger Jr., *Robert Kennedy and His Times*, 847-848.

[18] The telephone call between RFK and Dick Goodwin on the eve of the New Hampshire primary, with the exceptions noted below, is adapted from Goodwin, *Remembering America*, 516-517.

- Goodwin relaying McCarthy's "one term as president" offer to RFK if he endorsed McCarthy, RFK's refusal, Goodwin urging RFK to endorse McCarthy because, if McCarthy's campaign imploded, it would be easier for McCarthy supporters to rush to him, and RFK replying that "I just can't bring myself to tell people I'd really like to see Eugene McCarthy be president of the United States" is adapted from an actual conversation between RFK and Arthur Schlesinger. See Schlesinger Jr., *Robert Kennedy and His Times*, 847-848.

- RFK on McCarthy: "How can I endorse a guy that I think is totally unfit to be president?" See White, *The Making of the President 1968*, 158, 161, 175.

- New Hampshire's Democratic Governor John W. King (1918-1996) and U.S. Senator Thomas J. McIntyre (1915-1992) attacked McCarthy during their state primary. King made these comments about McCarthy:

  » A vote for McCarthy was a vote of support for the communist guerrillas of North Vietnam. See Stavis, *We Were the Campaign*, 27.

  » A victory for McCarthy would be "greeted with great cheers in Hanoi." See "1968: McCarthy Stuns the President," *Manchester Union Leader*, http://www.unionleader.com/apps/pbcs. dll/article?AID=/99999999/NEWS0605/110509966.

  » McCarthy is "a champion of appeasement and surrender." See Chester, Hodgson, Page, *An American Melodrama*, 98.

  » "The communists in Vietnam are watching the New Hampshire primary." Chester, Hodgson, Page, *An American Melodrama*, 98.

  » Senator McIntyre made these comments about McCarthy during his state's primary campaign:

  » McCarthy is the friend of "draft dodgers and deserters." See Chester, Hodgson, Page, *An American Melodrama*. 98.

  » McCarthy advocates legislation allowing draft dodgers to return to the U.S., which "will destroy the very fabric of our national devotion. This is fuzzy thinking about principles that have made our nation great." See "1968: McCarthy Stuns the President."

- Responding to King's and McIntyre's attacks, McCarthy called their accusations "lies" and "slanders upon my patriotism and loyalty." McCarthy said their efforts on behalf of LBJ "consisted of a single, shrill, irrelevant and false note—the implication that opposition to the President's policies is somehow disloyal." See "1968: McCarthy Stuns the President."

CHAPTER 9

[1]   "The President's [New Hampshire] promoters [Governor King and Senator McIntyre] had forecast a 3-1 victory [of LBJ over McCarthy]—and even that prediction was toned down from earlier 10-1 talk." See Associated Press, "McCarthy 4,000 Votes Behind Johnson," *Post Crescent*, Appleton, Wisconsin, March 13, 1968.

[2]   In his speech to the VFW convention on the night of the New Hampshire primary, LBJ joked, "You know, the New Hampshire primaries are unique in politics. They are the only races where anybody can run—and everybody can win. I think New Hampshire is the only place where candidates can claim 20 percent is a landslide, and 40 percent is a mandate, and 60 percent is unanimous. I had an early report from New Hampshire this morning on these 'unbiased' television networks. They had counted twenty-five votes there—the first twenty-five, and the vote for LBJ was zero. I said to Mrs. Johnson, 'What do you think about that?' She answered, 'I think the day is bound to get better, Lyndon.'" See "Remarks at a Dinner of the Veterans of Foreign Wars," *The American Presidency Project, Papers of Lyndon B. Johnson*, March 12, 1968, http://www.presidency.ucsb.edu/lyndon_johnson.php. See also Chester, Hodgson, Page, *An American Melodrama*, 80.

[3]   Since LBJ's name was not on the New Hampshire primary ballot, he could not control the number of pro-LBJ delegates running. With almost 50 of them vying for 24 slots, they dissipated the LBJ vote. By contrast, McCarthy fielded a tight list of 24 delegate candidates for the 24 slots. Thus, McCarthy won 20 out of the 24 delegate slots, even though LBJ beat him in the separate "beauty contest" vote. See, e.g., "1968: McCarthy Stuns the President."

4 "Despite its rural and small-town image, New Hampshire is a highly industrialized state with a large percentage of military and military-related industries." See McCarthy, *The Year of the People*, 62-63.

5 After counting the crossover votes, only 230 votes separated LBJ from McCarthy in the final statewide 1968 New Hampshire primary total. See McCarthy, *Up 'Til Now*, 186; White, *The Making of the President 1968*, 89 (McCarthy came within 230 votes of LBJ in "one of the most patriotic and warlike states of the Union.").

6 The apologetic comment to LBJ attributed to Governor King is adapted from actual comments made by King's fellow organizer of the New Hampshire LBJ write-in campaign, Senator Thomas McIntyre, during a post-primary press conference. McIntyre insisted that the New Hampshire outcome was not a repudiation of LBJ's policies, and instead excused the result as a "frustrated vote over Vietnam. The people of the State of New Hampshire are saying 'we don't understand, we wonder why we are not doing any better.'" See Associated Press, "Fury of Criticism."

7 LBJ's prediction as to how the press would interpret his 48 percent New Hampshire victory is adapted from Jack Bell's analysis of the vote: "While the President's supporters may dismiss as insignificant the verdict by about 53,000 Democrats in a state that is 2-1 Republican, the inescapable fact is that when he and his policies were tested at the polls for the first time in this presidential year, Johnson could barely manage to get 48 percent of the vote.... If McCarthy, little known in New Hampshire, could come close to beating the president, they will feel that there is a strong wind against Johnson's ship on its present course." See Associated Press, "Fury of Criticism."

8 An Associated Press reporter called LBJ's split decision over McCarthy "a narrow, empty victory[.]" See Associated Press, "McCarthy 4,000 Votes Behind Johnson."

9 In explaining LBJ's poor showing in New Hampshire, Governor King groaned to an aide, "What can you do? It was all those kids." See Chester, Hodgson, Page, *An American Melodrama*, 97.

Surprisingly, it wasn't only the peace advocates in New Hampshire that voted for McCarthy: voters who supported an increase in America's military presence in Vietnam voted for McCarthy over LBJ three-to-two. Kearns Goodwin, *Lyndon Johnson and the American Dream*, 338.

[10] Despite the entire state Democratic Party organization working for LBJ, McCarthy carried five of the state's ten counties. See "1968: McCarthy Stuns the President."

[11] The New Hampshire primary left LBJ and his camp stunned. Expecting to win two-thirds of the vote, LBJ garnered only 48 percent. Although it eclipsed McCarthy's 42 percent, McCarthy's strength shocked the political establishment. Overnight, the obscure Minnesota senator became a serious presidential candidate. "Some of McCarthy's voters were hawks fed up with Johnson's failure to win the war. Johnson supporters had underestimated the extent to which voters saw Tet as an American defeat, and overestimated gains to be made from describing a vote for McCarthy as a vote for [North Vietnamese communists]." See Dallek, *Flawed Giant*, 527.

[12] According to LBJ's official White House daily log for March 12, 1968, LBJ left the White House at 9:00 p.m. by motorcade for the VFW convention at the Sheraton Park Hotel. He began his remarks at 9:16 p.m. and completed them at 9:34 p.m. He departed the hotel at 9:40 p.m. and returned to the Oval Office at 9:50 p.m. See www.digital.lbjlibrary.org/transition_files/DD-19680312.pdf.

[13] After Governor King's term ended, he became a state superior court judge. A decade later, the current New Hampshire governor appointed King to the state supreme court. Two years later, he became chief justice. Robert McG. Thomas Jr., "John W. King, 79, Governor Who Instituted State Lottery," *New York Times*, August 14, 1996.

[14] RFK did not expect McCarthy to withdraw after he won the New Hampshire primary: see Schlesinger Jr., *Journals*, 280 ("RFK felt that McCarthy's success had boxed him in. Obviously he could not now expect Gene to withdraw. 'I don't blame him at all,' [RFK] said. 'Of course he feels that he gave me my chance to make the try, that I didn't and that he

has earned the right to go ahead. I can't blame him. He has done a great job in opening the situation up.'").

15   RFK refused to endorse McCarthy with the hope that, in making that gesture, McCarthy's delegates later would move to RFK once the McCarthy campaign flickered out: see, e.g., Schlesinger Jr., *Journals*, 279-280 (After Schlesinger urged RFK to endorse McCarthy with the expectation his delegates later would flock to him, RFK "listened but was not deeply impressed; he again cited the difficulty of saying, or seeming to say, that he really wanted Gene for president. We left, all perplexed and rather dejected, shortly after midnight." Journal entry of March 13, 1968.).

16   The discussion between RFK and Arthur Schlesinger over endorsing McCarthy the night of the New Hampshire primary is adapted from an actual event. See Schlesinger Jr., *Robert Kennedy and His Times*, 849.

17   "The campuses had always been considered as Kennedy's base. He had been nurturing this constituency for years; he lost it in a month." See Chester, Hodgson, Page, *An American Melodrama*, 98.

   McCarthy's success in New Hampshire had renewed RFK's interest in running. "McCarthy and his supporters were visibly—and justifiably—sour on the idea that RFK might take advantage of their effort by competing against their candidate after refusing to enter the race when Johnson looked unbeatable." See Sorensen, *Counselor*, 456-457.

18   After the New Hampshire primary, McCarthy said, "You know when I first thought I might have a chance? When I realized that you could go into any bar in the country and insult Lyndon Johnson and nobody would punch you in the nose." Kearns Goodwin, *Lyndon Johnson and the American Dream*, 338.

19   During McCarthy's New Hampshire primary victory speech, the assembled volunteers chanted, "We want Gene! We want Gene!" They sang the Wisconsin fight song and then added a chorus of "Happy Days Are Here Again." See Associated Press, "McCarthy Urges LBJ to Campaign," *Bridgeport Post*, Bridgeport, Connecticut, March 13, 1968.

McCarthy made his New Hampshire primary victory speech in the Bedford Room of the Wayfarer Inn. See Hoeh, *I Hear America Singing*, 488.

[20] In his New Hampshire primary election-night speech to his volunteers, McCarthy said, "People have remarked that this campaign has brought young people back into the system. But it's the other way around: The young people have brought the country back into the system." See Chester, Hodgson, Page, *An American Melodrama*, 100.

[21] The Associated Press quoted one of McCarthy's unnamed campaign advisers as looking ahead optimistically. "[P]eople will now join up who previously had discounted McCarthy's chances and did not want to be associated with a 'symbolic 5 percent fringe movement.'" See Associated Press, "McCarthy Urges LBJ."

[22] "I also rejected the offer of help from Senator Kennedy in Wisconsin. I did not need his money or his organization, I said. All I needed was running room." See McCarthy, *The Year of the People*, 93-94.

Arthur Herzog, who later became the McCarthy campaign's coordinator in the Oregon primary, wrote that when RFK called McCarthy in his hotel about 12:30 a.m. after the New Hampshire primary results came in, McCarthy was heard saying, "Oh, hi Bobby. Yes, it was great. Thanks. It was rough. Those factories—I tell you, I went through more factories than I've been through in twenty years of politics." He told RFK he would be in touch with him tomorrow after he returned to Washington. See Herzog, *McCarthy for President*, 98.

[23] In reality, Blair Clark was not the source of the "one dog stealing another dog's bone" description of RFK's expected late presidential campaign entry. It came from New Hampshire attorney Eugene Daniell, who had started a vigorous "Write in Robert Kennedy" during that state's 1968 primary. After RFK aide Ted Sorensen made a personal trip to the state and asked Daniell to cease the effort, the write-in campaign disbanded. When RFK announced he was entering the presidential contest following McCarthy's strong New Hampshire showing, a disgusted Daniell said he was through with RFK, and compared RFK's late entry to one dog

stealing another dog's bone. See Chester, Hodgson, Page, *An American Melodrama*, 93; see also Sorensen, *Counselor*, 454.

[24]   RFK and his team did not view McCarthy as a serious candidate. They believed McCarthy would never provide LBJ any meaningful opposition. Further, they also "knew" McCarthy would step aside if RFK entered the race. See Goodwin, *Remembering America*, 480-481.

If RFK entered the race, the political intelligentsia expected McCarthy to drop out. See McCarthy, *Up 'Til Now*, 192.

[25]   RFK's telephone conversation with McCarthy on the night of the New Hampshire primary, where RFK told McCarthy of his intention to enter the presidential race, is adapted from an actual event. See Schlesinger Jr., *Robert Kennedy and His Times*, 850, 855.

That same evening, after the voting results came in, RFK told the press, "I am actively reconsidering the possibilities that are available to me and I imagine that other people around the country are doing the same." RFK said that McCarthy's ability to run an issue-oriented campaign minimized his previous concern that his entry would produce a contest over personalities rather than over issues. See Associated Press, "Senator Gets 42% of Vote; President 48%," *Bridgeport Post*, Bridgeport, Connecticut, March 13, 1968.

The morning after McCarthy's New Hampshire primary win, RFK told the press he was "re-assessing" his previous decision not to run. See White, *The Making of the President 1968*, 162.

[26]   "Ironically, had Johnson refused to engage in New Hampshire, instructed his supporters not to campaign, and disavowed all efforts on his behalf, he might well have been renominated. But he believed what all 'informed' politicians believed, what they all told him: that [in New Hampshire] it would be an easy and decisive conquest [of McCarthy]." See Goodwin, *Remembering America*, 486.

CHAPTER 10

[1]   The day after the New Hampshire primary, Dick Goodwin flew back to Washington before rejoining McCarthy for the upcoming Wisconsin primary. While at his Georgetown hotel, he received a call asking him to attend a meeting of Kennedy advisers to discuss RFK's candidacy. Goodwin refused, citing his position with McCarthy. The next day, RFK called Goodwin at 6:00 a.m. and said he was running. The telephone conversations between RFK and Goodwin are adapted from actual events: see Goodwin, *Remembering America*, 517-518.

[2]   The telephone call in which Goodwin told RFK he was leaving for Wisconsin to help McCarthy, that RFK was not on the ballot in Wisconsin, and the defeat of LBJ there was as important to RFK as to McCarthy, is adapted from an actual event. See Goodwin, *Remembering America*, 520.

[3]   The vignette of the RFK-McCarthy meeting in RFK's Senate office is a compilation of two meetings that occurred over two days:

- On March 13, 1968, McCarthy returned to Washington from New Hampshire. Reporters met him at the airport and asked for his response to reports that RFK was about to announce his presidential candidacy. McCarthy declined to comment, saying it was just a rumor. When McCarthy reached the Capitol, he learned that RFK had called McCarthy's office several times asking to see him when he arrived. With reporters staking out the Capitol, McCarthy slipped into the Senate Gymnasium and then exited a side door for the prearranged meeting with RFK at Senator Edward Kennedy's office (Edward Kennedy was not present). During their encounter, RFK and McCarthy discussed RFK's earlier statement about him "reassessing" his position as to whether he would run. McCarthy said he believed it unlikely that he (McCarthy) could win the nomination, but if he won the White House, he wanted only one term. McCarthy did not promise to support RFK in 1972, nor did he ask for RFK's support in exchange for stepping aside four years later. RFK "did not specifically state his intention, but I got the definite impression that he was going to run." See McCarthy, *The Year of the People*, 88-89; see also McCarthy, *Up 'Til Now*, 189; Schlesinger Jr., *Journals*, 281-282.

- The next day, March 14, McCarthy left for Wisconsin to campaign in that state's primary. After a luncheon speech, McCarthy received word that Edward Kennedy wanted to meet with him privately. McCarthy reached the Norland Hotel in Green Bay that evening about 9:00 p.m. He learned that Edward Kennedy had missed a connecting flight in Chicago and was attempting to charter a private jet. By 11:00 p.m., the Green Bay airport reported no flight plan for a chartered airplane, so McCarthy went to bed. After 1:00 a.m., an aide awakened McCarthy and said that Kennedy was on his way over. Since reporters had staked out the location, the hotel manager escorted Kennedy to McCarthy's suite through a back entrance and a freight elevator. "Like the walrus and the carpenter, Senator Kennedy and I talked of many things," McCarthy later said of this meeting at which Edward Kennedy told McCarthy that RFK would announce his candidacy the following day. McCarthy told Edward Kennedy that RFK's decision would have no impact on his continued campaign for the nomination. McCarthy, *The Year of the People*, 92-93.

- According to the Library of Congress, in 1968 McCarthy occupied Room 411 of the Old Senate Office Building; Senator Edward Kennedy occupied Room 431 of the same building, and RFK occupied Room 3327 of the New Senate Office Building. Letter to the author from Terrance Lisbeth, Reference Assistant, Library of Congress, January 6, 2016.

[4] The Clark Clifford-Vietnam War commission vignette is based on an actual event. Just before announcing his presidential candidacy, RFK sent LBJ a private message: RFK would forego a presidential run if LBJ would (1) state publicly that his Vietnam War policies were a failure, and (2) appoint a ten-man commission to review these policies. Among the names RFK submitted for the commission were his own and eight other opponents of LBJ's escalation policies. In the actual meeting, both RFK and Ted Sorensen met with Secretary of Defense Clark Clifford to discuss RFK's proposal. After Clifford identified the problematic demand of LBJ admitting publicly his policies were a failure, RFK conceded the demand might be too strong. Prior to this meeting, there had been a reported expression of interest in the idea by the White House, but when Clifford met later with LBJ to discuss the matter (also attending that meeting were Vice President Hubert Humphrey and U.S. Supreme Court Justice Abe Fortas), they all agreed that LBJ should reject the proposition. For an account of the actual proposal and LBJ's response to it, see Schlesinger Jr., *Robert Kennedy and His Times*, 454-459.

Reporter Drew Pearson noted in his diary entry of March 18, 1968, "Bobby's reported plan to have a commission study the war and whether it should be dropped or escalated was based upon the idea that if Johnson accepted it, he, Bobby, would not run for president. The general impression I got was that this was political blackmail[.]" Pearson and Hannaford, *Washington Merry-Go-Round*, 552.

[5] The White House provided a swift response to McCarthy's unexpected strong showing in the New Hampshire primary. LBJ's press spokesman announced that everyone in the Johnson Administration would campaign against McCarthy in the Wisconsin primary, and that there would be a massive anti-McCarthy effort organized by state Party officials and directed by the Democratic National Committee. Among the administration officials sent to combat McCarthy in Wisconsin was his old friend and longtime Minnesota colleague, Vice President Hubert Humphrey. See, e.g., McCarthy, *Up 'Til Now*, 185.

[6] RFK announced his presidential candidacy at a press conference in the Senate Caucus Room at 9:00 a.m. on Saturday, March 16, 1968.

CHAPTER 11

[1]   On March 16, 1968, American soldiers were alleged to have murdered up to 500 unarmed men, women, and children in two Vietnamese hamlets, one of which was in Quang Ngai province. This atrocity, later known as the My Lai massacre, resulted in the court-martial of over two dozen soldiers. Only one, Lieutenant William Calley Jr., a platoon leader, was convicted. The My Lai massacre did not become public until November 12, 1969. Ironically, the story broke in the Associated Press by reporter Seymore "Sy" Hersh, Eugene McCarthy's original 1968 campaign press secretary.

[2]   Unlike the New Hampshire primary, which LBJ virtually ignored, the White House engaged heavily in the Wisconsin primary battle against McCarthy to avoid another embarrassment. LBJ's staff and Cabinet members blanketed the state in an effort to boost LBJ's chances. See McCarthy, *Up 'Til Now*, 187.

Almost two weeks after the New Hampshire primary, and only a week before the Wisconsin primary, the *New York Times* projected LBJ would win the nomination with about 65 percent of the delegate votes at the 1968 Democratic National Convention in Chicago. See Dallek, *Flawed Giant*, 528.

LBJ had no choice but to face McCarthy in the Wisconsin primary: unlike New Hampshire, Wisconsin placed all presidential candidates on the ballot automatically unless they filed a disclaimer of candidacy. "That means Johnson's name will be on the ballot." Associated Press, "McCarthy 4,000 Votes Behind Johnson."

[3]   Richard Nixon, campaigning for the 1968 Republican presidential nomination, believed RFK's candidacy put the New York senator into an

unsolvable conundrum: RFK jumped in at the last minute as a candidate for the nomination of a Party led by an incumbent president who hated him and who controlled all the national levers of Party power. See White, *The Making of the President 1968*, 145.

4   In announcing his support for LBJ's 1968 reelection, former President Harry S Truman chirped that Johnson's upstart challengers were just a "damned bunch of smart-alecks." See Sam Houston Johnson, *My Brother Lyndon* (New York: Cowles Book Company, 1970), 242; Schlesinger Jr., *Robert Kennedy and His Times*, 859.

Former President Dwight D. Eisenhower called RFK "shallow, vain and untrustworthy—on top of which he is indecisive." Eisenhower offered his appraisal of RFK in a letter to Robert Cutler, March 26, 1968 (reprinted in the *New York Post*, March 21, 1975); see also Schlesinger Jr., *Robert Kennedy and His Times*, 858.

5   Columnist Murray Kempton, a longtime RFK friend, blistered RFK for his late entry into the presidential race. In a column titled "Senator Kennedy, Farewell," *New York Post*, March 26, 1968, Kempton likened RFK to a coward coming down from the hills to shoot the wounded. "He has, in the naked display of his rage at Eugene McCarthy for having survived on the lonely road he dared not walk himself, done with a single great gesture something very few public men have ever been able to do: In one day, he managed to confirm the worst things his enemies have ever said about him. We can see him now working for Joe McCarthy, tapping the phones of tax dodgers, setting a spy on Adlai Stevenson at the UN [Stevenson, the 1952 and 1956 Democratic presidential nominee, was JFK's UN ambassador].... I blame myself, not him, for all the years he fooled me." Schlesinger Jr., *Robert Kennedy and His Times*, 861.

After RFK announced for president, Senator Edward Kennedy sent columnist Murray Kempton an invitation to join him and RFK for dinner. Kempton replied in a telegram, "Sorry I can't join you. Your brother's [presidential campaign] announcement makes clear that Saint Patrick did not drive out all of the snakes in Ireland." See Goodwin, *Remembering America*, 521.

In the weeks following RFK's assassination, a chastened Kempton took back his unkind words about RFK. See Schlesinger Jr., *Robert Kennedy and His Times*, 861.

6   After RFK became a presidential candidate, Chicago Mayor Richard J. Daley reiterated his support for LBJ. See Schlesinger Jr., *Robert Kennedy and His Times*, 859.

After RFK's entry into the 1968 campaign, Chicago Mayor Richard Daley told a friend that he wasn't "especially keen" on RFK, and as an organization man himself he couldn't understand a Democrat taking on an incumbent Democratic president of the United States. If RFK had any hope that Daley, who was privately a dove on the Vietnam War, might support him, those hopes were dashed three days after RFK announced, when Daley stated definitively and publicly, "the president could not be beaten" for the presidential nomination. See Chester, Hodgson, Page, *An American Melodrama*, 120, 127.

7   Despite the antiwar insurgencies of McCarthy and RFK, the mainstream Democratic Party was committed to continuing the war policies of the Johnson Administration. See McCarthy, *Up 'Til Now*, 199.

8   A few days after RFK announced his presidential candidacy, reporter Drew Pearson—a man who knew both RFK and LBJ well—recorded in his diary on March 20, 1968: "[P]revious to Bobby's getting into the race, I'd had doubts as to whether LBJ would run again. Now I was sure he would. The enmity between Bobby and the president is deeper and more vindictive than most people realize." See Pearson and Hannaford, *Washington Merry-Go-Round*, 554.

9   The actual assessment that the Wisconsin primary was "over" for LBJ, and that McCarthy could not be stopped, came not from Larry O'Brien, but from U.S. Senator (and future Vice President) Walter F. Mondale, who went to Wisconsin after the 1968 New Hampshire primary debacle to line up support for the Johnson-Humphrey ticket. "The Party leaders I met with, old friends of mine, told me it was hopeless [for LBJ].... They said it was over, that the White House could do nothing to stop [McCarthy]." See Mondale, *The Good Fight*, 71.

10   Late polls indicated McCarthy would trounce LBJ in Wisconsin, with McCarthy's lead at 60 percent as the election neared. See McCarthy, *Up 'Til Now*, 187.

When LBJ's 1968 campaign director, Lawrence F. O'Brien, visited Wisconsin on the eve of that state's primary, he noted sadly that "we drove by Johnson headquarters and found it dark and empty. A few blocks away we passed the McCarthy headquarters and saw perhaps one hundred young people hard at work inside. That was not a good sign." O'Brien reported back to LBJ that McCarthy would defeat LBJ badly in the Wisconsin primary. See O'Brien, *No Final Victories*, 229.

[11] In the Wisconsin primary, LBJ faced two major hurdles: first, Wisconsin had over 100,000 draft-age and politically active college students, and they found McCarthy's candidacy attractive on multiple levels. Second, Wisconsin allowed primary voters to "crossover," meaning Republican voters could vote for a Democrat. With Nixon having no meaningful Republican opposition in the Wisconsin primary, LBJ's campaign team predicted up to 200,000 GOP voters would cross over and vote for McCarthy to embarrass and weaken LBJ. For a summary of LBJ's Wisconsin problems, see Chester, Hodgson, Page, *An American Melodrama*, 137.

[12] As late as 1967, when antiwar Congressman George Brown (D-CA) introduced a non-binding resolution calling for an end to military operations in Vietnam, only 18 members of the House of Representatives voted for it. Almost 400 congressmen voted no. See Kearns Goodwin, *Lyndon Johnson and the American Dream*, 325.

[13] In a moment of candor, LBJ later told biographer Doris Kearns Goodwin that in 1968 he felt like he was being chased on all sides by a giant stampede of multiple threats: Vietnam, inflation, rioting blacks, demonstrating students, marching welfare mothers, squawking professors, and hysterical reporters. Then came the final straw: "The thing I feared from the first day of my presidency was actually coming true. Robert Kennedy had openly announced his intention to reclaim the throne in memory of his brother. And the American people, swayed by the magic of his name, were dancing in the streets. The whole situation was unbearable for me. After thirty-seven years of public service, I deserved something more than being left alone in the middle of the plain, chased by stampedes on every side." See Kearns Goodwin, *Lyndon Johnson and the American Dream*, 343.

[14]   On the eve of the Wisconsin primary, and realizing that his campaign in that state appeared hopeless, LBJ told former staffer Horace Busby, "If a president has to spend $10 million to get the re-nomination of his Party, then it's time for him and his Party and everybody else to go some other way. I don't want to go that way.... I can't get peace in Vietnam and be president, too." See Busby, *The Thirty-First of March*, 175, 194.

On the day before LBJ's March 31, 1968 bombing-halt speech, he received advance notice that the Gallup organization would release a poll just before the Wisconsin primary showing that LBJ's nationwide support had cratered to only 35 percent, which LBJ feared would drive more votes toward McCarthy in the primary. With two lost primaries and tanking poll numbers, LBJ foresaw the possibility that he might lose control of the Democratic Party. Once Party regulars found him unelectable, the pressure to dump him might prove too overwhelming. See Chester, Hodgson, Page, *An American Melodrama*, 8-9.

U.S. Senator (and future Vice President) Walter F. Mondale, who campaigned for LBJ in Wisconsin during that state's 1968 presidential primary, did not believe LBJ withdrew from the 1968 campaign so he would be free to pursue peace in Vietnam. "I believe Johnson timed his withdrawal to avoid an embarrassing primary loss [in Wisconsin]." See Mondale, *The Good Fight*, 71.

[15]   With the Wisconsin presidential primary only days away, LBJ invited to the White House a reporter who covered him for years. Later, the reporter wrote that when he entered the Oval Office, the president's physical appearance shocked him. "When I had last spoken to him, during the exuberant campaign of 1964, Lyndon Johnson had bestrode the nation's politics like a bronco-buster. Now he seemed exhausted. His eyes, behind the gold-rimmed eyeglasses, were not only nested in lines and wrinkles, but pouched in sockets blue with a permanent weariness.... The contour of his large body reflected his exhaustion as he slouched in a large rocking chair[.]" See White, *The Making of the President 1968*, 114.

[16]   On the night of LBJ's March 31, 1968 address to the nation, Humphrey was in Mexico City to sign a nuclear nonproliferation treaty. See Dallek, *Flawed Giant*, 529.

Humphrey listened to LBJ's March 31, 1968 withdrawal speech over the radio in the Mexican ambassador's study. See Humphrey, *The Education of a Public Man*, 359.

[17] As vice president, Humphrey and his wife Muriel lived in a co-operative apartment building at 550 N Street, S.W., in Washington, D.C. The two-bedroom unit at Harbour Square faced the Washington Channel.

[18] On the morning of LBJ's March 31, 1968 address to the nation, he made an unscheduled visit to Humphrey at the vice president's D.C. apartment just as the Humphreys prepared to leave for a treaty-signing ceremony in Mexico. Huddled in the bedroom, LBJ showed Humphrey the draft of his Vietnam speech, and then he handed him the two alternative endings from which LBJ would choose. The first announced LBJ's plan to seek reelection, and the second announced that he would not run again. LBJ told Humphrey he hadn't decided which one to use, and he suggested that Humphrey listen to his speech that evening to learn the answer. Humphrey followed LBJ's order not to tell anyone about their private discussion, including his wife. See Humphrey, *The Education of a Public Man*, 358-359; Ted Van Dyk, *Heroes, Hacks & Fools: Memoirs from the Political Inside* (Seattle and London: University of Washington Press, 2007), 62-63.

[19] After having met LBJ that morning in his home, and having seen the president's proposed language, Humphrey didn't believe that LBJ would forego reelection. Knowing LBJ for over 20 years, Humphrey dismissed the threat as another example of LBJ's penchant for drama. He didn't believe LBJ would ever surrender the White House. See, e.g., White, *The Making of the President* 1968, 119.

LBJ's longtime friend and adviser, James Rowe, did not believe LBJ would decline to run in 1968. He said that if he ever doubted LBJ would seek reelection, that doubt disappeared the day RFK announced he was running for president, because LBJ would never turn over America to RFK. Kearns Goodwin, *Lyndon Johnson and the American Dream*, 338.

Lawrence F. O'Brien, LBJ's 1968 campaign director, wrote that he never imagined LBJ would withdraw from the presidential race, "and I had not believed that Bob Kennedy could defeat him for the nomination. I had always expected Johnson to be the candidate, probably of a divided party, but, nonetheless, our candidate." See O'Brien, *No Final Victories*, 231.

[20] McCarthy's response to the news that LBJ pulled out of the 1968 election is adapted from actual events. See Chester, Hodgson, Page, *An American Melodrama*, 5-6.

McCarthy was speaking in the auditorium of Carroll College in Waukesha, Wisconsin, on March 31, 1968 when he learned that LBJ had dropped out of the presidential race. Fifty years later, in 2018, reporter Jules Witcover recalled that night: see Jules Witcover, "In 1968, LBJ Shook Nation, World in Decision That Reverberates Yet," *The Mining Journal*, March 30, 2018, https://www.miningjournal.net/opinion/columns/2018/03/in-1968-lbj-shook-nation-world-in-decision-that-reverberates-yet/.

[21] RFK's response to the news that LBJ pulled out of the 1968 election is adapted from actual events. See Chester, Hodgson, Page, *An American Melodrama*, 5-6.

CHAPTER 12

[1]   LBJ had barely completed his March 31, 1968 withdrawal speech when Humphrey's longtime executive assistant, Bill Connell, tried unsuccessfully to call Humphrey in Mexico. Unable to reach him immediately, Connell went to work without permission and called almost 100 labor officials, governors, senators, and other key Party leaders, asking each to avoid making any commitments prematurely. Surprisingly, when Connell made his calls, he found that either RFK or his brother, Senator Ted Kennedy, had already called most of the same people on Connell's list with the same request on behalf of the Kennedy campaign. See Humphrey, *The Education of a Public Man*, 359-360.

Bill Connell and other key Humphrey staffers called dozens of leading Democrats the night of LBJ's March 31 speech and attempted to gauge support for a Humphrey presidential candidacy. See Mondale, *The Good Fight*, 71.

[2]   As soon as LBJ finished his withdrawal announcement, telephone calls deluged the Mexico City embassy switchboard. Reporters covering the trip pounded on the study door and demanded to know if Humphrey was now a presidential candidate. See Van Dyk, *Heroes, Hacks & Fools*, 62-63.

[3]   Caught off guard by LBJ's March 31, 1968 announcement, Humphrey delayed making a decision about running. During this interval, primary filing dates came and went. With no decision yet made, the final deadlines past. If Humphrey ran, he would be forced to bypass the primaries and seek delegates by other means. This didn't concern Humphrey terribly: he knew that RFK wasn't running away with the nomination.

HHH believed that Kennedy had far less organizational support than most might have imagined, and McCarthy had even less. See Humphrey, *The Education of a Public Man*, 361.

[4]   LBJ's "surprise" withdrawal: In a conversation with Humphrey after his March 31, 1968 speech, LBJ chided Humphrey for not being very perceptive in failing to anticipate LBJ's withdrawal. Humphrey wrote later, "This was a lack of perception that I shared with much of America." See Humphrey, *The Education of a Public Man*, 361.

[5]   In contemplating a presidential campaign, Humphrey counted on longtime constituencies remaining loyal to him: civil rights leaders, pro-war Democrats, and organized labor. See Van Dyk, *Heroes, Hacks & Fools*, 67.

[6]   "A tide of goodwill came in the wake of the president's announcement on March 31 [1968]. The following day, April 1, Johnson saw a jump in his approval ratings from 36 percent to 49 percent. Those who had come to think of Johnson as power-hungry, warmongering, or deceitful were suddenly willing to give him the benefit of the doubt." Mark K. Updegrove, *Indomitable Will: LBJ in the Presidency* (New York: Skyhorse Publishing, 2014), 272.

Once LBJ withdrew, the response "was the most positive expression of national support since his landslide reelection in 1964. Democrats and Republicans alike described his decision as an act of selfless patriotism." In the days following his speech, Johnson's national approval rating rocketed to 57 percent. See Dallek, *Flawed Giant*, 530-531.

[7]   After RFK declared his candidacy in mid-March 1968, and before LBJ's withdrawal two weeks later, RFK took the fight directly to LBJ, calling him a sinister man who "call[s] upon the darker impulses of the American spirit." See White, *The Making of the President 1968*, 167.

The day after LBJ's withdrawal, and in a brazen act of chutzpah, RFK requested a private White House meeting with the president to ask that he not oppose him in the primaries. When told by an aide that RFK had requested the meeting, LBJ replied, "I won't bother answering that grandstanding little runt." Meanwhile, that same day, RFK had begun showering LBJ with public flattery. He told audiences that LBJ had shown "devotion to duty" and "leadership and sacrifice" in announcing his withdrawal. See Steel, *In Love with the Night*, 153.

[8] According to one of President Kennedy's closest aides, JFK would not have won Texas or any other Southern state without LBJ on the ticket, and thus would not have become president in 1960. See Sorensen, *Counselor*, 244.

[9] While vice president under JFK, LBJ learned that Attorney General RFK and First Lady Jacqueline Kennedy, in their private musings, gave LBJ and his wife the disparaging nicknames "Colonel Cornpone" and "Little Porkchop." See Guthman and Shulman, *Robert Kennedy in His Own Words*, 417.

[10] LBJ Secretary of Defense Clark Clifford, a rare "Kennedy Man" in LBJ's inner circle, was a credible witness to LBJ's longtime efforts to embrace RFK, only to have his kindness thrown back in his face. Clifford, who also served as JFK's personal attorney as well as chairman of JFK's Intelligence Advisory Board, said, "President Johnson made every effort after the assassination of President Kennedy to get along with the Kennedy family, and in almost every instance his overtures were rejected, and rejected in a manner that was thoroughly offensive and insulting. I thought the attitude of Robert Kennedy and the other members of the family was inexcusable, and I think President Johnson tried to the best of his ability to get along with RFK. He was gracious and courteous and handled it in statesmanlike fashion, and [RFK] and his followers rejected him at every turn.... [T]hey looked upon President Johnson as a usurper of the job that really belonged to them. Their attitude was exceedingly immature and one of the more unattractive chapters in the life of that particular family." See Heymann, *RFK: A Candid Biography of Robert F. Kennedy*, 367-368.

In assuming the presidency and consolidating power, "Where one might have expected bitterness—for all the slights received from some of these same men when he was vice president—Johnson showed only benevolence. He approached each of Kennedy's men individually and made his plea: Jack needed you; I need you more—and so does your country." Kearns Goodwin, *Lyndon Johnson and the American Dream*, 175.

RFK's younger brother, Senator Edward Kennedy, wrote shortly before his death in 2009, "Johnson was capable of kindness toward [Bobby], and courtesy, and political support." Edward M. Kennedy, *True Compass: A Memoir* (New York: Twelve/Hatchette Book Group, 2009), 227.

LBJ's vice president, Hubert Humphrey, wrote years later that LBJ "sought desperately and sincerely to continue the JFK programs, to assuage the Kennedy people who were bereft, to assure the nation that he could lead it well.... As he was heir to the presidency, he wanted, too, to be the heir to the affection of the Kennedy insiders as well as of the nation. When it was not readily forthcoming, he tried more desperately to succeed[.]" See Humphrey, *The Education of a Public Man*, 288-289.

[11]   At his first Cabinet meeting, President Johnson remarked that many men around the table had attended Harvard and Yale, but only one had graduated from Southwest Texas Teachers College in San Marcos. See Chester, Hodgson, Page, *An American Melodrama*, 55.

Although LBJ delivered the "Southwest Teachers College" line as a joke, behind the joke was a deep-seated sense of educational inferiority that was fueled by the sneers of the Eastern establishment-types that he had endured during his vice presidency under the urbane and Harvard-educated John F. Kennedy. Although JFK always treated LBJ with great respect, the snubs and belittling that LBJ endured from JFK's team—and especially from RFK—tattooed his ego permanently. Many years later, former LBJ White House Press Secretary George Christian said, "I really believe, in fact I'm damn sure, that if Bobby Kennedy had made an effort to be generous to Lyndon Johnson, Lyndon Johnson would have loved it. I mean, that's just the way Johnson was. If Bobby had treated him with some respect, instead of going around and calling him Colonel Cornpone, it would have been entirely different." See Heymann, *RFK*, 363-364.

As LBJ told Doris Kearns Goodwin, from that day in 1963 when "I took the oath, I became president. But for millions of Americans, I was still illegitimate, a naked man with no presidential covering, a pretender to the throne, an illegal usurper.... And then there were the bigots and the dividers and the Eastern intellectuals, who were waiting to knock me down before I could even begin to stand up. The whole thing was almost unbearable." See Kearns Goodwin, *Lyndon Johnson and the American Dream*, 170.

[12]   The extent of RFK's hatred for LBJ became clear many years later, when the John F. Kennedy Library released the extensive 1964 interviews RFK conducted for the Library's oral history project. In recordings not released until decades after his death, RFK said he didn't consider LBJ a "gentleman," nor even a "human being." Instead, he described LBJ as "mean, bitter, vicious—an animal in many ways." See Guthman and Shulman, *Robert Kennedy in His Own Words*, 417. At the very time that RFK was making these disparaging comments, he was trying to manipulate his way onto the 1964 Democratic ticket as LBJ's vice presidential running mate. See generally Humphrey, *The Education of a Public Man*, 290.

It wasn't only RFK or people in the Kennedy family orbit who had a negative personal assessment toward LBJ. George Reedy, LBJ's former White House press secretary and special assistant, once described his boss this way: "As a human being, he was a miserable person… a bully, sadist, lout, and egotist. His lapses from civilized conduct were deliberate and usually intended to subordinate someone else to his will." LBJ's reputation fared no better with Reedy's wife, who remembered LBJ as "a cold, conniving, demanding, cruel, and mean person." See Norman Sherman, *From Nowhere to Somewhere—My Political Journey: A Memoir of Sorts* (Minneapolis: First Avenue Editions, 2016), 227.

In a series of JFK Library oral history interviews, RFK suggested that LBJ was a pathological liar. "[M]y experience with [LBJ since his time as vice president] is he lies all the time. I'm telling you, he just lies continuously, about everything. In every conversation I have with him, he lies. As I've said, he lies even when he doesn't have to." In the same interview, RFK said that his brother, JFK, shared the opinion that LBJ was a consummate liar. RFK claimed that the night before JFK died, he told his wife Jacqueline that LBJ was "incapable of telling the truth." Robert F. Kennedy interview with Arthur M. Schlesinger, February 27, 1965, cited in Guthman and Shulman, *Robert Kennedy in His Own Words*, 26, 46. In another interview with Burke Marshall for the same oral history project, RFK quoted JFK as saying, "Can you think of anything more deplorable than [Johnson] trying to run the United States? That's why he can't ever be president." Robert F. Kennedy interviews with Anthony Lewis (with Burke Marshall present), December 4, 6, and 22, 1964, cited in Guthman and Shulman, *Robert Kennedy in His Own Words*, 153.

What accounted for RFK's utter disdain for LBJ? Some believed it dated back to 1955, when Joseph P. Kennedy supposedly approached LBJ and offered to help finance him in a 1956 presidential campaign if LBJ agreed to select his son, John Kennedy, as his running mate. The go-between in the discussion later reported that LBJ declining the father's offer infuriated RFK. See Dallek, *Flawed Giant*, 33.

In 1959, JFK sent RFK to the LBJ Ranch to sound out LBJ's presidential intentions for 1960. During the visit, LBJ insisted that RFK hunt deer with him on the ranch. Putting a shotgun in RFK's hands, he instructed RFK to fire at the distant quarry. Unfamiliar with firearms, RFK pulled the trigger. The recoil knocked him flat on the ground, leaving a cut above his eye. LBJ reached down to help him up, saying disparagingly, "Son, you've got to learn to handle a gun like a man." See Dallek, *Flawed Giant*, 33.

As the 1960 battle heated up between JFK and LBJ for the Democratic nomination, someone told RFK that LBJ had told reporter Peter Lisagor that JFK was "a little scrawny fellow with rickets and God knows what other kind of diseases." See Dallek, *Flawed Giant*, 33-34.

During that same campaign, RFK approached LBJ aide Bobby Baker and accused LBJ and his team of comparing RFK's father to the Nazis. (Before America entered World War II, Ambassador Joseph P. Kennedy argued against aiding Britain against the Nazis.) RFK also claimed LBJ was telling delegates falsely that JFK had Addison's disease. (JFK did have the disease.) At the end of his litany of complaints, RFK shouted at Baker, "You Johnson people are running a stinking damned campaign and you'll get yours when the time comes. We'll fucking kill you." See Heymann, *RFK*, 164.

Along with their feelings of mutual disdain, LBJ and RFK were mismatched physically and psychologically. A man who knew both, Arthur M. Schlesinger Jr., described their "immiscible" traits: he wrote that LBJ was 17 years older, six inches taller, coarse in language, with emotions near the surface. Schlesinger also described what others often called the "Johnson Treatment": LBJ "was all over everybody—always the grip on the shoulder, tug at the lapel, nudge in the ribs, squeeze of the knee. He was a crowder, who set his great face within a few inches of the object of his attention and, as the more diffident retreated, backed them across the room in the course of a monologue." By contrast, RFK liked people to keep their distance. Instead of LBJ's tall tales from the frontier, RFK was a study in "laconic irony." See Schlesinger Jr., *Robert Kennedy and His Times*, 623.

Kenneth P. O'Donnell, a member of JFK's "Irish Mafia" who was a brief LBJ White House holdover after the assassination, said that by the time LBJ was president, if RFK's name came up—even by accident—LBJ launched into a tirade about what a son-of-a-bitch RFK was. When it got back to RFK, he'd say something about LBJ. "These two men just didn't know each other," O'Donnell concluded, "and they'd built up this picture of each other which was just incredible." See Schlesinger Jr., *Robert Kennedy and His Times*, 647.

In 1967, reporter Drew Pearson recorded in his diary that Humphrey told him that despite LBJ's penchant for lecturing and bullying others, "he didn't think the president would lecture [RFK] because he knew that Bobby nursed grudges. 'Lyndon may scold me,' said Hubert, 'because he knows he can get away with it. Or he may scold you because you will take it, but he's too smart to ball out to Bobby.'" See Pearson and Hannaford, *Washington Merry-Go-Round*, 462-463.

[13]   A few weeks after JFK's assassination, LBJ raised the issue of an RFK-for-vice-president possibility in the 1964 elections: in a frank discussion with one of JFK's closest advisers, Kenneth O'Donnell, LBJ said he didn't want future historians to think he couldn't win without a Kennedy on the ticket. However, LBJ added, if he needed RFK to win in 1964, he'd take him. O'Donnell interpreted that to mean that only if the Republicans nominated a more liberal candidate than Barry Goldwater would LBJ need more support from labor and so-called Kennedy Democrats. See Kenneth P. O'Donnell and David F. Powers (with Joe McCarthy), *Johnny, We Hardly Knew Ye* (Boston: Little, Brown and Co., 1972), 445-447.

The 1964 RFK-for-vice-president concept enjoyed great support among rank-and-file Democrats. A few months before the 1964 Democratic National Convention, the Gallup Poll showed RFK the clear choice of Democrats for vice president, with 47 percent. Adlai Stevenson was in second place with 18 percent, and Humphrey trailed with 10 percent. See Schlesinger Jr., *Robert Kennedy and His Times*, 652; see also Steel, *In Love with the Night*, 112.

As LBJ later recalled, "Every day, as soon as I opened the papers or turned on the television, there was something about Bobby Kennedy... about what a great vice president he'd make. Somehow it just didn't seem fair. I'd given three years of loyal service to Jack Kennedy. During all that time I'd willingly stayed in the background; I knew this was his presidency, not mine.... And then Kennedy was killed and I became the custodian of his will. I became the president. But none of this seemed to register with Bobby Kennedy, who acted like he was the custodian of the Kennedy dream, some kind of rightful heir to the throne. It just didn't seem fair. I'd waited for my turn. Bobby should've waited for his. But he and the Kennedy people wanted it now. A tidal wave of letters and memos about how great a vice president Bobby would make swept over me. But no matter what, I simply couldn't let it happen. With Bobby on the ticket, I'd never know if I could be elected in my own right.... If they try to push Bobby Kennedy down my throat for vice president, I'll tell them to nominate him for the presidency and leave me out of it." Kearns Goodwin, *Lyndon Johnson and the American Dream*, 199-201.

LBJ's brother, Sam Houston Johnson, never believed LBJ gave serious consideration to RFK for the vice presidency for two reasons: 1) Lyndon hated Bobby, and 2) Bobby hated Lyndon. See Johnson, *My Brother Lyndon*, 159.

RFK wanted the 1964 vice presidential nomination. Eventually, "Johnson called Kennedy in and told him directly but privately that he would not be the [vice presidential] nominee." Humphrey, *The Education of a Public Man*, 290; see also Lyndon B. Johnson, *The Vantage Point: Perspectives of the Presidency* 1963-1969 (New York: Holt, Rinehart and Winston, 1971), 100.

Once conservative Senator Barry Goldwater won the 1964 GOP presidential nomination, LBJ knew he didn't need RFK as his running mate. He called RFK to the Oval Office and in a brief meeting told him he would not be on the ticket. According to LBJ's recollection, RFK told him, "I'm sorry you reached this conclusion, because I think I could have been of help to you." See Johnson, *The Vantage Point*, 100. However, in RFK's own dictated account of the meeting, he made no mention of expressing regret at the president's decision. See Schlesinger Jr., *Robert Kennedy and His Times*, 659.

After LBJ's announcement that he had decided not to consider any sitting Cabinet members for the vice presidency (at the time, RFK served in LBJ's cabinet as U.S. Attorney General), RFK joked with reporters, "I am sorry that I had to take so many nice fellows down with me." See Schlesinger Jr., *Robert Kennedy and His Times*, 662.

RFK claimed that in early 1964 LBJ called him to the White House and that the two men had a "bitter, mean conversation" about a Democratic national committeeman whom LBJ claimed was in New Hampshire trying to boost RFK for the vice-presidential nomination. RFK disclaimed any knowledge of such involvement and told LBJ that he didn't want to have this conversation with him. RFK told a friend, "[t]he one thing Lyndon Johnson doesn't want is me as vice president, and he's concerned about whether he's going to be forced into that.... I think he's hysterical about how he's going to try to avoid having me or having to ask me. That's what he spends most of his time on, from what I understand: figuring out how he's going to avoid me." Robert F. Kennedy interviews with John Bartlow Martin, March 1, April 13, April 30, and May 14, 1964, cited in Guthman and Shulman, *Robert Kennedy in His Own Words*, 406-407, 413-418.

[14] In 1964, as soon as RFK moved to New York and announced his candidacy for the U.S. Senate from that state, he shot to the top of the polls, pulling well ahead of incumbent moderate Republican Kenneth Keating. Crushing crowds greeted RFK everywhere. People pressed forward to touch him; they yanked buttons and cufflinks off his clothes for souvenirs. By day's end, scratches covered his hands and arms. "I feel like one of the Beatles," RFK told an aide. After covering the campaign, CBS News reporter Eric Sevareid said that the kindly and aged Senator Keating, a flesh-and-blood human being, was running against "witchcraft, a symbol of adulation and sorrow, memory of the deepest mass emotion of recent years, a fabulous ghost returned to earth." See Heymann, *RFK*, 379-380.

RFK knew that inherited adulation fueled his campaign appearances. At the end of one grueling campaign day, where massive crowds cheered and shrieked wherever he appeared, one of his aides told RFK that the audiences he drew were unlike those for any other candidate in America. "They aren't cheering me," RFK replied quietly. "They're cheering Jack." See, e.g., Steel, *In Love with the Night*, 118-119.

By October 1964, with the newness of RFK's Senate campaign entry fading, and with Republican opponent Kenneth Keating fighting back hard, the sudden specter of defeat loomed for RFK as Election Day neared. Polls showed him running six points behind Keating and dropping, while the same polls showed LBJ crushing Barry Goldwater in the state by a whopping two-to-one margin. New York Republicans put out thousands of buttons and brochures urging people to split their ticket. VOTE JOHNSON, KEEP KEATING—NEW YORK'S OWN (a reference to RFK's carpetbag Senate campaign). In a panic that victory might slip away, RFK swallowed hard and asked for LBJ's help. Despite all the slights, condescension, hostility, and insults, LBJ came to RFK's rescue. LBJ crisscrossed the state with RFK in tow—twice—and ended his effort for the troubled Senate candidate with a massive rally in Madison Square Garden. The Democratic National Committee, at LBJ's direction, plastered New York with "Johnson-Humphrey-Kennedy" posters, badges, and leaflets. Thanks to LBJ's help, RFK beat the Republican incumbent by over 700,000 votes, which was two million votes less than LBJ won in New York that same day. At the party celebrating RFK's landslide victory, RFK thanked his family, his friends, and his supporters in humble and emotional terms, but he never uttered one word of thanks to the man who carried him across the finish line, President Lyndon B. Johnson. Instead, he showed himself to be an ingrate. See Steel, *In Love with the Night*, 118-119.

During the 1964 election, "President Johnson roamed all over the Empire State giving his voice and his person to the [U.S Senate campaign of] Bobby Kennedy. When the votes were counted, the president had carried the state by over two million votes and Bobby Kennedy won by some 600,000. To the political pros, the coattails of the president had been long enough and strong enough to carry Bobby to victory over Senator Keating. Yet, somehow, somebody near Bobby must have cautioned him against giving any credit to the president. I sat with President Johnson in the Driskill Hotel in Austin on election night and we watched the returns.... As Bobby started speaking, he began to thank all those who made the victory possible.... At no time during this recounting of gratitude did he once mention the president. President Johnson made no outward sign that the omission struck him. His expression never changed throughout the speech by the senator-elect. But I felt the vacancy. I yearned for Bobby to say one word, just one, as a token of his appreciation for the hard stumping the president had done on his behalf, but no word came…. The president's demeanor masked whatever anger or disappointment he may have felt." Jack Valenti, *A Very Human President* (New York: W.W. Norton & Company, 1975), 149-150.

[15]   The April 1968 "summit" between LBJ and RFK (Ted Sorensen joined RFK at the meeting with LBJ) is adapted from actual events as recorded by first-person and reported sources. See Sorensen, *Counselor*, 461-462; see also Sorensen, *The Kennedy Legacy*, 146-147; Schlesinger Jr., *Robert Kennedy and His Times*, 863, 868-869; Johnson, *The Vantage Point*, 539-542; Dallek, *Flawed Giant*, 531; Steel, *In Love with the Night*, 153-154.

[16]   Soon after LBJ withdrew from the 1968 presidential race and met with RFK, he held a similar meeting with Humphrey and McCarthy. Many years later, McCarthy recounted that his discussion with LBJ was casual and pro forma until RFK's name came up. At the mere mention of Kennedy's name, LBJ said nothing, but he took his hand and made a slashing motion across his throat. See McCarthy, *Up 'Til Now*, 196.

CHAPTER 13

[1]   During his 1964 election campaign, after the U.S. conducted retaliatory strikes against communist guerrillas in the Gulf of Tonkin, LBJ promised voters he would not widen the conflict in Vietnam. However, after winning reelection in a landslide, guerrilla attacks continued against U.S. troop barracks in South Vietnam. LBJ called a Cabinet meeting and asked for advice. His new vice president, Humphrey, said that he opposed massive strikes and he urged caution. What Humphrey didn't understand at the time was that LBJ didn't want "advice" from him: he wanted validation. LBJ fumed privately over Humphrey offering an assessment counter to the president's private designs. Later, LBJ disregarded Humphrey's position and he ordered a full-scale bombing against North Vietnamese targets, thus commencing "Operation Rolling Thunder." Another war of sorts also began that day: an information war of attrition launched by LBJ against Humphrey for not agreeing with him. Humphrey learned quickly the price for offering honest assessments at Cabinet meetings. LBJ cut Humphrey out of the policy loop for years. LBJ forced his vice president to remain abreast of policy by having Humphrey's aides cull through diplomatic cable traffic, by personal initiative, and by begging information from friendly administration officials. Adding to the insult, LBJ directed that no Executive Branch resources be available for Humphrey's use unless cleared first by the White House chief of staff. See Van Dyk, *Heroes, Hacks & Fools*, 40-41, 43-44.

For years, LBJ excluded his vice president from senior war strategy sessions. The Pentagon and National Security Council, on orders from LBJ, provided Humphrey heavily abridged and edited intelligence reports. See, e.g., White, *The Making of the President 1968*, 7, 21.

[2]   In his diary, Humphrey recounted, "I wanted to be loyal to the president. My guts, my heart wouldn't let me do it any other way. I just couldn't yield to his critics.... I had a choice. Break with the President and be denounced as irresponsible. Or muddle through. Really no choice if I wanted to be president. And I do, how badly I do." See Humphrey, *The Education of a Public Man*, 5-6.

[3]   "Every time I'd make a statement [on Vietnam] with some little twist of my own, it would get shot down [by LBJ].... The president was impossible on the war. Such a fury when I showed him my task-force report on Vietnam." See Humphrey, *The Education of a Public Man*, 6.

[4]   After the January 1968 Tet offensive, LBJ finally invited Humphrey to a Cabinet meeting. Following that session, Humphrey met privately with LBJ and again expressed his reservations about LBJ's plan to increase the bombing of North Vietnamese targets. For that heresy, LBJ resumed his ban on Humphrey having access to White House resources. See, e.g., White, *The Making of the President 1968*, 7, 21.

[5]   After LBJ excommunicated Humphrey from White House strategy meetings in early 1965, Humphrey tried proving his loyalty by spending the next several years traveling the country promoting LBJ's "Great Society" domestic agenda. Increasingly, and despite his personal reservations over the escalating military conflict, Humphrey wanted to show loyalty to LBJ on Vietnam as well. As senior Humphrey policy adviser Ted Van Dyk later remembered, "Humphrey was genuinely torn.... He had not wanted the war escalated or the U.S. role in it expanded. But he was also a staunch anti-totalitarian.... Anxious to regain Johnson's favor, Humphrey made extravagant public statements on behalf of [LBJ's] Vietnam policy.... Humphrey returned to the capital having been restored at least partially to the president's graces. But he had seriously damaged his standing among Democrats, columnists, academics, and other leaders with doubts about the war." See Van Dyk, *Heroes, Hacks & Fools*, 47-48.

[6]   A U.S. Senate colleague of Humphrey's once said, "Humphrey likes people like an alcoholic likes booze. The warmth is not affected, it's real." See Chester, Hodgson, Page, *An American Melodrama*, 149.

[7] "In 1968, the great majority of delegates [to the Democratic National Convention] were selected and controlled by governors, bosses, confederations of county leaders, and so forth." See Goodwin, *Remembering America*, 514.

After scoring several early primary victories, McCarthy's campaign came to realize the math was not in their favor. As one of his campaign aides wrote later, "The primaries were crucial for establishing McCarthy as a national political figure. But, we suddenly realized, the number of delegate votes determined by these contests was actually quite low, perhaps only a quarter. The nomination would be decided by three-quarters of the delegates chosen without reference to primary contests. Having established McCarthy as a national figure, we now had to reach the delegates." See Stavis, *We Were the Campaign*, 150.

[8] To win the 1968 Democratic presidential nomination, a candidate needed 1,312 votes. On May 1, 1968—three days after Humphrey entered the race and almost four months before the convention, Humphrey's internal campaign poll showed that he already had 900 pledged delegates. On that same day, CBS News projected Humphrey had 1,000 delegates. As to why Humphrey delayed for almost a month his decision to seek the presidency after LBJ's March 31, 1968 withdrawal, longtime Humphrey friend and adviser Max M. Kampelman wrote, "We had a reluctant candidate, who, recalling [his loss to JFK during the 1960 Democratic primaries of] Wisconsin and West Virginia, did not want the public humiliation of another loss to a Kennedy, and Robert was running. His affection for John did not at that point extend to Robert Kennedy, and Humphrey assumed that Bobby could not be stopped. He simply didn't have the heart to try. We said, 'Go fast.' He said, 'Go slow.'" Max M. Kampelman, *Entering New Worlds* (Norwalk: The Easton Press, 1991), 163.

[9] Humphrey later wrote that McCarthy's Wisconsin victory was a bit overstated: the Republicans had no real primary contest, so large numbers of GOP voters crossed over and voted in the Democratic primary for the least likely nominee only to embarrass LBJ. See Humphrey, *The Education of a Public Man*, 364.

[10] For a summary of the post-Martin Luther King, Jr. assassination rioting statistics, see Schlesinger Jr., *Robert Kennedy and His Times*, 877.

[11] In 1969, McCarthy wrote that after LBJ's withdrawal, "I began to feel like a relay runner who after each lap had to face a different runner—starting in New Hampshire and Wisconsin, when I ran against President Johnson—first as a write-in and then under his own name, and now Indiana where I was to run against Senator Kennedy, after which, I anticipated, Vice President Humphrey would certainly be on the track." See McCarthy, *The Year of the People*, 105.

[12] Despite all the romance surrounding the Kennedy campaign, the antiwar activists drawn to McCarthy's cause viewed RFK's heavyweight senior campaign staff as a glamorized group of Democrat Party hacks. JFK's team of Cold Warriors were now Bobby's campaign brain trust: Pierre Salinger, Theodore Sorensen, and Larry O'Brien. As Jeremy Larner wrote, RFK did nothing to assuage these concerns: as soon as LBJ withdrew, RFK rushed to LBJ's side for a private White House visit to make up with the president. RFK also aired television spots featuring the endorsement of Robert MacNamara, JFK's and LBJ's Secretary of Defense and the chief architect of the Vietnam War. Also off-putting was RFK's penchant to stress "law and order" when campaigning in the white suburbs only, which young activists took as a racist appeal. See Larner, *Nobody Knows*, 69-70.

[13] Once LBJ left the race, RFK faced a dilemma: he now had to face McCarthy, who intended to show that Vietnam was a JFK Admnistration-produced mistake. As McCarthy told his chief campaign speechwriter, "So far [Bobby's] run with the ghost of his brother. Now we're going to make him run against it…. We'll make him run against Jack. And I'm Jack." See Larner, *Nobody Knows*, 63; see also Steel, *In Love with the Night*, 154.

After McCarthy learned that LBJ announced his withdrawal from the 1968 race, in the car ride back to his hotel McCarthy said, "Bobby will have to run against Jack now. Before, he could run against Lyndon." See Herzog, *McCarthy for President*, 120.

RFK had a response to McCarthy's strategy to paint Vietnam as traceable to the JFK administration. "Bobby was determined not to be sunk by JFK's, and his own, early enthusiasm for a war that everyone now wished would go away. It was not enough for him to disavow a disastrous war: John Kennedy had to be purged of it as well.... For this reason JFK was 'discovered' to secretly have changed his mind about Vietnam. Aides stepped forward to claim that he had told them he was secretly planning to withdraw in 1965, just as soon as he was safely reelected." See Steel, *In Love with the Night*, 154.

[14]   During the 1968 presidential campaign, McCarthy wanted his rest periods and his martini, even if he had to bootleg it in the motel kitchen. He liked a martini or a Scotch before dinner, but those close to him doubted he knew one brand of Scotch from another. He was not much of a drinker. See Herzog, *McCarthy for President*, 87, 112.

[15]   After RFK became a candidate, there was an expectation in his camp that McCarthy's supporters would defect to RFK in droves. Although there were some defections in the initial excitement, once the dust settled, McCarthy's support increased. As McCarthy later wrote, "The enthusiasm of the crowds was greater than it had been before Robert Kennedy's entrance, and within a week both the number of volunteers and unsolicited contributions increased greatly." See McCarthy, *Up 'Til Now*, 192.

[16]   At the end of 1968, a reporter from the *Boston Globe* asked McCarthy what would have happened if RFK hadn't entered the primaries against him at the last minute. McCarthy's answer surprised the reporter: RFK would probably have won the presidential nomination. When asked why he believed that, McCarthy said, "I would have beaten Johnson in four or five primaries and he would have looked weak, but the Democratic Party never would have nominated me. Bobby could have come in as a unifying force as a candidate who had not challenged LBJ." See Schlesinger Jr., *Robert Kennedy and His Times*, 856.

McCarthy believed that if RFK had stayed out of the primaries, McCarthy would have beaten LBJ in most of the contested primaries, and then RFK would have been nominated. See Herzog, *McCarthy for President*, 193.

[17]   RFK's political opportunism and slashing attacks aside, McCarthy had a more practical frustration with RFK's entry into the race: with neither

LBJ's nor Humphrey's names on any primary ballot, RFK's entry into the campaign pitted two antiwar candidates against each other. Meanwhile, Humphrey sat back and used the White House and the Democratic Party apparatus to scoop up the bulk of delegates to the nominating convention—with most of them selected by Party bosses loyal to LBJ, not by primary voters. See, e.g., McCarthy, *Up 'Til Now*, 196.

[18]   McCarthy thought RFK was "a spoiled, unintelligent demagogue." See Thomas, *Robert Kennedy*, 360.

[19]   McCarthy viewed RFK's penchant for salting his speeches and interviews with quotes from philosophers and poets as comical "exercises in intellectual self-improvement." See Schlesinger Jr., *Robert Kennedy and His Times*, 828-829.

After RFK announced his candidacy for president, McCarthy commented on the shaggy haircut RFK sported during his presidential campaign announcement speech. He told reporters that if he won the presidency, he would be glad to give RFK a job "licking stamps—provided he would cut his hair." Pearson and Hannaford, *Washington Merry-Go-Round*, 551.

[20]   When RFK and McCarthy squared off for the first time in the 1968 Indiana primary, McCarthy complained that RFK utilized the same underhanded campaign tactics of twisting and distorting his voting record, just as RFK had done to wrest a Senate seat from incumbent Kenneth Keating in 1964. "As [Kennedy's primary campaign against me] wore on, and as [RFK's] continued use of the dishonest attacks on my record remained in evidence, I began to have reservations [about him]." See McCarthy, *The Year of the People*, 124; McCarthy, *Up 'Til Now*, 193.

Twenty years after RFK's death, McCarthy still smarted from the underhanded primary campaign tactics RFK used against him, calling them "cheap and petty." See McCarthy, *Up 'Til Now*, 193.

[21]   The conversation between McCarthy and Dick Goodwin in which Goodwin quit the McCarthy campaign to join RFK's campaign is based on an actual event. See Goodwin, *Remembering America*, 526-528.

[22]   Unlike JFK's years of careful planning that led up to his White House race in 1960, RFK's campaign launch had all the organization of a spontaneous prison riot. As Kennedy friend Arthur Schlesinger noted, the day RFK announced, he had no campaign staff, no national organization, no delegates, and almost no promises of support. See Schlesinger Jr., *Robert Kennedy and His Times*, 858.

[23]   RFK's core constituency consisted of blacks, Hispanics, some blue-collar ethnics, and Camelot sentimentalists. He understood he had the star power to turn out the crowds, but to win the nomination he had to demonstrate his vote-getting ability with white voters, not just with minorities and students, and polls showed McCarthy beating him with voters in that necessary demographic across the board. After one published poll showed that McCarthy beat RFK among college-educated voters 44 percent to 18 percent, McCarthy cracked, "The better educated people vote for us." See Steel, *In Love with the Night*, 154, 179.

Pierre Salinger, a senior RFK campaign aide, said the central themes of RFK's campaign were poverty and blacks. See Schlesinger Jr., *Robert Kennedy and His Times*, 906.

[24]   "[F]ive days before the [Oregon] primary Drew Pearson and Jack Anderson reported that, as Attorney General, Kennedy had authorized the FBI to wiretap the now martyred Dr. King, a blow to both King's and Kennedy's reputations, and Kennedy's hopes to rally Adlai Stevenson liberals. The wiretaps on King had become known in December 1966. Kennedy denied then he had been aware of them, a denial FBI Director J. Edgar Hoover called 'absolutely inconceivable.'" Patrick J. Buchanan, *The Greatest Comeback: How Richard Nixon Rose from Defeat to Create the New Majority* (New York: Crown Forum, 2014), 263.

"The [*New York Times*'] James Reston found Kennedy either noncredible or noncompetent in 1966, writing, '[If] Mr. Kennedy didn't know [about the Martin Luther King, Jr. wiretaps], either he wasn't doing his job or [FBI Director] Hoover was going beyond his instructions. If he did know, he was condoning what he now condemns.'" See Buchanan, *The Greatest Comeback*, 263.

RFK told a reporter on his campaign airplane, "I've got every establishment in America against me." Chester, Hodgson, Page, *An American Melodrama*, 145.

The South was "solid in its hostility [to RFK, and] Northern Party regulars, except in New York and California, were on the whole just as cool." Chester, Hodgson, Page, *An American Melodrama*, 127-128.

25 RFK stressed his "law and order" credentials when campaigning in the white suburbs, which activists took as an appeal to racism. See Larner, *Nobody Knows*, 69-70.

When speaking before white, conservative, blue-collar audiences in his 1968 presidential campaign, RFK adopted conservative rhetoric:

- He attacked welfare programs and disparaged "the brutality of the welfare system itself [that] has done much to divide our people, to alienate us from one another."

- He attacked the welfare bureaucracy and centralization of power in Washington, proclaiming the need "to halt and reverse the growing accumulation of power and authority in the central government in Washington and return that power of decision to the American people in their own local community."

- He opposed a guaranteed national income for poor people, saying it rested on "a myth that all the problems of poverty can be solved by ultimate extension of the welfare system."

- He touted "the worth of individual effort and responsibility."

- He opposed forced school busing to achieve racial integration: "[C]ompulsory transportation of children over long distances, away from schools in their own neighborhood, doesn't make much sense and I am against it."

- He opposed "job preferences"—the precursor of the 1970s "affirmative action" quota system.

- He opposed national health insurance.

- He opposed trade sanctions against apartheid South Africa, saying it would end up hurting the oppressed black population there. See Steel, *In Love with the Night*, 165, 185.

A few years before running for president, in a sealed oral history interview for the JFK Library, RFK expressed this view on states rights and local control: "I think that it's well that all of that great power is not centered in Washington with the federal government." Robert F. Kennedy interviews with Anthony Lewis (with Burke Marshall present), December 4, 6, and 22, 1964, cited in Guthman and Shulman, *Robert Kennedy in His Own Words*, 99.

Because of the conservative positions RFK took when not campaigning before minority audiences, California Governor Ronald Reagan mocked RFK's 1968 rhetoric, saying, "Kennedy [is] talking more and more like me." See Steel, *In Love with the Night*, 165.

26   RFK's 1968 campaign manager Fred Dutton said that RFK walked a fine line between white and black audiences, and his campaign tried to find a way to put the two coalitions together. In doing so, RFK knew it did no good to push so far left that he won primaries and the nomination, only to lose the general election because a leftward movement pushed him out of the mainstream. Dutton recalled later, "[I]t was a worthwhile tradeoff.... In mounting [RFK's] 1968 campaign, we attempted to put together the anti-Vietnam forces and the civil rights forces with the hard hats, the redneck whites.... In our private discussions as we traveled around and in our speechwriting, we were looking for a way to bridge the George Wallace vote and the civil rights and peace movements.... [W]e thought we had to take both from the left and siphon from the Wallace movement as much as we could. That's what 1968 was all about.... Bridging the gap between the different segments of the population was Bob's concept, but his ideas were more 'feels' and 'gropes' than articulated. [His speechwriters could verbalize this], but this you didn't want to entirely verbalize. If you did, if you put it together, you'd lose the Wallace people [and] you'd lose the blacks." See Heymann, *RFK*, 477-480.

During the Indiana primary, RFK knew he needed to walk a careful high-wire act: attract black voters without alienating the blue-collar white voters. See Steel, *In Love with the Night*, 172.

27   RFK and his campaign team understood that the TV news footage of him reaching into crowds of ecstatic black voters who grasped frantically to touch him was off-putting to many white voters. With a high concentration of blue-collar white voters in Indiana, RFK ordered that his staff cut back his appearances in black communities. In a candid interview with journalist

David Halberstam, RFK explained the strategy. "So far in Indiana they seem to want to see me as a member of the black race—I don't think I can win if that happens." See Steel, *In Love with the Night*, 172.

[28] Many years later, RFK's 1968 campaign manager Fred Dutton said, "In the 1968 primaries, we were being driven to the left by the civil rights movement, by the students, by the crowds that turned out, by the emotionalism of that period.... Kennedy had no problem with that. He was not just bettering the world, he was advancing the Kennedy banner. He wanted to do good, but he was also a power animal. He didn't want to be a hero. He wanted to win." See Heymann, *RFK*, 477-480.

[29] RFK's campaign strategy was to blitz McCarthy in the primaries but avoid attacking him personally. RFK detested McCarthy and felt him unfit to be president, but he feared attacking him too fiercely would alienate the millions of young people rallying to McCarthy's cause. RFK needed those "McCarthy kids" in his corner once he dispatched McCarthy. Instead, RFK attacked Humphrey, a man he liked genuinely, as the stand-in for LBJ's Vietnam policies, but he also muted these attacks somewhat, for he knew he needed Humphrey's unwavering support after the convention if he won the nomination. RFK needed to win enough delegates to make the argument at the 1968 Democratic National Convention that he, not LBJ, McCarthy, or Humphrey, was the more electable nominee. See, e.g., White, *The Making of the President 1968*, 175-176.

[30] Even if RFK won every primary, it would produce only a small proportion of the delegates to seize the 1968 Democratic Party's presidential nomination. Most delegates that year came from the political machines of each state and not from the primaries. RFK hoped that if Humphrey failed to cobble together a majority on the first ballot, the Party elders would view Humphrey as a loser, and then they would switch their support to him as the most electable candidate. See White, *The Making of the President 1968*, 176.

[31] The conversation between Dick Goodwin and RFK, and Goodwin's outburst at RFK's campaign team, is based on an actual event. See Goodwin, *Remembering America*, 526-528.

In his diary entry of April 14, 1968, reporter Drew Pearson wrote, "Dick Goodwin jumped to Bobby because his speeches were not being used by McCarthy. He wrote one speech which was used. Mrs. McCarthy had advised her husband to let Dick go earlier since he was sure to jump anyway. Gene's writing his own speeches." Later, LBJ aide Jack Valenti told Pearson (diary entry of April 26, 1968), "[LBJ] has a sixth sense as to who's loyal to him and who isn't…. He knew Goodwin was not loyal. Later Goodwin left him—no loss—then went with McCarthy, then deserted McCarthy for Bobby." Pearson and Hannaford, *Washington Merry-Go-Round*, 568-569, 573.

CHAPTER 14

[1] During the campaign, an agitated RFK snapped at Peter Edelman for being too slow to fetch his shoes in the next room. See Thomas, *Robert Kennedy*, 381.

[2] After agreeing reluctantly to debate McCarthy following his Oregon primary loss, RFK refused to allow the debate to air on all three networks. Instead, the debate format was a one-hour special airing of ABC's *Issues and Answers* news show on June 1, 1968. See Herzog, *McCarthy for President*, 184.

[3] During RFK's presidential race, the candidate often treated his campaign staff as personal servants. "Kennedy staffers were expected to be [RFK's personal] valets[.]" RFK ordered a staffer to hold the Kennedy family dog's head out of the car window when the dog vomited. In one hotel, while Bobby snapped at a senior aide in his bedroom, he heard a few young staffers standing outside joking about something unrelated. Bobby charged out of the room in his boxer underwear. He told them off, saying all they did was goof around or play the guitar (one liked to strum Beatles songs on the campaign plane)—and that if they had nothing better to do, RFK told them, they should go ring doorbells. When one of the startled staffers tried to apologize, RFK slammed the door in his face. See Thomas, *Robert Kennedy,* 381. For another vignette of a stressed RFK screaming angrily at his staff in his hotel room, see O'Brien, *No Final Victories,* 241-242.

[4] As RFK prepared to run for president, senior campaign aide Pierre Salinger gave him this advice: "I told him he needed to soften his image…. Selling Bobby to the public was not unlike selling cans of tuna following

a botulism scare. Nobody dislikes tuna; it just has to be demonstrated it wouldn't harm anyone." See C. David Heymann, *Bobby and Jackie: A Love Story* (New York: Atria Paperback, 2009), 140.

5   McCarthy continued to challenge RFK to debate during the Oregon primary; RFK declined, telling his legislative assistant Peter Edelman that he "didn't want to raise McCarthy into a candidate of equal stature." See Heymann, *RFK,* 482.

6   McCarthy "seems to have felt the Kennedys were overrated, achieving their goals through an adroit use of public relations rather than by distinguished effort. Glamour, not ability, was paying off." See Herzog, *McCarthy for President,* 56.

7   Economist and Kennedy family friend John Kenneth Galbraith said that McCarthy thought he was "better qualified than the Kennedys. He had worked harder, studied harder, was a better economist and knew more about philosophy, poetry and theology—the elements of an educated man—than did either Bobby [or JFK]." John Kenneth Galbraith, in a recorded interview by Jean Stein, September 19, 1969, as quoted in Schlesinger Jr., *Robert Kennedy and His Times, 828.*

8   "The Portland Zoo Encounter": When McCarthy campaign aide Jeremy Larner saw that RFK was at the zoo the same time that McCarthy was there, he steered McCarthy and the press toward RFK hoping to get media coverage of the accidental confrontation between the candidates, especially since RFK had refused to debate McCarthy. See Larner, *Nobody Knows,* 100-101.

Arthur Schlesinger called RFK's refusal to debate McCarthy in Oregon his most serious mistake of the 1968 campaign. RFK "even dodged McCarthy personally when their schedules accidentally brought them together at the Portland Zoo." Jeremy Larner, McCarthy's principal speechwriter, followed Kennedy around the zoo, taunting RFK and calling him a "coward" for not debating McCarthy. See Schlesinger Jr., *Robert Kennedy and His Times,* 907.

When their schedules brought them together at the Portland Zoo, Blair Clark, McCarthy's campaign manager, said, "Bobby went scurrying in the direction of the nearest exit to avoid a face-to-face meeting with his adversary." See Heymann, *RFK*, 482-483.

At the Portland Zoo, when someone told McCarthy that RFK was nearby getting off the passenger train, McCarthy started walking toward RFK. Then, "Kennedy, hearing that McCarthy was approaching—they were now fifteen yards apart—said, 'Is he? That's too bad.' [Kennedy] jumped into his car and said to the driver, 'Let's get going.' From the crowd [as Kennedy escaped a confrontation] came the cry, 'Coward, coward' [from McCarthy supporters]." See Herzog, *McCarthy for President*, 170-171.

⁹   After RFK's Nebraska primary win over McCarthy, but before RFK's loss to him in Oregon, RFK campaign aide Pierre Salinger said McCarthy's candidacy was not "credible." See McCarthy, *Up 'Til Now*, 193; Chester, Hodgson, Page, *An American Melodrama*, 178.

The night RFK lost the Oregon primary to McCarthy, RFK concluded he had to debate McCarthy in California, saying, "I'm not in much of a position now to say [McCarthy's] not a serious candidate. Hell, if he's not a serious candidate after tonight, then I'm not a candidate at all." See Goodwin, *Remembering America*, 533.

¹⁰   After RFK lost Oregon to McCarthy, he knew he might lose in California as well. If that happened, his campaign for the nomination was over. See Sorensen, *Counselor*, 464-465.

RFK suggested to reporters that if he lost the California primary to McCarthy, he would pull out of the race. See Chester, Hodgson, Page, *An American Melodrama*, 334.

¹¹   According to McCarthy, during the Oregon primary RFK said that if he lost that state to McCarthy, he would withdraw from the race so that the antiwar forces could unite. After losing Oregon, RFK failed to keep his promise, and he moved on to the California primary. See McCarthy, *Up 'Til Now*, 197.

¹²   RFK tried his standard poverty-and-civil rights shtick in suburban Oregon. With a 98 percent white population, his speeches fell flat. He felt and received no traction. The frenzied, screaming, grasping mobs that

greeted him elsewhere were absent in Oregon. After another disappointing day on the campaign trail, RFK groused to an aide, "This ain't my group." See Heymann, *RFK,* 481.

"Kennedy knew he was in trouble in Oregon. 'If only we could move a ghetto up here, just for a day, then I know I could win it.' But there were no ghettos in Oregon. Minorities made up only 2 percent of the population. The entire state seemed like one sprawling suburb." See Goodwin, *Remembering America,* 533.

13   The local reaction to RFK's stripping down to his shorts and taking an impromptu dip in the Pacific Ocean demonstrated that "his personality was too intense for Oregon. His behavior offended unfathomable local sensitivities…. Apparently Oregonians never swam in the Pacific until August. They thought anyone who swam in May was a showoff or a fool." See Schlesinger Jr., *Robert Kennedy and His Times,* 906.

14   "Kennedy staffers were expected to be [RFK's personal] valets[.]" See Thomas, *Robert Kennedy,* 381.

15   Before his only debate with RFK during the California primary campaign, McCarthy stayed at San Francisco's Fairmont Hotel. See Herzog, *McCarthy for President,* 185. RFK had also lodged at the same hotel during his pre-debate preparation.

16   McCarthy drew this comparison between himself and RFK: "He plays touch football, I play football. He plays softball, I play baseball. He skates at Rockefeller Center, I play hockey." See Herzog, *McCarthy for President,* 141.

17   The story of Jon Fish luring away pro-RFK hecklers stationed outside the Fairmont Hotel in San Francisco is based on an actual event. One of McCarthy's young campaign organizers, Sandy Frucher, knew how to deal with Kennedy hecklers. One day during the 1968 campaign, and just as McCarthy prepared to leave his hotel, Sandy ran ahead and saw a squad of RFK partisans waiting outside near McCarthy's car to harass him for the television cameras posted outside. Quickly, Sandy reached into his pocket, pulled out his oversized "Kennedy" campaign badge, pinned it to his lapel, and ran over to the hecklers. "Hey, everyone," he shouted, "McCarthy's

sneaking out the side door—follow me!" Sandy then ran down the street and around the corner with the hecklers and reporters chasing behind him. A few moments later, McCarthy exited the hotel unmolested. See Larner, *Nobody Knows*, 88-89.

[18] From 1954 to 1985, KGO-TV broadcast from the old Eagle Building at 277 Golden Gate Avenue. After KGO moved to another location, the building fell into disrepair. In 2011, the building escaped its scheduled demolition. Today it houses 88 modern loft and studio apartments.

[19] At KGO studios on the day of the RFK-McCarthy debate, a large pro-McCarthy crowd awaited the arrival of the candidates. A few black hecklers waited to protest RFK's lack of black representation on his staff. McCarthy arrived amid the cheers of the crowd. After RFK received word that a hostile crowd stood outside the studio on Golden Gate Avenue, he entered the studio through a side door off the alley. See Chester, Hodgson, Page, *An American Melodrama*, 339.

[20] At their debate, both McCarthy and RFK took their seats on the set with the moderator and two reporters. "McCarthy looked composed, almost to the point of inertia. Kennedy looked rather edgy, and as usual, on the screen he looked almost a decade younger than he looked in the flesh." See Chester, Hodgson, Page, *An American Melodrama*, 339.

[21] Arthur Schlesinger called the McCarthy-RFK debate "an anticlimax." See Schlesinger Jr., *Robert Kennedy and His Times*, 911.

[22] During their debate, RFK threw a low blow for which McCarthy never forgave him. In a discussion about the ghettos, RFK suggested a plan to bring private capital into the slums. McCarthy objected, saying that such programs would still keep inner city minorities trapped in those areas—an "apartheid in our midst." RFK then swung back with a twisted interpretation of McCarthy's complaint—and a blatantly racist appeal to middle-class white voters: "[Y]ou are going to take ten thousand black people and move them into Orange County [the most conservative and white county in California].... [I]t is going to be catastrophic." RFK friend and journalist Jules Witcover called the assertion "political thuggery." Another close RFK associate, Arthur M. Schlesinger, admitted that

the comment "sounded, and was, demagogic." See Schlesinger Jr., *Robert Kennedy and His Times*, 911; Jeremy Larner, *Nobody Knows*, 54-55.

23   While RFK campaigned in California, he went to the Watts section of Los Angeles, the scene of a bloody race riot a few years earlier, to speak of black and white reconciliation—while Kennedy operatives slashed McCarthy with ads falsifying his sterling civil rights voting record. Later, while campaigning in heavily Republican Orange County, RFK made the preposterous claim that McCarthy wanted to relocate 10,000 blacks from the Watts ghetto of Los Angeles into their conservative and white bedroom communities. To veterans groups, RFK attacked McCarthy as weak and willing to negotiate with communists over Vietnam without mentioning that during his brother's administration, in which he served as a Cabinet member, he and JFK negotiated with communists from Russia to China to Cuba. When addressing non-Jewish groups, RFK claimed McCarthy would threaten Middle East peace by providing jets to Israel. When addressing predominantly Jewish groups, RFK pledged to provide Israel with jets. See McCarthy, *Up 'Til Now*, 195-197.

24   The so-called "Kennedy Citizen's Committee" issued a barrage of press releases and paid newspaper ads in the key primary states where RFK and McCarthy clashed. These ads falsified McCarthy's voting record on everything from civil rights to the war. During their debate, when McCarthy demanded RFK acknowledge his campaign's role in these smears, RFK denied both knowledge and responsibility. Despite RFK's denial, after his death one of RFK's key operatives told McCarthy that the source of the so-called "Citizen's Committee" was in fact RFK senior campaign aide Pierre Salinger. McCarthy, *Up 'Til Now*, 193-194.

25   During their primary battles, McCarthy felt that RFK ran the same kind of smear campaign against him that RFK had run against incumbent New York Senator Kenneth Keating in New York four years earlier. See McCarthy, *Up 'Til Now*, 193.

26   Twenty years after RFK's death, McCarthy still smarted over RFK's campaign tactics: McCarthy called them "cheap and petty." See McCarthy, *Up 'Til Now*, 193.

In 1968, *Washington Star* columnist Mary McGrory wrote, "Kennedy thinks that American youth belongs to him at the bequest of his brother. Seeing the romance flower between them and McCarthy, he moved with the ruthlessness of a Victorian father whose daughter had fallen in love with the dustman." See Herzog, *McCarthy for President*, 104-105.

[27] Surprisingly, McCarthy thought that losing the California primary to RFK might strengthen his own hand. McCarthy feared that if he defeated RFK in California, RFK would quit the race and surrender his delegates to Humphrey. See Steel, *In Love with the Night*, 192.

[28] Following their debate on the eve of the California primary, McCarthy decided he could not support RFK for the presidency. He concluded that RFK's dirty campaign tactics, his waffling on Vietnam, and his utter lack of judgment rendered him unfit for the presidency. See McCarthy, *Up 'Til Now*, 197-198.

McCarthy said that RFK's smear campaign against him showed he "was unfit to be president." See Herzog, *McCarthy for President*, 158.

CHAPTER 15

[1] The final Gallup Democratic voter preference poll taken before RFK's shooting showed him running third: 25 percent of Democrats favored RFK as their presidential nominee, 29 percent chose Humphrey, and 32 percent named McCarthy.

[2] As the California primary neared, some of McCarthy's staffers started trying to line up jobs with RFK in case their man lost badly and his campaign ended. See Stavis, *We Were the Campaign*, 125.

[3] *Walkin' around money*: cash given to local leaders to help get people to the polls. Also known as "street money" or "get-out-the-vote money," it is most commonly used in poor and large urban areas. Both parties use street money, but it is more common among Democrats, who tend to be better represented in the areas that rely on it. See Christopher Beam, "What's 'Street Money'?" *Slate*, October 23, 2008, http://www.slate.com/articles/news_and_politics/explainer/2008/10/whats_street_money.html.

During the California primary, to make sure black voters turned out for RFK, his campaign took to paying cash to grifting black ministers to get out the vote with their flocks. As John Siegenthaler, who helped run RFK's Northern California campaign noted, San Francisco Assemblyman (later Speaker) Willie Brown helped him negotiate the price. When a certain preacher came in, Brown warned Siegenthaler not to pay him over $250 to help turn out black voters. Sure enough, the pastor started the bidding at $500; Siegenthaler offered $100, and they settled right at Brown's $250 price. The local operation of State Assembly Speaker Jesse Unruh, the de facto California Democratic Party leader, warned Siegenthaler not to buy off the local black ministers too early, or else he'd have to buy them off again later. See Thomas, *Robert Kennedy*, 385.

[4]   RFK California campaign aide Dick Kline said later, "We had a lot of conflicts with the national staff. They wanted to get the candidate out among the Mexicans and in the black suburbs. We tried to tell them he was needed more in the middle class white suburbs, because he was going to get the black and Mexican votes anyway. What they didn't seem to realize was that the picture of Bobby surrounded by frenzied mobs pulling his shoes and shirt off was a violent picture, and it wasn't liked by the white voters who had been very frightened by the Watts riots three years before. I don't think the national staff ever understood why the West Side liberals in L.A. were so overwhelmingly for McCarthy." See Chester, Hodgson, Page, *An American Melodrama*, 323-324.

RFK tried to create an impression of "irresistible popularity, squeezing the crowds into cul-de-sacs or narrow streets to heighten the impact of congestion, a favorite Kennedy crowd-building technique." See Herzog, *McCarthy for President*, 146.

[5]   Two days before the California primary, RFK took a break from the campaign trail and took his children to Disneyland, where they rode the newly installed "Pirates of the Caribbean" ride. See Thomas, *Robert Kennedy*, 386.

[6]   West Side liberals in Los Angeles were overwhelmingly for McCarthy. See Chester, Hodgson, Page, *An American Melodrama*, 323-324.

[7]   Late Monday night, June 3, 1968, at the last public event of RFK's California campaign before the polls opened, RFK addressed a crowd of 3,000 in the ballroom of San Diego's El Cortez Hotel. During his speech, RFK almost collapsed from exhaustion. He sat on the edge of the stage and put his head in his hands as stunned onlookers watched. An aide escorted him quickly off the stage and into a nearby restroom, where RFK vomited. After a few minutes, he returned to the ballroom and finished his speech. See Thomas, *Robert Kennedy*, 26; see also John Wilkens, "RFK's Legacy Looms on the 50th Anniversary of His Assassination," the *San Diego Union-Tribune*, June 3, 2018, https://www.sandiegouniontribune.com/news/politics/sd-me-rfk-anniversary-20180531-story.html.

[8]   During Humphrey's 1960 primary campaign against JFK, RFK claimed falsely that Teamsters president Jimmy Hoffa and mobsters bank-

rolled Humphrey's effort. Of that smear, Humphrey later wrote, "Both [Bobby] and Jack knew the story was untrue and could have stopped it, but the rumor-mongering persisted despite our direct entreaties that it be stopped." See Humphrey, *The Education of a Public Man*, 209.

[9]   In 1960, Humphrey and his shoestring campaign staff jostled down the backroads of Wisconsin and West Virginia in a beat-up rented bus, while the deep-pocketed Kennedy family covered both states in a luxurious Convair 240 jet equipped with an office, full galley, bathrooms, bedroom, and a flight crew that included JFK's masseuse and private chef. See Heymann, *RFK*, 145, 157-158, 182.

[10]   RFK pressured Franklin D. Roosevelt Jr., the namesake of the revered late president, to attack Humphrey as a World War II draft dodger during Humphrey's 1960 West Virginia Democratic presidential primary campaign against JFK. See Schlesinger, *Robert Kennedy and His Times*, 199-200 and fn. p. 200; see also Humphrey, *The Education of a Public Man*, 475 n.4.

In recalling the 1960 West Virginia draft dodger smear years later, Roosevelt called his slur against Humphrey the biggest mistake of his life, and he blamed RFK directly for it. "I did it because of Bobby," Roosevelt said. Although RFK was a young man only in his mid-thirties, Roosevelt said RFK was "already a full-blown tyrant. You did what he told you to do, and you did it with a smile." See Heymann, *RFK*, 153-154.

In his February 12, 1975, diary entry, historian Arthur M. Schlesinger Jr. recorded that he discussed the 1960 West Virginia presidential primary the previous evening with his longtime friend, Franklin D. Roosevelt Jr. In discussing RFK's insistence on smearing Humphrey with his World War II record, Roosevelt told Schlesinger, "I made only one mistake [when I went to West Virginia to campaign for JFK against Humphrey].... That was bringing up Hubert's record during the war. Bobby had been bringing pressure on me to mention it. He kept calling—five or six calls a day. Finally I did. Then there was a lot of criticism, and Kennedy repudiated the statement and cut the ground out from under me. That was the beginning of the break between Bobby and me." See Schlesinger Jr., *Journals*, 399.

[11]   The night JFK beat Humphrey in the 1960 West Virginia primary and knocked Humphrey from the presidential race, RFK went to Humphrey's hotel room to make peace. As Humphrey recalled later, "When Bob arrived in our room, he moved quickly to Muriel [Mrs. Humphrey] and kissed her on the cheek. Muriel stiffened, stared, and turned in silent hostility, walking away from him, fighting back tears and angry words." Of RFK's behavior during the 1960 campaign, Humphrey wrote, "I didn't like him then. He seemed tough and hostile beyond the needs of political opposition. I suppose I never forgave him for that period[.]" See Humphrey, *The Education of a Public Man*, 221, 374.

[12]   When Humphrey declared his candidacy in 1968, he borrowed a line from a favorite John Adams passage about the way politics ought to be in America: the politics of happiness, the politics of purpose, and the politics of joy. It mattered not that RFK and Humphrey liked each other and considered each other friends. RFK pounced on the line and clubbed Humphrey with it throughout the campaign. "Any man who can find 'joy' in Martin Luther King's recent slaying or in the [sight] of young men brought home from Vietnam in body bags each week is not a man I want to see as president of the United States," RFK declared. It was "Bad Bobby" redux—a low blow—and the Humphrey campaign resented and protested it in vain. RFK kept repeating variations of the attack against Humphrey's "politics of joy" comment. Humphrey aide Ted Van Dyk later complained that "Robert Kennedy twisted [Humphrey's words], in all his campaign speeches, to say that at a time of war and dreadful poverty, Humphrey was just a vapid, silly, happiness candidate. It was a below-the-belt, stop-at-nothing kind of campaigning." See Heymann, *RFK*, 475-476.

In his November 16, 1966, diary entry, historian Arthur M. Schlesinger Jr., a friend to both men, noted that Humphrey and RFK "quite like each other, though that will not, of course, prevent either from cutting the other up tomorrow" if they ended up opposing each other in a presidential campaign. See Schlesinger Jr., *Journals*, 254.

[13]   Humphrey knew that if he won the 1968 Democratic presidential nomination, RFK would help him with the constituencies where he was weak: college students and minorities. Humphrey knew RFK would

campaign hard to bring them back to the Democratic Party in November. See Chester, Hodgson, Page, *An American Melodrama*, 405.

[14]   After LBJ withdrew as a presidential candidate, both Humphrey and RFK agreed that they would meet after the primaries and before the 1968 Democratic Convention to review their situation and see if they could work something out. In his 1974 memoir, Lawrence F. O'Brien—who directed the campaigns of both RFK and Humphrey that year—wrote that his understanding of their agreement was that if either Humphrey or RFK was clearly going to get the nomination, "the other might withdraw to avoid a bitter convention fight, that either one might instead accept the vice presidency on such a ticket." The suggestion came from Humphrey, and RFK "was in complete agreement and mentioned his sincere affection for Hubert. He said, 'The worst thing about all this is that we're in a fight with Hubert Humphrey. He's a great guy.'" See O'Brien, *No Final Victories*, 235-236.

[15]   On the evening of the California primary, Humphrey was on his way to the U.S. Air Force Academy in Colorado Springs. There he planned to stay overnight and then address the cadets the next morning. On the car ride from the airport, Ted Van Dyk asked Humphrey what he thought about the primary results starting to trickle in over the radio. Van Dyk expected Humphrey to prefer that fellow Minnesotan McCarthy beat RFK, since RFK appeared to loom as the more formidable rival for the nomination. Humphrey surprised Van Dyk with his reply. "I want Bobby Kennedy to win as decisively as possible. I want it to be so one-sided that McCarthy will be driven from the race entirely." When asked for the reason behind his unexpected analysis, Humphrey continued, "Bobby Kennedy and I understand each other. We've talked privately on a couple of occasions you don't know about. If I am nominated, he will campaign for me without reservation. If something should happen so that he is nominated, I'll campaign for him. But, if McCarthy stays in the game, he'll damage both of us. I know Gene and I have affection for him. But he is a spoiler. I want him gone—tonight." Humphrey could afford to be gracious: on the eve of the California primary, Humphrey had already secured almost enough delegates to win the nomination on the first ballot. See Van Dyk, *Heroes, Hacks & Fools*, 72.

On the day of the California primary, Humphrey said privately, "I want Bobby to win big [in California against McCarthy]. Number one, there are too many Party leaders opposed to him for him to have any real chance of winning the nomination. Number two, since [losing the Oregon primary to McCarthy], he can't use the argument that he went right through the primaries. And number three, he's a Party regular in spite of everything. If he does lose the nomination, he'll get together with me and work for me. Whereas, if Gene is my opponent—." Humphrey paused, and then he continued, "Gene's my friend. I've known him for twenty years. But if he wins tonight, he'll plague Bobby and me all the way to the convention." See Chester, Hodgson, Page, *An American Melodrama*, 402.

Humphrey didn't want RFK to lose the California primary to McCarthy because he knew that a loss there would knock RFK out of the race, and that would dissipate the Kennedy "magic" when RFK later campaigned vigorously for the ticket after Humphrey won the nomination. See Chester, Hodgson, Page, *An American Melodrama*, 309.

Humphrey's instincts that McCarthy would be a spoiler in the race proved correct. Two weeks after the California primary, McCarthy told reporters that it would be "very difficult" for him to back Humphrey if he won the nomination. See Chester, Hodgson, Page, *An American Melodrama*, 404.

RFK told Humphrey privately that he would withdraw from the race if he lost the California primary. See Chester, Hodgson, Page, *An American Melodrama*, 404.

"Had Bobby Kennedy lived, even with a narrow California primary victory, he knew he was second and had told Humphrey that he would support him after California if he didn't win [over McCarthy] by a substantial margin. [¶] As early as May, several months before the convention, a month before the California primary, Kennedy had Kenny O'Donnell, a long-time family political operative visit Humphrey.... [O'Donnell] then told Humphrey that if Bobby did not do well in California, he would withdraw, as he had promised, and immediately support Humphrey. A squeaker [for Kennedy in California] meant goodbye. Kennedy beat McCarthy by four points, 46 percent to 42 percent, hardly a game changing landslide." See Sherman, *From Nowhere to Somewhere*, 177.

[16]   RFK's candidacy did not worry Humphrey. He had confided to his staff that RFK had failed to seize the nomination the first week after LBJ withdrew from the race. Once LBJ had dropped out, RFK failed to consolidate his position as the presumptive nominee. With LBJ moving toward peace, and then McCarthy's strong showing in Wisconsin, RFK failed to lock it up, and by failing to do so, he had lost his chance for the nomination. See Chester, Hodgson, Page, *An American Melodrama*, 140, 144.

Although their names never appeared opposite each other on primary ballots, every time Humphrey faced RFK's forces in state convention fights—Pennsylvania, Vermont, Idaho, Iowa, and others—Humphrey won. Much of the money pledged to the Humphrey campaign came from business leaders in the state RFK represented in the U.S. Senate—New York—because they distrusted RFK. See Humphrey, *The Education of a Public Man*, 375.

As Humphrey aide Ted Van Dyk later related, Pennsylvania was the key state, with a huge cache of delegates. When RFK lost Oregon and Humphrey swept Pennsylvania, Humphrey knew he had RFK beaten. Even though RFK won California, it wouldn't have done anything for him had he lived. See Heymann, *RFK*, 494.

[17]   By the day of the California primary, Humphrey had secured almost enough delegates to win the nomination on the first ballot. See Van Dyk, *Heroes, Hacks & Fools*, 72.

By the time of the Nebraska primary on May 14, 1968, Humphrey campaign chairman Walter Mondale announced that Humphrey had 1,265 pledges on the first ballot in Chicago—only 47 short of a majority and the nomination. See Chester, Hodgson, Page, *An American Melodrama*, 178.

[18]   "That old bitch, luck." The conversation Chris Evans had with RFK in our story regarding a possible assassination attempt is adapted from an actual conversation RFK had with John Frankenheimer at the movie director's Malibu beach house eight days before the assassination. Frankenheimer told RFK that someone would try to kill him eventually. RFK replied, "There's no way of protecting a country-stumping candidate, no way at all. You've just got to give yourself to the people and to trust them. From then on, it's just that good old bitch, luck. You have to have luck

on your side to be elected president of the United States. Either it's with you or it isn't. I am pretty sure there will be an attempt on my life sooner or later. Not so much for political reasons; I don't believe that. Plain nuttiness, that's all. There's plenty of that around.... I told you, you can't make it without that good old bitch, luck." See Salinger, *P.S. A Memoir*, 185-187.

[19] CBS News, in an election-eve prediction, claimed RFK would beat McCarthy 52 percent to 39 percent. See Herzog, *McCarthy for President*, 189.

[20] The delegate projections favoring Humphrey, RFK's interpretation of them, RFK's frustration with having to waste time after the California primary to campaign hard against McCarthy in the upcoming New York primary, and RFK's need to "chase Hubert's ass" around the country are adapted from multiple conversations RFK held with his senior campaign staff on the evening of June 4, 1968. See Schlesinger Jr., *Robert Kennedy and His Times*, 913; Goodwin, *Remembering America*, 536-537.

Even as RFK's supporters savored their California victory in the Ambassador Hotel ballroom, Dick Goodwin knew RFK's primary win had limited meaning. "[O]utside the hotel, and beyond California, the Humphrey campaign, propelled by the single-minded power of Lyndon Johnson, was moving from state to state, persuading, coercing, calling in old debts and creating new ones, progressing toward control of the Chicago convention." See Goodwin, *Remembering America*, 536.

[21] Shortly before RFK went down to the ballroom to give his California primary victory speech in the Ambassador Hotel, Ted Sorensen brought RFK the disappointing projections from New Jersey and Ohio showing both delegations would probably break for Humphrey by next week. See Goodwin, *Remembering America*, 537.

[22] Ironically, RFK decided on the afternoon of the California primary that he would like to skip his election-night party at the Ambassador Hotel. RFK grew so relaxed at Frankenheimer's beach house that he suggested his family and staff bypass the hotel hoopla, watch the returns at the Malibu home, and invite the press over. When RFK later learned from his press

secretary, Frank Mankiewicz, that the television networks refused to haul their equipment out to Malibu, RFK decided reluctantly to go to the hotel to await the election returns. See Dan E. Moldea, *The Killing of Robert F. Kennedy: An Investigation of Motive, Means, and Opportunity* (New York: W.W. Norton & Company, 1995)

[23]   Before leaving for the Ambassador Hotel, and while still at the Frankenheimer home, Frankenheimer asked what RFK would do if he lost the California primary. RFK replied, "If I lose, I'll just go home and raise the next generation of Kennedys." See Goodwin, *Remembering America*, 536.

[24]   As John Frankenheimer drove RFK to the Ambassador Hotel on the night of the California primary, he raced his car down the Santa Monica Freeway. RFK chastised him for speeding, saying, "Take it easy, John. Life is too short." See Schlesinger Jr., *Robert Kennedy and His Times*, 913.

[25]   RFK beat McCarthy in the California primary 45 percent to 42 percent, with 12 percent for Humphrey's stand-in, California Attorney General Lynch. See Mailer, *Miami and the Siege of Chicago*, 102.

[26]   When RFK went down to the ballroom of the Ambassador Hotel to make his victory speech the night of the California primary, he did so believing that he had won more than 50 percent of the vote in the primary. He hoped that this showing might pressure McCarthy to leave the race. Because of the shooting, RFK never learned that late results gave him an unimpressive 45-42 margin over McCarthy.

In RFK's suite in the Ambassador Hotel on the night of the 1968 California presidential primary, and before RFK went downstairs to claim victory, Larry O'Brien, a longtime Kennedy family campaign strategist, gave RFK some unsettling but not surprising, news. While mobs had been snatching RFK's cufflinks and shoes in the small primary states, Humphrey had been traveling the nation and, quietly, lining up massive pockets of delegates in big states such as New Jersey, Pennsylvania, and Ohio. Unless RFK could find a way to shake loose those commitments, the nomination would not be his. Knowing that McCarthy's disdain for RFK was now so great that he would never step aside for him, RFK suggested throwing a "Hail Mary" pass. RFK asked Richard Goodwin, a

Kennedy staffer who doubled as a go-between for the two warring camps, to call McCarthy and suggest a deal: McCarthy leave the race tonight and endorse RFK, and if RFK won, he would name McCarthy as his Secretary of State. See Thomas, *Robert Kennedy*, 388.

[27] By the California primary, McCarthy's principal campaign speechwriter, Jeremy Larner, remembered that, "[I]t was now clear that McCarthy hated Bobby Kennedy, that on a personal level he preferred Humphrey [for the Democratic presidential nomination]." See Larner, *Nobody Knows*, 97.

[28] The vignette of McCarthy's concession speech, in which he said, "Winning isn't everything," and RFK's retort that such sentiment was not what his father taught the Kennedy children, actually occurred on the night of the Indiana primary a few weeks earlier, and not on the night of the 1968 California primary. See Chester, Hodgson, Page, *An American Melodrama*, 177.

[29] Pierre Salinger co-owned The Factory, a new Los Angeles discotheque, with Hollywood stars Paul Newman, Peter Lawford, and Sammy Davis Jr.

[30] Dick Goodwin intended to accompany RFK to the Ambassador Hotel ballroom for RFK's victory speech, but as the Kennedy party departed the suite, Goodwin took a last-minute call from a prominent McCarthy supporter that he had hoped to recruit. With Goodwin on the phone with the donor, RFK patted his shoulder and told him, "I'll go downstairs and do this, and then we can talk some more over at The Factory," which was an exclusive, invitation-only nightclub in West Hollywood where the Kennedy party had planned to celebrate their victory after his hotel speech. Goodwin nodded but didn't respond as RFK and his entourage headed down the hall for the elevator. See Goodwin, *Remembering America*, 538.

[31] The poster RFK autographed for campaign volunteer Michael Wayne as he entered the Ambassador Hotel ballroom for his victory speech was the last autograph he ever signed. Forty-four years later, Wayne sold the poster at auction for $2,550. https://www.greatestcollectibles.com/1968-robert-kennedy-signed-campaign-poster-autographed-b4-assassination/#.Xw3aHihKiUk.

CHAPTER 16

[1] A few minutes after RFK finished his Ambassador Hotel victory speech, Richard Goodwin (who remained in RFK's fifth-floor suite talking on the telephone) heard campaign manager Steve Smith's voice coming over the television. He looked up to see Smith standing at the lectern RFK had vacated only moments earlier. Steve sounded tense as he announced to the crowd, "The senator is hurt. Is there a doctor here?" See Goodwin, *Remembering America*, 538.

[2] McCarthy and his staff were in their suite at the Beverly Hilton hotel drafting a congratulatory telegram to RFK when they received news of the shooting. See McCarthy, *The Year of the People*, 173-174.

[3] McCarthy was one of the most religious men in American political life. See White, *The Making of the President 1968*, 36.

[4] How McCarthy responded upon learning the news of RFK's shooting is in conflict:

- When McCarthy heard of the shooting, Blair Clark reported hearing McCarthy say, "He [RFK] brought it on himself." Curtis Gans supposedly heard McCarthy mumble, "Demagoguing to the last." McCarthy later admitted that was how he felt at the time. Since RFK played up his support to Israel during their debate a few days earlier, McCarthy thought that might have provoked Sirhan Sirhan, a Palestinian refugee, to shoot RFK. See Dominic Sandbrook, *Eugene McCarthy and the Rise and Fall of Postwar American Liberalism* (New York: Anchor Books, 2005), 202-203.

- Another witness to McCarthy's Beverly Hilton suite that night, longtime Washington columnist Mary McGrory, reported it differently. McGrory wrote that as McCarthy and his senior staff drafted a congratulatory telegram to RFK, CBS News reporter David Schoumacher entered the room and said that RFK had been shot. McCarthy and others looked at him in total disbelief; someone said, "You're kidding." Schoumacher left to get more information and then returned a few minutes later to report that RFK had been shot in the hip. "McCarthy, sitting in a chair in the corner, put his hands over his eyes, and then looked up. 'Maybe we should do it [campaign] in a different way,' he said. 'Maybe we should have the English system of having the Cabinet choose the president. There must be some other way.'" Herzog, *McCarthy for President*, 189-190.

- Another McCarthy senior campaign worker, Arthur Herzog, wrote that after hearing the news, McCarthy—the color of ash—returned to the ballroom and told the remaining campaigners to go home and pray. See Herzog, *McCarthy for President*, 189-190.

- After RFK's death, McCarthy returned to Washington "a shaken man. He had not revered Kennedy in life, but he felt the shock, the outrage… the grief of the Kennedy family and friends." See Herzog, *McCarthy for President*, 193.

5   After RFK's shooting, McCarthy called the hospital several times and asked to speak to RFK's wife, Ethel Kennedy. She refused to take his call. McCarthy then went to the hospital directly. Instead of RFK's staff bringing him to see Ethel, Pierre Salinger and Dick Goodwin intercepted McCarthy. The two men brought him into a private hospital room and met with him for 15 minutes. During that discussion, Salinger and Goodwin had a bizarre request for the man they had defeated in the primary only two hours earlier. Given the circumstances, they asked him to fly to Washington immediately, meet with LBJ, and ask the president to announce he will be a candidate for reelection. Salinger and Goodwin told McCarthy that he couldn't win the nomination, and Humphrey couldn't win the general election. For the sake of the Democratic Party, they wanted McCarthy to urge LBJ to run again. "To his credit, Gene

McCarthy said he could see the logic in what we were saying, and he promised us he would think about it. Of course, he never did." See Salinger, *P.S. A Memoir*, 198-199.

[6]   When McCarthy arrived at Good Samaritan Hospital, the Kennedy family refused to see him. Instead, Dick Goodwin sat with him in the lobby. When told the name of RFK's assassin, Sirhan Sirhan, McCarthy said, "Sirhan Sirhan. It's just like Camus' *The Stranger*, the first name and the last name are the same." See Goodwin, *Remembering America*, 539.

[7]   Within a few minutes of RFK arriving at the hospital by ambulance following the shooting, campaign aides Pierre Salinger and Steven Smith tracked down Humphrey by phone at the Air Force Academy. They told him RFK had suffered a head wound; they didn't know the extent of the damage. They asked Humphrey to intercede and arrange immediate military transportation for an eminent Boston neurosurgeon to fly to Los Angeles to help the stricken candidate. Humphrey swung into action to process the request. Being at the Air Force Academy was fortuitous: Humphrey contacted the top brass assembled for the vice president's scheduled speech the next morning and he told them what he needed. A few minutes later, the base operations officer called and asked by what authority Humphrey was ordering a plane. Making up a position that did not exist, Humphrey shouted into the telephone, "I am Vice-Commander in Chief!" See Humphrey, *The Education of a Public Man*, 372.

After receiving the news that RFK had been shot, Humphrey "was on the phone talking to Pierre Salinger, a Kennedy aide, in Los Angeles. Tears rolled down [Humphrey's] cheeks as he learned how dire the situation was. Soon after the first call, Pierre called back to ask Humphrey's help in getting an Air Force jet to fly a neurosurgeon from Boston to Los Angeles. [¶] Humphrey called the Pentagon and told the duty officer what he wanted. The officer responded, 'Sir, under what authority are you ordering this plane?' Humphrey shouted, 'I'm Vice Commander-in-Chief.'" See Sherman, *From Nowhere to Somewhere*, 168.

As to Humphrey ordering a military transport plane under his authority as "vice commander in chief," a former Humphrey aide noted in his memoir, "It was an office that did not exist, but it worked." See Sherman, *From Nowhere to Somewhere*, 168.

[8]   After learning that RFK had been shot, Humphrey "received phone calls from Pierce Salinger and Steven Smith, who were with Kennedy at the Ambassador Hotel in Los Angeles. Kennedy was gravely wounded, they reported, but still alive. Could Humphrey arrange immediate military air transportation to Los Angeles for a Boston neurosurgeon who might be able to save him? Humphrey contacted Air Force brass who were present at the Academy for the next morning's speech. He gave them the doctor's name and phone number and said the doctor was standing by for instructions. Yes, they said, they would provide the transportation immediately. Five minutes later, however, Humphrey received another phone call. The White House had refused to approve Humphrey's request for the aircraft. It would not be available.... Humphrey rose and went briefly to his bedroom after receiving the news about the canceled aircraft. Observing his body language, I could see that he was humiliated and ashamed. The Kennedy family arranged the neurosurgeon's flight on their own." See Van Dyk, *Heroes, Hacks & Fools*, 70.

In his own 1976 memoir, Humphrey confirmed the story—to a point. After recounting the details of ordering the plane under his authority as "Vice-Commander-in-Chief," Humphrey wrote, "My intensity overcame [the operations officer's] reluctance and the doctor was flown to Los Angeles." At first glance, this appears to suggest that the Air Force, and not the Kennedy family, arranged transportation, but the phraseology Humphrey used remained ambiguous. Based on the evidence, the author believes that Van Dyk's detailed recollection is correct and that Humphrey left his version vague intentionally to spare LBJ's memory from such inexcusable pettiness. For Humphrey's version, see Humphrey, *The Education of a Public Man*, 372.

[9]   In reality, the bullet that killed RFK struck the mastoid bone behind the right ear, driving bullet and bone fragments into the right side of his brain. The damage was too severe to repair. One of RFK's surgeons noted that, had the bullet struck the bone at a glancing blow, he would have left the hospital and gone on his way in a few weeks. Another doctor said that if the bullet had struck just one centimeter to the right, RFK probably would have survived. See, e.g., Chester, Hodgson, Page, *An American Melodrama*, 357.

"[A] surgeon who operated on Kennedy reported that if the fatal bullet had hit him a centimeter further back he would have survived and spent several weeks recuperating before resuming his campaign." Thurston Clarke, *The Last Campaign: Robert F. Kennedy and the 82 Days that Inspired America* (New York: Henry Holt and Company, 2008), 273.

In the initial hours after the shooting, RFK's close associates had hope for his recovery. As Arthur M Schlesinger Jr. noted in his journal entry eight hours after RFK was shot, "When I caught the 8 a.m. plane back to New York, I was still reasonably hopeful. A brain specialist from Georgetown University had explained over ABC that the bullet had apparently entered a part of the brain that didn't much matter; and he was now being operated on." See Schlesinger Jr., *Journals*, 290-291.

[10]   Different resources offer slightly varying accounts of where the bullets struck RFK:

According to initial medical reports given to the press hours after the shooting, the first (and fatal) bullet struck RFK in the mastoid area of the right ear and lodged in the cerebellum, the second bullet grazed his forehead, and the third bullet struck him in the right armpit and lodged in the base of the neck. See, e.g., the medical diagram accompanying the article written by Ralph Dighton, Associated Press, "Doctors Pessimistic About Kennedy's Future," *Herald Dispatch*, Huntington, West Virginia, June 6, 1968, p. 11.

RFK's autopsy report prepared by the medical examiner, Dr. Thomas T. Noguchi, indicated that RFK was wounded three times. The first and fatal bullet struck RFK behind the right ear; a second shot hit RFK in the right armpit and exited near the right clavicle, and a third bullet entered the same armpit area and came to rest just under the skin at the base of the back of his neck. See Dr. Thomas T. Noguchi, Los Angeles County Chief Medical Examiner-Coroner, Autopsy Report on Robert F. Kennedy, Case #68-5731, Second Rough Draft, September 20, 1968.

[11]   In a 1985 article marking the centennial of Good Samaritan Hospital in Los Angeles, Ellis E. Conklin wrote, "At 1:43 a.m. June 6, [1968, Robert] Kennedy died inside a forty-foot-long, green-tiled intensive care

unit on the fifth floor, now the site of the hospital's print shop. The ninth-floor surgical unit is now just a heap of outdated equipment scattered randomly in darkened corridors.... There's now a paper-folding machine and booklet stitcher on the spot where Kennedy took his last breath. The track remains where the white curtains were pulled in a semicircle around the dying senator. [¶] A seventeen-year-old youth works several feet away on another printing machine. Overhearing his supervisor point the spot out to a reporter, the teenager said, 'What? That's where Bobby died?' His expression blazed in disbelief. It was like a ghost had fluttered past him." See Ellis Conklin, "Hospital Where Robert Kennedy Died Rich in Other History," UPI Archives, May 29, 1985, http://www.upi.com/Archives/1985/05/29/Hospital-where-Robert-Kennedy-died-rich-in-other-history/4136486187200/.

CHAPTER 17

[1]   The description of RFK feeling as though he had been electrocuted is adapted from the description given by Paul Schrade, a Kennedy campaign worker who suffered a nonfatal head wound in the Ambassador Hotel pantry that night. Schrade later described the event: "Bob [was] smiling and walking towards what I know now was a steam table. All of a sudden, I started shaking very violently. There were television cameras all around and cables all over the floor, and I thought I was being electrocuted. I just passed out. Other than the heavy trembling, I don't remember hearing anything or feeling anything. I just fell. My next sensation was feeling people trampling on me. I felt pain. Then, there was a doctor over me as I came to. He said, 'You're going to be all right. It's not serious.' I felt the blood streaming out of my head. At that point, I realized that I had been shot." See Moldea, *The Killing of Robert F. Kennedy*, 35.

CHAPTER 18

[No Endnotes]

CHAPTER 19

[1] After the 1968 Democratic National Convention, instead of endorsing Humphrey and campaigning for him that fall, McCarthy took an extended vacation on the French Riviera. When reporters greeted him upon his return, he told them he was not now endorsing Humphrey and would say nothing else on the matter until at least mid-October. Chester, Hodgson, Page, *An American Melodrama*, 645, 740, 744-745.

After the final primary in June 1968, McCarthy went on vacation and remained on his lengthy respite until the eve of the Democratic National Convention in late August. See Van Dyk, *Heroes, Hacks & Fools*, 71.

In his memoir of 1968, McCarthy wrote that when the primaries concluded, he traveled the country speaking to delegations in search of support. See McCarthy, *The Year of the People*, 179-181.

After RFK's shooting, McCarthy felt it would be in poor taste to campaign "circus style," but he continued to discuss the issues, which is what he felt the campaign was all about. He would speak only occasionally and with tortured restraint before audiences; he "would permit no hoopla, and no rallies, no real activity." McCarthy "would not campaign too hard, reserving several hours a day for writing poetry." McCarthy "felt he should not have to beg support from those who agreed with him ideologically, and he was often bitterly unhappy with the failure of the liberal politicians to get behind his campaign on their own." See Herzog, *McCarthy for President*, 196-197, 199, 221.

[2] In late July 1968, McCarthy packed Fenway Park in Boston, which seated about 40,000 people. Another 5,000 people with tickets were unable to gain admittance. It was perhaps the largest audience to date that ever appeared for a Fenway Park event. See Robert L. Turner, "Eugene

McCarthy Confidently Predicts Victory at Fenway," *Boston Globe*, July 26, 1968.

3   McCarthy had a great indifference to pursuing delegates at the convention. During convention week, his staff successfully coaxed him into visiting only five delegations, and when he did appear, he invited the delegates to consider his candidacy on a "take me or leave me" basis. See Chester, Hodgson, Page, *An American Melodrama*, 560.

During the 1968 Democratic presidential primaries, the total votes received were:

McCarthy	2,914,933	(38.73 percent)
RFK	2,305,148	(30.63 percent)
LBJ	383,590	(05.10 percent)
Humphrey	166,463	(02.21 percent)

https://en.wikipedia.org/wiki/Democratic_Party_presidential_primaries,_1968#cite_note-ourcampaigns.com-7

4   On the second day of the 1968 Democratic National Convention, August 27, 1968, McCarthy gave an interview to the Knight Newspaper chain in which he said he did not have the votes to win the nomination. Two decades later, and still stinging from criticism for this admission, McCarthy complained that stories of his aides scrambling to walk back the statement were "sheer nonsense.... I said what I did because I hoped that the statement might take the edge off the expectations of the young people who had come to Chicago and prepare them for defeat." See McCarthy, *The Year of the People*, 215.

In an interview with the Knight Newspapers syndicate, McCarthy said, "I think so" when asked if Humphrey had the nomination wrapped up. The headline in the morning *Chicago Daily News* blared MCCARTHY CONCEDES HE'S A LOSER. See Herzog, *McCarthy for President*, 266-267.

McCarthy sent shock waves through his delegates when, in what he thought was a private conversation with newspaper publisher John Knight, he said he had "zero" chance of winning the nomination. See White, *The Making of the President 1968*, 282.

[5]   In reality, after RFK died, it was McCarthy's appeal that grew in June and July as the Democratic Convention neared. His crowds grew by the tens of thousands, and he outpolled Humphrey in many states. Besides his original polling strength with the young, he also polled strongly with independents and center-left Republicans. See, e.g., White, *The Making of the President 1968*, 267.

[6]   With RFK dead, it was McCarthy who calculated that his chance for the nomination lay in proving to the delegates by polling data that he, and not Humphrey, could beat the Republican nominee. See, e.g., Herzog, *McCarthy for President*, 199, 209. McCarthy viewed Humphrey's strength as coming from three unnatural allies: Northern Democratic Party leaders heavily indebted to organized labor, the South, and LBJ. "If the proper wedges could be driven between Humphrey's forces his army might collapse in disarray.... The intention, then, was to break delegates away from Humphrey on issues other than the candidacy of Eugene McCarthy, to split the Humphrey camp into quarreling factions." Herzog, *McCarthy for President*, 202-204.

[7]   By mid-June 1968, the *New York Times* estimated Humphrey had 1,600 delegates, which was well beyond the 1,312 he needed to win the nomination. See Chester, Hodgson, Page, *An American Melodrama*, 403.

Longtime Humphrey senior adviser Max M. Kampelman noted in his memoir, "Humphrey announced for the presidency in April [1968] and had sewed up the necessary votes for nomination well before the convention. One of the continuing fictions of that year and since was that Bobby Kennedy would have received the nomination if he had lived, and that Humphrey was, therefore, the usurper of a tarnished prize. That was nonsense presented by instant revisionists, including some very bright writers like Theodore White. Before Bobby's death, Larry O'Brien and Kenny O'Donnell [longtime Kennedy family advisers], who were excellent vote counters, told Humphrey he would win and that they could not.

At a breakfast with Humphrey, Kenny said that Bobby would withdraw after the California primary if he lost either Oregon or California. Bobby himself had indicated to Humphrey that he would support Humphrey after the convention." Kampelman, *Entering New Worlds*, 164.

[8] For Humphrey, the Chicago convention timing was awful. The late August dates had been set originally by LBJ when he intended to seek reelection, and he chose those dates to coincide with his 60th birthday on August 27. As Humphrey later noted, "For an incumbent president, late is fine. For a non-incumbent, late is awful.... I desperately needed time to heal wounds, build Party organization, raise money—in short, to build a tightly knit campaign. I had lost the month of August, and the campaign started on Labor Day[.]" See Humphrey, *The Education of a Public Man*, 396.

[9] When McCarthy returned from his post-primary European vacation, and just days before the start of the 1968 Democratic National Convention, he met with Humphrey and said he knew that Humphrey would win the nomination. "'I should endorse you,' he said [to Humphrey]. 'You're the only one who can beat Nixon.' But he didn't.... Within a week of that meeting, McCarthy's people were out pushing for delegates again and the fight was on." See Mondale, *The Good Fight*, 75-76.

Two weeks before the convention, McCarthy told Humphrey he didn't expect to win the nomination and promised Humphrey he would come out for him sometime around the middle of September. See Humphrey, *The Education of a Public Man*, 376-377.

[10] If Humphrey accepted a dove plank at the convention, McCarthy said he might be able to support him. See Herzog, *McCarthy for President*, 238.

[11] Half of the 1968 Democratic Convention delegate votes came from the Southern states and from the labor unions. See Thomas, *Robert Kennedy*, 362-363.

[12] A large percentage of delegates to the Democratic Convention were the Party regulars: "mayors, governors, state Democratic Party officers, precinct leaders, and Party activists. Humphrey knew them all. He had

worked with a lot of them, done favors, raised money—he had a lot of chits to call in. They knew him and trusted him[.]" See Mondale, *The Good Fight*, 76.

"Humphrey came into Chicago [for the 1968 Democratic Convention] with nine-tenths of the organized Democratic Party—black support, labor support, Mafia support, Southern delegate support[.]" Norman Mailer, *Miami and the Siege of Chicago*, 111.

As for the non-primary selected delegates, "[t]he one element of politics they understood was loyalty. They understood their obligation to repay debts to the state organization: and the state organization usually had debts to Hubert Humphrey." See Stavis, *We Were the Campaign*, 151.

[13] In mid-May 1968, while on a flight to Maine to address the state Democratic Convention, Humphrey told Senator Edmund S. Muskie (D-ME) that he wanted Muskie as his running mate. Edmund S. Muskie, *Journeys* (New York: Doubleday & Co., 1972), 31-32.

In a 1982 handwritten letter to the author, former Senator Edmund Muskie shared his memories of how he ended up on the 1968 Democratic ticket with Hubert Humphrey. "Hubert first indicated his interest in a flight from Washington to Maine to attend the Maine Democratic Convention in May 1968. I was surprised and flattered but skeptical that political realities would permit him to choose a running mate from a small state like Maine. I remained skeptical until the day after his own nomination in Chicago. He asked me to come to his room in the Conrad Hilton Hotel. The invitation convinced me that I was about to be selected, which of course proved to be the case. As to my reaction, I was exhilarated and enthusiastic—notwithstanding the depressing events of the convention. We ended the campaign in the same spirit—and almost won! It was one of the greatest experiences of my life to be associated with Hubert Humphrey in such a venture!" Letter from Edmund S. Muskie to the author, December 9, 1982. See James E. Rogan, *And Then I Met... Stories of Growing Up, Meeting Famous People, and Annoying the Hell Out of Them* (Washington: WND Books, 2014), 305-306.

[14] As the 1968 Democratic Convention approached, Humphrey wanted to signal that he was now speaking for himself on Vietnam and not for an administration that had frozen him out of policy discussions. He set

up a task force of advisers to work up a draft peace proposal that would satisfy the McCarthy and RFK wings without alienating the pro-LBJ, pro-war forces, especially in the Southern delegations. Language calling for a unilateral and immediate withdrawal from Vietnam was off the table, but Humphrey indicated he might otherwise embrace the doves' call for peace and a swift conclusion to U.S. involvement in Southeast Asia. While the Humphrey drafting team put the final touches on this proposal, Humphrey learned from news reports that LBJ gave the order to renew massive bombing raids on the North Vietnamese—doubling the number of bombs dropped on them the previous year. This news enraged further the antiwar forces and buttressed their intent to descend on the Democratic Convention. See Van Dyk, *Heroes, Hacks & Fools*, 72-73.

[15]   Before Humphrey left for the 1968 Democratic Convention, he directed his top aides to meet quietly with RFK's and McCarthy's campaign representatives, along with LBJ's White House convention staff, to negotiate compromise language on Vietnam that would allow Democrats to unify over their Party's platform. Humphrey insisted that any proposal not undercut the peace negotiations, but he also wanted to reach out to the antiwar Democrats with his own belief that America needed to end its involvement quickly in Southeast Asia. After a day of round-the-clock negotiations, representatives from the various stakeholders found their compromise. An excited Humphrey followed LBJ's earlier order to "keep in touch with Secretary of State Dean Rusk over any Vietnam platform language. Humphrey tracked down Rusk and read him the proposal over the telephone. Rusk suggested a couple of minor changes, which Humphrey accepted readily. Rusk then told Humphrey, "We can live with this, Hubert. It isn't all we'd like, but under the circumstances, it's a sensible plank." Still wanting to cover his bases, Humphrey next called LBJ's national security adviser, Walt Rostow, and read him the draft. Rostow told Humphrey that the language sounded fine and he suggested no changes. See Humphrey, *The Education of a Public Man*, 387-388.

[16]   Unlike the 5,000 supporters greeting McCarthy's convention arrival at Midway Airport on Sunday, August 25, 1968, Humphrey arrived for the convention at O'Hare Airport, "but there was no crowd to receive him, just a few of the Humphrey workers." See Mailer, *Miami and the Siege of Chicago*, 89, 100.

During the convention week, Humphrey stayed in suite 2525A of Chicago's Conrad Hilton Hotel on Michigan Avenue.

[17]   Platform Committee Chairman Hale Boggs reviewed and accepted the compromise peace plank worked out by the Humphrey, RFK, McCarthy, and McGovern forces. See Sherman, *From Nowhere to Somewhere*, 173.

[18]   LBJ controlled every cell of the convention body. The Johnson people held such a tight rein on the 1968 Democratic Convention that they forced Humphrey's son-in-law to line up each morning with all the other delegates to plead for extra tickets from LBJ's convention lieutenant so that Humphrey's family could attend the proceedings. The White House had final say on schedule, who had podium credentials, how the communications lines were laid out, which people were appointed as the convention officers and sergeants-at-arms and custodians. Nobody received a gallery pass unless they went through the Democratic National Committee, which was a subsidiary of Johnson Inc. And, because he could, LBJ even oversaw the state delegations seating map. Since RFK won the bulk of delegates in California and Florida, the two most populated and powerful states in the Union ended up in the very back of the arena—and separated from each other as far as space allowed—just to keep the Kennedy family's most potent bases of strength dispersed on the floor. See White, *The Making of the President 1968*, 271-272.

According to Humphrey biographer Carl Solberg, LBJ's control of the convention arrangements was so complete "that Humphrey's son-in-law had to line up every morning for tickets for members of the Humphrey family." LBJ "micromanaged convention arrangements. He vetoed a suggestion from Humphrey that the convention be moved from Chicago to Miami, and he rejected all of Humphrey's recommendations for convention officers." As Solberg wrote, Johnson's control was so great that he "dictated the city, the date, the officers, the program of the convention." See Dallek, *Flawed Giant*, 574.

"Humphrey's son-in-law, for example, had to get in line with the general public to get [convention] tickets for the family... for the nominating session that night." See Sherman, *From Nowhere to Somewhere*, 172.

Lawrence F O'Brien, Humphrey's 1968 campaign director, recalled that as he prepared for the 1968 Democratic National Convention, "I discovered that nobody in the Humphrey organization had the remotest influence on the planning of the convention. Marvin Watson and a Johnson man at the [Democratic National Committee]... were in total control. We could get no information about the allocation of hotel rooms, access to the convention floor, telephones, any of the normal details of convention planning. The Johnson people had everything tied up. I found it ironic when the McCarthy camp began complaining that they were being discriminated against, being frozen out in favor of Humphrey, because we were receiving exactly the same treatment." See O'Brien, *No Final Victories*, 249.

[19] At the start of the 1968 Democratic Convention, LBJ's chief convention liaison Marvin Watson advised Humphrey that LBJ had rejected Humphrey's compromise peace language and that Humphrey must drop it. See Humphrey, *The Education of a Public Man*, 387-389.

[20] Shortly before Humphrey won the nomination, he presented LBJ with his proposed compromise peace language for the convention platform. LBJ rejected it outright, telling Humphrey that his proposal would injure the ongoing Paris peace negotiations. He accused Humphrey of playing politics with the peace process and said it would endanger the lives of U.S. troops—including his son-in-law currently serving in Vietnam as a Marine captain. LBJ ended his tirade by telling Humphrey that blood would be on his hands if he proceeded with his compromise language. During the convention, with platform negotiations proceeding, LBJ's chief of staff Marvin Watson warned Humphrey that LBJ expected him to "toe the line" on Vietnam policy. To hammer home the message, LBJ personally called Humphrey in Chicago and reiterated the expectation. Because of the squeeze, the peace platform negotiations collapsed. See Van Dyk, *Heroes, Hacks & Fools*, 74-77.

Before the start of the 1968 Democratic Convention, Humphrey showed LBJ his draft language that offered a compromise on Vietnam to placate the Kennedy-McCarthy wing of the Party. "Humphrey's proposed [language] angered Johnson." Humphrey later told an aide that, in a conversation with LBJ on July 25, and after Humphrey showed him the draft, LBJ said that he "would be jeopardizing the lives of his sons-in-law and endangering the chance for peace. [LBJ threatened that if] I announced this, he'd destroy me for the presidency." See Dallek, *Flawed Giant*, 571.

Humphrey negotiating with the McCarthy-RFK factions a compromise peace plank for the 1968 Democratic Party platform, Humphrey clearing the compromise language with Secretary of State Rusk and National Security Advisor Rostow, Marvin Watson telling Humphrey of LBJ's rejection of the language, and Humphrey's confrontation with both Watson and LBJ over the rejection is based on actual events. See Humphrey, *The Education of a Public Man*, 387-389.

[21]   After Humphrey explained to aide Ted Van Dyk that LBJ rejected vehemently the compromise peace language, Van Dyk asked if Humphrey believed LBJ's threat to denounce him publicly. Humphrey told Van Dyk that he had to believe him, and then he added this afterthought: "You know, I've eaten so much of Johnson's shit in this job that I've grown to like the taste of it." See Van Dyk, *Heroes, Hacks & Fools*, 74.

[22]   When LBJ ordered Humphrey to drop the compromise platform language, Humphrey's anger boiled to the surface. He told his staff that he wanted to stick with the negotiated compromise language, but before he could hold any further discussion on this strategy, the long and powerful arms of LBJ had already reached inside the convention hall. Within minutes of Humphrey's talk with LBJ, the Platform Committee chairman, Congressman Hale Boggs, rushed to Humphrey's suite and delivered the final blow: if the president opposed the compromise, then Boggs would instruct each committee member to follow the president's wishes. See Humphrey, *The Education of a Public Man*, 389-390.

The 1968 Democratic National Convention platform committee chairman, Congressman Hale Boggs, told Humphrey that he approved Humphrey's peace-plank language. Soon thereafter, LBJ called Boggs back to Washington and told him that America was on the verge of World War III because of the Soviet invasion of Czechoslovakia. Declaring it essential that America appear strong and with no doubts about our Vietnam policy, LBJ told Boggs, "You've got to go back there and this convention has got to stand behind me [on Vietnam] in order to preserve our nation." See Mondale, *The Good Fight*, 85.

When Humphrey proposed his compromise language on Vietnam to the Platform Committee, LBJ "hit the ceiling and forced a fight that produced a plank to his liking by a 1,567 to 1,041 vote." Years later, LBJ's Secretary of Defense, Clark Clifford, said that LBJ's victory in forcing the defeat of Humphrey's compromise language on Vietnam was a disaster for Humphrey. "At a moment when he should have been pulling the Party back together to prepare for the battle against Nixon, Humphrey had been bludgeoned into a position that had further split the Party and given more evidence of his own weakness." See Dallek, *Flawed Giant*, 575.

"Congressman Hale Boggs, chairman of the platform committee, originally supported the [compromise Vietnam peace] plank, but worked over by Johnson folk (maybe by the president himself) showed up in the [Humphrey] suite, well–oiled from a few too many drinks. He told Humphrey soberly that our peace plank would not get out of his committee. There was no negotiation possible; the decision was firm, final, and beyond discussion. He staggered off leaving despair behind." See Sherman, *From Nowhere to Somewhere*, 173. Lawrence F. O'Brien, Humphrey's 1968 campaign director, offered a similar account of the Boggs-Vietnam platform fight at the 1968 Democratic National Convention. See O'Brien, *No Final Victories*, 250-252.

[23] Some advisers urged Humphrey to resign the vice presidency, thereby distancing himself from LBJ's increasingly unpopular policies. At the 1968 Democratic Convention, all of Humphrey's foreign policy advisers continued urging that Humphrey break with LBJ over Vietnam and call for a bombing halt. Only then would Humphrey "establish his political independence and courage and liberal credentials beyond question." See Chester, Hodgson, Page, *An American Melodrama*, 153, 421.

[24] Senior Humphrey campaign advisers Bill Connell and Jim Rowe argued against Humphrey breaking with LBJ over Vietnam. They feared that if he called for a bombing halt, he would undermine the Paris peace negotiations. Why should North Vietnam negotiate for a bombing halt now, they asked, if Humphrey showed a willingness to give that concession to them for free if he wins? See Chester, Hodgson, Page, *An American Melodrama*, 641, 648.

[25] A trio of reporters covering the 1968 campaign wrote that only one person could bring escape to the Humphrey campaign from low polls,

poor crowds, poor morale, and a deep shortage of campaign contributions: "Hubert Humphrey had to do the leading himself. And the only way he could do that was by separating himself at last, clearly and unequivocally, from Lyndon Johnson." And the only issue that counted, Vietnam, "was the one of which Johnson was most spectacularly resentful of challenges." See Chester, Hodgson, Page, *An American Melodrama*, 641.

In the weeks leading up to the 1968 Democratic Convention, "[n] ewspaper columnists and Humphrey supporters were urging [Humphrey] to break with the president over the war, if he were to have any hope of being elected. It enraged Johnson." See Dallek, *Flawed Giant*, 570.

[26]   Bill Connell, Humphrey's 1968 Democratic Convention manager, said, "Nothing would bring the real peaceniks back to our side unless Hubert urinated on a portrait of Lyndon Johnson in Times Square before television—and then they'd say to him, 'Why didn't you do this before?'" See White, *The Making of the President 1968*, 271.

[27]   Stuck in his role as LBJ's vice president, Humphrey found that old friends and comrades in countless progressive battles now viewed him with a hatred and fury that left him shocked, hurt, and finally bitter. It was "as if his old record of twenty years [of] service to the liberal cause had been sponged away by the rewrite of history." See White, *The Making of the President 1968*, 270.

Humphrey's convention dilemma: what if he called for a bombing halt, and then the North Vietnamese launched a new major attack? The irony appeared horrid to him: Republican candidates standing loyally by LBJ and his effort to protect our troops, while his own vice president doesn't. If Humphrey split with LBJ now, how would such disloyalty look? As Humphrey's advisers reminded him, the nomination was in hand. Why do anything to risk it? This predicament is recounted in Chester, Hodgson, Page, *An American Melodrama*, 423-424.

Humphrey could win the nomination by supporting Johnson and the war. Delegates loyal to the White House made up the bulk of the votes at the convention. However, if he turned his back on the McCarthy-Kennedy delegates, he would essentially abandon a key voting bloc that would stay home in November. In close races in the urban and industrial states, such apathy threatened to give the election to the Republicans. If Humphrey went with a peace plank, he would unify the liberal-moderate factions of the Party at the expense of the Democratic Southern states. Chester, Hodgson, Page, *An American Melodrama*, 423-424.

28   On Monday, the first day of the 1968 Democratic National Convention, the Illinois delegation caucused at the Sherman House. Everyone expected Illinois to endorse Humphrey. Instead, after the caucus, Mayor Daley announced the delegation would remain uncommitted until Wednesday, which was the day of the balloting for the presidential nomination. See, e.g., "A Diary of Convention's Triumphs and Tragedies," *Chicago Tribune*, September 8, 1968, Section 1-A, p. 3.

Humphrey always assumed that he had a lock on Chicago Mayor Richard Daley and the entire Illinois delegation. Now, after the Illinois delegation caucused at the Sherman House the night before the convention opened, Daley announced that he would not commit the Illinois delegation to any candidate for the first 48 hours of the convention because he wanted "to see if something develops." See White, *The Making of the President 1968*, 280-281.

In his diary entry of April 4, 1968 (four days after LBJ withdrew from the 1968 presidential campaign), reporter Drew Pearson noted that a well-placed source told him, "The president had talked to Dick Daley of Chicago, who promised to be in Hubert's corner, even though Bobby is now claiming him." See Pearson and Hannaford, *Washington Merry-Go-Round*, 559-560.

29   After Chairman Boggs told Humphrey that the compromise Vietnam platform language was dead, Humphrey's conversation with his staff, in which a morose HHH tells them that it was futile to fight LBJ, is adapted from Humphrey's own description of his confrontation with Boggs over the compromise language at the convention. See Humphrey, *The Education of a Public Man*, 389-390.

30   During the convention pre-balloting, Humphrey learned that he picked up 110 more delegates from Kentucky, Utah and West Virginia, bringing his projected total delegate count to 1,642, not including California and Texas. See Chester, Hodgson, Page, *An American Melodrama*, 424.

[31] Author Theodore H. White summarized the political quicksand that trapped Humphrey: "Vietnam was a matter of conscience for candidate Hubert Humphrey. He was vice president of a nation at war; half a million American men fought in Vietnam—28,000 had died. He owed them a loyalty—to give their sacrifice a meaning. On this he could not, would not, run out. Knowing the intricate, persistent, unremitting effort of the American government to win peace by negotiation, he would not accept the thought that any magic formula would bring peace.... Humphrey, as vice president, could not attack his own administration—nor did he dare defend the issue before the electorate and his divided Party. Thus, a man of peace committed to a war, Humphrey waffled and wobbled." See White, *The Making of the President 1968*, 341.

The peace plank that the Kennedy, McCarthy, and McGovern camps drafted had received Humphrey's tentative acceptance at the Democratic Convention. The White House demanded Humphrey reject it, and he did. See Goodwin, *Remembering America*, 5-6.

Humphrey backed off an agreed-upon peace plank drafted for the 1968 Democratic National Convention and stood with LBJ instead. See Herzog, *McCarthy for President*, 266; see also O'Brien, *No Final Victories*, 249 (Humphrey met with LBJ intending to tell the president he would support a bombing halt, but he capitulated to LBJ's wishes on the Vietnam platform.)

"If Humphrey wished to win the election, his interest was to separate himself from the president. Since this was counter to Johnson's interest, the torture of Hubert Humphrey began.... [Humphrey's] horror was that he was wed to Lyndon Johnson.... Humphrey could not find sufficient pride in his liver to ask for divorce. His liver turned to dread. He came to Chicago with nobody to greet him at the airport except a handful of the faithful—the vice president's own [people]—those men whose salary he paid, and they were not many." See Mailer, *Miami and the Siege of Chicago*, 110.

For more information about the McCarthy/RFK/George McGovern peace plank compromise negotiated at the 1968 Democratic Convention, see generally Herzog, *McCarthy for President*, 254-255.

[32]   Stashed in a recess behind the amphitheater holding the 1968 Democratic Convention were thousands of rally signs captioned "We Love You LBJ," and "Happy Birthday Lyndon Johnson." See Chester, Hodgson, Page, *An American Melodrama*, 539.

[33]   "[Hubert Humphrey] had been for several months quite aware of the quality of Johnson's casual and contemptuous remarks about him to visitors. To one newsman the president, when asked to comment about Humphrey, had curtly remarked, 'He cries too much.' When the newsman pressed further, the president had only repeated, 'That's it—he cries too much.' In July [1968] the president had expanded on such criticism to another friend: 'Hubert's too old-fashioned, he looks like [and] he talks like he belongs to the past.' The president in this conversation observed that Hubert… didn't understand the changes going on in the country." One week before the 1968 Democratic Convention, LBJ "detained Humphrey for a 'Dutch Uncle' talk, a stern face-to-face lecture which rambled on about Humphrey's inadequacy as presidential timber, charged him with being too soft on foreign policy, with leaning over backward to placate Eugene McCarthy's doves, and accused him of stretching the patriotism of [Texas Governor] John Connally and the Southern delegates to the limit." The weekend before the start of the convention, Humphrey flew home to Minnesota, "not knowing whether the president was about to repudiate him even before the convention began[.]" LBJ's conversations "with so many visitors in derogation of Humphrey caused many in the Humphrey camp to believe that the president did intend to run again." White, *The Making of the President 1968*, 278-279.

[34]   On the eve of the 1968 Democratic Convention, LBJ met with Humphrey at the White House and lectured him, accusing Humphrey of being inadequate to the challenges of the presidency and being too soft on the peaceniks dividing the Party and American foreign policy. Although LBJ didn't say he was reconsidering his decision not to run in 1968, Humphrey came away from the White House stunned by that last-minute possibility. When he returned home to Minnesota the weekend before the convention, his suspicions amplified: he learned that copies of last-minute polls commissioned by the White House showed Humphrey running third behind George Wallace in key border states such as Tennessee, North Carolina,

Oklahoma, and Kentucky. The White House made sure that a copy of this poll was put under the hotel room door of every delegate arriving in Chicago. See White, *The Making of the President 1968*, 278-279.

During the summer of 1968, LBJ's conversations "with so many visitors in derogation of Humphrey caused many in the Humphrey camp to believe that the president did intend to run again. A successful summit conference with [Soviet Premier Alexei] Kosygin might well have incubated a genuine draft for Johnson on the [convention] floor.... There was the disturbance in mind of several of Humphrey's closest associates, provoked particularly by the sudden coolness of [Chicago Mayor] Richard Daley to the Humphrey candidacy... and, again, the White House's private, quick dissemination of the hopelessness of the Humphrey campaign as reported in polls from Oklahoma, Tennessee, Kentucky, North Carolina which indicated Humphrey would run third behind [American Independent Party candidate] George Wallace; and reports from the White House staff of mounting pressure on the president, from Southern governors, to run again. [¶] Humphrey himself was so disturbed by such reports that on Saturday evening before the convention he telephoned a New York friend from Minnesota to find out what the politically well-connected friend could tell him. The friend remembers Humphrey in this conversation as being as wounded, hurt, and baffled as a child who had just been beaten. Was the boss going to dump him? Humphrey wanted to know.... Not even after the election would Humphrey confirm or deny whether he felt himself under pressure of an imminent Johnson sell-out. 'I prefer to take the president at his word,' he said long later. 'I trust him.'" White, *The Making of the President 1968*, 279.

Longtime adviser to both LBJ and Humphrey, Ambassador Max M. Kampelman, noted in his memoir that LBJ had "frequent doubts about Humphrey [as a presidential candidate during the 1968 campaign], occasional anger, and some bitterness." Kampelman, *Entering New Worlds*, 170.

CHAPTER 20

[1] "After Robert Kennedy died, Johnson began thinking about whether he should reverse course and run again.... If, of course, he managed to end the [Vietnam] fighting before November or if it was sufficiently clear that peace was in the offing, a Johnson reelection was not farfetched." LBJ's White House press secretary, George Christian, said LBJ "fantasize[d] that the convention would be such a mess that he would go in on a flying carpet and be acclaimed as the nominee." See Dallek, *Flawed Giant*, 569-570, 573.

"During July [1968], Johnson acted as if he might run. He was concerned that the White House plan his public announcements more carefully and that the press office put out 'two good news stories daily.'" Texas Governor John Connally, a former LBJ congressional aide, longtime confidant, and one of Johnson's point men at the 1968 Democratic Convention, said in a 1990 interview that LBJ "very much hoped he would be drafted by the convention in 1968." He said that LBJ sent his chief of staff, Marvin Watson, to the convention "for the specific purpose of talking to delegates at Mr. Johnson's [direction]. I personally was asked to go to meet with the governors of the Southern delegations... to see if they would support President Johnson in a draft movement in 1968. Whether or not he really intended there to be a draft, who knows? Maybe it was a ploy to force Hubert Humphrey to support his Vietnam policy." Several of LBJ's principal aides acknowledged he was interested in being drafted. One LBJ Cabinet member, Joseph Califano, said that as the convention began, it was apparent that "LBJ hoped, and probably anticipated, that the convention delegates in Chicago would offer to draft him to be their Party's candidate[.]" Dallek, *Flawed Giant*, 570, 572.

[2]   Lyndon Johnson lived to acquire power his entire life, whether as a college student, a member of Congress, or as president of the United States, because "[t]he power he gained made good works possible, and good works, he believed, brought love and gratitude." Kearns Goodwin, *Lyndon Johnson and the American Dream*, x, 340.

"Lyndon Baines Johnson understood power on the atomic level. He knew what bills would fly in Congress, how to build coalitions, which lawmakers were undecided. He had an insider's knowledge of their egos and frailties." Patrick Healy, "An Exclusive Club Gets Included," *New York Times*, July 27, 2008. http://www.nytimes.com/2008/07/27/weekinreview/27healy.html

[3]   Once LBJ announced in March 1968 his decision to forego seeking reelection, the response "was the most positive expression of national support since his landslide [election] in 1964. Democrats and Republicans alike described his decision as an act of selfless patriotism." Soon after his speech, LBJ's national approval rating rocketed to 57 percent. By May, his popularity grew so much that his personal approval ratings no longer were underwater. Besides, a surprising 59 percent of Americans now felt Johnson's policies in Vietnam were "morally justified." See Dallek, *Flawed Giant*, 530-531, 570.

Regarding the "moral justification" of LBJ's Vietnam policies, former Vice President Walter Mondale wrote decades later, "[Today we] forget that many Middle Americans [in 1968] still feared communism and believed in loyalty to the president and the military. They were turned off by the radicals and the demonstrations.... I would look over Humphrey's [1968 campaign] mail—he got hundreds of letters on the war, much of it supporting Johnson and calling [Eugene] McCarthy a traitor." See Mondale, *The Good Fight*, 81.

[4]   After LBJ's withdrawal from the 1968 campaign, "[a] few days later, Hanoi agreed to negotiate in Paris. To many, it seemed that the road to peace might now be open. The polls showed a sharp increase in Johnson's popularity. And the president, who, a short time before, could speak publicly only at military installations, was once again cheered in the streets of Chicago.... [And he] took pleasure in the large numbers of schools which were asking him to speak: Yale, and even Harvard." Kearns Goodwin, *Lyndon Johnson and the American Dream*, 349.

5   When a reporter asked LBJ to comment on Humphrey as a presidential candidate, LBJ responded dismissively, "'He cries too much.' When the newsman pressed further, the president had only repeated, 'That's it—he cries too much.'" See White, *The Making of the President 1968*, 278.

After Humphrey showed LBJ his proposed compromise convention platform language on Vietnam and LBJ rejected it angrily, Secretary of Defense Clark Clifford said that LBJ branded Humphrey as weak and disloyal. "Johnson's discomfort with Humphrey on Vietnam strengthened his impulse to run again. Humphrey tried to blunt Johnson's antagonism with assurances that he was solid on Vietnam. But Johnson didn't trust him, and laid plans to become the nominee." See Dallek, *Flawed Giant*, 571-572.

During the 1968 campaign, LBJ told aide James Rowe, "I think Nixon is more for my policies than Humphrey." See Dennis D. Wainstock, *Election Year 1968: The Turning Point* (New York: Enigma Books, 2012), 169.

A few weeks before the 1968 Republican and Democratic Conventions began, LBJ told his Secretaries of State and Defense, and his National Security Adviser that he wanted to meet with Richard Nixon to discuss world affairs, saying, "When [Nixon] gets the nomination he may prove to be more responsible than the Democrats. He says he is for our position in Vietnam.... The GOP may be of more help to us than the Democrats in the next few months." See Dallek, *Flawed Giant*, 571.

LBJ thought Humphrey was too soft in his bid for the presidential nomination. "To offset charges that he was steamrolling the convention, Humphrey agreed to concede some delegates to Gene McCarthy. Johnson told him, 'The trouble with you, Hubert, is that you're just too damn good. Somebody comes along and kicks you in the face, and you pat their leg. I give them nothing.'" Dallek, *Flawed Giant*, 570-571.

6   LBJ thought that if he changed his mind and reentered the 1968 presidential race, it "might convince Hanoi to move sooner on negotiations rather than wait to see who the Democratic or Republican alternative would be." See Dallek, *Flawed Giant*, 570.

7   During the summer of 1968, and as the Democratic Convention approached, polls showed that in a general election matchup, Nixon would crush Humphrey by a whopping 16 points. By contrast, voters

favored LBJ over Nixon by a comfortable six-point margin. See Dallek, *Flawed Giant*, 570.

[8] With Humphrey's continued slide in the polls before the convention, one McCarthyite quipped, "Humphrey couldn't be elected mayor of Cairo against Arthur Goldberg." See Herzog, *McCarthy for President*, 230.

[9] Before the 1968 Democratic Convention, Humphrey promised the Southern state delegations he would support retaining the unit rule. At the convention, he reversed himself and supported its abolition. This infuriated Southern state delegations, and many of them viewed it as a reason to reject Humphrey outright and seek another nominee—preferably LBJ. See Chester, Hodgson, Page, *An American Melodrama*, 556-557.

On the first day of the 1968 Democratic Convention, the Southern state delegations held back endorsing Humphrey to pressure him into honoring his earlier pledge to support them on the unit rule battle. The Southern Democratic Convention delegations favored the "unit rule," which required the entire state delegation to vote for the candidate supported by the majority of delegates in the state. With the unit rule intact, blocs of smaller states, especially in the South, could flex muscle through their collective strength. See, e.g., Stavis, *We Were the Campaign*, 187; Jules Witcover, *Very Strange Bedfellows: The Short and Unhappy Marriage of Richard Nixon and Spiro Agnew* (New York: Public Affairs, 2007), 50.

[10] Shortly before the start of the 1968 Democratic Convention, presumptive nominee Humphrey wanted to change the convention venue from Chicago to Miami, where the GOP held their uneventful convention against a lovely backdrop a few weeks earlier. It was more than weather and scenery that motivated Humphrey's desire to change the site. As the Democratic Convention neared, labor unions plagued Chicago with various strikes, including electricians, telephone workers, and taxi drivers. This made candidate operations and media coverage a nightmarish experience for all involved. See Humphrey, *The Education of a Public Man*, 383-384.

LBJ vetoed Humphrey's last-minute request to move the 1968 Democratic Convention from Chicago to Miami. See Dallek, *Flawed Giant*, 574.

"[M]uch work went on behind the scenes to move the convention to Miami where the telephone and television lines were in, and Daley would be out. But Daley was not about to let the convention leave his city. Daley promised he would enforce the peace and allow no outrageous demonstrations, Daley hinted that his wrath—if the convention were removed, might burn away whole corners of certain people's support. Since Hubert Humphrey was the one who could most qualify for certain people, he was in no hurry to offend the mayor. Lyndon Johnson, when besieged by interested parties to encourage Daley to agree to the move, was rumored to have said, 'Miami Beach is not an American City.'" See Mailer, *Miami and the Siege of Chicago*, 103.

[11]   In our story, LBJ rejected suggestions that he reenter the 1968 presidential campaign by saying, "I don't want to be the Nelson Rockefeller of the Democratic Party. Rocky embarrassed himself this year[.]" This was a reference to three-term New York Governor Nelson Rockefeller vacillating about running for the 1968 Republican presidential nomination. First, after sending signals for months that he would run, Rockefeller announced that he would not be a candidate and would instead support another contender. Later, when that candidate dropped out, Rockefeller set up a campaign organization to run. At the press conference he called to announce his entry into the race, he shocked everyone by saying he would not run. One month later, Rockefeller reversed himself again and announced his candidacy for the presidential nomination. For more details on Rockefeller's indecisiveness regarding his 1968 presidential candidacy, see, e.g., Chester, Hodgson, Page, *An American Melodrama*, 220-223.

In 1968, three-term New York Governor Nelson Rockefeller vacillated about running for the Republican presidential nomination. First, after sending signals for months that he would run, he announced he would not be a candidate and would instead support another contender. Later, when that candidate dropped out, Rockefeller set up a campaign organization to run. At the press conference he called to announce his entry into the race, he shocked everyone by saying he would not run. One month later, Rockefeller reversed himself again and announced his candidacy for the presidential nomination. See Chester, Hodgson, Page, *An American Melodrama*, 220-223.

[12] "Nothing so raised the prestige of President Johnson in the years of the war in Vietnam as his meeting in June, 1967, with Soviet Premier Kosygin at Glassboro, New Jersey. Another summit, he felt, might do even better. In August, therefore, the key machinery at the White House and at [the State Department] was readying another conference. By Tuesday, August 20 [six days before the start of the 1968 Democratic National Convention], Assistant Secretary of State William Bundy had finished drafting a secret diplomatic note to be sent to all of America's major allies abroad informing them of the approaching summit and its purpose; George Christian, the president's press secretary, was on stand-by to inform the nation.... [A] quick flight would bring [LBJ] as peacemaker to a cheering convention in Chicago—and then, who could guess what might happen?" White, *The Making of the President 1968*. 277-278.

In June 1967, LBJ hosted the premier of the Soviet Union, Alexei Kosygin, at a summit conference in Glassboro, New Jersey to discuss the Middle East's "Six Day War" and possible joint cooperation on the Vietnam War. Although no meaningful compromises were reached, the "Spirit of Glassboro" was credited as improving U.S.-Soviet relations. See, e.g., https://en.wikipedia.org/wiki/Glassboro_Summit_Conference.

In July 1968, with Vietnam peace negotiations stalled in Paris, LBJ directed the State Department to advise the Soviet Union privately that he wanted to accept its earlier invitation to visit Moscow to discuss arms control and other areas of "mutual interest," meaning Vietnam. Johnson wanted the summit set sometime in the fall before the November presidential election. On August 19, one week before the start of the 1968 Democratic Convention, the Soviet Union cabled its invitation to Johnson for an October summit in Moscow. This historic trip would make LBJ the first American president to visit the Soviet Union. See Dallek, *Flawed Giant*, 555-556.

"A successful summit conference with [Soviet Premier] Kosygin might well have incubated a genuine draft for Johnson on the [convention] floor.... There was the disturbance in mind of several of Humphrey's closest associates, provoked particularly by the sudden coolness of [Chicago Mayor] Richard Daley to the Humphrey candidacy... and, again, the White House's private, quick dissemination of the hopelessness of the Humphrey campaign as reported in polls from Oklahoma, Tennessee,

Kentucky, and North Carolina that indicated Humphrey would run third behind [the Republican presidential nominee and American Independent Party candidate] George Wallace; and reports from the White House staff of mounting pressure on the president, from Southern governors, to run again." See White, *The Making of the President 1968*, 279.

Former Texas Governor John B. Connally, an LBJ protégé for over three decades, wrote in a memoir published shortly after his death in 1993: "What few were aware of at the time—and all but lost from the record since—is how fervently Johnson hoped he would be drafted by the convention in 1968.... In secrecy, he had sent [Marvin] Watson to assess his chances of being drafted as the nominee. [¶] His withdrawal statement notwithstanding, Watson was [sent to the 1968 Democratic National Convention in Chicago] for that specific purpose, talking with as many delegates as he could reach. My assignment was to ask the governors of the Southern delegations if they would support a movement to draft Johnson.... I believe in his heart he wanted that moment of drama, the emotion of a convention swept away as in olden times, and the vindication it would represent...." By the time LBJ left the White House and wrote his post-presidency memoirs, he had "resigned himself to the seclusion of his ranch, Johnson had convinced himself that he never held out hopes of a draft in 1968, nor did he want to appear at the convention. And yet I know he did. I know he wanted to hear the accolades—hear the sound of applauding hands[.]" John B. Connally with Mickey Herskowitz, *In History's Shadow: An American Odyssey* (New York: Hyperion, 1993), 203, 214.

[13]   Chicago Mayor Richard Daley withheld endorsing Humphrey at the opening of the 1968 Democratic Convention, and then he announced that he would host a 60th birthday party for LBJ at the convention, which was all done at LBJ's suggestion. This birthday party announcement sent shock waves through the Humphrey campaign's high command. See White, *The Making of the President 1968*, 280-281.

For the Tuesday Democratic Convention session, Mayor Daley ordered a massive "Happy Birthday LBJ" cake delivery to the Stockyards Inn, which Daley reserved for the week. That same night, convention officials planned to show a $125,000 film on the Johnson Administration's successes (and financed by the Democratic National Committee). See Chester, Hodgson, Page, *An American Melodrama*, 539.

"In August, [LBJ] gave serious thought to attending the 1968 Democratic Convention. The ostensible reason was to be honored by his fellow Democrats on his sixtieth birthday, August 27. Numerous Party leaders, including... Mayor Richard Daley... urged him to attend. In the days before and at the start of the convention, Johnson had his speech writers preparing an address for delivery in Chicago. [¶] It was to be a triumphant moment, but Mayor Daley and White House aide Jake Jacobsen believed it would be more than that. They foresaw a draft nomination if the president would just give the word. 'That's what I am for,' Daley said. 'I'm for a draft, and I'll start it if there is any chance he will do it.' White House aide Jim Jones reported: 'Jake says this convention is going to draft the president if there is the slightest indication the draft will be accepted.'" Dallek, *Flawed Giant*, 571-572.

14   Whenever LBJ flew to or from his ranch in Texas, he avoided using the large Boeing 707 usually designated as Air Force One. Because of its size, the Boeing had to land at nearby Bergstrom Air Force Base. Instead, LBJ preferred to fly on an Air Force JetStar, which could land on the small airstrip constructed 200 yards from the front door of his ranch house. See, e.g., James U. Cross, *Around the World with LBJ: My Wild Ride as Air Force One Pilot, White House Aide, and Personal Confidant* (Austin: University of Texas Press, 2009), 46-47.

In anticipation of LBJ making a surprise visit to the 1968 Democratic Convention on his 60th birthday, his presidential limousine was at the Chicago airport awaiting his arrival. See Herzog, *McCarthy for President*, 266.

15   Everyone in LBJ's personal orbit understood what it meant to get the "Johnson Treatment." Arthur Schlesinger described it this way: LBJ "was all over everybody—always the grip on the shoulder, tug at the lapel, nudge in the ribs, squeeze of the knee. He was a crowder, who set his great face within a few inches of the object of his attention and, as the more diffident retreated, backed them across the room in the course of a monologue." See Schlesinger Jr., *Robert Kennedy and His Times*, 623.

[16]   In our story, LBJ wanted to go to the 1968 Democratic Convention on his birthday, August 27, and announce a U.S.-Soviet summit in October. He hoped that this would lead to a groundswell of support for a draft. In reality, this *was* LBJ's original plan, but he aborted it because the Soviet and Warsaw Pact armies had invaded and occupied Czechoslovakia six days before the convention began. With the summit now scotched because of the invasion, LBJ instead hoped updated polling data from Lou Harris would show he was the only Democrat who could beat Nixon in November. However, as author Theodore H. White wrote, "If there was a Johnson boom, it died on Monday evening of the first night of the convention" after Lou Harris shared privately with LBJ his poll results before its release. The poll showed LBJ, Humphrey, and McCarthy all running six points behind Nixon. "[I]t was obvious that the polls would report publicly the next day that Johnson was no stronger a candidate against Nixon than Humphrey; and whatever plan, or boom, there had been for Johnson among Southern and Border states ended as word of the poll spread. By midnight on Monday the Southern governors, with all their votes, were falling in line again for the vice president against the peace candidates; and by late Tuesday evening, the next day, Humphrey's nomination was sure." White, *The Making of the President 1968*, 279-280.

[17]   A former chain smoker until suffering a massive heart attack in 1955, LBJ stopped smoking after this illness and did not revive the habit until after he left the White House. When he did smoke, his favorite cigarette brand was Winston. Archivist of the LBJ Library Barbara Cline, email to author, March 18, 2016.

[18]   The RFK and McCarthy delegates at the 1968 Democratic Convention introduced their own peace planks, which the convention's Platform Committee voted down handily. Instead, the committee passed a resolution supporting LBJ's Vietnam policies. The White House stacked the platform committee two-to-one with Johnson loyalists, and LBJ's senior aides were omnipresent to oversee the proceedings. See Van Dyk, *Heroes, Hacks & Fools*, 76-77.

[19]   At the 1968 Democratic Convention, McCarthy blasted the Johnson-Humphrey Vietnam plank, calling it "a reaffirmation of the policies of

the present Administration…. [Humphrey] has adopted a position which has been overwhelmingly rejected in primary after primary." See Herzog, *McCarthy for President*, 265.

[20]   On Tuesday night, the second evening of the 1968 Democratic National Convention, Mayor Daley announced his support for Humphrey, and then the Southern delegates joined him. For the McCarthy campaign, it was now over. See Stavis, *We Were the Campaign*, 188.

The following night (Wednesday), just before the balloting for the presidential nomination, U.S. House of Representatives Majority Leader (later Speaker) Carl Albert, the chairman of the convention, read to the delegates a message from LBJ asking that the convention not consider him for the presidential nomination. See Dallek, *Flawed Giant*, 573.

[21]   A pharmacist by training, as a young man Humphrey worked as a druggist at Walgreen's in Huron, South Dakota, from 1933-1937. http://www.encyclopedia.com/topic/Hubert_Horatio_Humphrey.aspx.

CHAPTER 21

[1]   Competing Vietnam War planks in the 1968 Democratic Platform divided the convention. The LBJ-supported version, adopted by the majority of delegates, rejected any unilateral U.S. withdrawal from Vietnam and "applaud[ed] the initiative of President Johnson which brought North Vietnam to the peace table." The "peace" plank, which failed to garner a majority, demanded an "unconditional end to all bombings in North Vietnam" and to negotiate an immediate withdrawal of U.S. forces out of Southeast Asia. For all of the divisiveness caused by these competing propositions, the *Chicago Tribune* noted the two planks were very close: the majority view (no unilateral end to bombing Hanoi until American troops were secure) vs. the minority view (end the bombing of Hanoi immediately). See "A Diary of Convention's Triumphs and Tragedies," *Chicago Tribune*, September 8, 1968, Section 1-A, p. 3.

[2]   For a summary of the Grant Park protests and riots, and for Humphrey's reaction to them as he watched the violence from his hotel window, see White, *The Making of the President 1968*, 294 et seq.

[3]   "Thousands of young people came to Chicago with no intention of violence [but to] show their deep feelings about the war. But there were revolutionaries and anarchists among them... who were capable and determined to play with aroused emotions, to escalate their own war, and manipulate a situation in which a sharp confrontation with the police was inevitable.... The clash was a microcosm of the whole year in our whole society.... [W]hen the hot coals of protest and dissent are already present and mobilized, bringing in a TV camera is like adding gasoline." See Humphrey, *The Education of a Public Man*, 385-386.

4   "Most of the police," Humphrey explained later, "like most of the demonstrators, were doing their 'thing'—theirs being to keep order. Some of the police came to those lines filled with anger and disgust, wearing Wallace for President pins." See Humphrey, *The Education of a Public Man*, 385-386.

5   At the 1968 Democratic Convention, Chicago Mayor Richard Daley "was only grudgingly for me for president." See Humphrey, *The Education of a Public Man*, 386.

6   After the 1968 election, and while reflecting on the violent riots and the fractured Party that nominated him at the Democratic Convention in Chicago, Humphrey said that securing the nomination didn't make him feel like a winner; he felt like a victim. What should have been the greatest moment of his life became one of the worst. Under normal circumstances, Humphrey lamented, he could have beaten Nixon: "But it's difficult to take on the Republicans and fight a guerilla war in your own Party at the same time." See White, *The Making of the President 1968*, 303.

7   A few hours before the roll call vote on the 1968 Democratic presidential nomination, key LBJ aides continued submitting to Humphrey proposed language for his acceptance speech—a speech the Johnson White House expected to find supportive of LBJ's policies. Among the LBJ staffers submitting drafts were LBJ's longtime aide Jack Valenti, his former White House Press Secretary Bill Moyers, and his Secretary of Labor, Willard Wirtz. See Van Dyk, *Heroes, Hacks & Fools*, 78.

8   In his 1976 memoir, Humphrey recounted the conversation he had with LBJ at the White House before LBJ offered him the vice presidential nomination in 1964. LBJ told him solemnly that they were old friends, but Humphrey must understand that this was to be a marriage with no chance of divorce. LBJ demanded complete and unswerving loyalty, saying that when a vice president steps out of line, it causes the president difficulties and embarrassment. LBJ said that is what he wanted in a vice president, and then he asked if Humphrey was that man. Humphrey replied that he was, and he told LBJ he could trust him. "I accepted [the vice presidency] under the conditions [Johnson] had set. I made a commitment

and I performed under the 'terms of the contract.' Whether my decision was the right one is something I suppose I cannot judge clearly. I think it was." See Humphrey, *The Education of a Public Man*, 301-303.

By mid-September 1968, pressure grew on Humphrey to break with LBJ over Vietnam. As reporter Drew Pearson noted in his diary entry of September 18, 1968, Humphrey refused, telling Pearson, "The president would be like a woman scorned. He doesn't help you much, but he can hurt you." Pearson and Hannaford, *Washington Merry-Go-Round*, 616.

During a 1984 dinner, which was 16 years after Humphrey's 1968 presidential campaign, JFK's and LBJ's Secretary of Defense, Robert S. McNamara, told historian Arthur M. Schlesinger Jr. that he and McGeorge Bundy (national security adviser to both presidents) "persuaded Hubert that he must repudiate Johnson on Vietnam and strike out on his own. An appointment was arranged for Hubert to go to the White House and explain to Johnson why he was doing this. Lyndon must have surmised what was impending. He kept Hubert waiting for forty-five minutes, thereby reducing him to a state of nerves. Hubert did not dare bring up Vietnam. The effort failed. If Hubert had been a stronger man, he would have been elected president." See Schlesinger Jr., *Journals*, 581.

[9] The vignette of Judge Terry Green exploding in anger at Humphrey is based on an actual event. A month after Humphrey became the nominee, he and his staff contemplated announcing a break with LBJ in a Salt Lake City speech set for September 30, 1968. The comments attributed to the fictional Judge Green character are adapted from those made by Humphrey staffer Ira Kapenstein while aides debated whether to announce the break in Humphrey's Salt Lake City speech. See White, *The Making of the President 1968*, 648.

[10] Shortly before the balloting for the presidential nomination began, Humphrey volunteers flooded the arena carrying Humphrey campaign banners and signs. Almost no McCarthy signs were in sight because shortly before the arena opened for the evening's nominating session, Chicago police "accidentally" tear-gassed the McCarthy sign storage area. The tear gas made McCarthy's signs unusable. See Chester, Hodgson, Page, *An American Melodrama*, 581.

[11]   LBJ's forces controlled all aspects of the convention, including the state delegation seating map. In the major states won by RFK and McCarthy, the Johnson forces seated those delegates in the back of the arena—and separate from each other—to keep them dispersed on the floor. See White, *The Making of the President 1968*, 271-272.

During the 1968 Democratic Convention, viewers watching the televised proceedings heard little of the booing and catcalls from the antiwar delegations. LBJ's and Mayor Daley's forces controlled seating and placement of the state delegations in the amphitheater, and they saw to it that those states populated heavily with McCarthy, RFK, and (later) George McGovern delegates "from New York, California, South Dakota, Massachusetts, Wisconsin and Oregon were placed far from the podium" and loud music from the band was used to drown out the rear delegations. See Mailer, *Miami and the Siege of Chicago*, 167-168.

[12]   The Pennsylvania delegation put Humphrey over the top at 11:47 p.m. An Illinois delegate then moved that the convention nominate him by acclamation. Ignoring the angry shouts of "no" from the floor, Chairman Carl Albert ruled that the motion had carried. See Chester, Hodgson, Page, *An American Melodrama*, 586.

[13]   After Humphrey won the 1968 Democratic presidential nomination, McCarthy called Humphrey and congratulated him. Humphrey told him that he appreciated the call, but he would appreciate more McCarthy's endorsement. It was not forthcoming. The day before, McCarthy told a reporter he would not support a nominee whose Vietnam views "do not come close to what mine are." Chester, Hodgson, Page, *An American Melodrama*, 562.

CHAPTER 22

[1] "If I am permitted to be president, I intend to be president. I've noticed most presidents are like that. They don't take orders from vice presidents or anyone else. Hubert Humphrey as vice president is a member of a team. Hubert Humphrey as president is captain of a team. There's a lot of difference." On March 24, 1972, during his campaign for the 1972 Democratic presidential nomination, Humphrey wrote out in longhand and signed this quotation for the author's political memorabilia collection while they stood on a busy San Francisco street corner, and Humphrey did so despite agitated Secret Service agents trying to hurry him along. See Rogan, *And Then I Met*, 17.

[2] At the 1968 Democratic Convention, Humphrey backed away from his compromise Vietnam War platform plank at LBJ's insistence. However, a month later, and with his campaign collapsing, Humphrey broke finally with LBJ and proposed a bombing halt in Vietnam. In our story, Humphrey's convention speech making this announcement is adapted from his actual Salt Lake City speech of September 30, 1968, when he announced a proposed unilateral bombing halt. See, e.g., Ronald H. Janis, "Stop the Bombing Says Humphrey," *The Harvard Crimson*, October 1, 1968, http://www.thecrimson.com/article/1968/10/1/stop-the-bombing-says-humphrey-pvice-president.

[3] On the last night of the 1968 Democratic Convention, one of Humphrey's representatives called McCarthy and asked that he appear on the platform after the acceptance speeches to show Party unity. McCarthy declined. "To accept would have been fine for a show of Party unity, but clearly inconsistent with the position I had taken both before and during

the convention. It certainly would have been a disillusioning betrayal of trust to so many of my supporters and would have eliminated the last slight possibility that by withholding support I might move the nominee of the Party after the convention to indicate his own position on the war and to assert his independence from the administration." See McCarthy, *The Year of the People*, 217-218.

After Humphrey's acceptance speech, McCarthy refused to join him on the platform at the 1968 Democratic Convention for a show of unity. See Chester, Hodgson, Page, *An American Melodrama*, 590.

Two weeks before the start of the 1968 Democratic National Convention, McCarthy promised Humphrey he would endorse him sometime around the middle of September. "I urged [McCarthy] to do it the night I got the nomination, if I did. Such a statement was the traditional thing to do, and would have demonstrated unity and solidarity, and is what I would have done for him. [¶] The tradition, like others, did not appeal to Gene, and he told me he wouldn't be able to do that. He was afraid, he said, that his supporters would revolt, that they would turn on him. What he was saying in his own, indirect way—and he almost always worked indirectly, was that it would take a little time to bring his people around. [¶] That didn't happen. After my nomination, some of his supporters came around on their own. If Gene tried to influence anyone to support me, I am not aware of it." Humphrey, *The Education of a Public Man*, 376-377.

4   At no time during RFK's presidential campaign did he ever expressly say he would support McCarthy if he had won the presidential nomination. See McCarthy, *The Year of the People*, 143.

During the 1968 Democratic Convention, after Humphrey won the nomination, McCarthy said to an aide, "It's no use being bitter about Hubert—he's too dumb to understand bitterness." White, *The Making of the President 1968*, 301.

5   Not only did McCarthy refuse to endorse Humphrey after HHH had won the nomination, but on the night of Humphrey's victory, McCarthy returned to his hotel and joined a large crowd of his dejected followers in the Grand Ballroom of the Conrad Hilton Hotel. McCarthy suggested to the crowd that if a large grassroots group of antiwar supporters broke off from the Democrats and formed a new party, he "might" support the

effort, although he declined to lead it. See Chester, Hodgson, Page, *An American Melodrama*, 586-587.

Following Humphrey's victory at the Chicago convention, many of RFK's supporters moved over and supported him. Since McCarthy refused to endorse Humphrey, a large number of McCarthy's troops followed his lead and sat on their hands. See, e.g., Van Dyk, *Heroes, Hacks & Fools*, 84.

Thirty years after Chicago, and writing about McCarthy's failure to endorse Humphrey after the convention, 1968 Humphrey campaign aide Ted Van Dyk still believed that McCarthy would have withdrawn from the race before the convention and endorsed Humphrey if the vice president had given him reason to do so. Based on what happened at the convention, when Humphrey backed LBJ's Vietnam platform language, Van Dyk blamed Humphrey for driving McCarthy away. Van Dyk, *Heroes, Hacks & Fools*, 99.

After Humphrey delivered his 1968 convention acceptance speech, McCarthy marginalized its significance to friends privately, telling them he saw no significant change in Humphrey's Vietnam position. Until Humphrey made a "significant" break with LBJ's war policies, he had no reason to deliver his endorsement. See, e.g., Chester, Hodgson, Page, *An American Melodrama*, 562, 742.

It was not until the eve of the November 1968 general election that McCarthy offered Humphrey an anemic endorsement. "These defections [of liberals away from the Humphrey campaign] were symbolized by Gene McCarthy's performance that fall [in refusing to endorse Humphrey after the 1968 Democratic Convention]. When he finally got around to endorsing Humphrey, his statement was so tepid as to be worthless." O'Brien, *No Final Victories*, 262.

[6]   In an interview with CBS News before the start of the 1968 Democratic Convention, a reporter asked McCarthy what kind of a president he thought Humphrey would make. "I think he'll be a good president," McCarthy replied. When asked to explain the apparent contradiction of that comment and his refusal to endorse Humphrey, he replied, "You can be a good president with bad policies." See Larner, *Nobody Knows*, 174.

In ending his campaign for president, McCarthy "had compromised nothing.... He had done it his way up to now, cutting out everyone from his councils who was interested in politicking at the old trough, no, his campaign had begun by being educational, and educational had he left it—he had not compromised an inch, nor played the demagogue for a moment, and it had given him strength, not strength enough perhaps to win, certainly not enough to win, but rectitude had laid the keel, and in that air of a campaign run at last for intelligent men, and give no alms to whores, he left." See Mailer, *Miami and the Siege of Chicago*, 100.

[7]   After serving almost 21 years in the United States Senate, President Jimmy Carter named Edmund Muskie as his Secretary of State in May 1980. Muskie served in that position until the conclusion of the Carter Administration in January 1981.

[8]   In our story, Humphrey tells RFK "this will make us even" for Wisconsin and West Virginia in 1960. While managing his brother's 1960 presidential primary campaign against Humphrey, RFK smeared Humphrey repeatedly. Reflecting on that time 16 years later, Humphrey confessed his dislike of RFK back then, calling him "hostile beyond the needs of political opposition." However, by 1968, their relationship had changed. Humphrey admitted that he had never forgiven RFK for "that period"—1960—but by 1968, Humphrey respected RFK and, in fact, liked him. Humphrey later wrote, "After his brother's death, I think Robert Kennedy became a man. Out of that tragedy, he developed concern and compassion and understanding that he seemed to lack previously. I campaigned for him in his New York senatorial race in 1964—and I did so out of respect for him, and not grudgingly…. By 1968, when he finally became a candidate for the [presidential] nomination, he excited the spirit of many people, often those who shared least in our society. He was a folk hero, as tough and competitive as ever but with a quality he had lacked a decade before: deep and sincere concern for those left out or forgotten." See Humphrey, *The Education of a Public Man*, 374.

Kenneth O'Donnell (1924-1977) had been RFK's college roommate when both were Harvard students. He later enlisted in JFK's first congressional race in 1946, and he remained one of JFK's closest aides throughout the president's brief White House tenure. A top campaign aide to RFK in 1968, O'Donnell visited Humphrey a few days before RFK's assassination. O'Donnell told Humphrey privately that if RFK lost the California primary to McCarthy, RFK would pull out of the race and endorse Humphrey. See Humphrey, *The Education of a Public Man*, 374-375.

9   By the 1968 Democratic Convention's nomination night, Humphrey ran 22 points behind Nixon in the polls. See Humphrey, *The Education of a Public Man*, 492.

In our story, Humphrey tells RFK, "Look, I'm probably going to lose this election. Not much I've done this entire year seems to have come out right. But win or lose, I've decided that I'm going to speak my mind, and I'm going to fight my fight. I'm not going to let Lyndon Johnson or anyone else deny me the right to be heard and say what I feel." This statement is adapted from what Humphrey told his staff as he sipped a beer just before he delivered his speech in Salt Lake City on September 30, 1968—the speech in which he broke with LBJ and said that he would halt the bombing of North Vietnam if elected. See Humphrey, *The Education of a Public Man*, 400; see also O'Brien, *No Final Victories*, 260-262.

10   Had RFK lived, would Humphrey have picked him as his running mate? Humphrey left us a clue. He and RFK "had not been close friends early on, but [by June 1968] Humphrey respected him and understood his political glamour. In an interview in late fall of 1967, [Humphrey] had told a reporter that if Johnson were to die and he became president, he would ask Robert Kennedy to be his vice president. He also said that, assuming a second term for Johnson and Humphrey, he thought 1972 was Kennedy's year. 'Bobby has everything going for him. He's young. He's got the name. There is what he has done in his own right.'" Sherman, *From Nowhere to Somewhere*, 169.

Lawrence F. O'Brien, JFK's 1960 presidential campaign director, the two-time chairman of the Democratic National Committee, and the 1968 presidential campaign director for LBJ, then (after LBJ's withdrawal) RFK, and finally (after RFK's assassination) Humphrey, wrote in his 1974 memoir that had RFK lived, "I would, at some point, have pursued the proposed Kennedy-Humphrey meeting after the New York primary. I'm sure it would have taken place because of the respect both men felt for the other. At such a meeting, Hubert would have had two goals: first, to persuade Bob to withdraw before the convention; second, to persuade him to run as the vice–presidential candidate.... Hubert could have agreed to support a peace plank acceptable to Bob at the convention. He would have done so knowing that Johnson might denounce him publicly, but... Bob's support in the campaign could have helped Hubert more than Johnson's criticisms could have hurt him." O'Brien, *No Final Victories*, 244-245.

[11]   Once LBJ suspected Humphrey might want to compromise with the Democratic Party's peace faction on Vietnam, LBJ ordered FBI taps on all of Humphrey's telephones. If Humphrey intended to break with LBJ on Vietnam, LBJ wanted to know about it in advance. See Dallek, *Flawed Giant*, 576.

PART TWO

The Republicans:
Prelude to Miami

CHAPTER 23

1   In 1968, writer Norman Mailer described New York Governor Nelson Rockefeller as having "an all but perfect face for president, virile, friendly, rough-hewn, of the common man, yet uncommon—Spencer Tracy's younger brother gone into politics." Mailer, *Miami and the Siege of Chicago*, 13.

2   "The scandalous news of Rockefeller's wedding in May of 1963 spread quickly. Nelson, who had divorced his first wife, [Mary Todhunter Clark], 18 months earlier, was finally tying the knot with the woman he had been having a relationship with for over five years, Margaretta 'Happy' Murphy. Public reaction to Nelson's divorce had been muted, but the headlines announcing his remarriage prompted the outrage and incredulity of many. Adding to the public's disapproval was the fact that in her recently settled divorce, Happy had surrendered custody of her four children. [¶] Yet the political impact of Nelson's second marriage was even more irreversible than its moral implications. The polls, which had given him a comfortable lead over other potential [1964 Republican presidential] candidates just weeks before, saw his popularity take a dive. Pundits called it an act of political self-destruction, noting that his presidential hopes seemed now more unattainable than ever. But the ever-confident Rockefeller forged ahead.... Rockefeller was still leading the [critical California primary] polls when, three days before the election, Happy gave birth to a baby boy, Nelson Jr. As Rockefeller interrupted his campaign to fly to New York, [Rockefeller's opponent, Senator Barry] Goldwater went into high gear, filling the airwaves with ads that touted his impeccable family background and questioned his opponent's morality. On June 2, [1964,] California [Republican primary] voters chose Goldwater over Rockefeller

by a narrow margin of less than three percent, ensuring the Arizona senator's nomination at the Republican convention[.]" PBS, "The 1964 Republican Campaign," *The American Experience*, http://www.pbs.org/wgbh/americanexperience/features/general-article/rockefellers-campaign/

After Rockefeller's divorce and remarriage in 1963, U.S. Senator Prescott Bush (R-CT), the father and grandfather of two future presidents, blasted Rockefeller's morals in a speech at a girls school, Rosemary Hall, on June 7, 1963: "Have we come to the point where a governor can desert his wife and children, and persuade a young woman to abandon her four children and husband? Have we come to the point where one of the two great parties will confer its greatest honor on such a one? I venture to hope not. [¶] Have we gotten so the American people will elect such a man? I venture to hope not.... Young ladies, I hope not, for your sake." Buchanan, *The Greatest Comeback*, 226-227.

3   At the 1964 GOP Convention, when Rockefeller rose to address the delegates, they booed him for 16 minutes. See Joseph E. Persico, *The Imperial Rockefeller: A Biography of Nelson A. Rockefeller* (New York: Simon and Shuster, 1982), 65-66.

4   When Rockefeller lost the GOP presidential nomination to Barry Goldwater in 1964, he refused to endorse Goldwater or to wear a Goldwater campaign button when someone offered one to him. Buchanan, *The Greatest Comeback*, 40.

5   "[C]onservatives generally found [Nixon] acceptable and preferable to the hated Rockefeller, whose big government, big spending, Eastern liberalism and failure to endorse the Goldwater ticket made him a 'party wrecker' in the eyes of the conservatives who had swept to power at the 1964 convention." Roger Stone, *Nixon's Secrets* (New York: Skyhorse Publishing, 2014), 319.

In 1964, "With Goldwater doing so poorly, and Rockefeller and Romney having eliminated themselves forever by sitting out the campaign, Nixon had become the favorite for the 1968 GOP nomination even before the 1964 election was held." Stephen E. Ambrose, *Nixon (Volume Two): The Triumph of a Politician 1962-1972* (New York: Simon and Shuster, 1989), 57.

[6]   As 1968 loomed, when asked by close friends if he would run for president again, Rockefeller growled, "Let them come to me. I'm here. They know my record." See White, *The Making of the President 1968*, 227.

[7]   With Rockefeller refusing initially to seek the 1968 GOP presidential nomination, saying, "Let them come to me," Theodore White noted later, "The Party was unwilling to come. And he was unwilling to seek." See White, *The Making of the President 1968*, 227.

[8]   Knowing that Republican activists blamed him for both splitting the Party in his fractious nomination battle with Barry Goldwater in 1964, and for Goldwater's annihilation at the polls in November, Rockefeller knew he had little hope of winning the GOP nomination in 1968. Thus, he repeatedly declared he would not be a presidential candidate in 1968. Instead, Rockefeller was content to be kingmaker, and the person he chose to push was Michigan Governor George Romney. See White, *The Making of the President 1968*, 38.

When pressed to drop his support of Romney and run himself, Rockefeller said, "I'm out of it. If we moderates want to preserve any chance of nominating a candidate who can win, we'd better stay behind George Romney," and he insisted that any effort to look elsewhere would deliver the nomination "to the other side"—meaning his old nemesis Richard Nixon. See Witcover, *Very Strange Bedfellows*, 4.

[9]   Did Rockefeller have an extramarital affair with a staffer prior to and during the 1968 presidential campaign?

- A few years after Rockefeller's death, longtime Rockefeller aide and speechwriter Emmet Hughes told historian Arthur M. Schlesinger that "Nelson was just compulsive about women. He made Happy [Mrs. Rockefeller] go through the misery of a divorce, and then two years later [he] was fooling around with a new girl in the office. In 1968 we were concerned all the time that the press might get on to this new involvement.... All his girls were the same type—the wholesome, hearty, simple, innocent American type. Except possibly the last one." See Schlesinger Jr., *Journals*, 513-514.

- Pat Buchanan, who worked for Richard Nixon as a campaign aide during that election, wrote in his memoir of the 1968 race: "Rockefeller was involved with a young staffer. After his divorce from his wife of many years, Mary, known as Tod, and his marriage to divorcee 'Happy' Murphy, who had given birth to his son three days before the California primary in 1964, which Rockefeller lost, another scandal would have dynamited any remote chance he had of being the nominee.... A source deep inside Rockefeller's office said it was true, and gave [Nixon's campaign team] the girl's name. The Albany press corps had to know this. Yet no one wrote it. Rockefeller was not a candidate and had declared he would not be a candidate.... Yet to announce for president with this rumor hanging out there seemed a huge personal and political risk." Buchanan, *The Greatest Comeback*, 222.

- As historian Arthur M. Schlesinger Jr. noted in his diary entry of December 7, 1967, Rockefeller had missed several meetings with Schlesinger in attendance at which Rockefeller was expected. "I was later told by Babe Paley (and by Joan Braden) that [Rockefeller] had another girl—his present secretary. Henry Kissinger [at the time a senior Rockefeller aide] said that, if this might have been true once, it was not presently the case. Nelson, he said, always requires the emotional support of women who work closely with him. He got this from [the current Mrs. Rockefeller]; and, when [she] moved on from secretary to wife, she removed herself from the picture and made some sort of local succession inevitable." Schlesinger Jr., *Journals*, 266.

- In his January 22, 1978, diary entry, Schlesinger discussed having dinner with Rockefeller and his wife, Happy Rockefeller, three nights earlier. As the Rockefellers bade the guests goodnight, Schlesinger noted that Mrs. Rockefeller showed "the remnants of a woman of spirit and charm crushed by [Rockefeller's] hyperactivity and infidelity." Buchanan, *The Greatest Comeback*, 446.

[10] For an overview of Rockefeller backing Romney for the presidential nomination in 1968, see White, *The Making of the President 1968*, 60-61.

[11] During his 1966 gubernatorial reelection campaign, Rockefeller renounced any future presidential ambitions. See Richard Norton Smith, *On His Own Terms: A Life of Nelson Rockefeller* (New York: Random House, 2014), 496.

"Rockefeller took himself out of the [1968 presidential campaign], saying one day after the [1966] election that he 'unequivocally' would not be a candidate." Ambrose, *Nixon (Volume Two)*, 100.

[12] 'As a former Rockefeller staffer and reporter who covered his tenure as New York governor noted, Rockefeller "had strong personal preferences, among them Dubonnet red wine, for an occasional drink at the end of a long day, and Oreo cookies.... These preferences, as a matter of routine, were accommodated at every stop[.]" Joseph H. Boyd, Jr. and Charles R. Holcomb, *Oreos and Dubonnet: Remembering Governor Nelson A. Rockefeller* (Albany: Excelsior Editions, 2012), 13.

[13] During the early days of the 1968 campaign, Rockefeller breezed past LBJ in the polls by not talking about the divisive national issues and keeping a low profile as a hard-working governor with no further interest in the presidency. Buchanan, *The Greatest Comeback*, 150.

CHAPTER 24

[1]   Prior to entering the 1968 presidential campaign, Nixon's law firm (Nixon, Mudge, Rose, Guthrie & Alexander) was located on the 24th floor of 20 Broad Street in Manhattan. See, e.g., Raymond Price, *With Nixon* (New York: The Viking Press, 1977), 16.

[2]   Rockefeller lived on the twelfth floor of 810 Fifth Avenue. After he divorced and remarried in the early 1960s, he purchased another full floor co-op in the neighboring building at 812 Fifth Avenue, which he combined with his original home at 810 Fifth Avenue. The floors of the two units were not at the same height, so he installed a six-step staircase to connect the units. The stairs were located behind what is now a bookcase in the library at 810 Fifth Avenue. Nixon and his family lived on the fifth floor of 812 Fifth Avenue, while Rockefeller lived eight floors above him. See, e.g., Mark David, "Rock It Like a Rockefeller," *Variety*, February 27, 2008, https://variety.com/2008/dirt/real-estalker/rock-it-like-a-rockefeller-1201227746/; see also https://en.wikipedia.org/wiki/810_Fifth_Avenue.

Nixon's Fifth Avenue apartment "was in one of those gracious older buildings facing Central Park that give Fifth Avenue its distinctive air as the Queen Mother of New York thoroughfares. At Sixty-Second Street, it overlooked… Fifth Avenue and Fifty-Ninth Street, where the Plaza Hotel holds court over the southeast corner of Central Park, while horse-drawn carriages wait for passengers in front of the graceful scoops of the Pulitzer Fountain. The apartment building was a co-op. Among the other owners [was] upstairs [neighbor] Nelson Rockefeller[.]" Price, *With Nixon*, 13-14.

In New York City, the Nixons lived "in a ten-room apartment that took up the fifth floor of a building at 62nd St. and Fifth Avenue, with a view of Central Park and the Plaza Hotel…. Only later did Nixon learn that the building belonged to Mrs. Mary Clark Rockefeller, who had taken possession as part of her divorce settlement, and that her ex-husband, Governor Rockefeller, and his new wife lived on the twelfth floor of the fourteen-story building." See Ambrose, *Nixon (Volume Two)*, 21-22.

[3]   According to RFK, the 1964 GOP opponent JFK feared the most was Michigan Governor George Romney. JFK thought Romney "would be difficult to soak" and would have great appeal both in the South and in the North. Robert F. Kennedy interviews with Anthony Lewis (with Burke Marshall present), December 4, 6, and 22, 1964, cited in Guthman and Shulman, *Robert Kennedy in His Own Words*, 76; see also Robert F. Kennedy interviews with John Bartlow Martin, March 1, April 13, April 30, and May 14, 1964, cited in Guthman and Shulman, *Robert Kennedy in His Own Words*, 343.

"In 1963, President Kennedy had confided to his close friend Paul Fay, 'The one fellow I don't want to run against [in 1964] is Romney.'" Benjamin Wallace-Wells, "George Romney for President, 1968" (*New York* magazine, May 20, 2012), http://nymag.com/news/features/george-romney-2012-5/.

[4]   In November 1966, Romney emerged as the national front-runner for 1968 and the strongest GOP candidate to face LBJ in 1968. See Buchanan, *The Greatest Comeback*, 93.

[5]   By 1967, Rockefeller turned over what was left of his 1964 presidential campaign operation, as well as all of his policy advisers—including foreign policy expert Henry Kissinger of Harvard—to Romney. Rockefeller became Romney's main cheerleader among their fellow Republican governors, and he pushed Romney's candidacy hard. See White, *The Making of the President 1968*, 60-61.

Rockefeller backed Romney for president in 1968, and he pledged significant Northeastern support to his candidate while also offering Romney the use of his policy staff. Wallace-Wells, "George Romney for President, 1968."

Rockefeller acted almost as a personal campaign manager for Romney, even reviewing Romney's speeches and press releases in advance, and making additions and deletions when they didn't mirror Rockefeller's own sentiments. At one point, a frustrated Romney rejected several of Rockefeller's changes, telling an aide, "I'm the candidate; he isn't." Smith, *On His Own Terms*, 497.

Some reports indicated that Rockefeller donated over $400,000 of personal money to the 1968 Romney-for-president campaign effort. See Witcover, *Very Strange Bedfellows*, 3.

6   In the spring of 1967, Romney's campaign staff "scheduled a series of weekend seminars, importing experts to meet with the governor at his summer home on rustic, carless Mackinac Island. The Romney camp had hired a young foreign-policy aide named Jonathan Moore, who one Friday evening arrived at the ferry dock to collect [Harvard Professor] Henry Kissinger, and with him the machinery of the modern presidential campaign. They were to return to the Romney home on a horse and buggy, and Moore signaled Kissinger over; the horse released a 'warm, moist' fart right into the professor's face. 'Kissinger gave a little cough,' Moore says, 'and then sort of looked off into the distance and said, "I see we have a lot of ground to cover."'" Wallace-Wells, "George Romney for President, 1968."

7   George Romney was the only 1968 presidential candidate not born in the United States. At the time of his birth, Romney's parents served as Mormon missionaries in Mexico. The family returned to the United States, where they struggled financially during the Great Depression. Romney worked at a variety of low-paying jobs and never completed college. Entering the business world, he joined the American Automobile Manufacturers Association, where he became their chief spokesman. Rising through the ranks, the American Motors Corporation named him chairman of the board in 1954. In 1962, he won the first of three terms as Michigan governor, and he developed a record as a popular Republican moderate in the Democratic state. His appeal to minorities, labor union members, and crossover Democrats made Romney appear as a strong alternative to Richard Nixon in the early handicapping for the 1968 Republican presidential nomination. See, e.g., Wallace-Wells, "George Romney for President, 1968." ("[R]ather than finishing college... [Romney] took a job as a stenographer... from there he moved into a career as a lobbyist

with Alcoa, and then went into the automotive industry. Three decades after his family went bust farming potatoes, Romney was overseeing Detroit's work.... After the war, Romney was hired as an assistant to the president of what would become American Motors, and eventually became president himself.")

8   Although Romney started as the front-runner for the 1968 GOP presidential nomination, after he began campaigning, he dropped dramatically in the polls, falling to last place behind Rockefeller, Nixon, and Reagan. By late 1967, LBJ ran 16 points ahead of Romney, and only 14 percent of Republicans wanted him as their nominee. See Buchanan, *The Greatest Comeback*, 133.

In Pat Buchanan's first-hand account of the 1968 Nixon campaign, he listed examples of the press taking the measure of Romney as a candidate:

- Don Oliver, the NBC News reporter covering Romney, told Buchanan that Romney was "a lightweight."

- Murray Kempton, one of America's most respected political columnists, wrote, "[Romney] is an off case. By every indication he is a successful governor; yet book him on a national tour, and he'll blow the option in two weeks. [¶] One finally decides he must have manufactured a splendid car at American Motors. You have to have a great product for George Romney to sell it."

- Godfrey Sperling of the *Christian Science Monitor* wrote: "[T]here are emerging doubts as to whether Mr. Romney has that 'something,' that necessary political charisma a presidential candidate must have to evoke enthusiastic public support.... [His] timing on jokes is bad. Often the audience is embarrassed. And when the governor tries to discuss issues in a quiet thoughtful way, he doesn't project too well. And he doesn't read speeches at all smoothly." Buchanan, *The Greatest Comeback*, 105-106, 108.

9   Thomas O'Neill of the *Baltimore Sun* wrote that other Republican governors bristled at Romney: "The nub of the complaint is that Governor Romney subconsciously, and perhaps unconsciously, approaches all others as inferiors." One GOP governor said that Romney possessed

a "superiority complex." Buchanan, *The Greatest Comeback*, 104.

[10] On August 31, 1967, in a taped interview with local talk show host Lou Gordon of WKBD-TV in Detroit, Gordon asked Romney, "Isn't your position [on Vietnam] a bit inconsistent with what it was, and what do you propose we do now?" Romney replied, "Well, you know when I came back from Vietnam, I just had the greatest brainwashing that anybody can get when you go over to Vietnam. Not only by the generals, but also by the diplomatic corps over there, and they do a very thorough job.... [A]s a result, I have changed my mind. I no longer believe that it was necessary for us to get involved in South Vietnam to stop aggression." Romney made this comment after supporting U.S. intervention in Vietnam for years—having once called his previous support "morally right and necessary." In rebuttal to Romney's "brainwashing" claim, eight other governors who accompanied him on that Vietnam trip disputed his characterization of the official briefings they received. See, e.g., Buchanan, *The Greatest Comeback*, 132-133; "The Brainwashed Candidate," *Time*, September 15, 1967.

"Brainwashing had a specific connotation [in the 1960s]: It was the term used to describe the ways in which the communist state sought to control people's minds; it conjured images of The Manchurian Candidate. The reference suggested that Romney was paranoid and naïve, and perhaps it also subtly reinforced the suspicion that his religion might be a cult. The Detroit News, for years his firmest supporter in the press, condemned him, and so did virtually everyone else.... In the Gallup poll, Nixon's lead [over Romney after the brainwashing comment] ballooned to 26 points." Wallace-Wells, "George Romney for President, 1968."

With his 'brainwashing" comment, "Romney, in effect, suggested that he was vulnerable to back-room pressure. And if he could be had by U.S. generals and diplomats in Vietnam, how would he stack up in the big leagues with de Gaulle and the British, with the Russians and the Chinese?" "1968: McCarthy Stuns the President."

Four days after Romney gave this interview to Lou Gordon, the *New York Times* carried the headline ROMNEY ASSERTS HE UNDERWENT 'BRAINWASHING' ON VIETNAM TRIP. Buchanan, *The Greatest Comeback*, 133.

[11] Instead of backing away from his devastating "brainwashed" comment, a defiant Romney reinforced it. When pressed about the comment, he told reporters, "Yes, I was brainwashed. We're all brainwashed. The administration simply does not tell us the truth about Vietnam. I'm glad I used that word. It woke up the country. Nobody was paying any attention when I only used words like 'snow job.'" In the aftermath of the gaffe's fallout, *Newsweek* reported that Romney decided to try and "brazen it out." Buchanan, *The Greatest Comeback*, 132.

Two days after making his "brainwashing" comment, "Romney appeared in Washington, where newsmen gave him a chance to get off the hook by asking whether he might have been misunderstood. 'I was not misunderstood,' he snapped. 'If you want to get into a discussion of who's been brainwashing who, I suggest you take a look at what the Administration has been telling the American people.'" See "The Brainwashed Candidate," *Time*; Buchanan, *The Greatest Comeback*, 145.

Thanks to Romney's brainwashing remarks, "[I]t is unlikely that his opponents in either party will allow him to forget his gaffe—not to mention the cartoonists, who henceforth will surely not miss a chance to picture the governor's cranium wreathed in detergent foam. And all can do it with impunity, since he did it to himself." See "The Brainwashed Candidate," *Time*.

"Describing Romney as an 'admittedly susceptible man,' the previously sympathetic *Chicago Daily News* asked whether the U.S. 'can afford as its leader a man who, whatever his positive virtues, is subject to being cozened, flimflammed and taken into camp.' More damaging yet, the Detroit News, long one of the Michigan governor's strongest supporters, announced in a lead editorial that it can no longer back him for the G.O.P. nomination and suggested that Romney quit the race in favor of New York's Governor Nelson Rockefeller, a man 'who knows what he believes.'" See "The Brainwashed Candidate," *Time*.

Romney's "brainwashing" comment was the beginning of the end for his campaign. Newspapers previously supportive now called on him to leave the race. Even his hometown paper, the Detroit Free Press, urged him to stand aside for Nelson Rockefeller. See Smith, *On His Own Terms*, 513.

Following the "brainwashing" gaffe, and after reporters rattled Romney repeatedly over Vietnam, Romney declared he would no longer answer questions about the war. As one columnist for the *New York Post* wrote, "[T]his self-imposed quarantine may help him arrest his virulent attack of foot-in-mouth disease." Buchanan, *The Greatest Comeback*, 107.

[12] Of Romney's brainwashing comment, Democratic presidential candidate Eugene McCarthy had a devastating retort: "I would have thought a light rinse would have done it." See Witcover, *Very Strange Bedfellows*, 5; Buchanan, *The Greatest Comeback*, 133.

[13] After the 1966 midterm elections, Nixon announced he would take a six-month moratorium from partisan politics, thus leaving the presidential campaign field to Romney. Concerned over this strategy, Nixon aide Pat Buchanan asked if it was wise to cede the field to Romney for a half-year with no flexibility. Nixon replied, "Let [the press] chew on [Romney] for a while." Buchanan, *The Greatest Comeback*, 93.

"'Let Romney take the point,' [Nixon] insisted. Nixon would maintain his moratorium on politics for six months, meanwhile traveling abroad on fact-finding missions." Ambrose, *Nixon (Volume Two)*, 105.

"The Sunday before the 1966 elections, during a CBS interview, [Nixon] announced one of his 'moratoriums'—this time a 'holiday from politics for at least six months.' [¶] What this meant was that other presidential candidates, particularly the front-runner, Governor George Romney, would be allowed time to put their feet in their mouths while Nixon dined with the famous in the great capitals of the world, letting pictures with prime ministers take the place of boring or dangerous words about the economy and Vietnam." Leonard Garment, *Crazy Rhythm: My Journey from Brooklyn, Jazz, and Wall Street to Nixon's White House, Watergate, and Beyond....* (New York: Times Books, 1997), 116.

Nixon told his staff that during his six-month moratorium from politics, "'While I am lying back I want you to work your tails off getting the job done. We will have to work harder and better than the other candidates to win.' He wanted the group to get going on putting together an organization in every state, complete with advanced men, fundraisers, and campaign managers. 'Don't give out any franchises,' he said, 'but get started contacting the power groups in each state.'" Ambrose, *Nixon (Volume Two)*, 105.

In early January 1967, Nixon held meetings with key supporters.

Although he planned on taking a six-month public moratorium from politics, he urged his supporters to get out and "work your tails off getting the job done." It was a calculated risk to let George Romney "be out front taking the heat from the press and the pundits while I continued my quiet planning and foreign travel." See Richard Nixon, *RN: The Memoirs of Richard Nixon* (New York: Grosset & Dunlap, 1978), 279.

[14]   Following the 1966 midterm elections, Nixon didn't want to be the "lead horse" coming out of the 1968 political starting gate. He believed that if he started 1967 as a presidential candidate, even an unannounced one, the press and public would grow tired of him and seek a fresh face. "It was a risky strategy and, judging by the results, a brilliant one." See Buchanan, *The Greatest Comeback*, 94, 101.

[15]   "Michigan Governor George Romney was advised not to challenge Nixon [in New Hampshire], and instead await the Wisconsin primary on April 2. It was believed by some advisers that the conservative nature of New Hampshire's Republicans and Nixon's popularity among its leaders and rank-and-file were too strong for Romney to overcome, and he should begin his quest for the nomination in a state closer in both ideology and geography. Romney was not dissuaded by such arguments and failed to realize that his not-quite-irresistible candidacy would collide with the immovable support from New Hampshire Republicans for Richard Nixon." See "1968: McCarthy Stuns the President."

CHAPTER 25

[1]   After his 1966 California gubernatorial victory, Reagan sat next to Rockefeller at a meeting of governors, and "Reagan didn't impress his vastly experienced New York counterpart by asking someone to define for him an ad valorem tax. ('Oh Christ, Ronnie...')." See Smith, *On His Own Terms*, 498.

[2]   Reagan joked that during his Hollywood days of making B-movies, the studios "didn't want them good; they wanted them Thursday." Lou Cannon, "Actor, Governor, President, Icon," *Washington Post*, June 6, 2004. http://www. washingtonpost.com/wp-dyn/articles/A18329-2004Jun5.html

[3]   For their National Governors Conference, 42 state governors boarded the liner S.S. Independence in New York City for a cruise to the Virgin Islands and back, October 16-24, 1967. See "In Unpath'd Waters," *Time*, October 27, 1967; see also *CQ Almanac 1967*, http://library.cqpress.com/cqalmanac/document.php?id=cqal67-1311523.

"Aboard the S.S. Independence this week in Manhattan, a bulwark-bulging guest list checked in for a voyage into 1968. As the governors of forty-two American states—twenty-one Democrats, twenty-one Republicans—and 700 aides and journalists sailed off on an eight-day cruise to the Virgin Islands[.]" "Anchors Aweigh," *Time*, October 20, 1967.

During the 1967 National Governors Conference, "[a]dding to the normal opulence of the [S.S. Independence's] staterooms and saloons were ballroom and calypso bands[.]" See "In Unpath'd Waters," *Time*.

[4]   The S.S. Independence, or "Indy," as she was affectionately known, was somewhat overshadowed by her newer sister, S.S. Constitution, which was glamorized in film and television roles, most notably *An Affair to Remember* with Cary Grant and Deborah Kerr, and the famous "porthole" episode of *I Love Lucy*. "Connie" was also famous for transporting Grace Kelly's wedding party to Monaco and was featured on the cover of *Life* magazine. Nonetheless, the Independence carried her share of dignitaries, including President and Mrs. Truman in the summer of 1958. See Jerome Aronson, The Life and Death of America's Last Cruise Ship the SS Independence, March 3, 2008, http://retardzone.com/2008/03/03/the-life-and-death-of-americas-last-cruise-ship-the-ss-independence; see also https://en.wikipedia.org/wiki/SS_Independence.

[5]   Rockefeller insisted to reporters aboard the S.S. Independence during the 1967 National Governors Conference, "I don't want to be president." See "In Unpath'd Waters," *Time*.

[6]   At a press conference aboard the Independence during the 1967 National Governors Conference, and after a reporter told him that Rockefeller announced earlier he didn't want to be president, Reagan replied, "'I have a carry-over from my previous occupation. I never take the other fellow's lines.' Then Ronnie lapsed into super-sincerity by saying that 'the convention, the Party and the people of the U.S. will make that decision. It is not relevant what someone's personal desires might be.'" See "In Unpath'd Waters," *Time*.

"At safety drill, [George] Romney and Ronald Reagan found themselves in the same lifeboat. Their fellow potential survivors showed up in the prescribed orange life jackets, but the putative rivals, jacketless, were plainly determined to either sink or swim on the strength of their own buoyancy." See "In Unpath'd Waters," *Time*.

[7]   During the 1967 National Governors Conference aboard the S.S. Independence, the attendees were treated to "enough rich food and free Virgin Islands rum (for those who tired of the domestic champagne) for a well-sated cruise[.]" See "In Unpath'd Waters," *Time*.

Aboard the S.S. Independence, "There was robust George Romney, up with the dawn and jogging about the sun deck in his sneakers, later

chiding asthenic reporters: 'I was up while you fellows were still asleep.'"
See "In Unpath'd Waters," *Time*.

8   While aboard the S.S. Independence during the 1967 National Governors Conference, "Nelson Rockefeller took Bonamine pills to ward off seasickness[.]" See "In Unpath'd Waters," *Time*.

9   A Gallup poll in late 1967 showed the "dream ticket" of Rockefeller-Reagan beating the expected Democratic ticket of Johnson and Humphrey 57 percent to 43 percent. See Smith, *On His Own Terms*, 497.

10   The lead article of *Time* magazine's "Dream Ticket" issue, featuring Rockefeller and Reagan on the cover, contained this observation: "'Nobody is so far ahead that he can't be beaten,' said a Republican state chairman from New England. 'Nor is anybody so far behind that he can't catch up—unless it is George Romney.' [¶] 'Romney's dead,' says Indiana's Republican state treasurer, John Snyder. 'The 'brainwash' remark didn't make all that much difference. People were already looking for a reason to turn away.' Most other G.O.P. strategists agree. From a commanding lead in the polls right after his impressive re-election victory in 1966, Michigan's Governor has reached a nadir; he is unlikely even to control the entire delegation from his own state." See "Anchors Aweigh," *Time*.

11   The dialogue between Rockefeller and Romney aboard the S.S. Independence, where Romney pleaded to end his presidential campaign after seeing the Rockefeller-Reagan "Dream Ticket" *Time* magazine cover, is based on actual events. "[Romney] had planned to attend the floating gathering of the National Governors Conference of 1967 on their autumn shipboard journey to the Virgin Islands. He appeared on the boat to join his basic constituents, the governors, like one of the walking wounded, pale, exhausted and dragging of foot. As the boat took off, a copy of *Time* magazine was placed under every door with a joint cover-picture story on Rockefeller and Reagan, writing Romney off as a fool unqualified for high office. Three times on board the boat, closeted with Rockefeller in Rockefeller's cabin on the sun deck, he pleaded with New York's governor to let him off the hook. He was through, Romney insisted; Nelson must run for president. But Rockefeller would not—the plan was for Romney

to run as the governors' candidate. He must go on with it." See White, *The Making of the President 1968*, 60-61.

"On a National Governors Conference cruise in the Virgin Islands, [Romney] visited Nelson Rockefeller's cabin three times, pleading with the New York governor to run so that he could drop out. Rockefeller wouldn't let him." See Wallace-Wells, "George Romney for President, 1968."

[12]   "Rockefeller has perhaps the greatest assets and the greatest liabilities of any man in the G.O.P. The assets make him the Party's most electable candidate; the liabilities make him its least nominable contender. Chief among the latter is the right wing's almost pathological hatred of Rocky.... 'I don't think Texans would vote for Rockefeller,' says Republican State Committeeman Albert Fay, 'if Jesus Christ were his running mate.'" See "Anchors Aweigh," *Time.*

"Nonetheless, there is some question whether the G.O.P.'s conservatives can ever bring themselves to condone Rockefeller's refusal to back Barry Goldwater in 1964." See "Anchors Aweigh," *Time.*

[13]   This dialogue between Rockefeller and Romney regarding Romney's desire to step aside as a 1968 Republican presidential candidate is adapted from letters Romney wrote to his son, future GOP presidential nominee Mitt Romney: "'[My father] wrote me lengthy letters when I was in my [Mormon] Mission about what was going on and what his experience was,' [Mitt] Romney recalled about his father. 'He had made a commitment to the Republican governors that he would be the standard bearer for the non-Nixon wing of the Party but if it didn't look like he could get the job done, he would withdraw. He concluded that following the brainwashing statement, the decline in the polls, and the rush of his key people to Rockefeller that his commitment to the other Republican governors was such that he needed to step aside. [¶] He did not want to step aside.... He wanted to keep fighting. He thought he could go forward and ultimately overcome the challenge, but he had made a commitment and felt that he needed to honor that commitment and give the Republican governors a chance to pick someone else. That was the way he described it to me in his letters.'" Hugh Hewitt, *A Mormon in the White House? Ten Things Every American Should Know About Mitt Romney* (Washington: Regnery Publishing, Inc., 2007), 36.

[14]   The luxurious S.S. Independence had everything, including high-end designer shops and branches of Fifth Avenue department stores. See "'The Independence': First U.S. Ship in Twelve Years Lacks Nothing but 3,000 Ashtrays," *Life*, February 19, 1951.

[15]   The S.S. Independence was equipped with ship-to-shore telephone service, including "bedside telephones from which a passenger can phone anyone within 5,000 miles." See "'The Independence.'"

[16]   During the early campaign season of 1967, while the press crucified Romney, his 20 year-old son Mitt, then on his Mormon mission in France, watched his father's ordeal from afar. See Buchanan, *The Greatest Comeback*, 108-109. In later years, Mitt Romney served as governor of Massachusetts and U.S. Senator from Utah. As the 2012 Republican presidential nominee, he lost his White House bid to President Barack Obama.

[17]   Before the 1968 New Hampshire primary, Rockefeller commissioned yet another poll to test Romney's strength in the Granite State against Nixon. When Rockefeller's staff analyzed the results, one of them "summarized the impression that George Romney had made. 'I guess the poll shows,' he said, 'that New Hampshire Republicans think George Romney is too dumb to be president of the United States.'" White, *The Making of the President 1968*, 60-61.

CHAPTER 26

[1]   Nixon was a Spartan campaigner. At the end of the day, he liked to sip a beer and then retire to bed quickly. See Buchanan, *The Greatest Comeback*, 210.

Nixon himself recognized the need to use alcohol sparingly on the campaign trail. "During the 1966 campaign, Nixon told a reporter that he sometimes had one beer after speaking, but never any alcohol of any kind before. 'When I'm campaigning,' he explained, 'I live like a Spartan.... I've seen a lot of people who drink. They get up there and talk too long. I speak without notes, and I can't do that without intense concentration before and during the speech.'" Ambrose, *Nixon (Volume Two)*, 85.

[2]   On January 31, 1968, a limousine took Nixon, Ray Price, Dwight Chapin, and Pat Buchanan to a private terminal at LaGuardia Airport where they caught a small plane to Boston's Logan Airport. Nixon's New Hampshire advance man, Nick Ruwe, picked them up at Logan and drove them to a New Hampshire motel, where he had registered Nixon under the name of "Benjamin Chapman." The men snuck Nixon into the motel through a side door. See Buchanan, *The Greatest Comeback*, 202.

[3]   On the day Nixon announced his presidential candidacy, he "strode to the microphones set up before assembled reporters in the meeting room of the Holiday Inn in Manchester, New Hampshire, and began: 'Gentlemen, this is not my last press conference.' He laughed, and the reporters tried to laugh, and he plunged on. He hit his main weakness head-on: 'Can Nixon win?' he asked. He wanted to be 'quite candid' in his answer, which turned out to be yes. [¶] He would win by demonstrating in the primaries that he was a winner. He got in a dig at Rockefeller, who had announced

again that he was withdrawing his name from the Oregon primary, but that he was open to a draft. Nixon said, 'I will test my ability... in the fires of the primaries, and not just in the smoke-filled rooms of Miami Beach.'" Ambrose, *Nixon (Volume Two)*, 135. See also Nixon, *RN*, 297 (Nixon declared his presidential candidacy on February 2, 1968, at the Holiday Inn in Manchester, New Hampshire, telling the assembled reporters, "Gentlemen, this is not my last press conference!"). [Author's note: In his memoir, Nixon wrote that he had declared his presidential candidacy on February 2, 1968. According to contemporary press reports, the correct date was February 1, 1968.]

"Richard Nixon... appeared at a Manchester Holiday Inn on a near freezing, foggy February day to tell the world" he was a candidate for president in 1968. See Jeffrey Frank, *Ike and Dick: Portrait of a Strange Political Marriage* (New York: Simon and Schuster paperbacks, 2013), 296.

4   The Hotel Wentworth, built in 1874, hosted the delegations from Russia and Japan at the suggestion of President Theodore Roosevelt in 1905. It was during their stay that the two nations negotiated and signed the Treaty of Portsmouth, which ended the Russo-Japanese War and earned Roosevelt a Nobel Peace Prize. See https://en.wikipedia.org/wiki/Wentworth_by_the_Sea.

5   As a presidential candidate, Romney "is already taking steps to soften the stiff, sanctimonious impression that he too often conveys. 'He's sure trying to be one of the fellas,' says an aide. 'He's even using a lot more *hells* and *damns* than he used to.' Even so, the newsmen who cover Romney still refer to him as 'Super Square.'" See "Anchors Aweigh," *Time.*

6   Prior to declaring his 1968 presidential candidacy, Nixon mailed a letter to 150,000 New Hampshire residents announcing that he would enter their state's primary. United Press International, "Nixon Begins His Presidency Fight," *The Times*, San Mateo, California, February 2, 1968.

7   The antiwar forces in the United States used the Eddie Adams photograph of General Loan shooting in the head a Vietcong terrorist to propagandize against the brutality of the South. One person who did not share that sentiment was the photographer. Thirty years after snapping

the iconic war photograph, Adams wrote a eulogy to the executioner that he had captured on film: "I won a Pulitzer Prize in 1969 for a photograph of one man shooting another. Two people died in that photograph: the recipient of the bullet and GENERAL NGUYEN NGOC LOAN. The general killed the Vietcong; I killed the general with my camera. Still photographs are the most powerful weapon in the world. People believe them, but photographs do lie, even without manipulation. They are only half-truths. What the photograph didn't say was, 'What would you do if you were the general at that time and place on that hot day, and you caught the so-called bad guy after he blew away one, two or three American soldiers?' General Loan was what you would call a real warrior, admired by his troops. I'm not saying what he did was right, but you have to put yourself in his position. The photograph also doesn't say that the general devoted much of his time trying to get hospitals built in Vietnam for war casualties. This picture really messed up his life. He never blamed me. He told me if I hadn't taken the picture, someone else would have, but I've felt bad for him and his family for a long time.... I sent flowers when I heard that he had died and wrote, 'I'm sorry. There are tears in my eyes.'" "General Nguyen Ngoc Loan," *Time*, July 27, 1998.

On February 2, 1968, the *New York Times*, the *Washington Post*, and the *Los Angeles Times* all carried the Eddie Adams photograph from Vietnam on page one of their newspapers. See Barbie Zelizer, *About to Die: How News Images Move the Public* (New York: Oxford University Press, 2010), 384.

8   The day before Nixon announced his presidential candidacy, Rockefeller addressed Nixon's upcoming entry into the presidential campaign. "Gov. Nelson A. Rockefeller of New York said Thursday he thought the entry of Richard Nixon in the New Hampshire presidential primary 'crystallizes the race,' but said Michigan Gov. George Romney is still his choice. [¶] He predicted Romney would win the New Hampshire race. [¶] Rockefeller, at a news conference, continually said, 'I'm not a candidate' in reply to questions on whether he might enter the GOP presidential nomination race. [¶] In reply to a question of what he would do if faced with a draft movement at the GOP convention, he said: 'If I was faced with a draft at the convention, I couldn't avoid it. That's something I

would have to face at the time.'" Associated Press, "Rocky Still Backs Romney," *Independent*, Long Beach, California, February 2, 1968; see also White, *The Making of the President 1968*, 229.

"As Romney struggled, Rockefeller's ambitions reignited, and when he let it be known he'd be available for a draft at the convention, he effectively gutted Romney from behind. The backstab came on February 24, 1968, after Rocky had addressed a Detroit fundraising luncheon for Romney. After first declaring his support for Romney, the press pressed: Would he be available for a draft? Rockefeller said 'Yes,' and that signaled the end of the Romney campaign." Hewitt, *A Mormon in the White House?*, 36.

[9]   Rockefeller's suggestion he would accept a draft left Romney deeply embittered. See White, *The Making of the President 1968*, 229.

"Dad [George Romney] was disappointed in Rockefeller. I think Rockefeller tried to sail a little too close to the wind and justified reversing his commitment. And he did it in a way that wouldn't look like he was reversing his commitment, that he was forced into the race." Hewitt, *A Mormon in the White House?*, 37.

[10]   In January 1968, a reporter asked Rockefeller what explained Romney's string of campaign gaffes. "Go ask a psychiatrist," Rockefeller quipped. See Chester, Hodgson, Page, *An American Melodrama*, 102.

[11]   Nixon believed that Rockefeller might be using Romney as a stalking horse for Rockefeller's own candidacy. See Nixon, *RN*, 289.

[12]   "One of [Romney's] backers later moaned, 'The minute George Romney lost his aura, [the New Hampshire people] literally wouldn't cross the street to meet him.'" See "1968: McCarthy Stuns the President."

"Nixon's New Hampshire campaign was stately, dignified, proud, and slow. In a complete reversal of his 1960 techniques, Nixon stayed away from factory gates, avoided shopping centers, made no effort to press the flesh, appeared in no high-school gyms, all of which Romney was doing to a maximum degree. But Nixon was well known in the state already (could there have been a voter in New Hampshire, indeed in the nation, who did not know Dick Nixon?) and he feared overexposure. When he did appear in public, it was only in large auditoriums, with audiences of never less than a thousand, some as large as twenty-five hundred. [¶] He made an effort to appear statesmanlike, dignified, experienced, and in command, and he succeeded. He spoke without notes, casually." See Ambrose, *Nixon (Volume Two)*, 137.

[13] "For two more months, with utmost bravery and great energy, George Romney campaigned through the snows of New Hampshire, stopping at bowling alleys, inspecting milk plants, hand-pumping in the sub-zero dawn outside factory gates, speaking to neighborhood groups, up early and to bed late." See White, *The Making of the President 1968*, 60-61.

[14] "By late February 1968, George Romney considered the race hopeless. The national polls indicated a decisive Nixon victory in New Hampshire, and Romney's private polls showed him trailing Nixon by more than five-to-one. In addition, contributions had fallen off considerably. Romney had already spent $1 million and his campaign would require another $2 million to carry him to the August convention." Wainstock, *Election Year 1968*, 44.

As the New Hampshire primary neared, "Romney had had it. His campaign's operating budget had been halved, and the line was that all of the remaining staffers were preparing memos explaining why the collapse was not their fault. Nixon flew into New Hampshire to give weekend speeches in front of crowds of 5,000; Romney trudged around milk plants." See Wallace-Wells, "George Romney for President, 1968."

"As the primary approached, Romney was being forced to compete not only with Nixon (who enjoyed massive leads in polls), but he was also confronted with the threat that an unauthorized write-in for Nelson Rockefeller (who had endorsed Romney) would overtake his own vote and leave him in a humiliating third [place]." See "1968: McCarthy Stuns the President."

Romney's pollsters told him that Nixon was beating him in New Hampshire among Republicans 70 percent to 11 percent, and nothing appeared able to change it. Chester, Hodgson, Page, *An American Melodrama*, 100.

The last of the New Hampshire polls, taken by Romney's favorite polling firm, Frederick Courier's Market Opinion Research, was completed the third week in February 1968. "Nothing had budged the Hampshiremen's minds; they were still for Nixon by six to one; the cause was hopeless." White, *The Making of the President 1968*, 60-61.

[15]   Two weeks before the New Hampshire primary, Rockefeller's secretly commissioned poll showed the results of his investment in Romney: Nixon beating Romney six-to-one. See White, *The Making of the President 1968*, 229.

"Most Republicans believed that [Nixon] had been a drag on the ticket in '52 and '56. He had lost to Kennedy in 1960 and to Pat Brown in 1962. No wonder Republicans across the country were saying, 'I like Nixon best, but he just can't win.'" See Ambrose, *Nixon (Volume Two)*, 104.

[16]   "Actually, the contested primaries will account for no more than 150 of the 1,333 delegate votes, and even if Nixon did win them all, he might still be denied the nomination Their chief influence, in fact, is psychological, and their major effect on the G.O.P. nomination is likely to be negative." See "Anchors Aweigh," *Time*.

"There were, in 1968, primaries in a dozen states, but some of those were already tied up by favorite-son candidates, most importantly California for the Republicans by Reagan. The majority of delegates would be picked in the non-primary states by the state committees." Ambrose, *Nixon (Volume Two)*, 104-105.

[17]   In a private meeting with Nixon during the 1968 campaign, Ohio Governor James Rhodes ridiculed Romney as a presidential candidate, telling Nixon that Romney "couldn't sell *%# on a troop ship." Buchanan, *The Greatest Comeback*, 108.

[18]   At a New Hampshire bowling alley photo-op, while his staff cringed and reporters laughed, Romney rolled 37 balls until he knocked down all ten pins. In recalling the incident later, reporter Jules Witcover wrote, "The episode was a metaphor for George Romney, the man who never knew when he was licked." See Buchanan, *The Greatest Comeback*, 211.

"George Romney may not be a hotshot bowler, but he is no quitter. To knock down all ten duckpins at an alley at Franklin, N.H., he took 34 balls. Pursuing his presidential hopes, Romney is proving every whit as persistent." "Romney Rediyivus," *Time*, January 26, 1968. [Author's note: compare this account to the previous footnote, where Buchanan wrote that Romney threw 37 balls to knock down all of the pins.]

"On and on the good man [Romney] went for the next few hopeless months, embrangling himself further with the press, whom he now regarded as a native American Vietcong.... [The press portrayed Romney] as a blunt, crude, unfeeling politician.... Romney could not win with the press." See White, *The Making of the President 1968*, 60-61.

As for Romney's campaign abilities, Ohio Governor James Rhodes told Nixon, "Dick, George Romney running for president is like a duck trying to *%# a football." Buchanan, *The Greatest Comeback*, 108.

[19] "On February 28, [1968,] while in Washington to attend the midwinter Republican Governors Conference, Romney announced to reporters that he was withdrawing from the [presidential] race.... He pledged his 'wholehearted support' to any new candidate his fellow Republican governors endorsed, but he did not name his choice." Wainstock, *Election Year 1968*, 44.

"In what would become the first 'technical knock-out' in primary history, the Michigan governor on February 28 withdrew from the race in a press conference in Washington, D.C." See "1968: McCarthy Stuns the President."

"George Romney took his decision forthrightly, openly, bravely, and on February 28 called an end to it, leaving behind the impression of an honest and decent man simply not cut out to be president of the United States." White, *The Making of the President 1968*, 60-61.

"George [Romney] really did think Rockefeller was going to support him for the presidential nomination in 1968, and Rockefeller in his inimitable fashion did nothing to disabuse him of that delusion. In the end, Rocky double-crossed him royally. He kept saying that he himself was not a candidate, that Romney would make an excellent candidate as the guardian of moderate Republican values, and Romney took him at his word. He went so far out on a limb, anticipating Rockefeller's full backing, which never materialized, and when his cumbersome campaign finally collapsed of its own dead weight Rockefeller was the only moderate left to pick up the ball and run with it. The only problem for Rockefeller, however, was that Romney self-destructed early—on February 28, 1968—

before Rocky was ready to launch a full-fledged primary campaign of his own. He was secretly hoping that Romney would fall apart closer to the convention so that he could be anointed as the candidate, rather than to have to earn it in the primaries." F. Clifton White and Jerome Tuccille, *Politics as a Noble Calling: The Memoirs of F. Clifton White* (Ottawa: Jameson Books, 1994), 176.

[20]   Lenore (Mrs. George) Romney was not forgiving of Rockefeller's treatment of her husband: "They saw each other after [Rockefeller] began saying he wouldn't rule out running for the presidency, [that] he'd be open to a draft and my mother saw him and he said, 'Oh, Lenore, how are you? I'm so sorry to hear that George has withdrawn,' and she said something to the effect that 'You are the cause of it, and you know you caused it.'" Hewitt, *A Mormon in the White House?*, 37.

[21]   Romney's son Mitt was still on his Mormon church mission in France when news of his father's withdrawal from the 1968 presidential campaign reached him. "'Your mother and I are not personally distressed,' George wrote his son [regarding his withdrawal from the campaign]. 'As a matter of fact, we are relieved.'" Wallace-Wells, "George Romney for President, 1968."

[22]   In early 1968, Maryland Governor Spiro T. Agnew set up a "Draft Rockefeller" operation in Maryland; a few days later, he announced the national "Draft Rockefeller" campaign had opened its doors, and Agnew had assumed the chairmanship of the movement. After Romney withdrew from the presidential race, he refused to play any part in Agnew's draft movement. Chester, Hodgson, Page, *An American Melodrama*, 102, 220.

CHAPTER 27

[1]   "For its campaign headquarters, the Nixon organization leased a five–story building at the corner of Park Avenue and Fifty-Seventh Street that previously housed the American Bible Society. It was dilapidated inside but imposing outside, one of those disappearing relics of a time when cities were built to human scale. I worked in a battered cubicle on the fourth floor. Around the walls on the first floor, in a single large room, Biblical quotations were painted in Gothic script on the moldings." See Price, *With Nixon,* 41–42.

Nixon's 1968 campaign headquarters, in the building previously occupied by the American Bible Society, was located in Manhattan at 450 Park Avenue. See David W. Dunlap, "New York Says Farewell to American Bible Society, and Its Building," *New York Times,* October 21, 2015, http://www.nytimes.com/2015/10/22/nyregion/new-york-says-farewell-to-american-bible-society-and-its-building.html .

[2]   Ray Price, one of Nixon's 1968 campaign speechwriters, described visiting the Nixons' ten-bedroom apartment that took up the entire fifth floor of 812 Fifth Avenue after he joined the team: "We went through the large foyer, through a sunny living room with a view of [Central Park], and settled into the small room off the living room that he used as a study. It, too, had a view of the park—it was the southwest corner that faced both the park and Sixty-Second Street. But the room's focus was inward, not outward, the furniture arranged with the backs to the windows. It had a comfortable, lived-in, worked-in look, with a small desk and desk lamp, bookshelves behind the desk that looked as though they were for reading, not display, a brown velvet overstuffed chair and matching ottoman, a couch, coffee table, a few chairs." Price, *With Nixon,* 14.

On occasion, and while traveling on his campaign airplane, Nixon drank vodka and Fresca. See Buchanan, *The Greatest Comeback*, 210-211.

[3]   Nixon coasted to an easy New Hampshire primary victory, winning 80,666 votes. See "1968: McCarthy Stuns the President."

After Romney withdrew, Nixon won New Hampshire with an impressive near-80 percent of the Republican vote. To minimize the victory, many pundits reminded everyone that he did so without opposition. See, e.g., Chester, Hodgson, Page, *An American Melodrama*, 101.

[4]   Reagan called Nixon's New Hampshire win "a hollow victory" because Nixon had no meaningful competition. See Associated Press, "What They Said," *Post Crescent*, Appleton, Wisconsin, March 13, 1968.

"Polling done for Nixon in 1967 told him that while the New Hampshire voters sampled considered the former vice president experienced, intelligent and able to deal with foreign policy matters and leaders, he was also perceived as a loser always running for the presidency but unable to achieve it, someone similar to Harold Stassen. Nixon had not won a general election in his own right since 1950, when he defeated Helen Gahagan Douglas for a United States Senate seat in California. Nixon had to overcome not only his loss to John Kennedy in 1960, but also his humiliating defeat by Edmund G. 'Pat' Brown for the governorship of the Golden State in 1962." See "1968: McCarthy Stuns the President."

Nixon was the first choice for the GOP nomination in almost every Gallup poll taken in 1967; in October 1967, Gallup showed Nixon beating Johnson for the first time, 49 percent to 45 percent. See Nixon, *RN*, 290.

A poll of every GOP county chairman showed they favored Nixon for the 1968 presidential nomination. See Buchanan, *The Greatest Comeback*, 21.

"Nixon is still the man to beat at the convention. In a poll taken last spring, G.O.P. county chairmen overwhelmingly endorsed him, 1,227 votes to 341 for Romney, 233 for Reagan, 119 for Percy and 67 for Rockefeller. He is the favorite of grass-roots Party workers, and even those who concede that he might not be the ideal standard bearer say nonetheless that they will vote for him in Miami Beach in deference to his experience and unflagging service. Nixon himself rejects the idea that any man should get the nomination in payment for his Party labors, insists that it should go to the strongest candidate.... [However], Nixon may have struck out too many times: his defeat in 1960 and in the 1962 California gubernatorial race have embossed him with a 'can't win' image that he may never fully erase." See "Anchors Aweigh," *Time*.

[5]   Nixon felt that Romney cheated him out of his massive New Hampshire primary victory. Commenting privately on Romney's last-minute withdrawal from the campaign, Nixon said, "Just like a businessman, no guts." See Buchanan, *The Greatest Comeback*, 213.

Nixon's plan to overcome the "loser" image was to enter all of the non-favorite son primaries and then argue, in essence, "If Nixon is such a loser, why don't the other Republicans enter the primaries against him and prove it?" The Nixon campaign believed the "loser" image would disappear once they started winning primaries. In a campaign memo sent to Nixon, aide Pat Buchanan wrote to his boss, "They can't very well say 'Nixon is a loser but he can beat the hell out of us.'" See Buchanan, *The Greatest Comeback*, 209.

Nixon decided the way to combat the "loser" perception was by entering all the primaries and prove otherwise. Nixon was disappointed when Romney dropped out, since he knew his New Hampshire victory would ring a bit hollow even though he had knocked Romney from the race. See Nixon, *RN*, 297.

By early 1967, "Romney looked to be [Nixon's] toughest opponent because of his big win in Michigan in 1966. This gave Nixon his opportunity. He doubted that Romney could 'hit big-league pitching,' meaning that when Romney was subjected to the national press corps he would crack. Thus it was to Nixon's advantage to build up Romney; then Nixon's victory, when it came, would be all the more dramatic." After Romney's "brainwashing" gaffe, "Nixon did all he could to keep the Romney candidacy alive through the early primaries, so that he would have someone to run against and beat." Nixon "needed momentum going into November 1968, and to get it he needed to prove that he could win, which he could do only through the primaries. There are risks... but Nixon had no choice." See Ambrose, *Nixon (Volume Two)*, 104-105, 127.

In noting that former Republican National Committee Chairman

Leonard Hall decided to back Romney for the 1968 GOP presidential nomination, Nixon told his law partner Leonard Garment, "Well, Hall has finally decided he's going with Romney—a hopeless candidate." See Garment, *Crazy Rhythm*, 117.

"Originally a firm supporter of the [Vietnam War] effort, [Romney] was beginning to have his doubts. His ambiguity cost him dearly when reporters began to press for answers. In the kind of situation in which Nixon excelled, Romney was an innocent lamb—just as Nixon had predicted would be the case." See Ambrose, *Nixon (Volume Two)*, 127.

6   Soon after Dwight D. Eisenhower selected Nixon as his 1952 vice presidential running mate, Nixon found himself embroiled in a scandal when the *New York Post* printed a story (September 18, 1952) claiming "Secret Nixon Fund! Secret Rich Men's Trust Fund Keeps Nixon in Style Far Beyond His Salary." Nixon labeled the story a smear, but pressure was brought to bear on him to resign from the ticket. Eisenhower was noncommittal when asked to defend his running mate. When Eisenhower finally reached Nixon by telephone, Ike said he had not decided what to do, then paused waiting for a reply. "Nixon let the line hang silent. Finally Eisenhower said, 'I don't want to be in the position of condemning an innocent man. I think you should go on a nationwide television program and tell them everything there is to tell....' Nixon, furious, said that there came a time to stop dawdling, that once he had made his speech, the general ought to decide. [¶] 'There comes a time in matters like this when you've either got to shit or get off the pot,' Nixon said." See Stephen E. Ambrose, *Eisenhower: Soldier and President* (New York: Simon and Schuster Paperbacks, 1990) 278-279.

"Nixon's big win on the Republican side in New Hampshire put the pressure on Rockefeller to announce that he was entering the primaries. Nixon expected Rockefeller to do so, and did not particularly fear it." Ambrose, *Nixon (Volume Two)*, 145-146.

7   One Republican, when speaking of Romney and Rockefeller, said, "While he personally had no objection to a couple of whores rejoining the church, he did hate like hell to see them leading the choir the first night." Buchanan, *The Greatest Comeback*, 47.

Conservatives never forgave Rockefeller for his refusal to help Goldwater in 1964. In that year, "Romney and Rockefeller had lit out for the tall grass. [Rockefeller] could support the nominee only if he was the nominee.... He had picked up his marbles and gone home. And few wanted him back in 1968." Buchanan, *The Greatest Comeback*, 18, 40.

8   The evidence points to Rockefeller having an affair with a staffer prior to and during the 1968 campaign.

- A few years after Rockefeller's death, longtime Rockefeller aide and speechwriter Emmet Hughes told historian Arthur M. Schlesinger that "Nelson was just compulsive about women. He made Happy [Mrs. Rockefeller] go through the misery of a divorce, and then two years later was fooling around with a new girl in the office. In 1968 we were concerned all the time that the press might get on to this new involvement.... All his girls were the same type—the wholesome, hearty, simple, innocent American type. Except possibly the last one...." See Schlesinger Jr., *Journals*, 513-514.

- Pat Buchanan, who worked for Richard Nixon as a campaign aide during that election, wrote in his memoir of the 1968 race: "Rockefeller was involved with a young staffer. After his divorce from his wife of many years, Mary, known as Tod, and his marriage to divorcee 'Happy' Murphy, who had given birth to his son three days before the California primary in 1964, which Rockefeller lost, another scandal would have dynamited any remote chance he had of being the nominee.... A source deep inside Rockefeller's office said it was true, and gave [Nixon's campaign team] the girl's name. The Albany press corps had to know this. Yet no one wrote it. Rockefeller was not a candidate and had declared he would not be a candidate.... Yet to announce for president with this rumor hanging out there seemed a huge personal and political risk." Buchanan, *The Greatest Comeback*, 222.

- As historian Arthur M. Schlesinger Jr. noted in his diary entry of December 7, 1967, Rockefeller had missed several meetings with Schlesinger in attendance at which Rockefeller was expected. "I was later told by Babe Paley (and by Joan Braden) that [Rockefeller] had another girl—his present secretary. Henry Kissinger [at the time a senior Rockefeller aide] said that, if this might have been true once, it was not presently the case. Nelson, he said, always requires the emotional support of women who work closely with him. He got this from [the current Mrs. Rockefeller]; and, when [she] moved on from secretary to wife, she removed herself from the picture and made some sort of local succession inevitable." Schlesinger Jr., *Journals*, 266.

• In his January 22, 1978, diary entry, Schlesinger discussed having dinner with Rockefeller and his wife, Happy Rockefeller, three nights earlier. As the Rockefellers bade the guests goodnight, Schlesinger noted that Mrs. Rockefeller showed "the remnants of a woman of spirit and charm crushed by [Rockefeller's] hyperactivity and infidelity." Buchanan, *The Greatest Comeback*, 446.

[9]   As Nixon surveyed the possible GOP candidates for 1968, he initially "judged that Romney was his chief rival, followed by Senator Percy of Illinois, and Governor Reagan. He gave Rockefeller no chance at all." See Ambrose, *Nixon (Volume Two)*, 104.

"I did not believe that after [Rockefeller's] performance at the [1964 Republican National Convention] and his refusal to endorse Goldwater he had a prayer of beating Nixon [in 1968]." Buchanan, *The Greatest Comeback*, 221.

[10]   Pat Buchanan sent Nixon a strategy memorandum a few months before the first primary, warning that Rockefeller had gained 30 points on LBJ—from 15 points behind to 15 points ahead. Buchanan reasoned it was because Rockefeller avoided television and kept his profile confined to print media. "With no presence on national television, Rockefeller's media consisted of what was written about him.... If he is not in the public eye declaring himself on Vietnam, on the riots, on civil rights, there is no reason for anyone to attack him. Rockefeller's team had stolen our playbook. He had declared his own moratorium on politics, indicated he had no further interest in the presidency, and was concerned only with being a good governor. And the press was buying it." Buchanan, *The Greatest Comeback*, 150.

[11]   In the summer of 1967, both Reagan and Nixon were members of the Owls Nest Camp at the Bohemian Grove. See Lawrence Berkeley National Laboratories Image Library, Collection Berkeley-Lab/Seaborg-Archive. "Breakfast at Owls Nest Camp, Bohemian Grove," July 23, 1967; see also http://imglib.lbl.gov/ImgLib/Collections/Berkeley-Lab/Seaborg-Archive/index/96B05411.html.

"When he was at the Bohemian Grove [in July 1967], Nixon had a talk with Governor Reagan. Nixon told Reagan that he had 'tentative' plans to enter the primaries and that his main goal was to unify the Republican Party so as to beat Johnson. Reagan solemnly agreed that the Party came before anything else. He confessed to Nixon that he was surprised, flattered, and somewhat concerned by the talk about his own presidential chances. Then Reagan showed that although he had been in politics for one year to Nixon's twenty-one, he could dissemble as well as the oldest pro. Reagan told Nixon he did not want to be a favorite son, but figured he would have to in order to assure Party unity in California." Ambrose, *Nixon (Volume Two)*, 118.

"Whatever Reagan's thinking or believing, from time to time he agreed to do something that might help his chance at the nomination.... By June of 1968, when it was much too late, Reagan began to be nibbled by the presidential bug. He had agreed to become a favorite son candidate in California which would allow him to run unopposed in the primary. His stated reason for running—and he believed it—was to avoid a divisive California primary fight between Nixon and Nelson Rockefeller. Others of us wanted him to run as a favorite son because it would give him a significant block of delegates if he ever decided to become a real candidate." Lyn Nofziger, *Nofziger* (Washington: Regnery Gateway, 1992), 71-72.

"A group of leading California Republicans had persuaded [Reagan] to let them place his name on the [California] primary ballot as a favorite son. Their point was to avoid a bruising primary contest among Nixon, Rockefeller, and Romney. That, they convinced Reagan, would only hurt the Republican Party and help the Democrats. So Reagan was on the ballot, but he continued to speak of himself as not a real candidate, while needing to avoid saying or doing anything that would truly have disqualified him from attention." William F. Buckley Jr., *The Reagan I Knew* (New York: Basic Books, 2008), 42-43.

[12] Nixon "campaigned in all eleven of the former Confederate states, and as [columnist David] Broder noted, 'the South provides a base of more than adequate dimensions for a serious [presidential] bid.' There were 279 delegates from the states of the old Confederacy, nearly half the total needed to nominate. Almost all had gone for Goldwater in 1964; in a race between Rockefeller, Romney, and Nixon, Nixon was almost sure to hold them all for himself in 1968.... Although the Southerners would prefer Nixon to either Rockefeller or Romney, their support for Nixon was soft and negative; they figured Nixon was the most conservative Republican candidate they could get who had a chance to win. But Reagan could steal the Southerners, and with them plus California he would be in the commanding position. Reagan then put out the word to key conservative Republican leaders to withhold announcing support for Nixon. Reagan said he was not yet a candidate himself, but his 'let's wait and see' advice convinced many observers that he was considering becoming an active candidate." Ambrose, *Nixon (Volume Two)*, 89, 118.

"[M]any Republicans... can imagine Rockefeller and Reagan deadlocking the convention[.]" See "Anchors Away," *Time*.

"If Rockefeller and Reagan could amass sufficient votes, they, along with favorite son candidates like Romney in Michigan and Governor Jim Rhodes in Ohio, could prevent a first-ballot nomination for Nixon and throw the convention wide open. Should that happen, there was a possibility that, given the conservative character of the post-Goldwater party of 1968, this could produce a stampede to Reagan, once delegates had been released from their obligations to vote for primary winners and favorite sons." Buchanan, *The Greatest Comeback*, 221.

"In late June, *Newsweek* reported its updated projected delegate count.... 'Nixon's followers are nervous about his convention staying power.' If Reagan and Rockefeller held their delegates firmly for two ballots, by the third ballot, 'many Nixon delegates would scatter.... Ronald Reagan... would inherit more than 300 Nixon votes.'" Gene Kopelson, *Reagan's 1968 Dress Rehearsal: Ike, RFK, and Reagan's Emergence as a World Statesman* (Los Angeles: Figueroa Press, 2016), 663.

[13] "I did not believe that after his performance at the Cow Palace in 1964 and his refusal to endorse Goldwater he had a prayer of beating

Nixon. But if a Rockefeller entry was followed by a Reagan entry, they could deadlock the convention." Buchanan, *The Greatest Comeback*, 221.

"By going after the campus radicals, Reagan was capturing the conservatives. And doing so actively, as he set off in the summer of 1967 on an extensive speaking schedule, concentrating on the Goldwater strongholds in the Mountain States, the Midwest, and the Deep South. He began broadening his subject matter and started speaking out on Vietnam." When Nixon saw Reagan "lecture to the university people about their responsibilities, Nixon knew who his chief competitor was, whatever he told the press about Rockefeller or Romney." Ambrose, *Nixon (Volume Two)*, 120.

It "was at Nixon's private January 1967 strategy meeting for 1968 where he had told his supporters that his major competition [for the Republican presidential nomination] would be from Reagan." Kopelson, *Reagan's 1968 Dress Rehearsal*, 362.

Nixon understood that "a surging Reagan would erode [Nixon's] support on the second ballot. Nixon's reputation as a loser would resurface as his candidacy faded on subsequent ballots, while a Reagan vs. Rockefeller battle ensued." Stone, *Nixon's Secrets*, 326.

[14]   Nixon's campaign celebrated its 1968 New Hampshire primary victory in the pine-paneled room of his new Park Avenue campaign office in New York, complete with a rock band, hot dog stand, beer, soft drink dispensers, and a bar. Nixon entered his victory party by walking past an "honor guard" of a dozen "Go-Go Girls for Nixon" in miniskirts. Associated Press, "Nixon Calls it 'Smashing Win'" *Bridgeport Post*, Bridgeport, Connecticut, March 13, 1968.

[15]   At the 1968 Republican National Convention, a candidate needed 668 delegates to capture the presidential nomination. For all of the psychological momentum given a candidate winning the first-in-the nation New Hampshire primary, that state sent a total of only eight delegates to Miami. See *1968 Republican National Convention Telephone Directory and Guide* (Miami: Systems Programing Services, Inc., 1968), 39.

[16]   In February 1968, with the Romney campaign fizzling, Maryland Governor Spiro Agnew announced the formation of a statewide "Draft Rockefeller" movement that he would head. Soon afterward, Agnew

expanded his horizons and formed a national Rockefeller for President Citizens Committee, and he named himself as its chairman. See Chester, Hodgson, Page, *An American Melodrama*, 220.

After the New Hampshire primary, Maryland Governor Spiro T. Agnew met with Rockefeller and came away believing that Rockefeller was ready to enter the presidential race. Rockefeller told Agnew that he would run for president if there was a broad base of support for his candidacy. See Witcover, *Very Strange Bedfellows*, 6.

[17]   In an effort to promote Rockefeller in the New Hampshire primary over Nixon, former New Hampshire Governor Hugh Gregg started a "Write-In Nelson Rockefeller" campaign. On election night, the effort tallied only 11,241 write-ins—a mere 10 percent of the vote. See "1968: McCarthy Stuns the President."

Sweeping 79 percent of the New Hampshire primary vote, Nixon "smother[ed] the last-minute write-in campaign" for Rockefeller. See Associated Press, "McCarthy 4,000 Votes Behind Johnson."

[18]   On Sunday, March 10, 1968, two days before the New Hampshire primary, Rockefeller held a secret meeting in his New York apartment with the leaders of the GOP's liberal wing: seven governors, three former Republican National Committee chairmen, five Members of Congress, three United States Senators, and New York Mayor John Lindsay. See White, *The Making of the President 1968*, 229-230; Chester, Hodgson, Page, *An American Melodrama*, 221.

[19]   After Nixon won the New Hampshire primary, Rockefeller told the press that Nixon deserved his victory and had worked hard for it, but, "[P]olitically I don't think it was very significant because there was no competition[,]" and that New Hampshire was "not a true test" of his strength. Associated Press, "Senator Gets 42% of Vote; President 48%," *Bridgeport Post,* Bridgeport, Connecticut, March 13, 1968.

[20]   Shortly before Rockefeller's final "war council" meeting on March 17, 1968, Rockefeller's senior campaign advisers told him that he had to decide: either he was a presidential candidate or he wasn't, and if he was, he had no choice but to go all out in the upcoming Oregon primary

on May 28. They estimated the cost of a successful Oregon campaign at $600,000. Before convening the war council meeting, Rockefeller met with a group of approximately 20 Oregon supporters. They delivered petitions signed by 51,000 Oregonians urging him to run, and they insisted that their state was winnable as long as Rockefeller committed at least 12 days of personal campaigning there. See Smith, *On His Own Terms*, 515.

21 Oregon Governor Tom McCall spoke for the majority of GOP governors in withholding any formal endorsement of George Romney because, in so doing, it might help get Rockefeller into the race. Smith, *On His Own Terms,* 497.

22 In 1968, if Rockefeller could win the GOP presidential nomination, he stood a strong chance of winning the White House. However, there was little reason to believe he could prevail at the convention. Although he enjoyed great popularity with voters generally, Republican voters did not share that view, and Rockefeller's standing was even worse with the GOP leaders from whose ranks would come the national convention delegates. A November 1967 Harris poll showed Rockefeller beating LBJ 52 percent to 35 percent; the same poll showed GOP county chairmen favored Nixon over Rockefeller five-to-one. One Republican activist, remembering how Rockefeller refused to endorse Barry Goldwater in 1964, said that in 1968 he knew Rockefeller would endorse the GOP nominee—as long as he's the nominee. Chester, Hodgson, Page, *An American Melodrama*, 219.

23 Near the end of the Rockefeller's March 17, 1968 political "war council" meeting, one of his senior aides composed a pair of statements, one announcing Rockefeller was entering the presidential contest, the other announcing he would not. Rockefeller grabbed the "positive" statement and "went flying off like an airplane with one wing." By the time the meeting ended, virtually everyone there expected Rockefeller to run. See Smith, *On His Own Terms*, 515-516.

24 Oregon Governor Tom McCall said he tried to keep the situation "fluid" and have the GOP governors remain uncommitted to Romney because "we can shake the tree and Rockefeller will fall out." Smith, *On His Own Terms*, 497.

CHAPTER 28

¹   A few days before Rockefeller's anticipated presidential candidacy announcement (set for March 21, 1968), Maryland Governor Spiro T. Agnew, the leader of the "Draft Rockefeller" movement, joined Rockefeller for a speech at a Greek Lodge convention. Before the speeches began, Rockefeller pulled Agnew aside and confided that he had decided to run for president. See Spiro T. Agnew, *Go Quietly... or Else* (New York: William Morrow and Co., Inc., 1980), 61.

²   On Monday evening, March 18, 1968, Rockefeller dined at the home of Senator Thruston Morton (R-KY). Rockefeller asked Morton to chair his anticipated presidential campaign. Chester, Hodgson, Page, *An American Melodrama*, 221.

On Tuesday, March 19, 1968, Senator Morton hosted a meeting of 17 senators to meet with Rockefeller to drum up support for his presidential campaign. See, e.g., Chester, Hodgson, Page, *An American Melodrama*, 221-222; see also Smith, *On His Own Terms*, 516.

³   Governor Agnew was not alone in believing Rockefeller would enter the presidential race at his March 21, 1968 press conference. The March 21 morning edition of the *New York Times* reported that Rockefeller would announce his White House bid that afternoon. Witcover, *Very Strange Bedfellows*, 8.

⁴   "Rockefeller appeared utterly calm as he made his [March 21, 1968] announcement [that he would not seek the GOP presidential nomination] to a press conference of between 400 and 500 newsmen, which was televised. Answering questions, he joked and smiled frequently." Associated Press,

"Rockefeller Won't Seek Nomination: N.Y. Governor Leaves Door Open to Draft," *Cumberland News*, Cumberland, Maryland, March 22, 1968.

Rockefeller held his March 21, 1968 press conference announcing that he would not seek the presidency before hundreds of reporters in the West Ballroom of the New York Hilton. White, *The Making of the President 1968*, 231.

[5] On March 21, 1968, Rockefeller told a press conference, "I have decided today to reiterate unequivocally that I am not a candidate campaigning, directly or indirectly, for the presidency of the United States.... We live in an age when the word of a political leader seems to invite instant and general suspicion. I asked to be spared any measure of such distrust. I mean—and I shall abide by—precisely what I say." Buchanan, *The Greatest Comeback*, 223–224; see also Smith, *On His Own Terms*, 517.

At his March 21, 1968 press conference, Rockefeller "left the door open, however, for a draft. He said: 'I have said that I stood ready to answer any true and meaningful call from the Republican Party to serve it and the nation. I still so stand. I would be derelict or uncandid were I to say otherwise. I expect no such call. And I shall do nothing in the future, by word or deed, to encourage such a call.'" He also said that he had ordered his name removed from the ballot for the Oregon presidential primary set for May 28, "filing with the Oregon Secretary of State, an affidavit that he is not a candidate. At the same time, the governor said, he has sent telegrams to the numerous draft-Rockefeller organizations that have formed across the country asking them to halt their efforts on his behalf." Associated Press, "Rockefeller Won't Seek Nomination."

[6] Maryland Governor Spiro Agnew "had invited the press to his office to watch what he expected to be Rockefeller's announcement of [his presidential] candidacy. After hearing Rockefeller's withdrawal, observers noted, Agnew 'just sat there frozen... his jaw open[ed] slightly for a second,' and 'a kind of barely perceptible sick grin [came] over his face for an instant.' 'It made Agnew look like a total fool,' recalled [Rockefeller aide Emmet] Hughes. 'He never forgave Rocky for it.'" See Wainstock, *Election Year 1968*, 51.

"So certain had been Governor Agnew of Governor Rockefeller's positive intentions that he had wheeled into his office a television set and invited capitol newsmen and several friends to watch the speech and kickoff of the Rockefeller campaign in which he would play a large role. Unwarned of the reversal, Agnew was humiliated as ignorant, too unimportant to be taken into the know." White, *The Making of the President 1968*, 231.

Reporter Jules Witcover wrote that with Rockefeller's announcement of non-candidacy, Agnew "was mortified. If ever there was a politician who climbed out on a limb and had it sawed off behind him, that politician was Spiro Agnew. It might not have been so bad had he not confidently invited the local press to share his moment of glory. But here he was, not only naked in his humiliation, but naked on television." See Buchanan, *The Greatest Comeback*, 224.

"Maryland's freshmen Governor Spiro T. Agnew, leader of the draft-Rockefeller effort among the governors, had invited reporters into his Annapolis office to watch [Rockefeller's] televised news conference. Agnew's face reddened [when Rockefeller withdrew his name from the 1968 presidential campaign]. He was placed in the most humiliating position a politician can occupy—a supposed Rockefeller insider, he had not gotten the word. The next day, [Nixon aide Robert Ellsworth] paid a courtesy call, heard Agnew's tale of misplaced trust and resentment, and arranged for the pride-stricken governor to visit Nixon in New York. From that moment, the draft-Rockefeller campaign was dead." Richard J. Whalen, *Catch the Falling Flag: A Republican's Challenge to His Party* (Boston: Houghton Mifflin Company, 1972), 125-126.

7 "An obviously disappointed Gov. Spiro T. Agnew said Thursday he would have to re-evaluate his efforts to draft New York Gov. Nelson Rockefeller for the Republican presidential nomination.... Only Tuesday, [Agnew] opened a national headquarters in Annapolis to coordinate the efforts of the various 'Draft Rockefeller' movements across the country. 'I question the ability of the volunteer groups to hold the enthusiasm that's pouring out all over the country in the face of his announcement today,' Agnew said. But the Maryland governor said he had not changed his position about Rockefeller. 'I think he is clearly the best possible candidate the Republican Party could offer to the electorate in November. I want to be again most candid in stating that I think the chances of his

becoming that candidate in the general election are diminished by what has taken place since the withdrawal of [Governor George Romney],' he said. As to the volunteer groups seeking to draft Rockefeller for the GOP nomination, Agnew said 'We're going to talk with our people, meaning the volunteer leadership over the country. I can't speak for what they're going to want to do, but we'll have a statement, I am sure, to make on the posture of the loose amalgam of volunteer organizations that [have] crystallized over the past week,' Agnew said. Asked whether he would continue his efforts to get Rockefeller into the campaign, Agnew said he wanted 'time to analyze the situation as it has developed. As I indicated to you, this comes as a complete surprise to me. I want a chance to think it over.'" Associated Press, "Disappointed Md. Gov. Agnew to Review Draft Rocky Drive," *Cumberland News*, Cumberland, Maryland, March 22, 1968.

"Gov. Spiro Agnew of Maryland, who had taken the lead among Rockefeller's fellow state chief executives in trying to get him to run, expressed both disappointment and surprise at his decision. 'Greatly disappointed and tremendously surprised,' was the way he put it." United Press International, "Decision Hard Blow to Rocky Backers," *Cumberland News*, Cumberland, Maryland, March 22, 1968.

8   As it turned out, Governor Spiro Agnew was not the only key Rockefeller supporter who believed Rockefeller would announce his presidential candidacy at his March 21, 1968, press conference, only to be left shocked by Rockefeller's eleventh-hour about-face:

- Kentucky Senator Thruston B. Morton, "who had been widely reported ready to run Rocky's [presidential] campaign, said in his Senate office that even he was both 'surprised' and 'disappointed' by the New York governor's news conference announcement. Morton, who didn't know of Rockefeller's negative decision until a telephone call finally reached him after the news conference in New York, said he thought Nixon's nomination was a 'pretty certain bet' now and predicted he would be 'the next president of the United States.'" See United Press International, "Decision Hard Blow to Rocky Backers."

- "Gov. Tom McCall of Oregon, an ardent Rockefeller booster, said in Salem he was 'shocked and dismayed.'" The announcement that Rockefeller would not run for president "caused a major political surprise, not least in Oregon, where leaders of the Draft Rockefeller committee obviously had no advance word. Only minutes before the governor's announcement, William F. Moshofsky, chairman of the committee, prepared a statement saying, 'Obviously we're tremendously pleased and excited about Gov. Rockefeller's announced candidacy.... Clearly he is the man of the hour.'" See Associated Press, "Rockefeller Won't Seek Nomination."

- "Backers of Gov. Nelson A. Rockefeller used two words over and over Thursday to describe how they felt about his decision against actively running for president—'disappointed and surprised.'" United Press International, "Decision Hard Blow to Rocky Backers."

[9] When Rockefeller began his March 21, 1968 press conference, Nixon declined to watch it. He instructed aides Pat Buchanan and Dwight Chapin to view it on their hotel room television and then report back to him with their complete impressions. When they rushed back to Nixon's room with the news that Rockefeller was not running for president, Nixon's response was, "It's the girl," which was a reference to Nixon's earlier statement that he heard Rockefeller had a girlfriend on the side. Buchanan, *The Greatest Comeback*, 224.

[10] On Saturday nights, Nixon like to unwind and talk sports at Toots Shor's, which was a famous Manhattan restaurant and bar located at 51 West 51st Street. See, e.g., Ambrose, *Nixon (Volume Two)*, 25; see generally https://en.wikipedia.org/wiki/Toots_Shor%27s_Restaurant.

[11] Shortly before Rockefeller's scheduled announcement on March 21, 1968, he had received the jarring news that more sophisticated and updated polling from Oregon showed Nixon beating him in that state. See, e.g., Smith, *On His Own Terms*, 516.

[12]   After Rockefeller met with a group of GOP senators in Washington on March 19, 1968, he became irritated by the "attitude, articulated with painful frankness by Senator Hiram Fong.… By all means let Rockefeller spend his money on the campaign, said Fong. It would bring the Party useful publicity and help to elect Dick Nixon." Chester, Hodgson, Page, *An American Melodrama*, 221-222.

Following Rockefeller's March 19, 1968 meeting with GOP senators, "it became painfully clear that most in attendance wanted Rockefeller to run merely to bolster the impact of Nixon's expected primary victories." Smith, *On His Own Terms*, 516.

Nixon campaign aide Pat Buchanan wrote that "[s]omething else might hold Rockefeller back [from announcing for president]: the primary calendar. Should he declare on March 21 [1968], Rockefeller would face Nixon in Indiana on May 7 and in the Nebraska primary on May 14. And Rocky was a mortal lock to lose both. Indiana, where Hannah Milhous had been born, was Nixon country, and Nebraska had been Nixon's strongest state against JFK. [¶] Not until May 28 did the Oregon primary come around, which Governor Rockefeller had won in 1964. But a thrashing by Nixon in Nebraska, two weeks before Oregon, would be a humiliation that would demoralize the Rockefeller supporters in Oregon. Rocky was boxed. For him to enter before the filing deadlines passed for Indiana and Nebraska would be suicidal, drawing him into battle on turf where Nixon not only held the high ground but held unassailable ground. And we were in touch with Nebraska Governor 'Nobby' Tiemann and his Secretary of State. We had their assurances that if Rocky delayed announcing for president until the filing deadline had passed in the Cornhusker State, they would open up the ballot and stick Rocky's name on it so Nixon could give him a thrashing on May 14." Buchanan, *The Greatest Comeback*, 222–223.

[13]   On March 21, 1968, as he was heading out the door of his office to announce his decision not to run for the presidency, Rockefeller told his longtime secretary Ann Whitman, "It's a no-go." Rockefeller asked that his key advisers—including Governor Spiro Agnew—be advised of the final decision before he made the public announcement that he would not run. The person tasked with calling Governor Agnew dropped the ball and

failed to do so. One writer claimed that longtime Rockefeller aide Ted Braun left Agnew off the call list intentionally because he felt Agnew was "notoriously indiscreet." For whatever reason, Rockefeller failed to notify Agnew in advance, which made the out-of-the-loop freshman governor the laughingstock of the Maryland press. Agnew never forgave Rockefeller for the omission, despite Rockefeller's repeated efforts to apologize. See Smith, *On His Own Terms*, 516-517.

14 "First Romney, then Agnew. Twice a crucial Rockefeller friend had become an enemy because of a [Rockefeller] slip[.]" Chester, Hodgson, Page, *An American Melodrama*, 223.

Jules Witcover wrote that almost immediately after Rockefeller humiliated Governor Spiro Agnew by not telling him of his change of plans, "political agents of Richard Nixon [got] in touch with Agnew, eager to field him on the first short bounce." Buchanan, *The Greatest Comeback*, 224.

"[Governor Spiro] Agnew's move towards Nixon began [the moment Rockefeller humiliated him following Rockefeller's March 21, 1968, press conference]." Wainstock, *Election Year 1968*, 51.

"Within a week [of Rockefeller's withdrawal press conference] Agnew was in New York meeting with Nixon." Buchanan, *The Greatest Comeback*, 224.

A week after Rockefeller announced he would not run for president, Nixon met with Agnew for two hours. Later, Agnew told reporters that he still liked Rockefeller, but he praised Nixon and acknowledged him as the undisputed front-runner. See Nixon, *RN*, 300.

15 At his March 21, 1968, press conference, Rockefeller told reporters, "Quite frankly, I find it clear at this time that a considerable majority of the Party's leaders want the candidacy of former Vice President Richard Nixon. And it appears equally that they are keenly concerned and anxious to avoid any divisive challenge within the Party as marked the 1964 campaign. It would therefore be illogical and unreasonable for me to try to arouse their support by pursuing the course of action they would least want and most deplore." Associated Press, "Rockefeller Won't Seek Nomination."

16 Despite Rockefeller's March 21, 1968, press conference, where he announced he would not seek the presidency, the Nixon team remained

unconvinced. "During his disavowal of any intention to run, Rockefeller decried the cynicism of the times and asked America to accept the sincerity of his words…. Well, we were suspicious of his motives, and we did distrust him, and we were right. Six weeks later, Rockefeller declared his availability and was fishing for an alliance with Reagan to block Nixon from being nominated on the first ballot." Buchanan, *The Greatest Comeback*, 224.

"Rockefeller's withdrawal astonished Nixon—'the Boss couldn't believe it,' Buchanan reported, and [Nixon] reacted with public praise of his rival's exemplary devotion to Party unity. But more than a shadow of suspicion lingered that Rockefeller had not really withdrawn. It was true enough, as Nixon told reporters, that the only remaining obstacle to his nomination would be 'my own mistakes.' But he realized that Rockefeller, by seeming to sacrifice personal ambition for the Party's sake, had positioned himself more strongly than ever to take advantage of any serious mistake." Whalen, *Catch the Falling Flag*, 127.

Nixon told the press he was "very much surprised" by Rockefeller's March 21, 1968, announcement that he would not run for president, but he added, "I'm not home yet. I don't take anything for granted." Associated Press, "Rockefeller Won't Seek Nomination."

Rockefeller's "original strategy had called for Romney to wear Nixon down in four contested primaries, after which the Michigan governor would step or be elbowed aside. Rockefeller then would enter the Oregon primary, score a spectacular victory, and ride into the convention aboard his cresting popularity in the polls. He would claim to be the only Republican who could win in 1968, and the delegates would put hopes of victory above revenge and nominate him. Romney's [early] collapse had wrecked the timetable and strategy for stopping Nixon." Whalen, *Catch the Falling Flag*, 126.

CHAPTER 29

[1]   During the 1968 campaign, "[Nixon] liked to use flying time for work, and sometimes just for thinking; when he wanted to talk, he would usually signal it by opening the conversation himself. Often he sat for long periods absorbed in thought, then suddenly launched into a conversation that might last moments, or might last hours." See Price, *With Nixon*, 20–21.

[2]   When traveling on commercial airlines, "Nixon would usually want me to take the aisle seat, so that I could provide a sort of a buffer between him and other passengers who might recognize him and would want to chat. For anyone as well known and readily recognizable as Richard Nixon, this could become a problem." Price, *With Nixon*, 20–21.
    Leonard Garment described his initial impression upon meeting his new law partner when RN joined the firm in the early 1960s: "Nixon was a figure out of history, still powerful and at the same time down-to-earth[.]" Garment, *Crazy Rhythm*, 69.

[3]   "On a plane, [Nixon] usually traveled with his briefcase on his knees, dipping into it for things he wanted, using it as a writing desk when it was closed, scratching ideas on the yellow legal pads that were his trademark." Price, *With Nixon*, 20–21.

[4]   On March 31, 1968, when LBJ announced we would not run for reelection in 1968, Nixon was flying aboard his chartered campaign jet. Since his plane was equipped with a radio, he and his staff heard the speech live, and that gave him time to contemplate a response for the press before landing at La Guardia Airport in New York. When he arrived, he made this comment: "I assume that this clears the way for someone with

President Johnson's viewpoints on Vietnam to enter the race." Although he didn't speculate on who that someone would be, Nixon knew: instead of LBJ now standing between him and the White House, it would be LBJ's vice president, Hubert Humphrey. See Chester, Hodgson, Page, *An American Melodrama*, 5-6.

5   Upon hearing the news that LBJ would not run, Nixon told reporters, "This is the year of the dropouts. First Romney, then Rockefeller, now Johnson." Buchanan, *The Greatest Comeback*, 232.

6   In late 1967, Nixon said, "Johnson will have it tough in '68. We had to run against his promises in 1964. Now we can run against his performance." See "Anchors Away," *Time*.

"If Nixon did win the nomination in 1968, [he believed] his almost certain opponent would be Lyndon Johnson. The prospect delighted Nixon, because Johnson was vulnerable on so many fronts and because Nixon, more than any other Republican, could goad LBJ into overreacting." Ambrose, *Nixon (Volume Two)*, 90.

"Gallup's most recent sampling shows that only 38 percent of the nation likes the way L.B.J. is handling the presidency—an all-time low for him and a long way from the 80 percent approval he enjoyed in January 1964." See "Anchors Away," *Time*.

7   After LBJ's withdrawal from the 1968 campaign, "[f]or a day or so, RN couldn't understand it. He had expected to face a bloodied, beatable opponent, either Johnson or Kennedy—preferably Bobby, because he wanted to beat a Kennedy. Johnson's withdrawal left him a bit scared. Now he couldn't be sure whether it would be Kennedy or Humphrey." Whalen, *Catch the Falling Flag*, 143.

8   "Bobby was nothing like his charismatic brother, nor had he any of JFK's conservative and centrist appeal. By 1968 he had moved far to the left to attract the students and antiwar movement and he was savaging his own president. I did not think he could unite his Party." Buchanan, *The Greatest Comeback*, 220-221.

"Nixon was greatly pleased by Robert Kennedy's plunge into the race and said two or three times: 'We can beat that little S.O.B....' If Kennedy were nominated, it would deliver the South to the Republicans.... Among other things, Kennedy had the liability of being a single-issue candidate. 'Johnson could take the war away from him in a minute—and then what..?' Throughout our conversation, it was clear that Nixon was not worried [about Robert Kennedy's candidacy]. If Bobby were nominated, he said, it would offer the chance to indict the whole JFK-LBJ tenure ('right back to the Bay of Pigs'). He showed no hesitancy about taking on the brother of the man who had beaten—and awed—him in 1960." Whalen, *Catch the Falling Flag*, 96-97.

Nixon campaign staffer John Ehrlichman related a cryptic comment from Nixon as he watched RFK declare his presidential candidacy. "On March 16, [1968,] evidently encouraged by the proof that Johnson was vulnerable, Senator Robert Kennedy entered the Democratic race. Nixon was in Portland, Oregon, that day; he watched Kennedy make his announcement on the hotel-room TV. John Ehrlichman, who was present, recalled that when the set was turned off, Nixon sat and stared at the blank screen. He finally shook his head and said, 'We've just seen some very terrible forces unleashed. Something bad is going to come of this. God knows where this is going to lead.'" Ambrose, *Nixon (Volume Two)*, 145; see also John Ehrlichman, *Witness to Power: The Nixon Years* (New York: Simon and Schuster, 1982), 40.

[9]   In his later years, Nixon recalled, "The Kennedys were not admirable people.... They simply were not nice. The legend is that Jack was always gracious, charming, dashing.... Bull. [JFK] spit on waiters and ignored or screamed at the help.... I remember attending a dinner once and watching Bobby [Kennedy]—who was the smartest and also the meanest [of the Kennedys]—throw his meal on the floor and right at a waiter because he didn't like it. [Longtime Nixon friend Bebe Rebozo] knew the Kennedys, and they used to socialize when they were in Key Biscayne. All of [the Kennedys] used to treat the help like crap, and I mean they were mean.... Bobby was the worst.... He was a bastard." Crowley, *Nixon Off the Record*, 32.

[10]   Nixon later said that LBJ "had guts, but not enough to run again in '68. He left me a mess, but at least he fought the goddamned North Vietnamese. A lesser president may have packed it in." Crowley, *Nixon Off the Record*, 18.

[11]   Nixon viewed LBJ as "tough, tough, tough…. He was a patriot, but he was a calculating bastard." Crowley, *Nixon Off the Record*, 17.

Nixon later described LBJ as "a totally political animal. He told me once, 'People don't support you because they like you. You can count on a person's support only when you can do something for him or to him.' He lived by that rule…. Johnson was not a good man, but he made decisions from his gut, and he tried." Crowley, *Nixon Off the Record*, 18.

[12]   After Lyndon Johnson announced that he would not be a candidate in 1968, Nixon speechwriter Ray Price wrote Nixon a memo: "We should now be laying whatever groundwork we can for enlisting at least [Johnson's] tacit support in November if the Democratic nominee should turn out to be Kennedy." Ambrose, *Nixon (Volume Two)*, 151.

[13]   LBJ, in contemptuous and unflattering remarks, told others he thought that Humphrey made a weak and unreliable presidential candidate, and that the Republicans would crush him in November. See, e.g., Dallek, *Flawed Giant*, 570-571; White, *The Making of the President 1968*, 278-279.

In later years, Rockefeller revealed that on April 23, 1968—three weeks after he withdrew from the 1968 campaign, LBJ snuck Rockefeller and his wife into the White House for a private dinner at which LBJ urged him to change his mind and run for president. LBJ told him he couldn't sleep at night thinking about Nixon becoming president, and he wasn't all that sure about his own vice president, Humphrey. See Smith, *On His Own Terms*, 528.

At their private White House dinner in early 1968, after lamenting the deficiencies of the Democratic candidates, LBJ told Rockefeller "he could only sleep well if Nelson Rockefeller were president." When Mrs. Rockefeller balked, LBJ took her for a walk around the White House; when they returned to where Rockefeller awaited, LBJ told him that he talked her into letting him run. "Rockefeller returned to Albany and the following week called a news conference and announced he had changed his mind and was running for president." Boyd and Holcomb, *Oreos & Dubonnet*, 79-81.

[14] LBJ took an unusual interest in the GOP nomination battle, albeit for a secret reason. His first choice for the presidency in 1968 wasn't a Democrat—it was a Republican: Nelson Rockefeller. "The two men had a high regard for each other. Johnson saw Rockefeller as a sensible moderate.... He also believed that Rockefeller was the one man who could beat Bobby Kennedy, no small asset in Johnson's mind." Dallek, *Flawed Giant*, 544.

[15] Rockefeller said that during his April dinner with LBJ, the president promised that if Rockefeller got into the race, he would never campaign against him. "He was very friendly about '68, and very supportive of me for '68," he recounted. Dallek, *Flawed Giant*, 545.

[16] On March 22, 1968, one day after Nelson Rockefeller withdrew from the presidential campaign, "a group sprang up like flowers out of a rock [telling him,] 'You can't let this happen!' The prime mover was John Hay Whitney [one of America's wealthiest men, who] managed to round up on behalf of Rockefeller a good cross section of the old-money WASP business aristocracy... of the country. [¶] Quite independently, a short while later, Rockefeller was approached by leaders of that other great financial oligarchy, the liberal Jewish business leaders in New York. These are not Republicans by habit and inheritance.... What they said, in effect, through various intermediaries, was: 'We would rather be with you than with Humphrey, but we have to be for someone who isn't Nixon. We have to know now, because if you don't go, we will have to go for Humphrey. Are you going to do it or not?'" Chester, Hodgson, Page, *An American Melodrama*, 379-380.

"The thing that most changed Nelson Rockefeller's mind between early March and late April [1968]... was that, for the first time, he felt he was being asked to run. For the first time in his life, he had widespread national support in the business world. [¶] By the middle of April, Rockefeller was again seriously considering running." Chester, Hodgson, Page, *An American Melodrama*, 380-381.

[17] LBJ gave this insight into how he saw Nixon's political chances in 1968: "Nixon can be beaten. He's like a Spanish horse who runs faster than anyone for the first nine lengths and then turns around and runs

backward. You'll see, he'll do something wrong in the end. He always does." Kearns Goodwin, *Lyndon Johnson and the American Dream*, 351.

"There were, in 1968, primaries in a dozen states, but some of those were already tied up by favorite-son candidates, most importantly California for the Republicans by Reagan. The majority of delegates would be picked in the non-primary states by the state committees." Ambrose, *Nixon (Volume Two)*, 104-105.

[18] In 1966, Nixon "carefully chose those districts in which he campaigned, and for the most part picked districts that were traditionally Republican but have been lost to the Democrats in the Goldwater catastrophe. With or without Nixon, most of these districts were going to go back to the GOP in 1966; by campaigning for the Republican candidate in such a district, Nixon could make it appear he was the only one who made victory possible." Ambrose, *Nixon (Volume Two)*, 80–81.

[19] "Rockefeller's professionals did not bother to keep up pretenses. They knew that Nixon had a long lead and that they had only one persuasive argument going for them. As a matter of preference, the great majority of Republican delegates would take Nixon if they could. Rockefeller's only hope was to persuade these men that taking him would make the difference between victory and defeat. His people had to put across the idea that Rockefeller could beat a Democrat and Nixon could not. [¶] There were two ways of selling this case. The first, the orthodox way, would be the direct method. Get out and make their pitch to the politicians.... It was not going to be easy. It was not even going to be possible unless [they] could produce evidence. [¶] Therefore, Rockefeller... had to appeal to the people over the heads of the politicians. But he was going to do it in a different way. The central idea of his strategy was simple, bold, and rational. It was too late to bind delegates by primary victories. And it was unlikely that he would be able to persuade enough delegates directly. Therefore, he must use the media to influence public opinion—for the opinion, it should be noticed, of Democrats and Independents as well as Republicans. That would be reflected in the polls, and the polls in turn could be used as a compelling argument with the delegates. But the whole venture turned on whether, at the end of the day, the polls showed, not merely that Rockefeller was more popular than Nixon, but that Rockefeller

could win and Nixon could not." Chester, Hodgson, Page, *An American Melodrama*, 381-382.

[20]   In a memo to Rockefeller from his new media team, they told him that his entire candidacy rested on the promise of giving the Republican Party a choice. It became their central task to make clear that Nixon's haziness on issues might be natural, but it was not accidental: "It is [Nixon's] deliberate intent to blur the issues between you and him. We must not conspire with him in doing this.... This means that your public utterances essentially must be aimed at your standing in the polls—not the presumed preconceptions of delegates.... The governor is not going to win delegates by sounding more and more like Richard Nixon. He cannot out-Nixon Nixon." Chester, Hodgson, Page, *An American Melodrama*, 385-386.

Rockefeller's 1968 presidential hopes rested on producing "sixty-second spot television commercials for early–and late–evening time in thirty key markets. These spots would be precisely aimed at the very people most likely to react favorably when questioned about Rockefeller by Gallup and Harris. [¶] [Rockefeller's media team] also recommended approximately three minutes a week of national network television advertising for the seven weeks of the campaign. Correctly used, they argued, television 'is the most emotionally evocative of all media....' Three network minutes a week, they calculated, would bring Nelson Rockefeller into 90 percent of all American homes." Chester, Hodgson, Page, *An American Melodrama*, 386.

"These were the two sides to Rockefeller's campaign: the orthodox campaign of direct delegate persuasion, and the effort to persuade indirectly through the polls. As soon as he announced, he set out on a furious three months during which he met and talked to delegates in forty-five states.... He tried to persuade them, not to come out for him, but to stay loose." Chester, Hodgson, Page, *An American Melodrama*, 382.

[21]   Rockefeller calculated that, at the Miami convention, he might have (at best) 400 votes; he needed a few hundred more to block a Nixon victory on the first ballot, and he knew where to get them. The success of his candidacy depended on two things: 1) Reagan entering the race, and 2) Reagan remaining in the race. Rockefeller needed Reagan to show strength in the Southern delegations; in tandem, the two combined might be able

to hold enough delegates to deny Nixon a first ballot convention victory. Ironically, the game plan for the conservative Reagan was the same as that of the liberal Rockefeller: ally to stop Nixon, and then take off the gloves as to each other. As Theodore White noted, "If both Rockefeller and Reagan did their best, they would meet after Nixon's destruction in Miami and clash for the soul of Party and country. It was Miami that would test their rival dreams." White, *The Making of the President 1968*, 236.

In 1968, "Rockefeller and Reagan shared a common strategy: to slow me down, brake my momentum, and buy time for a final attack at the convention in Miami Beach." Nixon, *RN*, 303.

According to the Rockefeller campaign projections, Reagan needed to collect 267 delegates to combine with Rockefeller's projected 400 for the Rockefeller-Reagan "blockage" theory to work. As the favorite son candidate from California, Reagan was assured of all 86 delegates from the Golden State. They would need 181 additional delegates for the anti-Nixon plan to prevail. See White, *The Making of the President 1968*, 239.

[22] In reality, the author found no evidence that Rockefeller considered Maryland Governor Spiro Agnew as a potential 1968 running mate. The person leading Rockefeller's list of vice presidential possibilities was moderate U.S. Senator Charles Percy (R-IL). See Smith, *On His Own Terms*, 636.

[23] When GOP activists howled over Rockefeller's change of heart and later entry into the presidential contest, he shrugged: "In 1960 they say I dropped out too soon; in 1964 they say I stayed in too long. Well, this year I've done both!" Smith, *On His Own Terms*, 529.

[24] "Governor Nelson A. Rockefeller, reversing his previous position, threw himself into contention Tuesday for the Republican presidential nomination and vowed to fight Richard M. Nixon for it, 'right up to the last vote.' [¶] 'I now commit myself to seeking this office—and so serve our nation—with all my heart and mind as well.... The country has changed. Never in history has so much changed in five weeks. Now I'm giving the people an option.' [¶] [H]e set forth four reasons for reversing himself: 1) 'The gravity of the crises that face us as a people.' 2) His conviction that 'to comment from the sidelines is not an effective way to present the alterna-

tives.' 3) He said many persons, 'within the Republican Party and outside it,' urged him to get in the fight. 4) 'Personally, I am deeply disturbed by the course of events—growing unrest and anxiety at home, and the signs of disintegration abroad....' The news conference, which was nationally televised, sounded at times like a combination of a victory celebration and a national nominating convention. The Red Room in the state capitol was jam-packed and so were the corridors outside. There were about 100 newsmen and perhaps double that many spectators and supporters of the governor in the room." Associated Press, "Rocky Reverses—'In Race to Win,'" *Salt Lake Tribune*, May 1, 1968.

"On April 30, [1968,] Nelson Rockefeller, who six weeks earlier had asked the nation to take his declaration of non-candidacy seriously, and not cynically, declared his availability for the Republican nomination. The filing deadlines for Indiana, Nebraska, and Oregon had passed. Rocky had ducked an open-primary fight with the man he and his staff had for years been calling a loser." Buchanan, *The Greatest Comeback*, 256–257.

The Associated Press offered these reactions from other candidates to news of Rockefeller's late entry into the 1968 campaign:

- Richard Nixon: Rockefeller's candidacy "will make for a more exciting convention and will result in a more meaningful discussion of the issues. He can conduct a very vigorous campaign from his strong position as governor of New York, but I think I'll win the nomination."

- Ronald Reagan: "Rockefeller's action does not change his own position that [Reagan] is not a candidate and cannot foresee any change before convention time. The California governor said, however, that Rockefeller's entry helps assure that no candidate will lock up the nomination before the national convention."

- Robert F. Kennedy: "Obviously it gives the Republican Party a choice, and that's good. It's a matter for the Republicans and I'm not going to have anything further to say on it."

- Eugene McCarthy: "Do I have to comment every time he comes in or out?" Associated Press, "Rocky Entry Sparks GOP Enthusiasm," *Salt Lake Tribune*, May 1, 1968.

"On April 30, Rockefeller announced that he was back in the race. Publicly, Nixon welcomed his entry. Privately, he worried not about Rockefeller but about Reagan. The California governor would certainly be tempted to join Rockefeller in a stop-Nixon movement. It was equally obvious that the right wing of the Party preferred Reagan to Nixon. [¶] Not that Nixon went into a panic; far from it. He showed a public confidence that was justified. All spring his chief delegate hunters… had been lining up Nixon votes…. Of course, they also made it clear that the bandwagon was under way, and that there would be a better spot on it for those who climbed aboard early." Ambrose, *Nixon (Volume Two)*, 153.

[25] On April 30, 1968, Rockefeller entered the campaign for the GOP presidential nomination. Massachusetts Governor John Volpe was an early Nixon supporter, but he insisted on running in the Massachusetts primary as a favorite-son candidate. Rockefeller humiliated Volpe by not only beating the incumbent governor in his own state, but he did it as a write-in candidate. This gave Rockefeller all 34 of the state's delegates to the national nominating convention and a great boost to his day-old campaign. See Nixon, *RN*, 302. [Author's note: What Nixon left out of this passage in his memoirs was that he had run a distant third as a Massachusetts primary write-in, trailing behind both Rockefeller and Volpe. See Associated Press, "Election Results Hint at Realignment," *North Adams Massachusetts Transcript*, May 2, 1968; see generally, Smith, *On His Own Terms*, 529.]

CHAPTER 30

[1]   Jerome Wolff, Leonard Matz, and Bud Hammerman were onetime close associates of Maryland Governor Spiro Agnew. When investigators discovered their participation in a bribery and kickback scheme with Democrat Baltimore County Executive Dale Anderson, the three former Agnew friends negotiated with the United States Attorney in Baltimore to mitigate their punishments. They agreed to implicate Agnew in exchange for leniency. By the time the allegations against Agnew became public, he was vice president of the United States. Several years after Agnew resigned the vice presidency following his plea of no contest to a single count of income tax evasion (October 10, 1973), he obtained documents relating to the federal investigation against him under the Freedom of Information Act. Only then did he learn about the prosecutorial pressure exerted on these and other investigatory targets. Agnew later said that if he had known this information, he would never have entered into a plea bargain. For more information on the Agnew case from both the prosecution's and from Agnew's perspective, see generally Witcover, *Very Strange Bedfellows*; see also Agnew, *Go Quietly... or Else.*

CHAPTER 31

[1]   On the campaign plane, and after one drink, Nixon once blurted out a spontaneous expression of affection for Asians: "I love those little brown people!" Nixon was not much of a drinker, and after one, it might appear to a listener that he had five. "Nixon worked so hard, was wound up so tight, was so exhausted from his work that, when he let down, all it took was one or two [drinks] to make it appear he was sloshed when his blood alcohol level night have passed a police sobriety test." Buchanan, *The Greatest Comeback*, 210-211.

Speechwriter Ray Price confirmed Nixon's uninhibited expression of affection for "those little brown people" after unwinding from a grueling schedule with a couple of martinis, no doubt due to Nixon's low tolerance for alcohol. See Price, *With Nixon*, 28.

[2]   Nixon's law partner and campaign aide Leonard Garment confirmed Nixon's low alcohol tolerance: On election night 1966, "One by one the senior members of the staff were invited to visit Nixon, who was alone, stretched out on the bed, a phone in one hand and a highball in the other.... Nixon [was] by then reasonably well oiled (it didn't take much to do the trick)[.]" See Garment, *Crazy Rhythm*, 115.

Nixon himself recognized the need to use alcohol sparingly on the campaign trail. "During the 1966 campaign, Nixon told a reporter that he sometimes had one beer after speaking, but never any alcohol of any kind before. 'When I'm campaigning,' he explained, 'I live like a Spartan.... I've seen a lot of people who drink. They get up there and talk too long. I speak without notes, and I can't do that without intense concentration before and during the speech.'" Ambrose, *Nixon (Volume Two)*, 85.

3   Bob Finch "was never welcomed into Reagan's inner circle in Sacramento, because he was more liberal than Reagan and 'his old ties to Nixon
made him suspect by the Reagan men looking toward the presidency.'
[¶] Finch's attitude for Reagan's favorite son status was described as a
'formality,' which was subject, 'like all such candidacies, to withdrawal
on later ballots or even, if the situation warranted it, before the balloting
began.'" Kopelson, *Reagan's 1968 Dress Rehearsal*, 619.

4   Longtime Nixon aide Ray Price described RN's personality: "One part
of Richard Nixon is exceptionally considerate, exceptionally caring, sentimental, generous of spirit, kind. Another part is coldly calculating, devious,
craftily manipulative. A third part is angry, vindictive, ill-tempered,
mean-spirited. [¶] Those of us who have worked with Nixon over the
years often referred to his 'light side' and his 'dark side.' The calculating,
devious, manipulative parts are ones that I assign to neither side: These
are necessary tools of statecraft.... Almost invariably, [Nixon's] rages were
directed at one aspect or another of the 'double standard'—the standard
that judged him harshly and his opponents leniently for the same actions.
He wanted to be trusting, but he had had his trust too often abused. He
had been burned too often by the press, and he reacted humanly rather
than superhumanly. He accumulated resentments. Most of the time he
hid them. Sometimes he let them show." Price, *With Nixon*, 29.

5   "That early primary season... [w]e developed a fairly general pattern:
two or three weeks of intense campaigning, then off for a weekend of rest,
recuperation, thinking, and planning in the Florida sun. Nixon had not
yet bought the house on Biscayne Bay that would later become the Florida
White House. Rather, he headquartered at the Key Biscayne Hotel. Key
Biscayne [in 1968] was still quiet, relaxed, informal, an unpretentious
barefoot haven a world away from the glitter and tinsel of nearby Miami
Beach." Price, *With Nixon*, 28.

6   President-elect John F. Kennedy traveled to the Key Biscayne Hotel to
meet Vice President Richard Nixon one week after the 1960 presidential
election. They met and conferred in Villa 69 of the hotel. See Merriman
Smith, United Press International, "Kennedy, Nixon Talk, Agree to Meet
Again," November 14, 1960, http://www.upi.com/Archives/1960/11/14/

Kennedy-Nixon-talk-agree-to-meet-again/9384085259041/.

"In his memoirs, Nixon said that Kennedy began their [post-election conversation at the Key Biscayne Hotel] by saying, 'Well, it's hard to tell who won the election at this point....' But former Nixon aide [General Don Hughes, who was with Nixon during this meeting with JFK] suspects there was another reason for the meeting. 'I think President-elect Kennedy wanted to be sure that perhaps there was not going to be a recount.... I think that was probably the real purpose of the meeting.' Nevertheless, Hughes says Nixon's choice to let the election results stand was wise. 'The whole country was in effect split down the middle if you will. It would have been harmful to the country to contest the election... to put our system on trial would not have been good for us.' Ultimately, Nixon himself was at peace with his decision. 'Then and all the times that I talked to him about it afterwards,' says [1960 campaign press aide Herbert] Klein, 'he never had any regrets. He felt it was the right decision for the country.'" "Nixon and the 1960 Election," ABC News 20/20, November 11, 2000, http://abcnews.go.com/2020/story?id=124208&page=1.

7   As the 1960 Republican presidential nominee, Vice President Nixon pledged to become the first candidate to campaign personally in all 50 states. He later regretted making and fulfilling the pledge, because he wasted valuable campaign time and resources traveling to states behind him solidly instead of concentrating on the swing states. See Nixon, *RN*, 216, 223; see generally White, *The Making of the President 1960*.

In 1968, "Relatively infrequent appearances in New Hampshire (he made twenty altogether) gave Nixon time to rest and to campaign elsewhere, which was one of the major benefits of the new strategy he adopted for 1968. An even greater benefit was that his changed techniques allowed him to go over the heads of the reporters and television commentators directly to the people. He found he liked doing that very much. He got his opportunity to do so by seizing on a plan that [chief of staff] Bob Haldeman suggested to him in a memorandum some months earlier. [¶] Haldeman's memorandum consisted of a brutal criticism of the 1960 campaign and a recommendation for new methods in 1968. No matter how hard a candidate worked, according to Haldeman, he could at best talk directly to a million or two voters, as Nixon had done in 1960. 'The reach of the individual campaigner doesn't add up to diddly-squat in votes.' Nixon's heroic physical effort had sapped his inner strength and vitality, pushed him beyond the realm of good judgment. 'We started Nixon off in 1960 sick and under medication and then we ran his tail off.' [¶] The right way, Haldeman wrote, was to use television to the maximum while keeping direct voter and reporter contacts to a minimum. One minute on the network evening news would reach more people than three months of barnstorming. Nixon would have to make only one speech a day to provide the necessary footage." Ambrose, *Nixon (Volume Two)*, 137-138.

8   In the autumn of 1967, Roger Ailes worked as a producer on the *The Mike Douglas Show* when he booked Nixon for a guest appearance on the program. While chatting with Ailes in the green room, "Nixon said it was a shame a man couldn't get elected president without a gimmick like TV. Ailes assured him the medium was here to stay. If Nixon didn't grasp that, and figure out how to turn it to his advantage, he would never get to the White House." The Nixon campaign hired Ailes to produce Nixon's television ads during the 1968 campaign, and "[t]he result was the *Man in the Arena* campaign.... Ailes staged a series of town meetings with selected audiences and prescreened citizen questioners who lacked the guile (and, in many cases, hostility) of the political press. *Man in the Arena* made it possible for Nixon to control his media environment." Zev Chafets, *Roger Ailes Off Camera* (New York: Sentinel, 2013), 32-33.

"Understanding the nature of [television] would be especially crucial to Nixon's 1968 campaign, for television, if misused, was the cruelest of all media.... Nixon the stump speaker—lawyerlike, earnest, intense, perspiring, forced—was Nixon at his absolute worst, all wrong for the cool television medium. On the other hand, Nixon more or less at ease, talking informally, one on one, was close to the 'personal' Nixon whom we found surprisingly congenial." Garment, *Crazy Rhythm*, 130.

"[T]he immediate problem was how to use Nixon effectively on [television]. Nixon's reputation was that he was experienced and able, but unelectable, because he handled television badly. When people thought of Nixon and television, they recalled... the 1960 debates with Kennedy, and the [1962] 'last press conference.' These were devastating images.... But if Nixon was not all that good by himself, or one-on-one, or with reporters, there were times when he was outstanding. Speaking to large audiences, he was smooth, professional, outgoing, and impressive. His punch lines would make the evening news, and have an impact. Nixon was also good in a small-group situation, so long as that group did not consist of reporters.... So the staff decided on a format that came to be called the Hillsboro approach, after the small town in New Hampshire where it was inaugurated. Nixon's people recruited a dozen or so citizens and gathered them together as a panel in the Hillsboro Town Hall.... Nixon sat down facing the group of panelists and took questions.... One great beauty of the whole format was that the staff could cut it up into five-minute segments for later broadcasting, leaving the embarrassing or awkward moments in the trash can.... With this format, Nixon could run a national campaign that relied exclusively on staged television events and excluded the press corps." Ambrose, *Nixon (Volume Two)*, 138-139.

Jules Witcover wrote, "In 1968 [Nixon] would severely limit his appearances.... With television becoming increasingly dominant in presidential politics, Nixon would hold relatively few public appearances each day, almost always well scripted, and timed early enough in the day and located conveniently enough to major airports for television crews to ship their film of the events by air to the network shows in New York." Stone, *Nixon's Secrets*, 302.

Pat Buchanan developed a thesis: "Nelson Rockefeller's rise in the polls was due to the absence of television exposure. If this were true, it raised the question whether Nixon really needed to seek access to the tube. TV commentators, magazine articles, and newspaper editorials were doing a much better job of selling Rockefeller than he could himself, Buchanan argued in a memo. 'The conservatives hate the old Rocky. But the old Rocky must have died because no one sees him in the flesh any more. We do read about a different person now, whom the press tells us about, a fellow without ambition, a happy family man, the most popular Republican in the country.' In Rockefeller's shunning of television, Buchanan saw lessons for Nixon. 'We don't need TV to prove we are the most experienced, most qualified and most able; we don't need TV to get ourselves known; we don't need it to demonstrate we have the looks and the glibness. Do we need the damn thing at all and do we want it? Yes. But only to do the job we want it to do. We want it controlled....' Buchanan urged that Nixon try to control the subject matter during his television appearances. 'To destroy the myth that RN is mean and that he places politics ahead of principles, RN ought to get on shows where he can kid himself, where he can talk about family, where he can crack jokes about past foibles. On other shows, he ought to talk about problems, dismiss questions about primaries.... In short, use TV to convey the impression that RN isn't thinking about New Hampshire or Wisconsin, but about Harlem and Appalachia.'" Whalen, *Catch the Falling Flag*, 62.

[9]   Senator Strom Thurmond softened his position on segregation, but the author was unable to find any reference to Thurmond "apologizing" for his past position (unlike Alabama's George Wallace, who later repented publicly his earlier support for segregation). However, Thurmond did change with the times, as even his most virulent critics acknowledged. "Thurmond never apologized for his segregationist past. But he did make some amends—and win some black votes—by becoming the first former Dixiecrat on Capitol Hill to hire an African-American staffer." David Welna, "Strom Thurmond at 100: Colorful South Carolinian Set Record as Oldest Living U.S. Senator," *National Public Radio,* December 5, 2002, http://www.npr.org/templates/story/story.php?storyId=865900.

"Clearly, Thurmond made shrewd accommodations late in life to changing times. In the 1970s, he became the first Southern senator to hire a black staff aide and to sponsor a black man for a federal judgeship. In the 1980s, he voted to reauthorize the Voting Rights Act (not because he agreed with it but in belated deference to 'the common perception that a vote against the bill indicates opposition to the right to vote.'). Strom also came to support making the birthday of Martin Luther King (about whom he'd once said, 'King demeans his race and retards the advancement of his people.') a federal holiday." Timothy Noah, "The Legend of Strom's Remorse," *Slate*, December 16, 2002, http://www.slate.com/articles/news_and_politics/chatterbox/2002/12/the_legend_of_stroms_remorse.html.

"Thurmond seemed to blame all of society's ills—'crime in the streets, a free rein for communism, riots, agitation, collectivism and the breakdown of moral codes'—on the 'Supreme Court's assault on the Constitution.'" Jack Bass and Marilyn W. Thompson, *Strom: The Complicated Personal and Political Life of Strom Thurmond*, New York: PublicAffairs, 2005, 200.

10   Former Governor and U.S. Senator Edwin L. Mecham (R-NM) (1912–2002) shared with the author this memory of the Senate attempting to pass the 1964 Civil Rights Act. Texas Senator Ralph Yarborough tried "to get a quorum for a subcommittee hearing to start consideration of the civil rights legislation. He would call a session with no quorum, get on the phone, send pages, and even go into the hall to try to find a subcommittee member to lure [into the hearing room]. One such was Strom Thurmond, who was resistant to Ralph's effort to pull him into the session. Strom decided the invitation had gone far enough, so he offered to wrestle Ralph in the hall of the beautiful Old Senate Office Building, with the loser to abide by the wishes of the other. Ralph agreed, and Strom then threw him in about three seconds. Ralph complained that Strom had a head start and wanted another fall. Strom agreed, and quickly threw Ralph again, helped him up, brushed him off, and walked away." E.L. Mecham, letter to the author, July 3, 1991: see Rogan, *And Then I Met,* 312-313.

11   "[Strom] Thurmond was the leading anti-communist in the U.S. Senate and was quite well-known across the South as an early segregationist. Importantly, he was also every bit as well known and revered in the South as [former Alabama Governor George] Wallace." Stone, *Nixon's Secrets,* 321.

At the 1968 Republican National Convention, a candidate needed 667 votes to win the nomination; 334 of those delegate votes came from the Southern states. See, e.g., Chester, Hodgson, Page, *An American Melodrama,* 434-438; see also "Anchors Away," *Time.*

12   "While [Harry Dent, aide to South Carolina Senator Strom Thurmond] had always liked Reagan, he believed Nixon would ultimately be the better candidate. It was tough to sell Thurmond on the proposition, however, for Thurmond was as enamored of the former movie actor has anyone. 'I love that man,' he once said [of Reagan]. 'He is the best hope we've got.' (Reagan had given a magnificent performance the previous year at a South Carolina GOP fund-raising rally in Columbia, stirring Republican hearts and erasing the Party's debt in one evening's work.)" Nadine Cohodas, *Strom Thurmond & The Politics of Southern Change* (New York: Simon & Schuster, 1993), 396.

In late 1967, the South Carolina Republican Party invited Reagan to

speak in Columbia "because the state Party had been $40,000 in debt....
[They] needed Reagan to come to South Carolina 'to get that note paid
off.' [¶] At the airport, Reagan received a 'big and enthusiastic greeting.'
Reagan was greeted by a crowd of 500. At the main event, the Republican
finance dinner held for 3,000 supporters at the Columbia Township
Auditorium, 'the auditorium rocked with the jubilation of a triumphal
political rally when Governor Reagan was escorted in.... [Thurmond
aide Harry Dent] recalled that Reagan had 'set Republican hearts afire.'
The $100-a-plate dinner had netted $150,000 and was described as 'the
largest political fund-raising event in state history.' The *New York Times*
reported that Dent was 'enthusiastically supporting Mr. Reagan for the
presidential nomination.' One newspaper reported that Reagan was 'the
greatest thing to come along since corn pone and hog jowls.'" Kopelson,
Reagan's 1968 Dress Rehearsal, 276-277

"[Reagan's] delirious [1967] reception in South Carolina two weeks
ago [shows] the apparent readiness of Southern Republicans to jilt faithful
old Dick Nixon if the charismatic Californian will only whistle[.]" See
"Anchors Aweigh," *Time.*

When Reagan met with Southern Republican Party leaders, although
he did not commit himself to running for president, "his personality and
conservatism made the Southerners hearts throb." Bass and Thompson,
Strom, 210-211.

"At any moment in 1967, had he chosen, Ronald Reagan might
have captured this bloc of Southern delegates and deadlocked the [1968
Republican presidential] nomination[.]" White, *The Making of the President 1968*, 239.

13 In late 1967, despite Reagan's continued denials that he was a candidate
for president, *Time* magazine noted, "Reagan's professed noncandidacy
[does not] jibe with his heavy speaking schedule in key primary states
and his decision to become California's favorite son. 'If the Republican
Party came beating on my door,' he admits, 'I wouldn't say, *Get lost, fellows.*'" See "Anchors Away," *Time.*

After the debt-retirement dinner for the South Carolina GOP, "Dent
and Thurmond met privately with Reagan... for the critical true purpose
of the trip.... The conversation went nowhere. Thurmond asked spe-

cifically and repeatedly as to Reagan's presidential plans. The governor's response was vague.... [A] critical opportunity with Thurmond was lost.... [H]ad Reagan affirmatively told them that he was running for president in 1968, the entire course of history might have been different.... 'Had [Reagan] asked for support in the atmosphere of the occasion, charged with his presence, the Californian would have received it from us then and there....' For Thurmond, although Reagan did not commit to running, 'his personality and his conservatism made hearts throb.'" Kopelson, *Reagan's 1968 Dress Rehearsal*, 277-278. 280, 530.

"Although [Reagan] had approved hiring [campaign staff for a possible 1968 GOP presidential nomination run] and putting out feelers, in his mind he was not, as he later admitted, ready to be president.... Despite all our efforts Reagan remained adamant about not running for president [in 1968].... In private Reagan did talk of being willing to accept a draft, and at that stage in his career he even believed that such a thing could be legitimate." Nofziger, *Nofziger*, 65-66, 69.

When Reagan's press secretary Lyn Nofziger and other aides tried to coax him into running in 1968, Reagan told them, "Feels kinda premature, fellows, I just don't think I'm ready." Edmund Morris, *Dutch: A Memoir of Ronald Reagan* (New York: Random House, 1999), 355.

"[L]ess than two years after being elected governor, Reagan launched a stealth, well-funded, tenacious, and hard-fought bid to snatch the presidential nomination from former Vice President Richard Nixon. He used Governor Nelson Rockefeller as a pawn to try to deadlock the convention so delegates would turn to [him]." Stone, *Nixon's Secrets*, 317.

To those who urged him to enter the presidential race, "Reagan said he was not yet a candidate himself, but his 'let's wait and see' advice convinced many observers that he was considering becoming an active candidate." Ambrose, *Nixon (Volume Two)*, 118.

As 1968 Reagan campaign surrogates Frank Whetstone and Anderson Carter "politicked through the West, they would drop the word that Reagan was running for president. Local reporters would call [Reagan press secretary Lyn Nofziger] in Sacramento, all excited at their scoops, and asked me if it were true. I would deny it, and they would write stories saying Reagan was going to run for president, even though his spokesman, Lyn Nofziger, denied it. I would then get ahold of Frank and Andy, tell them they'd done good work, and urge them to keep it up. Which they did." Nofziger, *Nofziger*, 68.

[14] "[In 1967], when Reagan met with [Southern GOP leaders], he was unwilling to go on record as a [presidential] candidate, clearing the path [to move South Carolina Senator Strom] Thurmond toward Nixon." Cohodas, *Strom Thurmond*, 396.

[15] "Nixon met with [Southern] Party leaders in Atlanta, and [Thurmond aide Harry] Dent made sure Thurmond attended. Nixon responded to questions about court appointments (he promised to appoint 'strict constructionists') busing of schoolchildren for purposes of integration, protecting the textile industry, law and order issues, communism, national defense, and building the Party in the South. Thurmond liked Nixon's answers. He rode in the car with Nixon to the airport and followed up the visit with a public commitment." Bass and Thompson, *Strom*, 210-211.

Following the Thurmond-Nixon meeting in Atlanta on June 1, 1968, "as the two men and their aides were standing in the hotel lobby ready to leave, Nixon asked Thurmond to accompany him to the airport. The senator accepted, and the ride immediately took on larger significance. When reporters saw the candidate welcome the symbol of the new Republican South into his car, they assumed the two men were in the midst of brokering a political deal to enhance Nixon's standing in the region. But [Thurmond aide Harry] Dent, who was intimately involved in the episode, had insisted that no such thing occurred. The airport ride was icing on the cake, the final thank-you. While that may have been true, the picture of these new allies huddled together in the car nonetheless sent a much louder message about political alignments. [¶] Thurmond was now ready to throw his support to Nixon—exactly what Dent believed was necessary to blunt a third party challenge from George Wallace. Who better to throw a body block against this rabid Southerner than an equally forceful Southerner who had once been a third-party candidate himself?" Cohodas, *Strom Thurmond*, 396-397.

[16] At the end of the workshop of Southern GOP leaders in Atlanta [held on June 1, 1968], Strom Thurmond told reporters that Nixon was a great man and a great candidate, but stopped short of an endorsement. United

Press International, "Wallace Through? Nixon Points Up," *Kingsport Times-News*, Kingsport, Tennessee, June 2, 1968.

"[Harry Dent, longtime aide to South Carolina Senator Strom Thurmond] had spoken to Thurmond and reaffirmed that the senator would support Nixon…. Nixon met with those Party leaders in Atlanta, and Dent made sure Thurmond attended. Nixon responded to questions about court appointments (he promised to appoint 'strict constructionists') busing of schoolchildren for purposes of integration, protecting the textile industry, law and order issues, communism, national defense, and building the Party in the South. Thurmond liked Nixon's answers. He rode in the car with Nixon to the airport and followed up the visit with a public commitment." Bass and Thompson, *Strom*, 210-211.

[17]   After the June 1, 1968 Southern GOP leadership workshop in Atlanta, Nixon came away with the endorsements of both the Tennessee and Oklahoma Republican state chairmen. These two states would send 50 delegates to the 1968 Republican National Convention. See United Press International, "Wallace Through? Nixon Points Up."

[18]   On June 1, 1968, Senator Strom Thurmond met with Nixon, and he liked Nixon's views on national defense and strengthening local and state governments. "Most important, [Thurmond] believed Nixon could win the 1968 presidential contest…. He also believed that only Nixon could win the election for the Republicans, and a GOP victory would move the country and the Supreme Court to the right." Bass and Thompson, *Strom*, 209.

On June 1, 1968, Nixon flew to Atlanta to meet with Senator Strom Thurmond and other Southern leaders. They discussed school busing, liberal federal judges imposing unending burdens on Southern states in the name of civil rights, and national defense policy. Nixon promised that they would be in on the consultations for, and have a say in, Nixon's selection of a vice president and Cabinet members, later federal appointments in their states, and he assured them that he would help build the blossoming GOP in the still-Democrat-dominated South. After reassuring the Southern leaders, Nixon left the meeting knowing he had secured the nomination. White, *The Making of the President 1968*, 138.

[19] "On June 22, [1968,] Strom Thurmond endorsed Nixon and announced that all of South Carolina's twenty-two delegate votes would be cast for him. He said he stood with Nixon on issues including domestic lawlessness, Vietnam, the rise in the cost-of-living, Supreme Court overreach, and the need for the nation to maintain its military strength. Thurmond said 'he did not agree with Nixon on every single issue,' but added '[h]e is the most acceptable and electable candidate.' Thurmond said he had 'no harsh words' for [third party candidate George] Wallace, but he knew the Alabama governor had little chance of being elected president." Stone, *Nixon's Secrets*, 323.

Thurmond endorsed Nixon after Nixon promised him a significant say in U.S. Supreme Court nominations and to take Thurmond's advice on defense-related matters. See Smith, *On His Own Terms*, 537.

During the 1968 campaign, Reagan campaign adviser F. Clifton White remembered "a conversation I had with Strom Thurmond after he came out for Nixon. 'Senator, what are you doing? Ronald Reagan is your kind of candidate.' [¶] 'Mr. White,' he answered in his courtly Southern manner of addressing everyone formally, 'if we don't get behind Dick now, that fellow Rockefeller's gonna make it.' [¶] 'That's not true, not true at all.' I was visibly agitated. 'I know most of these delegates and they'll swing over to Reagan.' [¶] 'Well, you may be right, son, but we just cain't take that chance and let Rockefeller slip in.'" White and Tuccille, *Politics as a Noble Calling*, 177.

CHAPTER 32

¹   "Reagan Welcome Rally / Governor and Mrs. Reagan Arrive Tonight, Saturday, August 3 [1968] / Rally begins at 8:00 p.m. / Governor Reagan's plane arrives at 8:30 p.m. / Come to the end of Concourse One, Miami International Airport / Dixieland Music and a Speech by Governor Reagan." Original flyer distributed by "Youth for Reagan" volunteers, 1968 Republican National Convention, August 3, 1968 (Author's collection).

"Reagan led the... California delegation into the convention city. They came in four planes from various sections of the state, Reagan arriving on a plane which left from Los Angeles. He plunged into meetings with leaders and will make a round of various state delegations before the opening gavel falls Monday morning." Walter Trohan, "Final Campaigns are Opened for Nomination," *Chicago Tribune*, August 4, 1968.

At the 1968 GOP Convention, the California delegation quartered in Miami's Deauville, Sherry Frontenac, and Monte Carlo hotels. See 1968 Republican National Convention Telephone Directory and Guide, 24.

²   CBS News taped their Sunday morning, August 4, 1968 *Face the Nation* broadcast with Ronald Reagan at Miami's Fountainbleau Hotel. See Kopelson, *Reagan's 1968 Dress Rehearsal*, 784.

On Sunday, August 4, 1968, the day before the start of the 1968 GOP Convention, Reagan appeared on the CBS News show *Face the Nation* and "calmly insisted that he was not running for the nomination against Nixon and Nelson Rockefeller. Nor was he interested in the No. 2 spot; he much preferred being governor of the nation's No. 1 state." See Morris, *Dutch*, 357.

3   "Although Nixon had a near lock on the Republican nomination well before the 1968 convention, in December of 1966 nobody had a lock on anything, or so a few of us around Reagan believed. Thus in early December a meeting convened in the Reagan residence to discuss the possibility of making the governor-elect, who had yet to serve a day in public office, the next president of the United States of America. [¶] The perpetrators of this affair were Tom Reed and [Lyn Nofziger]. Others present were Reagan [and five other senior advisers and donors]. The outcome of the meeting was that the fat cats agreed to let Reed enlist the aid of F. Clifton White to survey the situation and, if it seemed at all reasonable, to begin to put together some sort of a draft organization…. As a result of the December meeting a low-key, unofficial, and easily deniable 'Reagan for President' organization was hatched that functioned all the way to the 1968 Republican National Convention in Miami Beach." See Nofziger, *Nofziger*, 65-66.

Before the 1968 GOP convention, Reagan had Southern delegations flown to Sacramento to meet with him personally. As Nixon later related, Reagan made ideological appeals that were difficult for them to resist. Once the convention began, Reagan continued dropping in on their delegation meetings and charming them. See Nixon, *RN*, 309.

In late 1967, despite Reagan's continued denials that he was a presidential candidate, *Time* magazine noted, "Reagan's professed noncandidacy [does not] jibe with his heavy speaking schedule in key primary states and his decision to become California's favorite son." See "Anchors Aweigh," *Time*.

"Reagan traveled thousands of miles, gave dozens of speeches, and even reached out to arch-liberal Republican Governor Nelson Rockefeller in a bid to stop Nixon and turn the 1968 convention in his favor." Stone, *Nixon's Secrets*, 370.

As Frank Whetstone and Anderson Carter "politicked through the West they would drop the word that Reagan was running for president. Local reporters would call [Reagan press secretary Lyn Nofziger] in Sacramento, all excited at their scoops, and asked me if it were true. I would deny it, and they would write stories saying Reagan was going to run for president, even though his spokesman, Lyn Nofziger, denied it. I would then get ahold of Frank and Andy, tell them they'd done good work, and urge them to keep it up. Which they did." See Nofziger, *Nofziger*, 68.

[4]   For a more in-depth analysis of the 1952 Eisenhower-Taft Republican presidential nomination battle, and the role Nixon played in delivering the California delegates to Ike despite his pledge of support to California Governor Earl Warren, and William F. Knowland's refusal to abandon his pledge to Warren in exchange for the vice-presidential offer of Senator Taft, see Gayle B. Montgomery and James W. Johnson, *One Step from the White House: The Rise and Fall of Senator William F. Knowland* (Los Angeles: University of California Press, 1998); see also Stone, *Nixon's Secrets*, 77-89.

[5]   During the 1968 GOP Convention, Reagan's campaign command center was on the 16th floor of the Deauville Hotel. See White, *The Making of the President 1968*, 240.

[6]   At a press conference on the opening day of the 1968 GOP Convention, former Senator William F. Knowland told reporters that he had proposed the California delegation resolution urging Reagan to become an active candidate "because many delegates from other states told him they would back Reagan if they were sure [he] was an outright candidate. Knowland told a news conference... that many delegates had asked him if Reagan 'actually is going to let his name stay in.'" Associated Press, "California Delegation's Resolution Forced His Hand, Reagan Claims," *Santa Cruz Sentinel*, Santa Cruz, California, August 6, 1968.

[7]   Reagan press secretary Lyn Nofziger "would tell the story of how he managed to launch Ronald Reagan's first presidential campaign [in 1968]. He and Tom Reed had been plotting this moment since 1966, despite repeated demurrals from [Reagan].... Funds had been coaxed out of [two major donors], a network of paid or pledged operatives established nationwide, and a secret campaign office opened in San Francisco. [¶] All that was lacking, as the primary season got underway, was a public gesture from the governor that would give him gravitas and turn him overnight from a favorite son with eighty-six convention delegates into a major contender with three hundred or more. Such a gain could only come at the expense of Richard Nixon, whom Nofziger and Reed saw as

a vulnerable front-runner, banking on many political IOUs and tagged with the image of a loser." See Morris, *Dutch*, 355.

In 1968, "[m]y feeling was that Reagan had to strike while the iron was hot, to put it tritely. I was afraid that if he waited too long, like, for instance, until 1972, it would be too late—if a Republican were elected president in 1968 Reagan would have to wait until 1976 to run. And by that time, after two terms as governor if reelected in 1970, he would be wearing ten years worth of political scars. He would also be sixty-five which, in my innocence, I thought a little too old to be seeking the presidency. In contrast, in 1966-67 he was a hot political figure, the natural successor to the aging and irascible and forever defeated Barry Goldwater." See Nofziger, *Nofziger*, 67.

8   Clif White, who directed the Barry Goldwater delegate operation in 1964 and now trolled the 1968 GOP convention state delegations for Reagan, nose-counted only 550 firm first-ballot votes for Nixon. With 667 votes needed to nominate, this was good news for Rockefeller, especially when CBS News estimated Rockefeller had 400 votes without having entered any primaries. See Smith, *On His Own Terms*, 530.

"Reagan at the top of the ticket becomes more of a possibility when it is realized that the South and West will have more votes than the Midwest and the Northeast at [the 1968 GOP convention in] Miami Beach (682 to 634)." See "Anchors Aweigh," *Time*.

9   During the 1968 GOP convention, reporters overheard Reagan chief delegate counter Clif White say optimistically, "All we need is just one break—one state switching to Reagan—and we've got him." Chester, Hodgson, Page, *An American Melodrama*, 457.

10   "Former Sen. William F. Knowland, now a California newspaper publisher, introduced the Reagan resolution at a closed caucus of the 86-vote California delegation yesterday afternoon. It was adopted without debate. Reagan did not attend the meeting. 'After consulting and canvassing the floor, I went to Gov. Reagan personally,' Knowland said. '[Reagan] said this is a matter for the delegation to decide.'" Associated Press, "California Delegation's Resolution Forced His Hand, Reagan Claims," *Santa Cruz Sentinel*, Santa Cruz, California, August 6, 1968.

[11]   On the opening day of the 1968 Republican National Convention, at a hastily called press conference in the Napoleon Room of the Deauville Hotel, William F. Knowland announced that the California delegation had passed a resolution asking Reagan to end his favorite-son status and seek the presidential nomination actively. See Kopelson, *Reagan's 1968 Dress Rehearsal*, 789.

[12]   Lyn Nofziger, Reagan's 1968 press aide, remembered that at the 1968 GOP Convention, "On nomination day the late William Knowland came to me with an idea. Knowland was a former U.S. senator, a one-time Senate majority leader, and publisher of the *Oakland Tribune*, and a man who had seen his own presidential hopes dashed when he lost a gubernatorial race to Pat Brown in 1958. At the moment he was a member of the California delegation. [¶] His idea was simple. Reagan should announce that he was no longer just a favorite son and throw his hat in the ring in earnest. I said, let's go see Reagan. We did. Reagan liked the idea and made the decision without further consultation. It was dumb of me to take Knowland to Reagan without bringing in… any of the [senior strategists]. And it was dumb of Reagan not to call [them]. After all, Knowland had proved in 1958 that he wasn't the smartest politician around. But the decision was made and Reagan became a full-fledged candidate, nearly a year too late and well over a dollar short…." Reagan's last-minute presidential candidacy "put [his] friend and fellow governor, Paul Laxalt of Nevada, in an awkward spot. Even though he was pledged to Nixon, Laxalt had agreed to second Reagan's nomination as a favorite son candidate, but when Reagan announced he was running in earnest Laxalt came to him and said he could no longer second him. It was the proper thing to do but his decision upset the people around Reagan." Nofziger, *Nofziger*, 73-74.

At the 1968 GOP Convention, Reagan "indeed tossed his hat in, impulsively, believing that Nixon could not win on the first ballot." Morris, *Dutch*, 358.

"Another declared opponent entered the field against Mr. Nixon when Gov. Ronald Reagan of California announced he was a real, rather than a favorite-son, candidate. This surprised virtually no one[.]" Tom Wicker, "Nixon Makes a New Gain as Republicans Convene; Reagan Avows Candidacy; Drops Favorite Son Role," *New York Times*, August 5, 1968.

"California Governor Reagan dropped his coyness and formally announced his candidacy for the nomination. Reagan and his forces had been active during the summer, courting Southern state delegations and siphoning off support [from Nixon].... Columnist Rowland Evans told him that Ohio Governor James Rhodes said after Reagan's announcement, 'It's a new ball game.'" Bass and Thompson, *Strom*, 213.

"To no one's surprise, on August 5 [1968] Reagan flew into Miami to announce that he had dropped his favorite-son status to become an avowed contender for the nomination. Playing the role of drafted candidate, Reagan summoned up all his onstage shyness as he professed to have been bowled over by the spontaneous and unsolicited support he had received." Ambrose, *Nixon (Volume Two)*, 169.

[13] "Reagan was smiling and full of pep when he made his [1968 presidential candidacy] announcement, remarking, 'this is the year of political surprises.'" Associated Press, "California Delegation's Resolution Forced His Hand, Reagan Claims," *Santa Cruz Sentinel*, Santa Cruz, California, August 6, 1968.

"As of this moment," Reagan declared at a press conference on the first day of the 1968 GOP Convention, "'I am a candidate before this convention.' With that statement, the 57 year-old first-term governor abandoned the favorite son role he had played for more than a year while traveling throughout the nation for Republican appearances.... Reagan moved after the California delegation voted 85 to 0 to ask him to declare his active candidacy." Associated Press, "California Delegation's Resolution."

[14] At his 1968 GOP convention presidential campaign announcement press conference, Reagan said he decided to run "at the delegation's request and not as part of a preconceived plan. 'I want you to know that the resolution came as a complete surprise out of the blue,' Reagan said." Associated Press, "California Delegation's Resolution."

CHAPTER 33

¹ "On July 21 [1968], with the Republican Convention only two weeks away, Nixon showed how confident he was of winning the nomination by disappearing from public view. He flew out to Los Angeles and stayed in a private oceanside home at Newport Beach. [Aide Bob] Haldeman told the press [Nixon] was working on his acceptance speech.... On July 26, Nixon flew to Washington, at the president's request, for a briefing on Vietnam from Johnson.... From Washington, Nixon flew to New York and drove to the eastern tip of Long Island, where he sequestered himself in a five-room cottage at Montauk Point. There he went to work on his legal pads, creating a Republican platform. On his walks along the beach, he thought about his acceptance speech." Ambrose, *Nixon (Volume Two),* 166.

While Nelson Rockefeller and Ronald Reagan "assumed battle line commands [in Miami] in their drives for the Republican presidential nomination[,] far off in the wings—at Montauk on Long Island—Richard Nixon appeared to be displaying supreme confidence in his own candidacy by staying away from this convention city until Monday." Walter Trohan, "Final Campaigns are Opened for Nomination," *Chicago Tribune,* August 4, 1968.

"In his fishing village retreat [at Montauk] on Long Island, Nixon's phone has been busy. He has talked to key members of various state delegations and been in touch with his strategy team." Russell Freeburg, "Rocky's 'Halt Nixon' Plan—Secret Hot Line to Reagan Camp Set Up at Parley: Staff Ordered to Shadow Leading GOP Figures," *Chicago Tribune,* August 4, 1968.

Nixon spent nearly three days secluded in a rented cottage at the east end of Long Island before the start of the 1968 GOP Convention.

Among other things, he told reporters he spent his time "sorting out the great issues." Russell Freeburg, "Bartlett Withdraws, Endorses Nixon," *Chicago Tribune*, August 4, 1968.

2   Richard Nixon wrote his 1968 Republican Convention nomination acceptance speech in Skippers Cottage at Gurney's Inn, Montauk, New York. See Natasha Wolff, Room Request! Gurney's Montauk Resort & Seawater Spa, *DuJour Newsletter*, http://dujour.com/lifestyle/room-request-gurneys-montauk-resort-seawater-spa/.

3   "Nixon had gone into seclusion at Montauk, there to walk the beach, inhale the salt air he loved, and compose his acceptance speech. Each of the writers had been asked to contribute material for the speech, but Nixon intended to assemble it unassisted. (When reporters asked what the candidate was doing, [Pat] Buchanan said the Boss was fine. 'He called this morning, said "send over more yellow pads," and hung up.')" See Whalen, *Catch the Falling Flag*, 194.

4   "Some of Nixon's supporters were fearful that Reagan would steal the South at the last minute, and grumbled that Nixon's absence at a time when he should have been leading the fight might cost him the nomination. [¶] Nixon stayed calm. When he arrived in Miami... he was smiling and confident, and the confidence was justified. The Nixon juggernaut was functioning smoothly. [His delegates] were holding the line." Ambrose, *Nixon (Volume Two)*, 169.

    "While Nixon secluded himself at Montauk Point, Rockefeller and Reagan managed to create some anxiety and thus provide some badly needed suspense to the convention. Rumors ran rampant—Reagan was supposed to have swayed this or that Southern delegation, Rockefeller to have hidden strength here and there. Senator Percy, to Nixon's surprise, endorsed Rock-efeller. [¶] Nixon stayed on Long Island. He relied on [his] political staff to keep his delegates in line." Ambrose, *Nixon (Volume Two)*, 167.

5   "One complication [at the 1968 GOP Convention] is that fifteen men, controlling 666 votes (one short of the needed 667 [votes to win the nomination]), will be going to the convention as favorite sons." See "Anchors Away," *Time*.

6   Reflecting back on Nixon's convention strategy, Pat Buchanan wrote in 2014, "Even if we came up short on the first ballot, the favorite-son delegations would then be released, and there were Nixon loyalists in every one, including Rockefeller's New York, Romney's Michigan, and Reagan's California. We would go over the top on the second ballot. As for a Rockefeller-Reagan alliance, I did not see how it worked. Reagan's people would never accept the nomination of Nelson Rockefeller, who had damaged and then deserted Barry Goldwater. And to Rockefeller's people, Reagan was the Goldwater of 1968. My sense was that if Rockefeller started gaining traction, Reagan's forces would throw in with us. And if Reagan looked like he was about to stampede the convention, the moderates and liberals would panic and come to us. The Rockefeller and Reagan forces might be working together, but neither would accept the other's man. And neither Rockefeller nor Reagan would take second spot on the other's ticket. Had they thought this through to the end game? [¶] Indeed, if the two should stop Nixon and deadlock the convention, the delegates would be looking to a centrist candidate who could unite the Party. That would bring them back to Nixon. Their dilemma: If they stopped Nixon they would get Nixon. The Boss was yet again in the catbird seat." Buchanan, *The Greatest Comeback,* 302–303.

7   On the first day of the 1968 GOP Convention, Monday, August 5, Maryland Governor Spiro T. Agnew dropped his favorite-son status and endorsed Nixon. United Press International, "GOP Convention Opens Amid Fast and Furious Politicking," *Panama City News-Herald,* Panama City, Florida, August 6, 1968.

On the first day of the 1968 GOP Convention, "gossiping delegates and reporters [saw as significant] Mr. Nixon's gains—particularly the announcement of Gov. Spiro T. Agnew of Maryland that he would support the former vice president. Informed sources reported that the Maryland governor's final decision was made when he got Mr. Nixon's promise that he could make the formal nominating speech Wednesday night." Wicker, "Nixon Makes a New Gain."

8   "This is Your Invitation to Meet Dick Nixon and His Family / Arrival Reception Monday Night 7:00 p.m. / Hilton Plaza Hotel / 5445 Collins Avenue / Miami Beach." (Author's collection). As of 2021, the old Hilton

Plaza Hotel building still stands, but it has been converted into rental vacation suites and condominiums. See, e.g., https://designsuitesatcastlebeach.com/about-us/.

[9] "Outside the Hilton, Nixon's convention headquarters, the hired man dressed in an Uncle Sam costume walked about on stilts. The hired brass band blared away, and a gaggle of Nixonettes lured by the prospect of being noticed, pranced and cheered. The neatly dressed crowd at the entrance raised limp hurrahs, but mostly they gawked at perspiring musicians, the stilt-walker, and the inevitable baby elephant." Whalen, *Catch the Falling Flag*, 192-193.

Author Norman Mailer recounted Nixon's arrival at the Hilton Plaza in Miami for the 1968 GOP convention: "Nixon had come in earlier that day. A modestly large crowd, perhaps 600 at the entrance to the Miami Hilton, two bands playing 'Nixon's the One,' and the Nixonettes and the Nixonaires, good clean blonde and brown-haired Christian faces... a cluster of 2,000 balloons going up in the air... and Nixon himself finally in partial view at the center of the semicircle of camera's held overhead. Just a glimpse: he has a sunburn—his forehead is bright pink." Mailer, *Miami and the Siege of Chicago*, 34.

[10] "During the 1960 campaign, an elephant had relieved itself in front of the platform from which [Nixon's] vice-presidential candidate Henry Cabot Lodge was to speak. The crowd, standing downwind, thinned quickly, leaving Lodge puzzled and upset. Then his patrician nostrils twitched, and he too fled. The episode prompted a contingency plan. Now the advance men in Nixon campaigns, following instructions in their manual, gave every prop-elephant a precautionary enema. [At the 1968 GOP Convention] I crossed this beast's path without mishap and entered the Hilton." Whalen, *Catch the Falling Flag*, 192-193.

[11] During the 1968 GOP Convention, Nixon stayed in the penthouse on the 18th floor of the Hilton Hotel. See Whalen, *Catch the Falling Flag*, 196.

"Nixon was said by aides to be working on his speech accepting the nomination [in] his penthouse on the eighteenth floor of the Hilton Plaza hotel[.]" Associated Press, "Nixon Holding Lead as Balloting Begins:

Tabulation Shows Top Commitment," *Florence Morning News*, Florence, South Carolina, August 8, 1968.

During the 1968 Republican National Convention, Nixon's campaign hierarchy occupied the top four floors of the Hilton hotel. "To prevent incursion by the press and our opponents, we took stringent security measures, including fencing off the fire escapes, to safeguard the top four floors, where Nixon... and our convention staff would have offices." Ehrlichman, *Witness to Power*, 41.

Nixon speechwriter Richard Whalen has a slightly different memory than campaign manager John Ehrlichman of how many Hilton floors the Nixon team occupied. "The enormous Nixon staff had taken over three floors in the Hilton (the overflow was scattered among smaller hotels), and we were carefully sorted, filed, and labeled. My room was on the seventeenth floor, reserved for Nixon's personal staff, and a large sign over the door bore my name. (This proved to be a great convenience in the early-morning hours as we returned, unsorted and unfiled, from the nightly roundup of un-Republican parties.) There were several telephones in the room, variously connected to the hotel switchboard, the 'secure' Nixon switchboard in the eighteenth floor solarium, the research-and-writing command post, and others on the Nixon staff." Whalen, *Catch the Falling Flag*, 193.

During his research, the author attempted to determine in which suite of the Miami Hilton Plaza Hotel Nixon stayed and worked on his acceptance speech. The answer, Penthouse B, came from two sources. Former *Life* magazine photographer David Douglas Duncan, covering the 1968 GOP Convention for NBC News, knew Nixon since their days stationed overseas during World War II. His photographs taken of Nixon watching himself nominated for the presidency, putting the final touches on his acceptance speech, and meeting with GOP leaders to discuss his vice presidential choice, show that Nixon used Penthouse B of the Hilton Plaza Hotel. See David Douglas Duncan, *Self-Portrait U.S.A.* (New York: Harry N. Abrams, Inc., 1969), 63-87. The Associated Press reported that Nixon worked on his acceptance speech in Penthouse B of the Hilton Plaza Hotel in Miami. See Associated Press, "Like a Space Shot, Pat [Nixon] Says," *Florence Morning News*, Florence, South Carolina, August 8, 1968.

[12] "When Nixon got to his penthouse suite at the Hilton Plaza Hotel, he called [campaign manager John] Mitchell. 'John, what's the count?' he asked. [¶] Mitchell chuckled and replied, 'I told you that you didn't need to worry, Dick. We've got everything under control.'" Ambrose, *Nixon (Volume Two)*, 169.

[13] "The corridors and stairways [of Nixon's hotel headquarters] were patrolled by private guards from the Wackenhut Corporation in powder blue uniforms and snappy Air Force-type hats. We at once dubbed them 'the Wackenhut SS,' which wasn't quite fair. Many of them were college students and all were unfailingly courteous. Indeed, they were a bit embarrassed to be jumping up and challenging us at every turn. (Soon, girls on the staff began fraternizing and passing soft drinks and sandwiches to the guards stationed on the sweltering stairwells, and our working environment became less 'secure' but more human.)" Whalen, *Catch the Falling Flag*, 193.

[14] The day Reagan dropped his favorite-son candidacy and announced he would seek the presidential nomination, "[California] Lt. Gov. Robert H Finch, who managed Nixon's 1960 presidential campaign and is now a California delegate, said many of the California delegates feel that Reagan's announcement eliminates the commitment they made to support him as a favorite son. Asked if Reagan's decision ends the favorite son commitment, Finch replied, 'Many of the delegates feel that way. That will be discussed in our caucus.' Finch said the 'California delegates will vote for Reagan on the first ballot, but the problem will come after the first ballot when delegates want to cast their own votes....' Reagan acknowledged rumors that Nixon supporters on his state slate are restive, but denied he jumped into the race to hold the delegation behind him." Associated Press, "California Delegation's Resolution Forced His Hand, Reagan Claims," *Santa Cruz Sentinel*, Santa Cruz, California, August 6, 1968.

The California delegation's deputy chairman, William French Smith, a Reagan loyalist, "told the press that his delegates were holding firm for their favorite son, Reagan, with 'absolutely no' defections." Kopelson, *Reagan's 1968 Dress Rehearsal*, 780.

[15] Nixon thought the impetus of Reagan's entry into the nomination contest came from "the people around him [wanting] him to run. He

hadn't made up his mind. So far as Nixon could tell, the Goldwater forces were not flocking to him. If [Reagan] didn't enter the primaries… he would be asking the convention to take him on image and faith. Goldwater had told Reagan bluntly that the Democrats would destroy him on the issue of experience. Reagan, like Rockefeller, was an attractive but unreal candidate, whose chance might come only if Nixon faltered." Whalen, *Catch the Falling Flag*, 12.

[16]   When Richard Nixon arrived in Miami Beach for the 1968 GOP Convention, South Carolina Senator Strom "Thurmond was there to greet him and ready to warn him of serious problems. The *New York Times* had run a story that morning speculating that if nominated, Nixon would choose as his running mate one of three men—New York's Rockefeller, New York City Mayor John Lindsay, or Illinois Senator Charles Percy. All represented the Party's liberal wing." This developed "confusion and panic among Nixon's Southern delegates. The *New York Times* story 'went through [the convention floor] like wildfire….' [T]he slogan of Reagan supporters was: 'The double cross is on, the double cross is on.'" Bass and Thompson, *Strom*, 212.

[17]   Interestingly, the telegram Senator Strom Thurmond sent to Southern delegates in an effort to get them to hold fast for Nixon made no mention of the vice-presidential running mate panic caused by that morning's *New York Times* story speculating that Nixon would choose a liberal as his running mate: "Richard Nixon's position is sound on law and order, Vietnam, the Supreme Court, military superiority, fiscal sanity, and decentralization of power. He is best for unity and victory in 1968. Our country needs him, and he needs our support in Miami. See you at the convention. Strom Thurmond, U.S. Senator." Stone, *Nixon's Secrets*, 328.

[18]   "[A] new catchword began making the rounds in Miami Beach: *erosion*. Both Rockefeller and Reagan had an interest in convincing delegates that I had not yet sewn up the nomination, and they joined forces to attempt to show that my strength was eroding and that I was losing delegates…. [T]he marriage of convenience between Rockefeller and Reagan was now operating at full force. Rockefeller worked the Northern and Midwestern states while Reagan tried to breach my Southern flank."

Strom Thurmond and John Tower held the Southern delegates for Nixon. Tower called it "the thin gray line that never broke." Nixon, *RN*, 309.

[19]   Even the *New York Times* conceded that it was "difficult to continue describing as a loser a man who is so overwhelmingly powerful that no challenger will even take him on." Buchanan, *The Greatest Comeback*, 213.

Ward Just of the *Washington Post* wrote: "What is the trouble with Richard Nixon? He wins the presidential primaries in New Hampshire, Wisconsin, Indiana and Nebraska by staggering majorities—in each case by more than 70 percent of the vote. He forces George Romney out of the race, then lures Nelson Rockefeller into an in–out–and–in–again performance so indecisive and amateurish Adlai Stevenson looks in retrospect like Napoleon.... [Nixon] must be America's only major political figure who can win 70 percent of a state's vote and have the analysts talking about his opponent's 23 percent. Yet it happened in Nebraska with Gov. Reagan." Buchanan, *The Greatest Comeback*, 260–261.

In a shot at Rockefeller's dithering, when Nixon announced his presidential candidacy, he said that every candidate should make their case "in the fires of the primaries." Buchanan, *The Greatest Comeback*, 209.

After Nixon checked into his suite at Miami's Hilton Plaza for the 1968 GOP convention, South Carolina Senator Strom Thurmond shared his concern about the rumor Nixon might choose a liberal running mate. Nixon dismissed the senator's worries. He also wasn't bothered by Reagan's candidacy, assuming that any move toward Reagan would cause Rockefeller supporters to move his way. Later, Thurmond aide Harry Dent told Nixon that the *New York Times* article claiming Nixon would pick a liberal had caused numerous defections all day to the Reagan camp. "Dent recalled that Nixon was 'startled' by the Reagan gains. Others in the room similarly felt Nixon truly was 'stunned' by the news of the onslaught of more and more defections in the South, and then the meeting suddenly became 'panicky.'" Kopelson, *Reagan's 1968 Dress Rehearsal*, 792, 795.

"Called the loser, he had entered and won every primary. Told Rockefeller was stronger, he took the lead from Rocky among independents. Told he could not win the fall election, he was showing up in the Gallup polls as the strongest candidate. Yet still came the carping that the Republican Party must turn to someone else. 'What the hell are we supposed to do?' Nixon exploded in exasperation. 'Paint our asses white and run with the antelopes?'" Buchanan, *The Greatest Comeback*, 261.

20   "Nixon spent [Tuesday, August 6, 1968] visiting various delegations, especially Southern ones. The *Miami Herald* planted a tape recorder in one caucus room, and later printed parts of the transcript. The secret recording was relatively harmless, as Nixon told the Southern delegates in private what he had already said in public, that he would not pick as a running mate anyone who 'is going to divide this Party,'" meaning he would not pick a liberal Republican like Rockefeller. Ambrose, *Nixon (Volume Two)*, 169.

Strom Thurmond worked as a "fire brigade… to extinguish any insurgency [among Southern delegations that] Reagan got going. Thurmond insisted again and again that Nixon would select no running mate who would 'split this Party.'" Stone, *Nixon's Secrets*, 331.

21   Nixon's political strategy was to follow the so-called Eleventh Commandment: Thou shalt not speak ill of another Republican. He avoided any public criticism or attack on Romney, Rockefeller, or Reagan. "By focusing his attacks on Johnson, and on Humphrey and Robert Kennedy for rendering aid and comfort to protesters and urban rioters, Nixon unified his Party." Buchanan, *The Greatest Comeback*, 212.

CHAPTER 34

[1]   Strom Thurmond visited each Southern delegation and pleaded his case for Nixon over Reagan: "'A vote for Reagan is a vote for Rockefeller...' he told his fellow Republicans, who would agree to follow his lead. 'We have no choice, if we want to win, except to vote for Nixon.... We must quit using our hearts and start using our heads. I have been down this road, so I know. I am laying my prestige, my record of forty years in public life, I'm laying it all on the line this time.... Believe me, I love Reagan. But Nixon's the one....' Everywhere Reagan operatives went, [Thurmond aide Harry] Dent brought in Thurmond—he called him his 'big cannon'— right behind him. Dent would warm up the group, reminding them of the senator's stellar conservative credentials, his loyalty to the South, and his willingness to put it all on the line for Nixon. Then Thurmond would speak for a few minutes, extolling Nixon's virtues. After the senator left, Dent followed up with last-minute exhortations." Cohodas, *Strom Thurmond*, 397-399.

"I am laying it all on the line this time. Are any of you making a comparable sacrifice?" Thurmond pleaded with the Southern delegates. "Do any of you have so much to lose..? Believe me, I love Reagan, but Nixon's the one." Chester, Hodgson, Page, *An American Melodrama*, 447-448.

"Thurmond... told sympathetic [Southern delegation] chairmen that he 'loved Ronnie Reagan' and that 'he would support him next time' but it was crucial to nominate Nixon, who could be competitive in every region in the country, while Goldwater had only scored in the South and the West.... When Reagan inroads were reported in Georgia, Congressman Bo Callaway introduced Thurmond to their caucus. [Thurmond] told them, 'We have no choice, if we want to win, except to vote for Nixon.

We must quit using our hearts and start using our heads. I love Reagan, but Nixon's the one.' Thurmond showed up after Reagan addressed each delegation to argue why staying with Dick Nixon was the right thing to do.... Thurmond was not alone in fighting this final Reagan surge, either. Bill Buckley's role as a Nixon supporter and key support from Barry Goldwater, Senator John Tower, and Congressman Bill Brock also helped Thurmond repulse Reagan's attempts to stampede the Southern delegates committed to Nixon or held in place by the unit rule." Stone, *Nixon's Secrets*, 328, 332-333.

"When slippage for Nixon was reported in the Florida delegation, Thurmond rushed to be with them at the Doral Country Club, holding a majority for Nixon in the delegation that voted by unit rules, where a majority would determine the full vote of the entire delegation. Elsewhere, he worked to shore up weak spots and to recruit uncommitted delegates. [¶] Thurmond was not alone in holding the South for Nixon. He visited the Mississippi delegation, and so did Barry Goldwater, also a Nixon supporter." Bass and Thompson, *Strom*, 217.

2   Of the 334 Southern convention delegates, if left to their own emotions, at least 300 would have voted for Ronald Reagan. This explains why Nixon's wooing of Strom Thurmond remained so critical to his campaign for the nomination. See Chester, Hodgson, Page, *An American Melodrama*, 434-438.

Even after Strom Thurmond announced his support of Nixon for the 1968 presidential nomination, he did not have an easy time convincing fellow South Carolina delegates to follow him. "Reagan's strength in the South ran deep. At a meeting of the South Carolina delegation in early June, all twenty-two delegates were 'unanimous for Reagan.' It took all of Thurmond's cajoling to convince them otherwise.... Southern delegates had their arms twisted and shifted to Nixon, although some of those arms would get untwisted at Miami Beach." Kopelson, *Reagan's 1968 Dress Rehearsal*, 655.

3   On Tuesday, August 6, 1968, the second day of the convention, and "before meeting with the South Carolina delegation, Reagan met privately with [South Carolina U.S. Senator Strom] Thurmond in the senator's hotel room. Reagan asked [Thurmond aide Harry Dent] to leave, believing

that one-on-one he could persuade Thurmond to support him. Asked a few minutes after the meeting what he told the California governor, Thurmond said, 'I told him I would support him next time.' Dent said that Thurmond was unimpressed with Reagan, finding him shallow, and told Reagan of his commitment to Nixon. 'That's something Reagan never understood even though he was told,' Dent added." Bass and Thompson, *Strom*, 216-217.

During the 1968 GOP Convention, "Reagan went to see Senator Thurmond at his hotel. They spent nearly an hour together and the senator expressed his high regard for Governor Reagan but he had given his word to Nixon. It was that iron-clad commitment that was keeping the Southern delegations in line. The high respect in which Strom Thurmond was held throughout the South made him the real power at this convention." F. Clifton White and William J. Gill, *Why Reagan Won: The Conservative Movement 1964-1981* (Chicago: Regnery Gateway, 1981), 123.

"'Young man,' [Senator Strom] Thurmond said prophetically to the fifty-seven-year-old Reagan [during their meeting], 'you'll be president someday but not this year.' Thurmond, like Goldwater, was solidly in Nixon's camp and worked hard and successfully to keep Southern delegates with Nixon even though in their hearts they wanted Reagan." Nofziger, *Nofziger*, 71-72.

At the 1968 GOP Convention, "Reagan met privately with Thurmond in the senator's hotel room. Reagan asked Thurmond aides to leave so the two men could be alone. Asked a few minutes after the meeting what he told the California governor, Thurmond said, 'I told him I would support him next time.' Reagan could not move 'Ol' Strom.'" Stone, *Nixon's Secrets*, 332.

CHAPTER 35

1   Although quiet rumors persisted for many years, news of Senator Strom Thurmond's mixed-race daughter did not surface in the mainstream press until six months after his death in 2003. Essie Mae Washington-Williams (1925-2013) then came forward and revealed that he was her father. Her mother, a 16 year-old black servant working in the Thurmond family home, became pregnant by Thurmond when he was 22. Although Thurmond never acknowledged publicly Ms. Washington as his daughter, he paid for her college education and helped her financially over the years. In 2005 she wrote a memoir about her life and their relationship. See Essie Mae Washington-Williams, *Dear Senator: A Memoir by the Daughter of Strom Thurmond* (New York: HarperCollins, 2005).

2   Most histories of Rockefeller's 1968 presidential campaign report that he visited 45 states in his three-month bid for the nomination; in his address to the Republican National Convention on Thursday, August 8, Rockefeller said he campaigned in 46 states. See "The Honorable Nelson A. Rockefeller, Governor of the State of New York, Addresses the Convention," *Official Report of the Proceedings of the Twenty-Ninth Republican National Convention Held in Miami Beach, Florida* (Republican National Committee, 1968), 401-402.

Rockefeller arrived for the 1968 GOP Convention at Opa Locka Airport aboard an American Airlines 727 jet that carried him, during his 12-week campaign, 65,000 miles into 45 states. See Mailer, *Miami and the Siege of Chicago*, 11.

"'Keep in mind that Nelson is not of the liberal wing of the Party,' says New York's Senator Jacob Javits, [a Rockefeller supporter] who decidedly is. 'He is more of a moderate Republican than he is a liberal.'" See "Anchors Away," *Time*.

³   Just before the start of the 1968 GOP Convention, the *Washington Post* headlined the Harris poll ROCKY TOPS ALL CANDIDATES. At the same time, the Crossley poll showed Nixon running ahead of Rockefeller by only two points nationally, but with Rockefeller enjoying a lead in seven out of the nine key swing states. See Chester, Hodgson, Page, *An American Melodrama*, 391-393.

⁴   On the eve of the GOP convention, as delegates departed for Miami, the Gallup organization released its last pre-convention poll, headlined NIXON OVERTAKES HUMPHREY AND MCCARTHY; ROCKY RUNS EVEN AGAINST BOTH DEMOCRATS. After spending millions, Rockefeller's polls showed him tied with Humphrey and enjoying only a bare margin over McCarthy. The poll was, in the words of one Rockefeller campaign aide, "devastating." Rockefeller's team put out the results of their own Harris and Crossley polls to contradict Gallup, but its message was lost in the vapors. See Chester, Hodgson, Page, *An American Melodrama*, 391-393; see also Witcover, *Very Strange Bedfellows*, 25; Whalen, *Catch the Falling Flag*, 190.
    Nixon found good news in the final Gallup poll issued before the delegates selected their nominee at the 1968 Republican National Convention: "[A] final preconvention Gallup poll to be published in the next morning's *Miami Herald* showed that Nixon alone among Republicans could comfortably defeat [any of the Democratic candidates]. That seemed to remove the last shadow of doubt that Nixon would be nominated—and it also removed his incentive to do anything even slightly risky." Whalen, *Catch the Falling Flag*, 190.

⁵   "Rockefeller's whole effort had been staked on his faith that the polls would convince the Republican delegates that he could win and Nixon could not. The flat contradiction between the [Gallup and Harris] polls meant that neither of them would convince the delegates of anything—least of all something they did not want to believe." Chester, Hodgson, Page, *An American Melodrama*, 391-393.

⁶   Nelson Rockefeller "did everything but enter the campaign at the right time, fight it out in the primaries, or design his attack for the mollification of Republican fears." Mailer, *Miami and the Siege of Chicago*, 31.

Once Rockefeller announced his candidacy on April 30, 1968, he learned that running for president was one thing; getting media attention was another. During May and into June, most of the political press pointed their spotlight on the McCarthy-Kennedy Democratic presidential nomination battle. During the five-week period following Rockefeller's entry, McCarthy and Kennedy squared off in six major statewide primaries. To Rockefeller's dismay, the best he could attract were second-string reporters trailing him as he campaigned. See White, *The Making of the President 1968*, 233.

With Romney out of the race before New Hampshire, and Nixon left with no direct Republican primary challenger, press attention turned to the Kennedy-McCarthy battle. See Buchanan, *The Greatest Comeback*, 216.

[7] Writer Norman Mailer compared Rockefeller's 1968 presidential effort to "a general who had mounted the most massive offensive of a massive war but had neglected to observe that the enemy was not on his route, and the line of march led into a swamp." Mailer, *Miami and the Siege of Chicago*, 31.

[8] Nixon put Richard Kleindienst, an Arizona lawyer, in charge of delegate care and feeding during the 1968 Republican Convention. Nixon's aides nicknamed Kleindienst, "The Genghis Khan of Miami." White, *The Making of the President 1968*, 135.

[9] Nixon needed 667 votes to win the nomination; the preconvention projections from the major news networks put Nixon's estimated delegate count between 619 and 657. See White, *The Making of the President 1968*, 239.

[10] By the time of the balloting at the 1968 GOP Convention, key favorite-son candidates frustrated Nixon in their refusal to release their delegates. "The continued denial of Ohio and Michigan delegates to Mr. Nixon encouraged supporters of Governor Reagan and of Governor Rockefeller of New York in their efforts to stop the nomination of Mr. Nixon on the first ballot. If they can do that, each of the governors believes, one of them will go on to victory." See Wicker, "Nixon Makes a New Gain."

On the eve of the 1968 GOP Convention, "United Press International gave Nixon 674 votes…. The UPI found that Nixon had lost seventeen votes during the past week, but Nixon forces do not agree." See Freeburg, "Rocky's 'Halt Nixon' Plan."

On July 31, 1968, the *New York Times* reported that Nixon had lost ground in the South to Reagan, claiming that 15 to 20 delegates had abandoned Nixon for Reagan. Rockefeller's camp claimed the actual number of Nixon defections to Reagan was 40 delegates. See Kopelson, *Reagan's 1968 Dress Rehearsal,* 758.

In its August 2, 1968, final count, CBS News showed Nixon with 644 votes—still 23 votes short of victory. See Kopelson, *Reagan's 1968 Dress Rehearsal,* 754.

On August 5, 1968, *Newsweek* magazine's final poll showed "Reagan had 'picked up at least forty delegates' and was 'gaining much more rapidly than Rockefeller.' Their tabulation showed Nixon had lost ground, now fully seventy-six votes shy of a first ballot victory." Kopelson, *Reagan's 1968 Dress Rehearsal,* 754.

[11]   The governor of Kentucky, Louie Nunn, said he held 22 of his 24 delegates for Nixon, but if Nixon didn't prevail on the first ballot, most of those votes would move to Reagan. Similarly, in Texas, Nixon's commitments over Reagan stood 41 to 15; if the fight went to the second ballot, most expected Reagan to grab the bulk of the delegates. See Chester, Hodgson, Page, *An American Melodrama,* 457.

National Review's William Rusher said that if Nixon did not win on the first ballot, his delegate numbers "would shrink like a scoop of ice cream in the hot Miami sun." Kopelson, *Reagan's 1968 Dress Rehearsal,* 754.

[12]   Since Rockefeller entered too late to battle Nixon in the primaries, he launched (in Nixon's words) a "ludicrous 'battle of the polls.'" Rockefeller's pollsters tried to show that their candidate, and not Nixon, stood the best chance of beating the Democrats in November. "[Rockefeller] hired a polling firm—and then spent millions of dollars on a massive national advertising campaign in an obvious attempt to affect public opinion at the time his polls were being made. Just before the convention, Rockefeller began releasing the results of the polls, which showed him

ahead of [Nixon] in the key electoral states." Nixon, *RN*, 306.

Rockefeller had spent, it was said, $10 million in his failed attempt to win the 1968 GOP presidential nomination. Mailer, *Miami and the Siege of Chicago*, 32.

13   At the 1968 GOP Convention, the Maryland delegation quartered in Miami's Sans Souci Hotel. See *1968 Republican National Convention Telephone Directory and Guide*, 34.

14   During the 1968 GOP Convention, Strom Thurmond "had obtained assurances from Nixon that no vice-presidential candidate intolerable to the South would be selected." Mailer, *Miami and the Siege of Chicago*, 69.

15   Seeking to undercut any Reagan tide, the Nixon team leaked (falsely) that Nixon had already offered the vice-presidential nomination to Reagan and that he had accepted. When word of this reached Reagan, he reacted sharply. His campaign sent emergency telegrams to every state delegation denying the rumor. In interviews, he insisted he would not accept the vice presidency. "Even if they tied and gagged me," he said with a grin, "I would find a way to signal by wiggling my ears." Chester, Hodgson, Page, *An American Melodrama*, 465.

16   "Astonishingly, in view of Nixon's troubles with his 'secret fund' when he became the Republican vice-presidential nominee in 1952, Nixon did not ask Agnew any questions about his finances, or whether he had any skeletons in his closet. Nor did Nixon make any attempt to conduct a private investigation of Agnew's actions as governor of Maryland (when he had been taking bribes on a regular basis)." Ambrose, *Nixon (Volume Two)*, 174.

One of Rockefeller's biographers claimed that Rockefeller knew in early 1968, or perhaps even earlier, that Agnew was suspected of pocketing money from contractors and others doing business with the state. See Smith, *On His Own Terms*, 636.

CHAPTER 36

[1]   At 5:04 p.m. Wednesday, August 7, 1968, the permanent Republican National Convention chairman, Congressman Gerald Ford of Michigan, called the 1968 GOP Convention to order to begin the process of placing names in nomination for the presidency. "Then followed dreariness.... [F]or nine long hours the Republican convention proceeded with the ancient rituals of nominating a president of the United States, as tacticians, political freaks and publicity-hungry politicians abused the patience of the delegates and national audience alike with speeches, demonstrations, seconding speeches, more speeches, more demonstrations.... [T]he names of nominees went on and on: Reagan of California, Hickel of Alaska, [Governor Winthrop] Rockefeller of Arkansas, Romney of Michigan, Carlson of Kansas, Fong of Hawaii, [Governor Nelson] Rockefeller of New York, Case of New Jersey, Richard M. Nixon, Rhodes of Ohio, Stassen of Erehwon, Thurmond of South Carolina, twelve in all." White, *The Making of the President 1968*, 247.

[2]   On Wednesday, August 7, 1968, there was a mind-numbing 45 nominating and seconding speeches made for presidential candidates and favorite sons at the 1968 GOP Convention. For a list of each speaker and nominee, see *Twenty-Ninth Republican National Convention*, 479-480.

Balloting for the 1968 GOP presidential nomination did not begin until 1:19 a.m. Thursday morning, August 8, 1968. White, *The Making of the President 1968*, 246; see also Kopelson, *Reagan's 1968 Dress Rehearsal*, 823.

[3]   "It was after nine [p.m.] before Governor Shafer of Pennsylvania stood up to put Nelson [Rockefeller's name in nomination for the presidency].

More than two and a half hours had elapsed between the end of Reagan's presentation and the beginning of Rocky's. Reporters had left the convention hall, and were huddled backstage in places like the Railroad Lounge where free sandwiches and beer were available[.]" Mailer, *Miami and the Siege of Chicago*, 63.

4   Maryland Governor Spiro Agnew closed his nomination speech of Nixon before the 1968 GOP Convention: "It is my privilege to place in nomination for president of the United States the one man whom history has so clearly thrust forward—the one whom all America will recognize as a man whose time has come—the man for 1968, the Honorable Richard M. Nixon." See "The Honorable Spiro T. Agnew, Governor of the State of Maryland, Nominating the Honorable Richard M. Nixon for President," *Official Report of the Proceedings of the Twenty-Ninth Republican National Convention*, 332-334; see also Mailer, *Miami and the Siege of Chicago*, 64.

CHAPTER 37

[1] At 7:00 p.m. on Wednesday, August 7, 1968, Nixon sat in Penthouse B of the Hilton-Plaza, "having finished a cheese omelet, milk and ice cream, to watch the [presidential nominating speeches], sipping Seven-Up." White, *The Making of the President 1968*, 250.

Watching the convention's roll call vote with Nixon in his hotel suite were his wife Pat, daughters Tricia and Julie, future sons-in-law Edward Cox and David Eisenhower, Nixon's longtime secretary Rose Mary Woods, and campaign aides Bob Haldeman, Pat Buchanan, Dwight Chapin, Ray Price, and Leonard Garment. Nixon, *RN*, 310.

At the 1968 GOP Convention, "Shortly after midnight, the roll call of the states began.... Nixon sat alone in the center of the [hotel suite], watching the television set. The others were on the sofas, around and behind him. He kept score on a yellow legal pad[.]" Ambrose, *Nixon (Volume Two)*, 170.

[2] The announcement of Wisconsin's vote by Governor Warren Knowles put Nixon over the top and gave him the nomination: "Mr. Chairman, Wisconsin is proud to cast its thirty votes for the nominee of this Party, Richard M. Nixon." See *Twenty-Ninth Republican National Convention*, 377.

[3] Despite having run in and won every primary, and facing two convention opponents who spent all year foreswearing any interest in the presidency, Nixon's margin of victory at the convention was "agonizingly—almost insultingly— small.... [H]e did not go 'over the top' until the next-to-last state, Wisconsin, was called." Chester, Hodgson, Page, *An American Melodrama*, 434.

After the New Hampshire primary, the *Cleveland Plain Dealer* wrote a story quoting a top Nixon campaign official that Ohio Governor Jim Rhodes would "absolutely not" be considered for Nixon's running mate. Pat Buchanan later called the remark "gratuitous and stupid." Since 1966, Nixon always had Buchanan tout Rhodes as a "short list" vice presidential possibility. Rhodes, holding Ohio's delegation as a favorite son, would control one of the single largest blocs of delegates at the convention. Because of the unfounded statement by the aide, "When we got to the convention in Miami Beach, Rhodes would refuse to release his Ohio delegates on the first ballot. Had he done so, we would not have needed to sweat all the way down the roll call to Wisconsin to win the nomination." Buchanan, *The Greatest Comeback*, 216.

Ignoring an almost two-year secret Reagan for-president-effort that came very close to upending Nixon's nomination, Reagan friend William F. Buckley Jr. perpetuated Reagan's later claim that he never sought the nomination seriously. In a posthumous memoir about his friendship with Reagan, Buckley wrote, "In August [1968], in Miami, the movement for Reagan was distinct. A number of delegates in addition to the California ones had pledged their support for Reagan, and his name was actually put in nomination. Notwithstanding that he was not an official candidate, his votes on the first ballot came in at 182.... [¶] I had written that Reagan was not a genuine candidate, that he had permitted the use of his name on the floor only to satisfy GOP conservatives, that he was a willing participant in the political exercises ahead aimed at electing Nixon." Buckley, *The Reagan I Knew*, 42-43.

One former Nixon campaign aide claimed that Nixon had a buffer. "The hope of Rockefeller and Reagan supporters that Nixon would fall short of the 667 votes required on the first ballot, producing switches and a deadlock, proved to be forlorn. So ample was Nixon's cushion that his floor managers released some secretly committed delegates, being held in reserve, to vote as local pressures dictated." Whalen, *Catch the Falling Flag*, 201.

4   "Nixon won the nomination on the first ballot, and [South Carolina Senator Strom] Thurmond was widely credited with playing a major role in the nominee's victory. Political analysts dubbed him Nixon's 'kingmaker.' *The State* told the story through an interview with [1968

Thurmond aide and South Carolina GOP Chairman Harry] Dent, who said, 'Richard Nixon can thank a man named Strom Thurmond for the nomination. I know what he did. Richard Nixon knows what he did. Nelson Rockefeller knows what he did and Ronald Reagan knows what he did.' As part of its convention coverage, *Newsweek* told of delegates who ended up 'eyeball to eyeball with Strom' as he raced from delegation to delegation on Nixon's behalf." See Cohodas, *Strom Thurmond*, 399.

5   After Nixon won the nomination, Youth for Reagan activist Pat Nolan ran into CBS News reporter Mike Wallace. Pat asked Wallace if he thought Reagan had a chance to be elected president in the future. With the "certainty of declaring a three-day old corpse dead," Wallace's answer was immediate: "He's finished. He is way too old to run for anything but reelection as governor." Kopelson, *Reagan's 1968 Dress Rehearsal*, 843.

6   How close did Reagan get to taking away the nomination from Nixon at the 1968 Republican National Convention? Very close—between one and eight delegate votes.

- The nomination of either Nixon or Reagan may have come down to the 34 member Florida delegation. Under Florida's "unit rule," the entire delegation was bound to vote for the wishes of the majority. One group of reporters described the delegation as "crazy for Reagan." With the Reagan and Nixon forces working the delegation feverishly, only when Strom Thurmond and Harry Dent told the Floridians that Nixon had given Thurmond 'veto power" over a vice-presidential pick did the delegation vote—barely—to stand by Nixon. The final Florida vote was Nixon, 19; Reagan, 14; Rockefeller, 1. A switch of three votes in Florida would have obliged the entire delegation to vote for Reagan, and barring any additional switches, this would have denied Nixon a first-ballot victory, and the history of the 1968 GOP convention might have ended differently. "[I]f Florida would successfully get out of its pre-convention commitment to Nixon, then likely the rest of the South… would hop on the Reagan bandwagon…. It all depended upon getting just three delegates to change. Reagan ultimately actually may have convinced two to switch, because according to historian Jules Witcover, Clif White [Reagan's chief convention delegate hunter] recalled later that actually it had come down to just one Florida delegate. [¶] So the American presidency hinged on one—possibly three—Florida delegate(s) switching and voting with his/her heart." Kopelson, *Reagan's 1968 Dress Rehearsal*, 803-804.

- Before the convention, Reagan's delegate counter, F. Clifton White, met with the chairman of the Florida Republican Party, Bill Murfin. After stating the obvious—that Reagan had significant support within the delegation, White asked Murfin, "If I get sixteen of these thirty-three delegates, will you make it seventeen?" White later recalled that Murfin "thought it over for a minute and then said, 'Yes. I'll do that.' We both knew this meant that under the unit rule the entire delegation, with the exception of [Governor] Claude Kirk, who was refusing to abide by the rule, would vote for Reagan if I got sixteen delegates from Florida. Of course, Murfin didn't think I could get the sixteenth or he would not have given me his pledge so readily.... I did get the sixteen votes we needed for Bill Murfin to make the seventeen. But instead Murfin threatened to resign as state chairman if the delegation refused to hold for Nixon. They reaffirmed the unit rule by the margin of a few votes and it was really on that action that [Reagan's 1968 presidential hopes] were lost." White and Gill, *Why Reagan Won*, 119, 123-124.

- Reagan's biographer, historian Edmund Morris, wrote that Reagan's bid against Nixon failed because "he had been a 'non-candidate' too long. Nevertheless, he came within eight votes of [blocking Nixon's first ballot win]." Morris, *Dutch*, 358.

- "The swing of just eight votes at the 1968 Republican convention would have nominated Ronald Reagan for president, ended the comeback bid of Richard Nixon, and the trajectory of history would have been changed." Stone, *Nixon's Secrets*, 336

7   The Reagan convention team had created a "high-tech communications command center and clandestine rolling field office, planning room, opera-

tions and strategy center,' which was housed inside a brand-new forty-five foot Mayflower moving van semi-trailer. The van was constructed by select members of Lockheed Aircraft's Skunk Works in Burbank, whose role was to create electronic and anti-eavesdropping equipment. The trailer had twenty stations for field commanders who had at their disposal the latest in walkie-talkies, radiophones and hard-wired secure telephones.... The van itself was the ultimate piece of subterfuge. After it was driven 3,000 miles to Miami Beach, it was positioned [on] the outside of the convention center against a solid concrete wall. The wall had a 'movie-set style loading dock painted on the outside of the building.' This gave the impression to the opposition that Reagan's supposedly true trailer would come in as soon as this moving van would finish unloading its cargo. But of course the moving van in fact was the true Reagan communications trailer. As soon as the disguised van arrived next to the painted wall, as all the wireless equipment was being readied for use, [technicians ran] phone lines to each delegation that was hooked up to the communications trailer." Kopelson, *Reagan's 1968 Dress Rehearsal*, 771-772.

[8]   Convention Chairman Gerald Ford recognized seven states and allowed them to change their vote to Nixon before he recognized California for the same purpose. After recording all its votes for Nixon, a California delegate asked Ford to allow Reagan to address the convention briefly. Ford refused, saying, "There is no provision in the Rules for anyone to move to the platform and be recognized at this time." See *Twenty-Ninth Republican National Convention*, 381.

After twice refusing to allow Reagan to move Nixon's nomination by acclamation, Convention Chairman Gerald Ford recognized 27 more states for vote changes before recognizing the California delegation. Delegate William French Smith rose and said, "Mr. Chairman, the State of California believes that now is the time to start unity in the Republican Party looking towards November. In order to accomplish that at this point, I would move the unanimous suspension of the Rules in order to permit the governor of the State of California to appear on the platform and give his views to this assembly." Ford required two states to second the motion before putting it to a vote and allowing Reagan to speak: "Under the rules of the convention, two other states must second the move to suspend the rules. Do I see two other states?" Maine and Virginia called out their seconds, requiring Ford to put it to a voice vote. After an overwhelming shout of approval, Ford recognized Reagan. See *Twenty-Ninth Republican National Convention*, 386-387.

During the convention balloting, Reagan watched the proceedings from his campaign's communications trailer outside the convention hall with aide F. Clifton White. As White recalled later, "When Wisconsin put Nixon over the top I asked [Reagan] if he wanted to go to the rostrum and make the nomination unanimous. Reagan knew it was a necessary gesture to unite the Party and he said he would do it. [¶] We went into the convention hall together and made our way to the rostrum. But we were stopped just behind the platform. [Republican National Committee Chairman] Ray Bliss was throwing his vaunted power around that night and he didn't want Reagan stealing the show.... [I told the convention parliamentarian] to inform Bliss that if he didn't let Governor Reagan speak he would go down to the floor and make his announcement from there. Bliss finally relented and Reagan touched off the most delirious demonstration of the convention when he went to the rostrum and moved that the nomination of Richard Nixon be declared unanimous." White and Gill, *Why Reagan Won*, 127.

When Convention Chairman Gerald Ford recognized Reagan for his motion, Reagan's speech was brief: "Mr. Chairman, fellow delegates, fellow Republicans: We are gathered here with one common bond uniting us, and that is the knowledge that this great nation cannot stand or survive four more years of the policies that have been guiding us for too many of the recent years. Therefore... I hereby and proudly move on behalf of my fellow Californians that this convention declare itself as unanimously united behind the candidate, Richard Nixon, as the next president of the United States, and I so move." See *Twenty-Ninth Republican National Convention*, 387.

After Nixon went over the top on the first ballot, "magnanimous candidate Ronald Reagan ascended the platform. As he walked up, there was a 'giant wave of applause.' [Convention Chairman Gerald] Ford would not let Reagan come to the rostrum, citing convention rules. So while Reagan waited, and waited, Ford again thwarted Reagan by continuing to recognize delegations, one by one. Finally, Ford recognized a motion...

to suspend the rules, and he let Reagan address the convention." Reagan then asked the convention to declare Nixon its nominee by acclamation. Kopelson, *Reagan's 1968 Dress Rehearsal*, 825.

Instead of putting to a vote Reagan's motion to declare Nixon the nominee by acclamation, Convention Chairman Gerald Ford thanked Reagan, announced the total vote, and then closed the convention with a benediction. See *Twenty-Ninth Republican National Convention*, 387-389.

Whether the Ford-Reagan encounter at the 1968 GOP Convention (which actually occurred) caused a mutual disdain between the two men is speculative. However, eight years later, with Ford in the White House after Nixon's resignation, Reagan challenged Ford for the GOP presidential nomination in a bruising primary campaign. Reagan came within reach of beating the incumbent president. Blaming Reagan for his later loss of the White House to Jimmy Carter, the ex-president maintained a disdain for Reagan to the end of his life. See, e.g., Thomas M. DeFrank, *Write It When I'm Gone: Remarkable Off-the-Record Conversations with Gerald R. Ford* (New York: The Berkley Publishing Co., 2007).

[9]   After Nixon went over the top in the delegate count, Rockefeller called to congratulate him, and he laughed as he told Nixon, "Ronnie didn't come through for us as we expected." Nixon, *RN*, 311.

When Nixon won the GOP nomination in 1968, Rockefeller called and congratulated him. After a brief discussion, "Nixon told his entourage it was 'nice of him to call.... He couldn't have been nicer.... He said he gave me a good run.... He said Ron [Reagan] didn't come through as good as he thought he would.' Nixon allowed himself a little shiver of delight. He lifted his eyes to the ceiling, brought them down, and broke into a mischievous grin." Ambrose, *Nixon (Volume Two)*, 170.

[10]   "Nixon spoke of [Nelson Rockefeller] with a mixture of dislike and respect. He had experience and impressive qualifications.... But he would not enter the primaries and could not be nominated. Goldwater would lead his people out of the convention [in protest had Rockefeller won the 1968 presidential nomination]." Whalen, *Catch the Falling Flag*, 11.

11   After Nixon won the nomination, Senator Thurmond "managed to get Reagan and Nixon together at the Fountainbleau [Hotel in Miami]. Nixon said, 'Well, Ron, you're a young man. You'll have another shot at this.' Reagan countered, 'Mr. Vice President, you're three years older than I am.'" [Author's note: This quotation appears in Kopelson, *Reagan's 1968 Dress Rehearsal*, 827. Dr. Kopelson cites as its source an oral history given by Reagan aide Michael Deaver. In fact, Reagan was almost two years older than Nixon. The author attributes the discrepancy to Mr. Deaver's faulty recollection of what was said.]

12   "The day after Nixon was nominated Reagan told me what he apparently was to tell a number of people in the ensuing two or three weeks, namely, 'I'm not disappointed that I didn't get the nomination. I wasn't ready for it.' [¶] And that was what had bugged him all along, that was why he had fought becoming an active candidate until he finally got caught up in the excitement of the convention, and that was why he was able to campaign enthusiastically for Nixon and go back to his governorship a happy and relieved man." Nofziger, *Nofziger*, 74.

"In the end, considering Reagan's late entry as a bona fide presidential candidate, the margin of victory for Nixon [at the 1968 Republican National Convention] was embarrassingly slim. I had obtained secret pledges for many Southern delegates to switch to Reagan if Nixon failed to win on the first ballot. Many were aware of Dick's well-known penchant for retribution, and were afraid of what might happen to them if they threw their support to Reagan prematurely and Nixon won." White and Tuccille, *Politics as a Noble Calling*, 178.

13   In reality, Nixon chose Spiro Agnew as his running mate in 1968, and both won renomination and reelection in 1972. In 1973, federal prosecutors in Baltimore indicted Agnew, and he resigned the vice presidency later that year. Agnew met with Nixon on the afternoon in 1973 that the scandal broke in the press: "Nixon reviewed in a monologue what [Attorney General Elliot] Richardson had told him about Agnew's troubles.... Nixon 'seemed sympathetic and solicitous—indignant about the investigation in Baltimore. He said he understood the pressures on a governor to raise money for the ticket, and he understood where and how that money had to be raised. During all this, [Agnew] had no opportunity to do other than

briefly interject a word of agreement or a nod of understanding....' Nixon asked him: 'Can you function effectively as vice president?' Agnew replied that he could. He then reviewed his own version of the case against him; of old business associates who, he told Nixon, 'were caught in a tax evasion problem and they saw a hell of a good way to extricate themselves from it by dragging me in.' The Baltimore prosecutors had the goods on them, he said, and told them 'if you will just deliver Agnew to us, things will be a lot easier for you....' [Agnew] repeated his belief that most of the governors in other states had followed practices such as those common in Maryland. He emphasized that he had always awarded contracts on the basis of merit, and he felt that the amounts he had received had been so small that no reasonable critic would claim that they could have influenced him to make a decision that contravened the public interest. He said that he could not see that what he had done was unethical.... [At Agnew's final meeting with Nixon before he resigned the vice presidency, Agnew remembered later], 'As I was leaving, Nixon put his arm around my shoulders, shook his head, and said again how awful it all was. Incongruously, I suddenly had the feeling that he couldn't wait to get me out of there.'" Witcover, *Very Strange Bedfellows*, 310-311, 342–343.

[14]   Near the end of his life, Nixon told aide Monica Crowley, "[A]ny effective leader has got to be a son-of-a-bitch." Crowley, *Nixon Off the Record*, 4-5, 51.

Nixon often quoted former British Prime Minister William E. Gladstone's admonition that to be an effective prime minister, one needed to be "a good butcher." See, e.g., Rogan, *And Then I Met*, 139; see also Buchanan, *The Greatest Comeback*, 366. [Author's note: in Mr. Buchanan's book, Nixon attributed the quotation to British Prime Minister Herbert Henry Asquith. Nixon was correct that Asquinth did use the quotation, but Asquinth credited its origin to Gladstone. According to Winston Churchill, "When offering me Cabinet office in his government in 1908, [Asquinth] repeated to me Mr. Gladstone's saying, 'The first essential for a prime minister is to be a good butcher,' and he added, 'There are several who must be pole-axed now.'" See "Duty of a Prime Minister," *The Spectator*, February 19, 1942, p. 14, quoting from Churchill's essay on the first Earl of Oxford and Asquinth in *Great Contemporaries*.]

CHAPTER 38

1   "Midway through the balloting [for the presidential nomination at the
1968 Republican National Convention] pages had begun to deliver notes
to selected Republican dignitaries at the convention. 'I would appreciate
it,' read the typewritten slips, 'if you could meet with me tonight in my
room in the Hilton-Plaza as soon as possible after the end of the balloting.
Arrangements to escort you to my room will be handled by Mr. Hamilton at
the reception desk on the fifteenth floor of the Hilton-Plaza. So as to avoid
any possible confusion, please bring this memorandum with you. (signed)
Dick [Nixon].'" White, *The Making of the President 1968*, 250-251.

2   "At two-ten a.m. Thursday, Nixon had the nomination. By two-
fifteen, sprawled in an armchair in the solarium of his Hilton penthouse
suite, he was deep in talks with the vanguard of the army of politicians he
and his staff were to 'consult' in the course of the night. [¶] The structure
of this group, and the one which followed it, is interesting not only for
Nixon's apparent assessment of who holds power within the Republican
Party, but because each group was so precisely balanced.... There were
twenty-four people present at that first meeting, thirteen staffers and
eleven outside political advisers.... Nixon did the talking—the meeting
lasted only fifteen minutes or so—as he defined what he wanted of his
nominee: the unimpeachable virtues of competence and loyalty." Chester,
Hodgson, Page, *An American Melodrama*, 485-486.

3   Nixon's post-nomination penthouse meeting with GOP leaders "was
a jovial meeting, as the leaders treated themselves to well-earned bourbon
and Scotch and considered their advice." White, *The Making of the President 1968*, 251.

4   In the early morning hours after Nixon won the presidential nomina-
tion, he held three different meetings of GOP leaders in his Penthouse
Suite. In each meeting, he invited a mix of conservatives, moderates, and
liberals. At the first meeting, those attending included Senators Barry
Goldwater (AZ), Strom Thurmond (SC), Paul Fannin (AZ), John Tower
(TX), Hiram Fong (HI), and Karl Mundt (SD); former Senator William
F. Knowland (CA), Lieutenant Governor Robert Finch (CA), former
Governor Thomas E. Dewey (NY), Governor Jim Rhodes (OH), former
U.S. Attorney General Herbert Brownell, Congressman John Rhodes
(AZ), former Republican National Committee Chairman Leonard Hall,
and Nixon's law partner John Mitchell. See Duncan, *Self-Portrait U.S.A.*,
86. Others attending the meetings included Senate Republican Leader
Everett Dirksen (IL), and House Republican Leader Gerald Ford (MI).
See White, *The Making of the President 1968*, 252.

5   "If I want to win this," Nixon said to the GOP elders in his penthouse
shortly after securing the nomination, "I'm going to have to win it on my
own." Chester, Hodgson, Page, *An American Melodrama*, 485-486.
    In making his vice-presidential selection, Nixon wanted a man who
would hurt him the least, telling an aide, "The vice president can't help
you. He can only hurt you." Some on his staff thought Nixon wished he
could run with no running mate. Ambrose, *Nixon (Volume Two)*, 163.

6   During the conclaves in Nixon's penthouse suite after he won the
1968 GOP presidential nomination, the moderates and liberals "were for
Lindsay; but the others at the gathering were overwhelmingly conservative.
Barry Goldwater declared he could under no circumstances accept Lindsay;
Thurmond would not have Lindsay; neither would the lesser conservatives.
Lindsay was out." White, *The Making of the President 1968*, 251.

7   Besides John Lindsay, other moderate or liberal potential running
mates suggested to Nixon during his penthouse meeting with GOP leaders
were Senators Charles Percy of Illinois and Mark Hatfield of Oregon. See
White, *The Making of the President 1968*, 251.

8   At the penthouse meeting of GOP leaders to discuss a running mate
for Nixon, "[s]everal Northerners observed that the North and the indus-

trial states could not accept Ronald Reagan (Strom Thurmond's favorite) any more than the South could accept Lindsay." White, *The Making of the President 1968*, 251.

Senators Strom Thurmond and Barry Goldwater rejected the liberal names under consideration for vice president, while key moderate governors and Nixon campaign advisers urged rejection of the right-wing choices. See Chester, Hodgson, Page, *An American Melodrama*, 487.

After winning the nomination, Nixon "took a first sampling of opinion from the twenty-four men of his operational staff in the solarium. There were few new vice presidential names to be added to the ones so long and so often discussed. There were the liberals—Lindsay, Percy, Hatfield. There were the conservatives—Reagan above all others[.]" White, *The Making of the President 1968*, 251.

Former GOP presidential nominee Barry Goldwater arrived at the 1968 Miami convention and endorsed a Nixon-Reagan ticket. United Press International, "GOP Convention Opens Amid Fast and Furious Politicking," *Panama City News-Herald*, Panama City, Florida, August 6, 1968.

9 "The second [meeting of Party elders to consider a vice presidential nominee] opened at two-forty-five a.m., before another well-structured audience of Party satraps.... Everyone had names. The conservative choices were Reagan, Senator John Tower of Texas, and Senator Howard Baker of Tennessee. The liberals were Romney, New York Mayor John Lindsay, and former Pennsylvania Governor William Scranton. Senator Strom Thurmond's list was the subject of rather more attention. At its head, inevitably: Reagan." Chester, Hodgson, Page, *An American Melodrama*, 486-487.

10 "At 6:30 [a.m.], Mr. Nixon went to bed and awoke at 8:30 to descend to the Jackie-of-Hearts Room (so named for Miami's favorite adopted son, Jackie Gleason). Nixon had promised he would announce to the nation the name of his new vice president at about eleven in the morning, but he was no nearer a decision than ever. The nine-o'clock session in the Jackie-of-Hearts Room was, in effect, a rump session of eleven elders who had not been able to make the all-night session in the Penthouse Suite. Relatively rested and refreshed, these gentlemen, full of vigor, gave one

another a hard time, beginning all over again with the same list of names that Mr. Nixon had heard chewed over twice before since his nomination. Again the record turned, the same tune was heard, and the needle stuck: the Southerners in the group absolutely refused to consider Lindsay—or Percy, or Romney, or Hatfield. The Northerners, who wanted Lindsay, absolutely refused to consider Reagan or Tower.... Wilson of California, having given up on Lindsay, suggested Congressman Gerald Ford—because Ford was in the room. Senator Everett Dirksen suggested Senator Howard Baker of Tennessee—his son-in-law. Senator George Murphy suddenly, out of nowhere, suggested Robert Finch again—because Finch was in the room." White, *The Making of the President 1968*, 252.

[11]   Since these multiple meetings of Party elders to give advice on a running mate "were rapidly getting non-productive, Mr. Nixon finally withdrew. Summoning his own uppermost inner circle together, they retreated to the Penthouse Suite again, whither a dozen Seven-Ups, a dozen Coca-Colas and two buckets of ice were quickly sent." White, *The Making of the President 1968*, 252.

[12]   Running as a third-party presidential candidate in 1968, former Alabama Governor George Wallace "had locked up most of the Dixiecrat states that had gone for Goldwater—South Carolina, Georgia, Alabama, Mississippi, Louisiana. Four of these had gone for Strom Thurmond in 1948. The battle for the remaining six—Texas, Florida, North Carolina, Virginia, Tennessee, Arkansas—would likely be between Nixon and Wallace. We needed help on the Southern front and it had to come from our vice presidential choice." Buchanan, *The Greatest Comeback*, 295.

"We needed to peel away Wallace votes—and Reagan was the man to do it. Not only was he a tremendous campaigner... [but] Nixon needed a vice president to 'take the heat and lightning in order to spare and conserve the prestige of the man in the White House.' Our arguments pointed straight to Reagan." Buchanan, *The Greatest Comeback*, 295–296.

Pat Buchanan supported Reagan for vice president strongly: he felt Reagan would be a voter boon in the South, act as an effective counter to Wallace, and would free up Nixon to campaign in the East. See Witcover, *Very Strange Bedfellows*, 22.

[13]   During the vice-presidential selection meetings, Texas Senator John Tower opined that "perhaps half of Wallace's strength in some states might be sheared away by a determined assault from the right," and then he argued that the only conservative who might achieve this feat was Ronald Reagan. See Chester, Hodgson, Page, *An American Melodrama*, 489.

[14]   During Nixon's post-nomination meeting with GOP leaders, when Reagan's name came up repeatedly as a running mate, Nixon dismissed it. "'I've had polls on these glamour boys,' he said confidently. 'If they help you in one place, they hurt you in another....' [During these meetings] Nixon [confined] himself to sniping at the 'glamour boys[.]'" Chester, Hodgson, Page, *An American Melodrama*, 485-487.

"Glamour boy" was Nixon's private and dismissive nickname for Reagan during his meetings with GOP leaders to discuss the selection of a 1968 running mate. White, *The Making of the President 1968*, 251.

With several of Nixon's advisers trying to convince him to select Reagan as his running mate, "[t]he more attractive [they] made Reagan, the less Nixon would consider him.... Nixon waved them off, saying, 'Reagan's just an actor.' Nixon's private phrase for Reagan was 'Glamour Boy.'" Kopelson, *Reagan's 1968 Dress Rehearsal*, 832.

In these discussions about a vice-presidential running mate, 1968 Nixon campaign aide Richard Whalen recalled, "The more attractive we made Reagan appear, the less he appealed to Nixon, who would suffer from the inevitable side-by-side comparison." Whalen, *Catch the Falling Flag*, 179.

[15]   During the final meeting with Nixon on a vice presidential nominee, "Robert Finch observed that Reagan simply would not accept the offer.... Between four and five in the morning, the meeting broke up in indecision, all having waited for Mr. Nixon's decision, while he waited on their advice." White, *The Making of the President 1968*, 251.

In issuing an adamant denial to the Nixon campaign's false rumor that he would accept the vice presidency, Reagan told delegates, "Even if they tied and gagged me, I would find a way to signal 'no' by wiggling my ears." White and Gill, *Why Reagan Won*, 123.

"Nixon's people even went so far as to circulate rumors that Reagan would be their candidate's choice for vice president in an effort to keep the delegates in line. After all, if Reagan were going to be on the ticket anyway, what was all the fuss about? This proved to be a clever and effective tactic. It forced Reagan to state repeatedly that he would not consider the vice presidency under any circumstances to keep his presidential bid alive. [¶] 'Even if they tied and gagged me I would find a way to signal no by wiggling my ears,' Reagan said, delivering the best one-liner of the convention." White and Tuccille, *Politics as a Noble Calling*, 178-179.

[16]   When Nixon held his final meeting with senior campaign staff to finalize his 1968 running mate selection, it was aide John Sears who "led off with a superb analysis of Reagan's strengths and weaknesses, supplemented by a detailed, state-by-state breakdown of a Nixon-Reagan ticket's likely electoral success against Hubert Humphrey and two quite different running mates: Edward Kennedy or John Connally.... [His analysis] judged 1968 as a 'center-right' year. It identified the South as by far the most volatile region of the country, showing extreme sensitivity to the vice presidential choices of the major parties and very probably being the decisive battleground.... [The] analysis advanced the case for Reagan as 'the only officeholder in the country who can outtalk and outcampaign George Wallace....' [T]he choice of Reagan could not, for example, guarantee a Republican victory in California. But Reagan could at once tie down and stir up the conservatives who were the GOP shock troops, and he could breach Wallace's Southern citadel like no other Republican. His all-important function, Sears concluded, 'should be to relieve the burdens on RN so that RN can spend the vast majority of the campaign in eight or nine critical states.'" Whalen, *Catch the Falling Flag*, 177-178.

[17]   "[Pat] Buchanan, in still another memo, declared that 'the Nixon campaign is confronted with the old German problem—the two-front war.... We're going to have to stave off the assaults of Wallace from the right, keep him from making any further inroads, and we're going to have to defeat the challenge of Humphrey in the center of American politics. It is almost impossible for one candidate to do both of these things well at the same time.' Reagan would free Nixon of 'the burden of fighting George Wallace, a burden we would otherwise have to assume totally, a burden which would necessarily cost us something in the center.'" Whalen, *Catch the Falling Flag*, 177-178; see also Buchanan, *The Greatest Comeback*, 295.

[18]   "Historian Peter Hannaford noted that political considerations aside, the two major reasons Nixon did not [want] Reagan [as his running mate] were rooted in jealousy: Reagan would upstage him and Reagan was taller." Kopelson, *Reagan's 1968 Dress Rehearsal*, 832.

[19]   Nixon's final meeting to select a running mate "produced no strong consensus for any candidate, but they did gradually tend to eliminate [people]. Before finally deciding, I asked two of my close friends and long-time associates: would he himself be my running mate? [¶] The first was Bob Finch. Bob was probably my closest friend in politics, and after winning the lieutenant governorship of California in 1966, he had become a rising star in the Party. I was sure of his answer, but I told him, 'You have many of Lindsay's best attributes. You have youth and freshness, and you would have great appeal to the Party and to independent voters.' He was deeply moved by my suggestion, but he strongly rejected it, arguing that the leap from lieutenant governor to vice president would be perceived as too great. Besides, he was my former aide and a long-time personal friend, and there would be charges of cronyism. Also, he and Reagan had already developed a rivalry in California, and Reagan's supporters would be extremely irritated if he were chosen." Nixon, *RN*, 312-313.

[20]   "Nixon himself preferred [as his running mate], above all others, Robert Finch of California. Finch was to him a younger brother, closer, more trusted, conspicuously more able and more visionary than any other man he had known over the years. He had telephoned Finch with a hard offer several weeks before the convention. But Finch would not— he felt he simply was not yet ready to carry, as he put it, 'the other end of the stick' in a campaign so important as the presidency.... In the early morning hours after winning the nomination, Nixon met with his closest [advisers to make] the final decision on a running mate. When Nixon threw Bob Finch's name out for consideration, Finch left the room when they discussed him.... Mr. Nixon emerged to give the message to Mr. Finch—that the group wanted him, that he himself wanted to have him.... Friends [described Finch] as appalled [at the news]; the world waited for Nixon's decision, press and TV clamored for the name of the vice president. All this should have been settled hours ago. The choice of his name, Finch now said, would smack of nepotism. Finch felt he could

be a better friend and adviser than a running mate to the old companion who now offers him partnership. The upshot: Finch refused. The meeting resumed to consider the names of the finalists. White, *The Making of the President 1968*, 250, 252-253.

"Robert H. Finch owned a historic footnote not widely known but confirmed by Richard Nixon in his presidential memoir: when Nixon won the 1968 Republican nomination, he asked Finch to be his running mate. Because of Finch's one-word answer to that question, when I met him in 1988 he was a solo-practicing lawyer in a small Pasadena office. Had Finch given a different answer, today there would be a Robert H. Finch Presidential Library, and Gerald Ford would be the name of an obscure former Michigan congressman. (By the way, in later years Finch hosted a fundraising lunch for me when I ran for the state legislature. After he introduced me, I told this story, and then made this astute observation: 'If Bob had said yes instead of no, today he'd be the former president of the United States—and I could have charged all of you a hell of a lot more than the lousy 50 bucks you paid to get in here!')" As Finch related to the author a quarter-century after 1968, "It's true that when Nixon won the 1968 Republican presidential nomination, he asked me if I would be his running mate. After discussing the option with my friends and family, I turned him down.... I felt being a lieutenant governor did not give me sufficient national exposure to bring strength to his ticket." Rogan, *And Then I Met*, 129-130.

[21]   During Nixon's discussion with his senior staff regarding a running mate selection, aide John Sears again suggested Reagan. Nixon asked him, "But what kind of a president would he make?" Sears replied, "Oh, I've got this all wrong. I thought *you* were going to be the president. I thought we were talking about the vice president." Witcover, *Very Strange Bedfellows*, 22.

[22]   When Nixon finally settled upon a running mate, he did not personally call the man he selected. Instead, Nixon delegated the call. It was a Nixon campaign staffer that advised Nixon's choice that he would be the 1968 GOP vice presidential nominee. Nixon, *RN*, 313.

Nixon announced the name of his 1968 vice presidential running mate at a 1:00 p.m. press conference in the ballroom of Miami's Hilton Plaza

Hotel on August 8, 1968. See, e.g., Ambrose, *Nixon (Volume Two)*, 174.

"Just before one o'clock the next afternoon, [Pat] Buchanan and I met at the door of the ballroom where Nixon was to announce his choice of a running mate. He winked and said, 'We have a pope.' Before he could whisper the name, Secret Service men stepped between us and ordered the aisles cleared." Whalen, *Catch the Falling Flag*, 202.

[23] "From Miami, the Republican [presidential and vice-presidential] nominees, their entourages, and the press flew to Southern California and a resort called Mission Bay.... At the San Diego airport, the band, balloons, and the crowd waited to greet the victorious favorite son.... After telling the crowd how wonderful it felt to be coming home, Nixon led a motorcade to [Mission Bay].... The announced purpose of Nixon's weeklong stay in California was to plan the forthcoming campaign. In fact, the operational plans [had been completed] in advance. The actual purpose was to yield the spotlight to the Democrats and the inevitable civil war at their approaching convention in Chicago. In contrast, Nixon intended to project an image of calm, order, and unity as Republicans of every ideological stripe came to pay him homage." Whalen, *Catch the Falling Flag*, 208.

On August 10, 1968, two days after the end of the 1968 Republican National Convention, Nixon arrived at the Bahia Resort Hotel at Mission Bay in San Diego to begin a ten-day stay. Nixon and his senior campaign staff took 40 rooms at the Bahia, with the remainder of his staff and traveling press using 110 additional rooms at the nearby Catamaran Hotel on Mission Bay. See United Press International, "Nixon, Aides to Spend 10 Days in San Diego," *Chicago Tribune*, August 9, 1968.

PART THREE

Prelude to November

CHAPTER 39

[1] The FBI was originally named the Bureau of Investigation after Congress created it in 1908. It became the United States Bureau of Investigation in 1932, and rechristened as the Federal Bureau of Investigation in 1935. See https://en.wikipedia.org/wiki/Federal_Bureau_of_Investigation.

"Helen Gandy had worked for [J. Edgar Hoover] since 1918, six years before he even became [FBI] director, briefly as a clerk, then as his secretary, and, since 1939, with the title of executive assistant. Like her boss, she had never married, having devoted her full life to the FBI." In the 54 years she worked for Hoover, never once did he call her by her first name. Curt Gentry, *J. Edgar Hoover: The Man and the Secrets* (New York: W.W. Norton & Company, 1991), 24.

[2] Hoover's era as FBI director covered the gamut of twentieth century crime, from John Dillinger to Ma Barker, Alvin Karpis, Machine Gun Kelly, the Rosenbergs, Alger Hiss, Pretty Boy Floyd, and the assassinations of JFK, RFK, and Martin Luther King, Jr. See Gentry, *J. Edgar Hoover*, 33.

[3] Actor Efrem Zimbalist Jr. starred as FBI Inspector Lewis Erskine in the television series *The F.B.I.* on ABC from 1965 to 1974. See https://en.wikipedia.org/wiki/The_F.B.I._(TV_series).

[4] A senior FBI official later described Hoover's files on politicians as "drawers full of political cancer." See Gentry, *J. Edgar Hoover*, 30-31, 50-52.

Hoover kept salacious and "explosive material [on high-level officials and notables] in his personal files, which filled four rooms on the fifth floor of [the FBI's Washington] headquarters." See Sullivan and Brown, *The Bureau*, 50.

[5] Journalist Victor Navasky noted J. Edgar Hoover's "genius" in making people believe he knew about their indiscretions. See Heymann, *RFK*, 217-218.

"[T]here was only one way the Kennedys could assure Hoover's continued silence about [JFK's World War II affair with suspected Nazi spy] Inga Arvad and certain other extremely embarrassing items in his files. No one needed to spell it out. It was simply understood by everyone concerned. And since it was unstated, no one could call it blackmail.... Hoover was continually reminding JFK, albeit indirectly, of his comprehensive and assiduously updated files." See Gentry, *J. Edgar Hoover*, 471, 479-480.

"Neither Jack nor Bobby [Kennedy] ever doubted that Hoover was actually a powerful and relentless enemy, and they kept their distance." Sullivan and Brown, *The Bureau*, 55

JFK knew Hoover could destroy him with the FBI files the director had compiled on him. "Less than three weeks after [JFK won the 1960 Democratic presidential nomination], on August 4, 1960, the *New York Times* reported, 'During a series of news conferences on his lawn today, Senator Kennedy was asked whether, if elected, he would retain J. Edgar Hoover as director of the Federal Bureau of Investigation.... He replied that he would, of course, retain Mr. Hoover and planned no major changes within the agency.'" See Gentry, *J. Edgar Hoover*, 471.

[6] "'Every month or so,' RFK recalled in 1964, J. Edgar Hoover 'would send somebody around to give information on somebody I knew or members of my family or allegations in connection with myself. So that it would be clear—whether it was right or wrong—that he was on top of all these things....' [E]very such tale was a subtle reminder of what the FBI director had in his own files on [JFK]." See Gentry, *J. Edgar Hoover*, 471, 479-480.

J. Edgar Hoover sent someone from the FBI to meet with RFK regularly and give him information on RFK's family and friends, including frequent reports that JFK caroused weekly with a group of girls at the LaSalle Hotel. RFK felt Hoover did this just to let him know the FBI kept tabs on everybody. See Robert F. Kennedy interviews with Anthony Lewis (with Burke Marshall present), December 4, 6, and 22, 1964, cited in Guthman and Shulman, *Robert Kennedy in His Own Words*, 128-129.

[7]   In 1941, FBI Special Agent Frederick Ayer Jr. sat in a hotel room taping and monitoring the activities of the woman in the adjoining room—suspected Nazi spy Inga Arvad, a 28 year-old former Miss Europe—and an unidentified male. Ayer knew his report on her activities would be hand-delivered to FBI Director J. Edgar Hoover personally. "The panting over, the couple were lazily conversing when Ayer suddenly froze. He recognized the man's voice; there was no mistaking it; it belonged to one of his former Harvard classmates[:] John Fitzgerald Kennedy." The FBI later bugged young JFK and Arvad on multiple occasions. When they rendezvoused in South Carolina, the FBI arranged for the hotel front desk clerk to assign them to a pre-bugged room. See Gentry, *J. Edgar Hoover*, 467-469.

J. Edgar Hoover's memos and wiretaps on JFK dated back to World War II, when the FBI began surveillance on suspected Nazi spy Inga Arvad. With her room bugged, young Navy Lieutenant John F. Kennedy made his way to her room on more than one occasion. When the Navy learned about it, JFK faced expulsion from the service. JFK's father, Joseph P. Kennedy, intervened with his longtime friend Hoover to save his son's naval career, and Hoover came through. See, e.g., Heymann, *RFK*, 217-219.

J. Edgar Hoover was a good friend of Joseph P. Kennedy, and they used to keep in touch. Robert F. Kennedy interviews with Anthony Lewis (with Burke Marshall present), December 4, 6, and 22, 1964; cited in Edwin O. Guthman and Shulman, *Robert Kennedy in His Own Words*, 119.

[8]   Miss Helen Gandy maintained a private index to J. Edgar Hoover's secret files. Even if someone accessed her file cabinets, they would likely have been unable to locate the secret files without her private index to them "because a number of the especially sensitive holders were deceptively titled. One on the current president, for example, appeared not under NIXON, RICHARD but under OBSCENE MATTERS." When J. Edgar Hoover died in 1972, acting United States Attorney General Richard Kleindienst ordered Hoover's private office secured to protect the treasure trove of "secret files" Hoover was known to possess on the powerful. The assistant FBI director told Kleindienst he had secured Hoover's office and changed the locks to protect against intrusion. "What [he] neglected to tell the acting Attorney General was that no [sensitive] files were kept in Hoover's private office. The FBI's most secret files were in the office of his

secretary, Miss Helen Gandy. [¶] And now, only hours after [Hoover's] death... Miss Gandy had already begun to go through those files, culling and separating them, marking some for destruction by shredding, setting others aside for special handling." A list of files Miss Gandy turned over to another close Hoover aide, W. Mark Felt, totaled 17,750 pages, categorized within 167 files, and stored in 12 combination-lock file cabinets in Felt's office. Before the new director moved into Hoover's office suite, "Helen Gandy transferred the contents of at least thirty-two more file drawers into cardboard boxes [that were] not given to Mark Felt. Instead, by means of Bureau trucks and drivers, they were moved all the way across Washington, to the basement recreation room of [Hoover's home].... In addition to the boxes, at least six—and possibly as many as twenty-five file cabinets were also moved to Hoover's home during this same period." See Gentry, *J. Edgar Hoover*, 30-31, 46, 50-52.

9 J. Edgar Hoover reached the mandatory retirement age of 70 on January 1, 1965. On that day, he would be forced to retire unless the president of the United States gave him a personal exemption. See Gentry, *J. Edgar Hoover*, 536.

Since J. Edgar Hoover reached the age of mandatory retirement for federal employees in 1965, "he stayed in office only because of a special waiver which required [LBJ's] signature each year. That waiver put Hoover right in Johnson's pocket. With that leverage Johnson began to take advantage of Hoover, using the Bureau as his personal investigative pawn. [LBJ's] never-ending requests were usually political, and sometimes illegal." Sullivan and Brown, *The Bureau*, 60.

10 "Johnson and Hoover had their mutual fear and hatred of the Kennedys in common—and more. As neighbors in Washington since the days when Johnson was a senator from Texas, they had been frequent dinner guests in each other's homes. They remained close when Johnson served as vice-president[.]" Sullivan and Brown, *The Bureau*, 60.

11 When J. Edgar Hoover sent RFK a report on communists in government, RFK told JFK aide Kenneth O'Donnell, "Look at this shit. Hoover's gone mad. All this nonsense about the Communist Party in America. What a supreme and utter waste of time." RFK then added his

opinion of the director personally: "He's a fucking cocksucker. Any day I expect him to show up for work wearing one of [First Lady Jacqueline Kennedy's] dresses by [French clothing designer Christian] Dior." Heymann, *RFK*, 215.

Near the end of his tenure as Attorney General in 1964, RFK told reporters he thought that J. Edgar Hoover was dangerous, senile, and something of a psycho. Heymann, *RFK*, 219.

[12]   The day after JFK's assassination, J. Edgar Hoover ordered disconnected the direct telephone line that ran from his desk to RFK's desk in the Attorney General's office. See Heymann, *RFK*, 368.

RFK later lamented that after JFK's assassination, J. Edgar Hoover no longer had "to hide his feelings, and he no longer had to pay any attention to me." After Dallas, Hoover bypassed RFK and dealt directly with LBJ. Robert F. Kennedy interviews with Anthony Lewis (with Burke Marshall present), December 4, 6, and 22, 1964, cited in Guthman and Shulman, *Robert Kennedy in His Own Words*, 127.

Within a few days of JFK's death, J. Edgar Hoover went to the White House and passed out FBI security dossiers on senior Kennedy Administration appointees. Robert F. Kennedy interviews with Anthony Lewis (with Burke Marshall present), December 4, 6, and 22, 1964, cited in Guthman and Shulman, *Robert Kennedy in His Own Words*, 127.

[13]   On September 24, 1968, LBJ told Secretary of Defense Clark Clifford that he doubted Humphrey had the guts to be president. He said he would respect his vice president more if Humphrey "showed he had some balls." See Dallek, *Flawed Giant*, 577.

Nixon campaign aide Pat Buchanan did not see RFK as a formidable threat in 1968, because even if he had lived to win the presidential nomination, "Robert Kennedy as nominee would have made Johnson a silent partner of Nixon, so great was the animosity between him and RFK. That animosity dated to Robert Kennedy's resistance to Johnson's selection as vice presidential nominee in 1960, and RFK's contemptuous treatment of 'Uncle Cornpone' during his brother's presidency. Some Kennedy loyalists saw Johnson as a usurper, an illegitimate heir to the martyred JFK. And LBJ's animosity could only have been deepened by Bobby's having fallen upon him in his moment of maximum vulnerability after New Hampshire, when RFK piled on and accused the president of calling up 'the darker impulses of the American people.' Nor did Gene McCarthy bear any great love for his fellow Catholic who had lacked the courage to take on Johnson until he, McCarthy, had wounded the president in the Granite State." Buchanan, *The Greatest Comeback*, 265–266.

[14]   Shortly before the 1968 Republican National Convention, LBJ set up a private meeting with Richard Nixon. Before the meeting, Johnson told aides, "When [Nixon] gets the nomination he may prove to be more responsible than the Democrats.... [H]e is for our position on Vietnam.... The GOP may be of more help to us [on that issue] than the Democrats." Dallek, *Flawed Giant*, 571.

At this LBJ-Nixon secret White House meeting, LBJ fumed against liberal Democrats that demanded he order a bombing halt in Vietnam. As Nixon later recalled, LBJ asked rhetorically, "Do I tell that [American combat soldier fighting in Vietnam] that we'll stop bombing and let thirty percent more trucks filled with ammunition and guns come south so that [the North Vietnamese] will have a better chance to kill him?" Nixon, *RN*, 307-308.

In October 1968, when White House aide Jim Rowe passed along to LBJ a request from Humphrey for the president to campaign for him in Texas, New Jersey, and key border states, LBJ refused, telling Rowe, "Nixon is following my policies more closely than Humphrey." See Dallek, *Flawed Giant*, 580.

Shortly before the 1968 Democratic Convention began, when Humphrey showed LBJ his proposed compromise platform language on Vietnam, LBJ exploded. He said that Humphrey was not only jeopardizing the lives of his sons-in-law in combat in Vietnam, but also jeopardizing the chance for peace. LBJ threatened to destroy Humphrey if he pursued this policy. LBJ's Secretary of Defense, Clark Clifford, later said that after seeing Humphrey's proposal, LBJ branded his vice president as disloyal. See Dallek, *Flawed Giant*, 571-572.

As Humphrey related many years later, LBJ viewed American combat soldiers as "my boys": "When bombing raids [over North Vietnam] were going on, [Johnson] frequently stayed up late to hear whether all the planes returned. He thought of every bomber that went out, every flight crew, as if it were his own personal family or property. Some mornings, looking drawn, he would put an arm around my shoulder, almost for support, and say, 'Hubert, I lost five of my boys last night. How am I going to explain to their families why they had to die?'" See Humphrey, *The Education of a Public Man*, 340.

After leaving the White House, LBJ told biographer Doris Kearns Goodwin, "Everything I knew about history told me that if I got out of Vietnam and let [the communists] run through the streets of Saigon, then I'd be doing exactly what Chamberlain did in World War II. I'd be giving a big fat reward to aggression. And I knew that if we let communist aggression succeed in taking over South Vietnam... [it would] kill my Administration, and damage our democracy.... [And there] would be Robert Kennedy out in front leading the fight against me, telling everyone I had betrayed John Kennedy's commitment to South Vietnam. That I had let a democracy fall into the hands of the communists. That I was a coward—an unmanly man. A man without a spine. Oh, I could see it coming, all right." Kearns Goodwin, *Lyndon Johnson and the American Dream*, 252-253.

[15] LBJ saw potential international catastrophe in accepting the Humphrey-Kennedy-McCarthy brand of Vietnam War appeasement. He believed that once the Soviet Union and communist China saw that we were weak in Vietnam, they "would move in a flash to exploit our weaknesses. They might move independently or they might move together. But move they would—whether through nuclear blackmail, through subversion, with regular armed forces or in some other manner.... [T]hey couldn't resist the opportunity to expand their control over the vacuum of power we would leave behind us [in Vietnam]. And so would begin World War III. So you see, I was bound to be crucified either way I moved." Kearns Goodwin, *Lyndon Johnson and the American Dream*, 253.

JFK's and LBJ's Secretary of State, Dean Rusk, told Nixon that U.S. withdrawal from Vietnam would leave Red China as the only major power on the Asian mainland, thus creating a panic among our allies. See Nixon, *RN*, 308.

In reality, after Humphrey delivered his September 30, 1968 speech in Salt Lake City in which he announced his break with LBJ's Vietnam policies, LBJ believed that Humphrey's proposal made the South Vietnamese "extremely nervous and distrustful of the Johnson-Humphrey Administration and of the entire Democratic Party." LBJ also felt that Humphrey's speech made South Vietnam believe it was in their interest to drag their feet, not cooperate with Johnson's peace negotiations, and hold out for a better deal under a Nixon Administration. It so irritated Johnson that he later refused to see Humphrey." See Dallek, *Flawed Giant*, 579-580.

[16] LBJ grew furious over Humphrey's continued suggestion of a North Vietnam bombing halt. On September 4, 1968, LBJ told the members of his National Security Council that if U.S. negotiators in Vietnam maintained a hard line and continued the bombing, "we can convince the North Vietnamese that they won't get a better deal if they wait" to join in peace negotiations. Further, LBJ did not want to order a bombing halt until North Vietnam accepted three conditions: 1) respect the demilitarized zone; 2) quit attacking South Vietnamese cities; and 3) allow South Vietnam to join the peace negotiations. Dallek, *Flawed Giant*, 577.

[17] In a conversation with Nixon, J. Edgar Hoover referred to RFK as "that sneaky little son-of-a-bitch." See Heymann, *RFK*, 219.

[18] By the late 1960s, "muckraking" journalist Drew Pearson's *Washington Merry-Go-Round* column was printed in over 650 newspapers and had an estimated 60 million readers. See https://en.wikipedia.org/wiki/Drew_Pearson_(journalist).

CHAPTER 40

[1] Jack Wallace (George Wallace's brother) recalled that his family grew up as poor farmers: "We grew most of our own food, and in the summer we spent a good bit of our time helping Mother shell peas and snap beans. There was very little you had to buy at the store." George Wallace put himself through school shoveling coal and waiting tables in boarding houses for 25 cents an hour. When he married his wife Lurleen, their first home was a reconverted chicken house. See Chester, Hodgson, Page, *An American Melodrama*, 263-264.

[2] Wallace always maintained that his stand in the schoolhouse door at the University of Alabama was not based on racism, but rather to raise a constitutional sovereignty objection to federal encroachment over states rights. "I stirred the people up about the court system, not against black folks," Wallace said. "I said that the white and black people of Alabama can work these problems out themselves. We don't need the Justice Department to tell us everything to do and what time frame to use. We can do that ourselves in Alabama." Wallace's first press secretary, Bill Jones, said Wallace "knew that integration was coming.... He felt that the way to keep violence down and prepare the people to accept what they were going to have to accept was to say repeatedly—repeatedly: 'Let me do it, let me stand for you'—not only in the schoolhouse door, but in every way, such as in the courts and everything. He realized that he could be a catalyst for getting the thing accepted finally that he knew was going to be forced down the South's throat, whether they wanted it or not." In any event, Wallace later came to regret his "schoolhouse door" defiance, saying, "I made a very bad mistake in saying 'segregation forever....' [T]hat day at the University of Alabama, carried nationwide [on radio and

television], gave me a bad image and was not good for the state's image.... If I had it to do over, I would not have stood in the schoolhouse door at all. I would have prevented violence on campus in some other manner." As his biographer noted, "the irony of ironies—that within a year [of the schoolhouse door incident], Wallace's Alabama was integrating at a rate as fast as or faster than most other states in the Union, much less the South." Lesher, *George Wallace*, 167, 238, 240.

Although a segregationist in the early 1960s, Wallace insisted he was no racist. He was, like most Southerners of his and earlier generations, a separatist. In later years, as Wallace's views softened, he apologized publicly for his segregationist past, saying it was the only way of life he knew growing up. Apology accepted: in his final race for Alabama governor in 1982, Wallace won a fourth term with over 90 percent of the black vote. Tuskegee University, a historically black college founded by Booker T. Washington, awarded Wallace an honorary degree. James Hood, one of the two black students whose entrance into the University of Alabama Wallace had attempted to block in 1963, grew to admire Wallace as "'one of the most astute Southern politicians this country will ever know.' Although he did not agree with Wallace's attempt to deny him entry to the University of Alabama, Hood maintained that Wallace's position 'had nothing to do with race,' but, rather, with constitutional questions, just as Wallace asserted. Hood even called Wallace's act 'courageous' and 'very noble' because the governor had been ready to risk being jailed to keep his promise to his constituents and raise the issue of states rights. And Hood did not think Wallace was a racist." Lesher, *George Wallace*, 234.

There is a persistent claim that after losing his 1958 race for Alabama governor, Wallace said that he would never let another political opponent "out-nigger" him. This canard has been debunked. As Stephen Lesher noted in his critical and seminal biography of Wallace in 1994, the source of this claim came from "Marshall Frady in his scantily documented biography of Wallace [quoting] an unnamed observer" who claimed that Wallace made this comment to a room filled with supporters after losing his 1958 gubernatorial race: John Patterson out-nigguh'ed me. And, boys, I'm not goin' to be out-nigguh'ed again..... That harsh, cynical line, in one form or another, clung to Wallace like a sweat-soaked shirt throughout his career. Despite the inability of any other reporter to find a single credible source who could or would say that Wallace made the remark, it was repeated so often in articles about Wallace that it took on the coloration of gospel truth. After the statement appeared in the Frady book, Joseph P. Cumming, then the chief of *Newsweek*'s Atlanta bureau, could not confirm that Wallace had ever uttered it.… Cumming did, however, report that some people (also unnamed) remembered that Wallace said he would never be 'out-segged' again. Wallace always denied having said anything remotely like being out-niggered or out-segged. He maintained that using the word nigger was uncharacteristic for him… and of the second term, he said, 'The phrase [out-segged] is not even a Southern phrase—I have never heard of that expression before. I never said anything like that in my life.'" Lesher, *George Wallace*, 128-129.

With no verifiable witnesses to Wallace ever using the phrases "out-niggered" or "out-segged," and despite Wallace's oft-repeated denial that he ever used the phrases, Wallace's 1998 *Washington Post* obituary resurrected the claim that he said he wouldn't be "out-segg'd" by his next political opponent. See Richard Pearson, "Former Ala. Gov. George C. Wallace Dies," *Washington Post*, September 14, 1998, https://www.washingtonpost.com/wp-srv/politics/daily/sept98/wallace.htm.

[3] Wallace pondered whether to run in the 1968 Democratic primaries or instead form a third party and run as an independent. He decided that challenging LBJ in the primaries might allow him to embarrass the president in one or more primaries, but since LBJ controlled the Party machinery, it was foolish to think he could deprive him of the nomination. Instead, by running as an independent, he could attack both the Democrats and the Republicans—and "he would remain in the spotlight for the duration of the campaign—all the way to Election Day in November 1968." See Lesher, *George Wallace*, 387-388.

Susanna McBee wrote in *Life* magazine, "Wallace raids into the alien North have found a welcome among many people of substantial place and means. But his primary pitch seems targeted dead center on middle-class and on lower-middle-class whites. Here lie resentments about high taxes, inflation, and crime, along with the sullenness of people who feel that they are left out in the cold while the country's leadership pampers the undeserving shiftless. In both North and South, Wallace appears to be tapping the powerful underground stream of frustration and discontent." Lesher, *George Wallace*, 413-414.

[4]   At his presidential candidacy announcement on February 8, 1968, Wallace said that if he won, he would gather "all [the] briefcase-toting bureaucrats... and throw their briefcases in the Potomac River." He promised that he would make it possible to walk Washington's streets safely, even if he "had to keep thirty-thousand troops standing on the streets two feet apart with two-foot-long bayonets." Urban rioting and open support for America's Vietnamese enemies, he said, were led by "activists, anarchists, revolutionaries, and communists" whom he would arrest and jail. See Lesher, *George Wallace*, 400-401.

[5]   In October 1967, polls showed Wallace at 10 percent of the vote. By July of 1968, he stood at 16 percent. Pollster George Gallup reported, "If the presidential election were being held today, the strong possibility exists that third party candidate George Wallace would deny either major party candidate the electoral votes needed to win." Chester, Hodgson, Page, *An American Melodrama*, 293.

[6]   During a campaign rally, when a heckler in the rear of the hall "emitted a shrill yell... [George] Wallace's schoolyard retort—'Show that fellow where the little boys room is'—was applauded." Lesher, *George Wallace*, 291-292.

When hecklers once tried to drown out a Wallace speech, he shouted back, "These are the folks that people like us are sick and tired of. You've been getting a good lesson in what we've been talking about. They talk about free speech but won't allow it to others." Lesher, *George Wallace*, 414.

Once, during his 1964 presidential primary campaign, when a parade of hecklers tried to interrupt Wallace, he raised his voice and told his wildly applauding audience, "There are more good people like you in this country today than there are these little pinkos running around outside, but we must band together. When you and I start marching and demonstrating and carrying signs, we will close every highway in this country!" Lesher, *George Wallace*, 271.

During his 1968 presidential campaign, Wallace told a rally audience,

"When I become your president, I'm going to ask my Attorney General to seek an indictment against any college professor who calls for a communist victory [in Vietnam]. That's not dissent. That's not free speech. That's treason." Lesher, *George Wallace*, 420-421.

7   When Wallace brought his presidential campaign to Dartmouth College, student protesters threw plastic bags full of urine at him. White, *The Making of the President 1968*, 347.

When Wallace campaigned at Northern college campuses, "the very sharpness of emotions he aroused amplified his voice. Students, bearing peace placards, would beat him over the head; they would rock his car, trying to overturn it; and the publicity spread his message." White, *The Making of the President 1968*, 345.

8   In one of his stump campaign speech lines in 1968, Wallace told cheering audiences that if any demonstrator ever tried to stop his motorcade by lying down in front of his car, he would run right over them. See, e.g., Ambrose, *Nixon (Volume Two)*, 185.

During a campaign swing through Maryland, Wallace told reporter Jim Bennett, who covered the race for the Birmingham Post-Herald, that if any protesters ever lie down in front of his car, "that's the last car they will ever lie down in front of." Jim Bennett, "I Covered George Wallace's Presidential Races in the '60s," *Alabama Media Group*, March 16, 2016, http://www.al.com/opinion/index.ssf/2016/03/i_covered_george_wallaces_pres.html.

"Greeted by stink bombs in some places... by brawls and gun threats in yet others, [the Wallace campaign] found that the greater the violence against them the more ready and numerous were the faithful of the underground to come out and work" for him. White, *The Making of the President 1968*, 347.

By October 1968, Wallace's campaign mailing address—P.O. Box 1968, Montgomery, Alabama—received a cascade of campaign donations, often reaching 20,000 letters each day. See Chester, Hodgson, Page, *An American Melodrama*, 651.

9   One of Wallace's stock lines during his 1968 campaign was, "You can take all the Democratic candidates for president and all the Republican

candidates for president. Put them in a sack and shake them up. Take the first one that falls out, grab him by the nape of the neck, and put him right back in the sack. Because there is not a dime's worth of difference in any of them." Wallace, *Stand Up for America*, 121.

"If George Wallace hates anything, it is not Negroes—it's the federal government of the United States and its 'pointy-head' advisors, the 'intellectual morons,' the 'guideline writers' of Washington who try to upset the natural relation of races and force Negroes and whites to live together in unnatural mixing." White, *The Making of the President 1968*, 345.

At one campaign speech, Wallace proclaimed, "Crime has risen in our country at an astronomical rate, and the court system now has ruled that you can hardly convict a criminal. If you are knocked on the head on a street in a city today, the man who knocked you on the head is out of jail before you can get to the hospital.... And they can't tell me that we can't adopt a system in this country that will protect the individual liberties and freedoms of our people and, at the same time, incarcerate the man who is a self-confessed murderer." Lesher, *George Wallace*, 294.

In testimony before the House Judiciary Committee in 1964, Wallace denounced the U.S. Supreme Court for banning prayer in school: "We are being manipulated by the courts in a gigantic socialist conspiracy." He claimed the Court has made a "hollow mockery" of the Bill of Rights in a decision "as sweeping and deadly as any ever issued by any dictatorial power," and he noted that the 1928 platform of the U.S. Communist Party demanded the abolition of religious instruction in schools. Lesher, *George Wallace*, 292.

In a 1967 interview with James J. Kilpatrick, Wallace predicted, "By the fall of 1968, the people of Cleveland and Chicago and Gary and St. Louis will be so goddamned sick and tired of federal interference in their local schools, they'll be ready to vote for Wallace by the thousands. The people don't like this trifling with their children, telling them which teachers to have to teach in which schools, and busing little boys and girls half[way] across the city just to achieve 'the proper racial mix....' I'll give you another big [issue] for 1968: law and order. Crime in the streets. The people are going to be fed up with the sissy attitude of Lyndon Johnson and all the intellectual morons and theoreticians he has around him. They're fed up with the Supreme Court that [is] a sorry, lousy, no account outfit.... Anytime the federal government lays down the law for people... fixing the terms and conditions on which they can sell their own homes... folks won't stand for it. And there's nothing about the sale of private housing in the Constitution either.... [On Vietnam], [w]e've got to win this war." White, *The Making of the President 1968*, 346.

During his 1968 campaign, Wallace "denounced the hippies, rioters, and campus anarchists with a populist rhetoric Nixon could not match. He was a demon campaigner with a brutal but effective humor. Everywhere he went the crowds were big and excited. While he had only 9 percent of the national vote in a Gallup poll in April, by July, he was at 16. See Buchanan, *The Greatest Comeback*, 291-292.

[10]   Lurleen Wallace, Wallace's first wife, explained her husband's popularity by noting that when they hear him express his opinions on the issues, ordinary people "listen to him and think, 'That's what I would say if I were up there.'" Lesher, *George Wallace*, 390-391.

[11]   David Azbell, Wallace's former press secretary, recalled in 2014, "When I worked for the governor, he was 77 years old and still smoked the Garcia y Vega cigars that were his trademark throughout his career. In fact, a local tobacco wholesaler would deliver five boxes each week, and he would smoke them all before the next batch arrived, which translated to 150 cigars a week that he smoked. My wife would complain each night when I returned home from work because I reeked of cigars from being next to him all day." David Azbell, *American Political Items Collectors Facebook Page*, July 18, 2016, https://www.facebook.com/groups/apicusa/search/?query=azbell%20wallace%20cigar.

[12]   Columnist James Kilpatrick wrote, "[Wallace] can strut sitting down.... He is full of nervous stage business: standing up, sitting down, the horn-rimmed glasses on, the glasses off, lighting his cigar, licking his cigar, spitting in the wastebasket. There is never a moment of stillness.... I had met some mighty talkers. But George Wallace is the greatest nonstop talker of them all." Kilpatrick added that whether traveling, dining, or chatting with Wallace during one concentrated period, it made him feel as though he was "spending seventeen hours in the middle of a juke box." Lesher, *George Wallace*, 391.

[13] "The first Gallup poll after the [1968 Republican National Convention], in mid-August, put Nixon ahead by 45-29, a margin of 16 points over Humphrey that Nixon had never known before. Wallace was at 21, closer to Vice President Humphrey than Humphrey was to Nixon." Buchanan, *The Greatest Comeback*, 317.

From 9 percent in the national polls in April-May 1968, Wallace moved to 16 percent by June, and 21 percent by mid–September. "If the trend continued unbroken, [Wallace could] reach close to 30 percent" by Election Day. If that happened, "no candidate would have a majority of the Electoral College. And in a time of war, a leaderless America would wait for weeks, perhaps months, on the Electoral College or the politics of the House [of Representatives]" to produce the next president. White, *The Making of the President 1968*, 347-348.

[14] Wallace claimed that if he could deadlock the election in the Electoral College, the election would never reach the House of Representatives, because "he would direct his electors to vote for the major party candidate who allowed Wallace a say in selecting the Cabinet and future Supreme Court nominees." Lesher, *George Wallace*, 401.

[15] "In 1968, George Wallace publicly offered to barter with his electoral support. Wallace's electors pledged in writing to vote as he told them to. In a celebrated press conference on February 19, 1968, he named his price for delivering the presidency to someone else: the criminal indictment of anyone advocating Vietcong victory; the elimination of the federal anti-poverty program; cuts in foreign aid to any nation that refused to support the United States in Vietnam; a tough stand on law and order; the repeal of all civil rights legislation; the appointment of 'differently oriented' judges to the Supreme Court; and a return to the states of all power over housing, school, and hospital integration, over reapportionment, and over congressional redistricting." Laurence H. Tribe and Thomas M. Rollins, "Deadlock," *The Atlantic Monthly*, October 1980, http://www.theatlantic. com/past/docs/issues/80oct/deadlock.htm.

[16] In 1968, the South had a quarter of the national population. Chester, Hodgson, Page, *An American Melodrama*, 702.

"If, as they hoped at their September peak, Wallace did carry seventeen states, then, they felt, a longer-range perspective would open to them. His victories would so terrify local politicians everywhere that in [the midterm elections of] 1970 scores of congressmen, perhaps more than 100, would run in alliance with George Wallace's American Independent Party. With such a congressional base, all perspectives would change." White, *The Making of the President 1968*, 351.

The Wallace campaign hoped to place their American Independent Party on the ballot in every state. This proved problematic, since each of the 50 states has their own special laws relating to ballot access. The immense power and popularity of Wallace's campaign became frighteningly apparent to the political class when his supporters navigated the labyrinthine election laws of every state and qualified him for the November ballot in each one—making him the first third party candidate in American history to achieve that feat. "To create a third party in America, one must mount a transcontinental assault on habit, tradition, emotion and, above all, 50 different election laws." White, *The Making of the President 1968*, 346.

As reporter Don Holt noted, the Wallace campaign "is like the air. You can't see it, but it is all around you." Lesher, *George Wallace*, 414-415.

[17]   "People who threw rocks, bottles, and other dangerous objects at my rallies were called 'demonstrators.' Those who did the same thing during Nixon or Humphrey rallies were correctly called hoodlums, thugs, and anarchists." Wallace, *Stand Up for America*, 125.

Under Alabama law, Wallace could not run for reelection in 1966 because governors at that time were limited to a single four-year term. After Wallace tried unsuccessfully to change the law, his wife, Lurleen B. Wallace, ran in his place and succeeded her husband. Sixteen months into her term, she died of cancer on May 7, 1968. See, e.g., Glenn T. Eskew, "Lurleen B. Wallace (1967-1968)," Encyclopedia of Alabama, updated September 30, 2014, http://www.encyclopediaofalabama.org/article/h-1662.

During one campaign rally, Wallace excoriated the press in attendance: "*Life* magazine comes out against my wife. You know them, though. They think you're degenerates.... And [t]he *Saturday Evening Post* [is] with us here today. They take a lot of pictures, then they pick out the worst one and put it in there…. *The Wall Street Journal* made fun of my wife on the front page because she used to be a dime-store clerk and her daddy was a shipyard worker. The liberals and beatniks and socialists have gotten together and said, 'We're not gonna have any more of Wallace,' and that's why the national press is here—to see if you are going to repudiate what we have done. I'm not fighting the federal government. I'm fighting this outlaw, beatnik crowd in Washington that has just about destroyed the federal government—and I'm trying to save it." Lesher, *George Wallace*, 361.

[18]   Throughout the 1968 campaign, Wallace "insisted he was not a racist, that he did not dislike any person because of color, and he did 'not recommend segregation in any phase of our society in any state in this union' but rather 'that the states… continue to determine the policies of their domestic institutions themselves, and that the bureaucrats and the theoreticians in Washington let people in Ohio and New York and California decide themselves… what type of school system they are going to have.'" Lesher, *George Wallace*, 389.

At another campaign speech, Wallace declared, "Now, you may want to bus your children across to some other school just to meet the plans of some social engineer in Washington for racial balance in the classroom because they say that's good. I don't object to that if that is what you want to do. But you people here in Maryland ought to decide that for yourselves, not some bureaucrat sitting in Washington." Lesher, *George Wallace*, 298.

[19]   During the 1968 campaign, in Cicero, Illinois, Wallace told a rally, "Some of these newspaper editors—they look down their nose at every workingman in Cicero, on every workingman in the United States and calls them a group of red-necks or group of punks because we want to defend America…. [W]hen we're talking about 'domestic institutions,' we're talking about schools, we're talking about hospitals, we're talking about the seniority of a workingman in his labor union, we're talking about ownership of property, that's what we're talking about. I want to say this about the school system of Alabama and Illinois. We don't have any recommendations to make in Illinois about what kind of schools you ought to have in Cicero. You people are intelligent enough in this city and this state to determine for yourselves what's in the interest of your

child, where he should go to school. And we don't need guidelines to tell us, and we don't need half a billion dollars being spent on bureaucrats in Washington of your hard-earned tax money to check every school system, every hospital, every seniority list of a labor union. And now after the election they're going to check even on the sale of your own property.... One of the first things I'm going to ask the Congress [to do after I am elected president is] to repeal this law about the sale of your own property and let them know that a man's home is still his castle." White, *The Making of the President 1968*, 349.

20   Wallace said he opposed the 1964 Civil Rights Act not because of any opposition to black rights, but because it was a massive federal bureaucratic intrusion upon the states and communities. During an interview on NBC's *Meet the Press*, he rejected accusations of racist motivations by himself and like-minded opponents: "'I don't believe there is a backlash in this country because of color. I think that's a journalistic expression. I think it was coined by the news media. I think there's a backlash against the theoreticians and the bureaucrats in national government.... There is a backlash against big government in this country.... I'm not fighting the federal government. I'm fighting this beatnik mob in Washington that has just about destroyed the federal government.' And one day, in the middle of 1967, he hit upon the sentence that was to be an applause line in 100 speeches because his audiences loved it so: 'Our lives are being taken over by bureaucrats, and most of them have beards!'" Chester, Hodgson, Page, *An American Melodrama*, 280.

At another campaign rally, Wallace said that, because of the so-called civil rights laws now on the books, "Every businessman would have to keep records on the race, color, religion, and creed of his employees to prove that he is not discriminating. Because if he has one hundred employees and only two of them are Chinese Baptists, but there are 4 percent Chinese Baptists in the place where he lives, he is going to have to show some federal bureaucrat why he doesn't have four of them working for him—and then fire someone and hire them." Lesher, *George Wallace*, 298.

21   Wallace told reporters he would stop urban riots by "shooting looters and arsonists on the spot." Lesher, *George Wallace*, 414.

"Speaking in Detroit, Newark, Los Angeles, cities ravaged by rioting and looting, [Wallace] told his audiences: 'We don't have riots in Alabama. They start a riot down there, first one of 'em to pick up a brick gets a bullet in the brain, that's all. And then you walk over to the next one and say 'All right, pick up a brick. We just want to see you pick up one of them bricks, now.'" George J. Marlin, "Is Trump Repeating George Wallace's '68 Disaster?" *Newsmax*, November 7, 2016, http://www.newsmax.com/George-J-Marlin/george-marlin-george-wallace-1968-cautionary-tale/2016/06/11/id/733409/.

In one campaign speech, Wallace told the crowd that when he won the White House, "I am going to give the moral support of the presidency to the police and firemen in your city and through your state. Let me tell you something: if it wasn't for the police and firemen of your city, you wouldn't be able to even ride down your streets, much less walk down them." Lesher, *George Wallace*, 420-421.

[22] Author Theodore H. White speculated that Wallace might "have gone down as a major figure in the new South. Heavy appropriations for more schools (fourteen new junior colleges authorized), more hospitals, mental institutions, nursing homes and clinics, free textbooks, increased Social Security benefits for state employees, [and] the largest road-building program in Alabama's history were his achievements. They might have marked him as one of the South's outstanding progressive governors" but for the racist accusations that swirled around Wallace during most of his public life. See White, *The Making of the President 1968*, 344.

As governor, Wallace was (by Southern standards) a "big spender": he built roads and schools, worked to attract more business to Alabama, and increased money for health programs substantially. Chester, Hodgson, Page, *An American Melodrama*, 267.

During the 1968 campaign, Wallace denounced the Ku Klux Klan, saying he had no use for the group, and called them, "just a bunch of thugs." Chester, Hodgson, Page, *An American Melodrama*, 29.

"[W]hen a Gallup poll of America's most admired men was published, Wallace placed seventh—just below Pope Paul VI and just ahead of Richard Nixon. Hubert Humphrey did not make the list." Lesher, *George Wallace*, 423.

[23] During one press interview, Wallace said, "'The American people are sick and tired of columnists and TV dudes who get on the national networks and, instead of reporting the news as it is and shame the devil, which is what they are supposed to do, trying to slant and distort and malign and brainwash this country.' After the program, the CBS reporter Dan Rather, one of the panelists, rushed up to Wallace and said earnestly, 'Governor, if you ever have an instance where CBS has distorted news about you in any way, I want you to call me collect and let me know—and I will see that that is corrected.' Wallace looked at him, grinned, and replied, 'Dan, I can't do that; it would bankrupt CBS.'" Lesher, *George Wallace*, 309.

CHAPTER 41

[1]   Regarding Humphrey's continued demand that Nixon debate him, "Nixon charged that his rival had been on 'both sides' of every important issue, and concluded, 'In fact, my friends, it appears that the Great Debate this year is going to be Humphrey vs. Humphrey, and I'm going to have to ask for equal time.'" Ambrose, *Nixon (Volume Two)*, 184.

[2]   After Nixon turned down Humphrey's debate challenge, this gave Humphrey another issue. Throughout the remainder of the 1968 presidential campaign, he taunted Nixon as "Richard the Chicken-Hearted" and "Richard the Silent." Nixon, *RN*, 319.

[3]   Near the end of the 1968 presidential campaign, after Humphrey mocked Nixon for refusing to debate him, "[a] reporter asked Nixon if he was afraid to debate his opponent. Nixon's face flushed as he snapped in reply, 'I'm not afraid of anybody. So that's the way it's going to be and don't plant any words in my mouth to the effect that I'm afraid to debate Mr. Humphrey. I've [debated] before and I'll do it again and we'll win next time.'" Ambrose, *Nixon (Volume Two)*, 192-193.

[4]   In a 1968 campaign memorandum to Nixon, aide Pat Buchanan wrote, "Debate challenges are for losing candidates" in reply to other staffers urging Nixon to debate McCarthy during the early primary stages to attract publicity. Buchanan, *The Greatest Comeback*, 195-196.

[5]   Years later, when Nixon penned his memoirs, he discussed his refusal to debate Humphrey during the 1968 campaign. Since Humphrey ran far behind after the conventions, Nixon believed that any debate would benefit Humphrey. He wrote that if he agreed to debate, Humphrey

would insist that Wallace be included—and Wallace was bleeding support from the Republicans more than from the Democrats. "Anything I did to elevate Wallace would be self-destructive. It was not fear but self-interest that determined my decision on the debates." Nixon, *RN*, 319.

6   Although this fact remains relatively unknown, even to historians, Reagan and RFK actually debated one time before a live worldwide television audience. They faced off via satellite (Reagan in Sacramento; RFK in Washington, D.C.) and took questions from a panel of international students based in London. The program, *Town Meeting of the World: "The Image of America and the Youth of the World,"* was broadcast over the CBS television and radio network on Monday, May 15, 1967, from 10:00-11:00 p.m. EDT. CBS News reporter Charles Collingwood moderated the forum. For the complete transcript, see http://reagan2020.us/speeches/reagan_kennedy_debate.asp.

7   Initially, Reagan did not want to participate in the CBS debate *Town Meeting of the World* until he heard that his opponent would be RFK, and then he "jumped at the chance." See Joseph Lewis, *What Makes Reagan Run?* (New York: McGraw-Hill 1968), 196-197.

Reporter Bill Boyarsky, who had noted that Reagan had 'bombed out' at the Gridiron Club when both he and RFK spoke there in early 1967, felt that Reagan 'had to prove himself' against Kennedy this time. Reagan press secretary [Lynn] Nofziger agreed that Reagan should go for it.... Such a debate opportunity might be the only chance he would ever have at least to question RFK's changing policies on Vietnam, whose new dovish tones Reagan so detested." Kopelson, *Reagan's 1968 Dress Rehearsal*, 205.

8   Reagan and RFK "first met in person at the prestigious Gridiron Dinner on March 11, 1967, in Washington, D.C. Walter Trohan of the *Chicago Tribune* was club president, and he had invited as speakers Reagan for the Republicans and RFK for the Democrats. The dinner turned out to be a bipartisan series of parities, skits, songs, and self-deprecating humor." Kopelson, *Reagan's 1968 Dress Rehearsal*, 182-183.

9   "The comments at the Gridiron Dinner traditionally were off-the-record, but some observers did make subsequent comments. Kennedy

introduced Reagan as 'the "acting" governor of California.' [1968 Reagan campaign strategist Thomas C. Reed] commented that Kennedy 'was masterful; his jokes were self-deprecating one-liners about himself, his family, and his problems with President Johnson. His timing was great and his humor was perfectly attuned to that Washington in-crowd.' Reagan's performance was 'light and his jokes good, but they were too California-oriented. They did not make much sense to the Washington insiders. Reagan tried to wind up with a short, serious pitch, but it failed....' For Reagan and RFK, in their first in-person head-to-head encounter, Reed reflected, 'Bobby won. Reagan departed as a country bumpkin not yet ready for prime time. As a pro, however, he had learned some lessons.'" Kopelson, *Reagan's 1968 Dress Rehearsal*, 183–184.

10   Reagan believed that, because of his support for Nixon over John F. Kennedy in the 1960 presidential campaign, Attorney General RFK went after him using the power of the Justice Department. First, RFK sought to bring antitrust charges against Reagan's employer, General Electric, for whom Reagan hosted the television show *General Electric Theater* since 1954. After RFK settled the case against GE due to lack of evidence, his Justice Department ordered an IRS audit of both Ronald and Nancy Reagan's tax returns for the prior ten years. "But despite Kennedy's harassment of the Reagans in the grand jury room and in arranging for the IRS audits, no charges were filed against anyone." Kopelson, *Reagan's 1968 Dress Rehearsal*, 41-43.

"Thomas Reed, who managed and directed Reagan's California gubernatorial bids, as well as his 1968 presidential nomination drive, writes in his book The Reagan Enigma that the animosity [between RFK and Reagan] began in 1962, when [RFK had Reagan] hauled before a federal grand jury to be questioned about using his influence as then-president of the Screen Actors Guild.... [The] Department of Justice, which Kennedy headed as Attorney General, after that appearance promptly 'subpoenaed' Reagan's tax returns.... And a few months later, Kennedy tried to get Reagan fired from *General Electric Theater*, Reagan believed[.]" Cathy Burke, "Bobby Kennedy Was Ronald Reagan's 'Supreme Villain,'" *Newsmax*, October 7, 2015, http://www.newsmax.com/Politics/Robert-Kennedy-Ronald-Reagan/2014/12/05/id/611395/.

[11]   Reagan's son Michael told campaign aide Tom Reed, "Dad told us he had just lost his job with GE. He said "Dad told us he had just lost his job with GE. He said [GE President] Ralph Cordiner had called him earlier to report that [Cordiner] had been contacted by Bobby Kennedy, who had said: 'If you want government contracts, get Reagan off the air.' Getting even with Kennedy was on his agenda, Reed said.... [The] animosity between Reagan, as Screen Actors Guild president, and then-Attorney General [Robert] Kennedy is consistent with what Reagan's daughter Maureen wrote in her memoirs, *First Father, First Daughter:* 'I've always suspected, and I'm sure Dad agrees with me on this one, that Bobby Kennedy had a hand in [having Reagan subpoenaed before the grand jury, having his tax records audited, and getting him fired as host of *General Electric Theater*]. I think the Kennedy Administration saw in Dad's [political speeches and] remarks a backhanded slur against their way of doing things.'" See Burke, "Bobby Kennedy Was Ronald Reagan's 'Supreme Villain.'"

According to Reagan's son Michael, when General Electric was negotiating several contracts with the federal government, RFK dictated new terms to the company: if GE wished to do business with the U.S. government, they would have to get rid of *General Electric Theater* and fire Reagan. Kopelson, *Reagan's 1968 Dress Rehearsal*, 43–44.

[12]   "In pure irony... [Robert F.] Kennedy had launched Reagan's political career by coercing General Electric and CBS to cancel *General Electric Theater* in 1962, as Michael Reagan [said] his father had believed[.]" Kopelson, *Reagan's 1968 Dress Rehearsal*, 182.

Thomas Reed said decades later that Reagan's presidential campaign in 1968 was fueled by a desire to get even with Kennedy. "It really accounts for why Reagan, who was sort of casual about whether he was going to run for president in '68, came alive. In March of '68, Johnson is out, Kennedy is in, and Reagan puts the throttle full forward. And he is now a real candidate, going hammers and tongs." After RFK's assassination in June 1968, "Reagan sort of lays back and goes through the motions, but he is changed.... Bobby Kennedy was the supreme villain in Ronald Reagan's life." See Burke, "Bobby Kennedy Was Ronald Reagan's 'Supreme Villain.'"

[13]   In 1967, when he set up the Reagan-RFK debate for his television program, CBS producer Don Hewitt "did not want the well-known Republicans, such as Nixon or Rockefeller, to oppose Kennedy. Rather 'the network people just saw Reagan as somebody that was articulate and formidable… so they asked him.' On the other hand, some may surmise that the liberal network may have thought they had arranged the perfect ambush, expecting Kennedy easily to triumph over Reagan." Kopelson, *Reagan's 1968 Dress Rehearsal*, 206.

[14]   In recalling the Reagan-RFK debate almost 40 years later, RFK's 1968 campaign press secretary, Frank Mankiewicz, wrote that he thought RFK debating Reagan was a wonderful idea, and that he had embraced the opportunity for his boss eagerly: "I saw no downside, and thought RFK would virtually destroy this 'B-movie actor' who had somehow stumbled into the governorship of California." Frank Mankiewicz, "Nofziger: A Friend With Whom It Was A Pleasure To Disagree," *Washington Post*, March 29, 2006, http://www.washingtonpost.com/wp-dyn/content/article/2006/03/28/AR2006032802142.html.

CHAPTER 42

[1] "On Monday, May 15, 1967, Reagan sat silently as he prepared to enter a television studio in Sacramento [to debate RFK on the CBS program *Town Meeting of the World*]. He seemed tense and did not hear the 'chatter of his assistants.'" Kopelson, *Reagan's 1968 Dress Rehearsal*, 203.

"Inevitably, the Ronnie-Bobby show turned out to be the first eyeball-to-eyeball test of two men who may very well meet on the road to the White House." See "The Ronnie-Bobby Show," *Newsweek*, May 29, 1967, 26.

[2] Reagan prepared for his May 1967 debate with RFK "by studying a 12-page memorandum. Assistant Press Secretary Clyde Beane had prepared the fact-based paper and recalled decades later that Reagan 'carried it around in his suit pocket—took it out and studied it in the limo or whenever he wanted to.'" Kopelson, *Reagan's 1968 Dress Rehearsal*, 204.

"By the testimony of his own staffers, [Robert] Kennedy made no special preparations for [his 1967 debate with Reagan]. Reagan prepped by studying a special twelve-page Vietnam memo drafted by his aides[.]" See "The Ronnie-Bobby Show," *Newsweek*, 31.

[3] In his monumental book on Reagan's 1968 presidential campaign, Dr. Gene Kopelson uncovered a treasure trove of evidence showing that former President Dwight D. Eisenhower coached and tutored Reagan during the early days of his political career. Ike remained heavily involved in schooling Reagan during the period leading up to and during his 1968 campaign for the Republican presidential nomination. See generally Kopelson, *Reagan's 1968 Dress Rehearsal*.

[4] In 1968, television station KXTV operated as the local CBS affiliate at 400 Broadway Street, Sacramento, California.

[5] "At first, CBS planned that Reagan would be in a studio in Sacramento and Kennedy at a studio in Syracuse, New York, with the student audience being taped in the afternoon local time in Great Britain. Later the plans for RFK were changed to Washington, D.C.... Host Charles Collingwood was on the London set with the eighteen students. It was the latest in Telstar, also called Early Bird, satellite television transmission technology at the time, although Telstar was a generic name.... Reagan and Kennedy were shown in color but [moderator] Collingwood and the students were shown in black-and-white; indeed the images of the latter had a grainy appearance. The students were sitting in two rows with name placards of their country of origin. [American student and panelist Bill] Bradley recalled that the television and satellite formats were indeed novel to him but he remembered he could see clearly both Kennedy and Reagan on large television screens in front of the students.... [At] the beginning [Kennedy and Reagan] were shown together on a split-screen." Kopelson, *Reagan's 1968 Dress Rehearsal*, 206-207.

[6] In preparing for his debate with RFK, Reagan "rehearsed at a Q and A session on the day before the taping. Beyond that, he could call on years of on-camera experience as an actor and TV pitchman and on rhetorical set--pieces polished in thousands of speeches he made as a free-enterprising huckster for the General Electric Co. It all paid off." See "The Ronnie-Bobby Show," *Newsweek*, 31.

"On the final preparatory day [before his March 1967 debate with RFK], Ed Meese had helped [Reagan] with a rehearsal dry-run. But probably Reagan's greatest hidden asset was the mentoring on Vietnam and global affairs he had received from Eisenhower, most recently at their March meeting." Kopelson, *Reagan's 1968 Dress Rehearsal*, 204.

[7] "The students [on the 1967 Reagan-RFK 1967 debate panel], attending universities in Great Britain, were from Europe, Asia, and Africa.... The one American student was named Bill Bradley.... In the mid-1960s, Bradley's name was a household word to American television audiences. He had been a Princeton University basketball star, held

many Ivy League and Princeton basketball records and had won an Olympic gold medal in basketball.... At the time of the debate, Bradley was a second-year Rhodes Scholar at Oxford but also worked for CBS radio's London office. His being familiar to the CBS London office staff is what prompted his invitation as the one American student participant." Kopelson, *Reagan's 1968 Dress Rehearsal*, 207.

8   Frank Mankiewicz, RFK's 1968 campaign press secretary, thought debating Reagan on live worldwide television was a great opportunity for RFK. Almost 40 years after their debate, Mankiewicz recalled, "I saw no downside, and thought RFK would virtually destroy this 'B-movie actor' who had somehow stumbled into the governorship of California." See Mankiewicz, "Nofziger."

9   The author estimates that in 1968, 101 million viewers might have watched a debate between the Republican and Democratic presidential and vice presidential nominees. Eight years earlier, 70 million viewers tuned in to the first Kennedy-Nixon 1960 debate (see "Kennedy-Nixon Presidential Debates, 1960," *Encyclopedia of Television*, http://www. museum.tv/eotv/kennedy-nixon.htm), when there were approximately 52 million television sets in the United States (see Winthrop Jordan, *The Americans* (Boston: McDougal Littel, 1996), 798. By 1968, the number of television sets in the U.S. rose to 78 million (see "1968 in Television," Wikipedia, https://en.wikipedia.org/wiki/1968_in_television).

10   "Some of the initial student questions centered on dissent and draft dodging, in which RFK had made blanket answers and statements that dissent was in fact patriotic. But Reagan countered, 'When dissent takes the form of actions that actually aid the enemy... such as avoiding the draft, refusing service, blocking troop trains and shipments of munitions... this is going beyond the dissent that is provided by our present governmental system.'" Kopelson, *Reagan's 1968 Dress Rehearsal*, 211.

11   An intimate of RFK said after his debate with Reagan, "Bob was talking to the students, Reagan was talking to the American TV audience. That's why Reagan was the big gainer." See "The Ronnie-Bobby Show," *Newsweek*, 31.

¹² "Reagan detested moral equivalency and took it on each time it reared its ugly head during [his 1967 debate with RFK]. Kennedy did not." Paul Kengor, "The Great Forgotten Debate," *National Review*, May 22, 2007, http://www.nationalreview.com/article/220949/great-forgotten-debate-paul-kengor.

¹³ "Truthfully, [the 1967 Reagan-RFK faceoff] was not a debate between Ronald Reagan and Bobby Kennedy. Rather, it descended into a venomous America-bashing session by a panel of extremely rude international students, who seemed to bask in their big chance to unleash their torrent of anger on the two available representatives of the country they despised…. [Panelist and American student Bill Bradley] appeared troubled and overwhelmed by the level of bile directed at his country. Also among [the panelists] was a beaming Soviet student, clearly thrilled with what he was witnessing from this group of young dupes who had obviously swallowed every dose of Kremlin propaganda hook, line, and sinker." See Kengor, "The Great Forgotten Debate."

"The students made it easy for Reagan. Their questions about the U.S. were almost universally hostile (except for a sympathetic offering by ex-Princeton basketball star Bill Bradley, now at Oxford and the only American on the panel)." See "The Ronnie-Bobby Show," *Newsweek*, 26.

In writing about the 1967 Reagan-RFK debate 40 years later, Professor Paul Kengor noted, "Reagan and Kennedy ended up debating the group of students, not one another. And it was there that Reagan was so effective, whereas Kennedy was passive, meek, and apologetic. Alarmed viewers looking for a defense of the United States as anything other than history's greatest purveyor of global misery were frustrated by Kennedy's lame responses but buoyed by Reagan's strong retorts." See Kengor, "The Great Forgotten Debate."

During his debate with Reagan, "Kennedy never seemed to dispute the premises nor supposed facts of the student questioners. Rather he seemed to join them in turning the meeting into one long critique of America and its policies…. Reagan on the other hand seemed quite at ease in defending his country…. On screen, Kennedy… sympathized with the anti-American students. Although his initial answers reminded the students that the goals of the U.S. had been to bring self-determination to the people of South Vietnam, his subsequent answers almost always were apologetic in nature. Clearly he felt he had to apologize to the students, and possibly the world, for America and his own role in creating those exact policies that the students, and now he, decried.... Then apparently attempting to side with the students [again] against American policy, when the second student cited that the U.S. was 'spending $20 billion a year destroying the country,' Kennedy corrected him to the upside: 'It's about $25 billion' and smirked. Then Kennedy continued his apologies: 'I said in the beginning that there were mistakes and things done that I would disagree with in South Vietnam....' Ronald Reagan remained fiercely pro-American. He saw the war being mismanaged and wanted to win. He knew that not only were America's goals in Vietnam laudatory, the original policies had been established while RFK was his brother's closest adviser." Kopelson, *Reagan's 1968 Dress Rehearsal*, 208-210.

When one student exaggerated that a million civilians had been killed in Vietnam, RFK didn't dispute the comment. More often than not, Kennedy "agreed with the students' sharply worded critiques" about his nation's policies, and he "seemed essentially sympathetic to the students' complaints about U.S. involvement in Vietnam." See "The Ronnie-Bobby Show," *Newsweek*, 31.

[14] "[O]nscreen to millions of American viewers and potential voters, governor and presidential candidate Ronald Reagan showed himself a steely debater [against RFK in 1967]. Reagan's knowledge of Vietnam was 'encyclopedic.'" Kopelson, *Reagan's 1968 Dress Rehearsal*, 210.

After the Reagan-RFK debate, *Newsweek* magazine reported, "To those unfamiliar with Reagan's big-league savvy, the ease with which he fielded questions about Vietnam may have come as a revelation. In response to other questions, [Reagan] effortlessly reeled off more facts and quasi-facts about the Vietnam conflict than anybody suspected he ever knew." See "The Ronnie-Bobby Show," *Newsweek*, 31.

During his debate with RFK, "[Reagan] was so thoroughly briefed by air time that he could correct the statistics of one of his questioners." Lewis, *What Makes Reagan Run?*, 196-197.

[15] During the Reagan-RFK debate in 1967, RFK "often was found looking into the wrong lens, while Reagan kept his gaze riveted on the

right camera. Kennedy tried to recover with an upbeat quote that he had used before, but Reagan came right back with one of his set pieces about man reaching for the stars, and Kennedy gulped in restrained agony." Lewis, *What Makes Reagan Run?*, 196-197.

During their debate, "[w]hile Reagan or the students spoke, Kennedy watched them on the studio monitor—so it seemed to the home audience as if he was deflecting his gaze. Reagan focused his eyes earnestly on the cameras—missing the monitor picture—but appearing to those at home as if he was carefully following every nuance." See "The Ronnie-Bobby Show," *Newsweek*, 31.

RFK's 1968 campaign press secretary Frank Mankiewicz later recalled that during the Reagan-RFK debate, "When the first question came in from London, about Vietnam, I sensed we were in trouble. Kennedy, predictably, thought about his answer, mentioned that there were difficult questions involved. He came down on the right side, to be sure, but only after a lengthy explanation and a good deal of thought, during none of which did he make eye contact with the camera. [Reagan] stepped into the camera and, making instant eye contact, answered clearly and quickly." See Mankiewicz, "Nofziger."

In his memoirs, 1968 Reagan campaign aide F. Clifton White recalled, "If I myself had any doubts about Reagan's [presidential] prospects, they were dispelled when I saw a televised debate between him and Bobby Kennedy that was filmed at Oxford. Reagan, to everyone's surprise, including Bobby's wife Ethel, [longtime NBC News political correspondent] Sander Vanocur and his wife, and others not exactly biased toward Reagan, slaughtered Bobby Kennedy. According to [Sander Vanocur], whose wife viewed the debate at a party, Ethel Kennedy kept shouting at the television screen, 'Do something, Bobby! He's killing you, he's killing you!'" White and Tuccille, *Politics as a Noble Calling*, 168.

[16] At his 1967 debate with Reagan, "Robert Kennedy was in a difficult position, as many of America's Vietnam policies had been promulgated by himself and his now-slain brother, President John F. Kennedy, and then had been continued by President Johnson.... [As] the students hammered away about Vietnam, Kennedy's demeanor became noticeably sullen and he looked quite uncomfortable as the representative of the United States

having to defend the Johnson policies." Kopelson, *Reagan's 1968 Dress Rehearsal*, 208-210.

[17]   At the end of his debate with RFK, "Reagan closed on an uplifting note to the students and the American audience by stating the ideals he had shared with Eisenhower and Churchill and the Republican Party... [while] Robert Kennedy 'gulped in restrained agony' and 'had little to say.'" Kopelson, *Reagan's 1968 Dress Rehearsal*, 213.

[18]   "Reagan himself credited his own careful [RFK debate] preparation, saying, 'That was one time when woodshedding really paid off.'" Kopelson, *Reagan's 1968 Dress Rehearsal*, 217.

Michael Deaver, one of Reagan's longtime aides, was in the Sacramento studio watching his boss debate RFK in June 1967. Writing in his memoir almost 35 years later, Deaver remembered that the moment the debate ended, "the lights went out in the studio in Sacramento, Reagan looked at me and smiled. He didn't say anything and I don't think the debate ever came up again." Michael K. Deaver, *A Different Drummer: My Thirty Years with Ronald Reagan* (New York: HarperCollins, 2001), 165-166.

"Reagan spoke publicly about the debate for the first time a few days later at Chico State College. Reagan said it had been 'shocking' to hear the diatribes against America uttered by the students. Reagan told his listeners that first he had thought the Oxford students might have been brainwashed. Then he had thought that America had failed to sell its image. But Reagan told his audience that instead he concluded that America had been trying to 'buy love in the world when we should have been earning respect.' America should stand tall and proud that it was helping the Vietnamese remain free." Kopelson, *Reagan's 1968 Dress Rehearsal*, 217-218.

[19]   1968 Reagan campaign aide Thomas Reed said that, at his debate with RFK, Reagan gave "a brilliant performance, a nice recovery from the dismal Gridiron Club face-off with RFK just two months before, and it was done before an audience of millions." Kopelson, *Reagan's 1968 Dress Rehearsal*, 216.

In his debate with RFK, Reagan had "beaten him decisively. [Reagan] was anything but intimidated by the Kennedy mystique, while Nixon was." White and Tuccille, *Politics as a Noble Calling*, 177.

[20]   RFK's 1968 campaign press secretary Frank Mankiewicz later recalled that the Reagan-RFK debate "was a disaster for our side. Reagan, a master of on-camera speaking developed through years of introducing the *General Electric Theater*, was in command from the beginning.... As the questions continued... it only got worse [for Kennedy]." See Mankiewicz, "Nofziger."

In later years, RFK's 1968 campaign press secretary Frank Mankiewicz reflected that the Reagan-RFK debate was "'the most one-sided, awful debate I have ever seen.... It was chaos.' Kennedy's bitterness about the debate would last almost to the end of his life." Kopelson, *Reagan's 1968 Dress Rehearsal*, 216-217.

[21]   "Robert F. Kennedy was 'furious' immediately after [his debate with Reagan], shouting, 'Who the fuck got me into this?' and telling his aides never again to put him on the same stage with 'that son-of-a-bitch....' [L]ater, when RFK saw his press secretary who had arranged his participation in debating Reagan, Frank Mankiewicz, Kennedy castigated him saying, 'You're the guy who got me into that Reagan thing.' But RFK's debate loss to Reagan clearly irked Kennedy to such a point that RFK would bring it up frequently from then on. Indeed Mankiewicz recalled that for the remaining year of RFK's life, whenever RFK and his 1968 campaign team would debate the pros and cons of a certain campaign activity, RFK would turn to Mankiewicz and ask ruefully, 'Aren't you the fellow who urged me to debate Ronald Reagan?'" Kopelson, *Reagan's 1968 Dress Rehearsal*, 217; see also Mankiewicz, "Nofziger."

Reporter and Reagan biographer Lou Cannon wrote that after the Reagan-RFK debate, RFK asked, "'Who the fuck got me into this?' Weeks later Kennedy upbraided Frank Mankiewicz by saying, 'You're the guy who got me into this Reagan thing.'" Lou Cannon, *Governor Reagan: His Rise to Power* (New York: Public Affairs, 2003), 260.

"Kennedy himself conceded defeat to Reagan, telling his aides after the debate to never again put him on the same stage with 'that son-of-a-bitch.' Kennedy was heard to ask immediately after the debate, 'Who the f— got me into this?' Frank Mankiewiz was that aide, as Kennedy was quick to remind him a few weeks later: 'You're the guy who got me into that Reagan thing.'" See Kengor, "The Great Forgotten Debate."

Reagan aide Michael Deaver, who was with Reagan in the Sacramento studio when he debated RFK on May 15, 1967, later wrote in his memoir, "Naturally I thought Reagan got the better of Kennedy, but I never really gave the session much thought until about twenty years later when I was at a charity dinner in Boston. There I met an attorney who had been on Bobby's staff at the time of the debate.... [At the end of the debate], Bobby looked at him and said, 'Don't ever, ever put me on the same stage with that son-of-a-bitch....' Like a lot of political sophisticates, Robert F. Kennedy paid a heavy price for underestimating Ronald Reagan." Deaver, *A Different Drummer*, 165-166.

RFK huffed after his debate with Reagan, "Don't ever put me on stage with that son-of-a-bitch again." See Burke, "Bobby Kennedy Was Ronald Reagan's 'Supreme Villain.'"

In 1981, at a White House ceremony, President Reagan bestowed posthumously on RFK the Congressional Gold Medal. In his prepared remarks, Senator Edward Kennedy, the last surviving Kennedy brother, told Reagan that after RFK debated him on international television in 1967, "[M]y brother Bob said that Ronald Reagan was the toughest debater he ever faced, and, obviously, he was right." Kopelson, *Reagan's 1968 Dress Rehearsal*, 852.

[22]   In later years, Nixon told aide Roger Stone that at the 1968 Republican National Convention in Miami, "The convention's heart belonged to Reagan." Nixon said that Reagan would have captured the presidential nomination had he stumbled. Stone, *Nixon's Secrets*, 328.

Near the end of the 1968 presidential campaign, "Humphrey was getting to Nixon with his 'Richard the Silent' and 'Richard the Chicken-Hearted'" taunts for Nixon's refusal to debate. Ambrose, *Nixon (Volume Two)*, 192-193.

[23]   After the Reagan-RFK debate, fans deluged Reagan "with thousands of letters of support for his 'standing up for America.' Those letters were used by [Reagan aide Thomas] Read and his team to 'begin determining who might be for Reagan throughout the nation.'" Kopelson, *Reagan's 1968 Dress Rehearsal*, 217.

[24] "There was total agreement, including among media sources who revered Bobby Kennedy, from the *San Francisco Chronicle* to *Newsweek*, that Reagan overwhelmingly won the debate...." Kengor, "The Great Forgotten Debate."

Newsweek magazine reported that, after their 1967 debate, "it was political rookie Reagan who left old campaigner Kennedy blinking when the session ended." See "The Ronnie-Bobby Show," *Newsweek*, 26.

"Reactions to Kennedy's performance uniformly were poor whereas Reagan's were excellent." Kopelson, *Reagan's 1968 Dress Rehearsal*, 215-217.

In a tongue-in-cheek commentary on the Reagan-RFK debate, William F Buckley Jr. wrote, "I mean, it is more than flesh and blood can bear: Reagan, the moderately successful actor, the man ignorant of foreign affairs, outwitting Bobby Kennedy in a political contest. It's the kind of thing that brings on... nightmares." William F. Buckley Jr., "Reagan and California," *National Review*, November 28, 1967.

Writing about the Reagan-RFK 1967 debate, Reagan biographer Lou Cannon wrote that Reagan gave "a stellar performance against Senator Robert Kennedy.... Reagan clearly bested Kennedy[.]" Lou Cannon, *Ronnie & Jesse: A Political Odyssey* (Garden City: Doubleday & Company, Inc., 1969), 264. Over 30 years later, in a subsequent Reagan biography, Cannon again emphasized that Reagan "bested Kennedy.... The press verdict that Reagan won the debate was virtually unanimous. [Historian] David Halberstam wrote that Reagan had 'destroyed' his opponent." See Cannon, *Governor Reagan*, 260.

Regarding his debate with RFK, Joseph Lewis wrote that Reagan "deflated another magnetic personality, Robert F Kennedy, on *CBS Town Meeting of the World*. While Kennedy anguished through questions about the war from hostile European students, the tanned and relaxed governor talked easily and precisely without a hint of uncertainty or hostility.... By the end of the show Kennedy looked as if he had stumbled into a minefield." See Lewis, *What Makes Reagan Run?*, 196-197.

[25] "Reagan performed so well [against RFK in their debate] that his [1968] presidential boosters sought to use clips from the debate during the 1968 Oregon presidential primary, and requested a copy from CBS.

Kennedy, however, reportedly did not want the video to be made available; CBS, naturally, acceded to his request." See Kengor, "The Great Forgotten Debate."

After the Reagan-RFK debate, "The sponsors of Reagan's campaign in the 1968 Oregon primary sought to use a portion of the CBS program in a political commercial. The Kennedy camp refused to give permission." Cannon, *Governor Reagan*, 260.

"[R]eportedly at Kennedy's behest, [CBS News] refused to make the program [of the Reagan-Kennedy 1967 debate] available for Reaganites to use during the 1968 Oregon primary, which ironically was the only campaign that Kennedy ever lost." Cannon, *Ronnie & Jesse*, 264.

1968 Reagan campaign aide F. Clifton White recalled that after the Reagan-RFK debate, "I obtained a tape of the performance and played it at Republican gatherings so people could see for themselves just how effective Reagan was. It was an education for everyone who saw it." White and Tuccille, *Politics as a Noble Calling*, 168.

CHAPTER 43

¹   In 1968, while campaigning at the Ford Motor Company plant in Flint, Michigan, Humphrey, who had been supported throughout his entire career by union members, noticed man after man on the assembly line wearing hats with a "Wallace for President" logo. It was then that Humphrey knew his longtime labor base was in jeopardy. Humphrey, *The Education of a Public Man*, 379.

²   After McCarthy dropped out of the 1968 presidential contest, a number of his college-aged supporters backed Wallace instead of Humphrey. One McCarthyite "explained that he had been disillusioned and embittered after the [1968] Democratic National Convention; he wasn't so much pro-Wallace as antiestablishment." Lesher, *George Wallace*, 417.

³   Following the disastrous 1968 Democratic Convention, "Bobby Kennedy and Gene McCarthy supporters were so furious about the tactics used against them [by Mayor Daley's police] that they not only refused to [support Humphrey after he won the presidential nomination], they actively went after Humphrey." Ambrose, *Nixon (Volume Two)*, 185.

⁴   Both before and during the 1968 presidential campaign, LBJ humiliated and harassed Humphrey repeatedly:

- During his vice presidency, Humphrey reserved the presidential yacht for a Potomac cruise with friends and supporters. When Humphrey's high-powered guests arrived at the dock, LBJ instructed White House Chief of Staff Marvin Watson to cancel the cruise. See Humphrey, *The Education of a Public Man*, 427.

- After Nixon defeated Humphrey for the presidency in November 1968, Nixon met with FBI Director J. Edgar Hoover, who surprised him by revealing that LBJ ordered FBI wiretaps on Humphrey during the 1968 campaign. Ambrose, *Nixon (Volume Two)*, 235.

- During the fall 1968 campaign, Humphrey told reporters he thought American troops in Vietnam could be drawn down in 1968 and 1969. After hearing Humphrey's assessment, LBJ ordered Secretary of State Dean Rusk to issue an immediate denial of that likelihood. The next day, in a speech to the American Legion, LBJ personally rejected Humphrey's comment, saying that nobody in the administration is in a position to predict when U.S. troops will start coming home. White, *The Making of the President 1968*, 334-335. The day after this humiliating rebuke, Humphrey recorded in his diary, "Wonder why Johnson shot me down when I said that troops would be withdrawn in 1969? I was right. I got the information from the White House. Ruined my credibility, made me look like a damn fool. It hurt. Never [recover] from that." Humphrey, *The Education of a Public Man,* 8.

- According to Humphrey aide Ted Van Dyk, during the 1968 race, LBJ refused to invite Humphrey to attend Executive Branch policy meetings and briefings at which the vice president normally would be expected. Adding to the insult, LBJ refused to brief Humphrey individually on Vietnam developments. He insisted that both Nixon and Wallace be included on any conference call briefings. LBJ further isolated Humphrey by withholding all official administration diplomatic cables. Humphrey's team had to glean intelligence through backdoor channels, forcing the Democratic nominee to rely on friends at the State Department and CIA to provide policy information. At one point Van Dyk had to abandon the campaign trail and fly overnight to Washington, where he paid a secret visit to the home of Bill Bundy (Assistant Secretary of State for Asian Affairs) to examine key Vietnam cables that LBJ ordered withheld from Humphrey. Van Dyk, *Heroes, Hacks & Fools,* 68-69.

- Did LBJ want Nixon to defeat his own vice president, Hubert Humphrey, for the presidency in 1968? Two senior Democrats close to LBJ thought that was the case. Shortly before Election Day 1968, LBJ's Secretary of Defense, Clark Clifford, conferred privately with his old friend, former Governor Averell Harriman (D-NY). At the time, Harriman was LBJ's ambassador to the Paris Peace Talks and the lead negotiator trying to end the Vietnam War. As Clifford and Harriman discussed the campaign, "Harriman wonder[ed] aloud whether Johnson might actually want Nixon to win the election. 'If you agree it is just between you and me,' replied the defense secretary, 'I believe you are right. The president wants to see [Humphrey] defeated.' Harriman was furious to think he was put in the position of merely holding the line [on Vietnam peace talks] for Nixon in Paris. If he knew that to be the case, he said, he would quit." Rudy Abramson, *Spanning the Century: The Life of W. Averell Harriman 1891-1986* (New York: William Morrow and Co., 1982), 668.

- "According to an unnamed official in the Johnson White House interviewed by Seymore Hersh, Johnson was angry at Humphrey for breaking with him on the war, and thus 'had no interest in defeating Nixon. He wasn't going to do anything for the purpose of seeing Nixon discredited.'" After reviewing the various theories, Ambrose concluded the charge that Nixon prevented a Vietnam peace in November 1968 was false. See Ambrose, *Nixon (Volume Two)*, 210-216.

[5] Near the end of the 1968 presidential race, and after Humphrey staked out his own position on Vietnam and separated himself from LBJ's policies, the protesters and hecklers who stalked his public appearances virtually disappeared. On the road with Humphrey during the campaign, adviser Ted Van Dyk noted that from Humphrey's breakout Vietnam speech in Salt Lake City (September 30, 1968) until Election Day, Humphrey received no major heckling on the war. "It was as if someone had thrown a switch," Van Dyk later wrote. Also, Humphrey's crowds grew in both size and enthusiasm. Van Dyk, *Heroes, Hacks & Fools*, 88; see also Humphrey, *The Education of a Public Man*, 403.

6   Nixon aide Pat Buchanan noted in his memoir of the 1968 presidential campaign, "Clearly, Nixon had a back channel to Johnson and [Secre-
tary of State] Dean Rusk of which some of us were unaware." Buchanan,
The Greatest Comeback, 321.

7   Humphrey adviser Ted Van Dyk recalled that shortly before Election
Day 1968, "Humphrey had attempted to see Johnson briefly one Saturday
morning during the vice president's last pre-election visit to Washington,
D.C.... I called Jim Jones, then LBJ's chief of staff, from New York the
day before to request the meeting. Johnson initially turned down the
request. When I persisted, Jones said LBJ would see Humphrey promptly
at noon in the Oval Office. Humphrey must be prompt, however, because
Johnson was leaving immediately thereafter for a weekend at Camp David.
Humphrey had a campaign rally that morning in Prince George's County,
Maryland. Rather than going directly to the White House, he stopped
en route at his apartment to change his shirt. At 12:01 p.m. I received a
call from Jones: 'Humphrey is late. The meeting is canceled.' From my
window, I could see the vice president alighting from his limousine at
the West Wing basement entrance. 'He is thirty seconds away, Jim,' I
said. 'Please ask the president not to cancel the meeting.' When Humphrey arrived at the Oval Office door, however, Jones blocked his way
and indicated that the president would be unable to see him. Humphrey
turned and walked back to his... office. 'I told Jim [Jones] I was trying
to run for president and was a couple minutes late,' [Humphrey] said. 'I
said I'd had enough of this stuff and the president could just cram it. I
could see Johnson through the door and I know he heard me. I hope he
did.'" Van Dyk, *Heroes, Hacks & Fools*, 89–90.

As Election Day neared, Humphrey made an appointment to meet
LBJ at the White House in October 1968. When Humphrey arrived, LBJ
refused to see him because he was a few minutes late. When given the news,
Humphrey recalled later, "I asked [White House aide Jim] Jones if he would
carry a message from me to the president. He agreed. And I described in
terms that the president would understand what they could do with their
meeting." Humphrey, *The Education of a Public Man*, 404-405.

Humphrey set up a meeting with LBJ in October 1968. When
Humphrey arrived at the White House, LBJ refused to meet with him.

Humphrey later told his aide Ted Van Dyk, "That bastard Johnson—I saw him sitting in his office. Jim Jones was standing across the doorway, and I said to him: 'You can tell the president he can cram [the meeting] up his ass.' I know Johnson heard me." See Dallek, *Flawed Giant*, 580.

In October 1968, "When Jim Jones, a top aide and later congressman from Oklahoma, met Humphrey in the [White House] driveway and told him the meeting [with LBJ] had been canceled, Humphrey asked Jim if he would take a message to the president. 'Tell him to kiss my ass.' It is probably the only time during the campaign that Humphrey spoke up angrily. Whether the invitation was delivered is unclear, although it is unlikely since Jones remained on the staff." Sherman, *From Nowhere to Somewhere*, 191.

[8]   Following the Republican National Convention, Nixon visited the LBJ Ranch in Texas for a personal briefing on Vietnam from Johnson. Ambrose, *Nixon (Volume Two)*, 178.

In his diary entry of August 9, 1968, reporter Drew Pearson noted, "LBJ dropped something of a political bombshell late yesterday when he called Nixon on the telephone and invited him to lunch at the [LBJ] ranch on Saturday. This is going a bit beyond the call of bipartisanship.... The general reaction among Democrats, however, was that LBJ was almost throwing [Humphrey] to the wolves." Pearson and Hannaford, *Washington Merry-Go-Round*, 602-603.

[9]   A few days before the start of the 1968 Democratic National Convention, Ambassador Sol Linowitz told reporter Drew Pearson privately that Humphrey "was very down over the treatment given him by LBJ and wonders whether the president doesn't really want the Republicans to follow him in office.... [T]he president may want a Republican to succeed him, first to carry out his war policy and second to show the country the contrast between his regime and Nixon's.... Hubert is livid over the so-called neutrality of the Johnson Administration. Not one cabinet member has spoken out for him." Pearson and Hannaford, *Washington Merry-Go-Round*, 607.

[10]   The LBJ Library was 50 miles west from Bergstrom Air Force Base. Robert A. Caro, *The Years of Lyndon Johnson: The Passage of Power* (New York: Alfred A. Knopf, 2012), 503.

11   It was "a Texas ritual [for special guests of the president at the LBJ ranch]: the presentation of big gray 'ten-gallon' Stetsons to the guests[.]" Caro, *The Years of Lyndon Johnson*, 509.

12   Driving across the LBJ ranch in a big convertible, the president and his guests "[bumped] along rutted trails and lurch[ed] across gullies." Caro, *The Years of Lyndon Johnson*, 504.

When giving a tour of his Texas ranch, LBJ showed visitors "the livestock loading pens and chutes. 'That's where the cattle go out and the money comes in,' he explained." Caro, *The Years of Lyndon Johnson*, 506.

LBJ's car at his Texas ranch, a big white Continental convertible, "was fitted out with a bullhorn which, at the touch of a button on the dashboard, emitted a loud moaning sound—Oo-OOH-gah, Oo-OOH-gah—like that of a bull in distress. Suddenly veering off the dirt track, the president would nose the Lincoln up to one of the Herefords, sounding the horn to try to get the bull to move. If it wouldn't, he would sometimes inch the car so close that its bumper touched the big, stolid animal, chewing solemnly on its cud. He would sound the horn again. The Hereford, alarmed at last, would amble away. Johnson would sound the horn in triumph." Caro, *The Years of Lyndon Johnson*, 515.

LBJ liked to show his Herefords off to guests visiting his Texas ranch. Sometimes he would "go up to a bull, kick its hindquarters ('That's where the best steaks come from.'). 'But that's not why I bought him,' he would explain with a grin, lifting up the bull's tail to display his huge testicles. 'This one's a steer,' he would say of another animal, giving his explanation that 'A steer is a bull who has lost his social standing.'" Caro, *The Years of Lyndon Johnson*, 515.

13   "[W]hy conservatives supported Nixon [for the 1968 GOP presidential nomination] was no mystery, nor was it opportunistic; they flocked to Nixon because they liked what he said on Vietnam—no compromise, war to the finish, total victory." During the fall 1968 campaign, "[Nixon] absolutely refused to discuss Vietnam [publicly], as that would undercut the president." Ambrose, *Nixon (Volume Two)*, 61-62, 183.

In 1968, on the subject of Vietnam, Nixon maintained a statesman's (and safe) position: while negotiations continued in Paris by the American negotiators, the GOP nominee would not discuss Vietnam nor inject it into his campaign. See White, *The Making of the President 1968*, 372.

[14] By the 1960s, the Democratic Party was vulnerable to charges of being "soft" on communism. A frail and dying Franklin Roosevelt appeased Soviet dictator Josef Stalin at their Yalta conference in the closing days of World War II, where FDR allowed Stalin to scoop up seven Eastern European nations and lock them in the strangling yoke of Soviet communist domination. A few years later, after Mao's communist army drove the Chinese Nationalists from Mainland China to the island of Taiwan during the Truman Administration, Democrats again smarted over the accusation that they "lost" China to the reds. Had John Kennedy or Lyndon Johnson surrendered a democratic government to the communists, he would become the third Democratic president in 20 years to face that accusation.

[15] When Nixon watched Humphrey's Salt Lake City speech on September 30, 1968 (in which Humphrey broke with LBJ over Vietnam), Nixon feared privately that this would help Humphrey unite the Democratic Party. Publicly, he mocked Humphrey's contradictions: "Humphrey either has to be for a bombing halt," RN told the press, "or he has to support the [administration's peace] negotiations in Paris.... I am not sure which side he is on." Wainstock, *Election Year 1968*, 169.

[16] As Nixon's 1968 campaign aide Pat Buchanan noted, "For Humphrey, victory in Vietnam was no longer an option. He had gone over to the peace camp. No longer a hawk in the aviary of LBJ, he was now sharing a nest with the doves who had sought to dump Johnson with the candidacies of McCarthy and Kennedy." Buchanan, *The Greatest Comeback*, 348.

"Humphrey was trapped. [Before the 1968 Democratic Convention he] could not break with Johnson, and thus he could not attack Nixon on Vietnam. This allowed Nixon to support Johnson on the bombing, while criticizing him on his conduct of the war. The only alternative for the voter was George Wallace, whose policy was to increase the bombing.... [I]t worked very much to [Nixon's] benefit." Ambrose, *Nixon (Volume Two)*, 182.

[17] LBJ bristled whenever someone called the battle between North and South Vietnamese a "civil war." He said it is a civil war when one nation

fights its own citizens, but South Vietnam was a separate country with a separate border created and internationally recognized by the Geneva Accords. When North Vietnam started aggression against South Vietnam, LBJ analogized it this way: "When a man walks into your house with a gun and its hammer pulled back, that's aggression. And that's exactly what North Vietnam did when it walked into the house of South Vietnam. It's just perverted history to claim that it's a civil war[.]" Kearns Goodwin, *Lyndon Johnson and the American Dream*, 328.

[18] On September 15, 1968, Nixon dispatched Reverend Billy Graham to meet with LBJ to deliver a private message to the president on his behalf. During his talk with LBJ, Graham passed along Nixon's message: Although the campaign required Nixon to point out weaknesses in the Johnson Administration, Nixon wanted LBJ to know that he would never embarrass him personally. Nixon relayed that he felt LBJ was "the hardest working and most dedicated President in 140 years," adding that he respected LBJ as a man and as the president, and if Nixon won the election, once he settled the Vietnam War, he intended to give LBJ the lion's share of credit—because LBJ deserved it. Graham later reported to Nixon that LBJ appeared deeply appreciative. See Dallek, *Flawed Giant*, 578.

In September 1968, "Nixon made certain that Johnson was aware of how much Nixon was doing on his behalf, by spelling it out in detail for his friend Billy Graham, with explicit instructions to Graham to pass it along to Johnson. As Graham made notes, Nixon said, 'I (Nixon) promise never to embarrass him (Johnson) after the election. [¶] I respect him as a man and as a president. [¶] He is the hardest working and most dedicated president in 140 years. [¶] I want a working relationship with him and will seek his advice continually.' [¶] Nixon said he would send Johnson on 'special assignments after the election, to foreign countries.' [During the campaign, Nixon] would be forced to 'point out some of the weaknesses and failures of the administration, but I will never reflect on Mr. Johnson personally.' He promised that when Vietnam 'is settled I will give you (Johnson) a major share of the credit, because you deserve it.' [¶] In conclusion, 'I will do everything to make you (Johnson) a place in history because you deserve it.' [¶] Graham flew to Washington the following week for a private meeting with Johnson. He read his notes, 'point by point.' Johnson was 'touched and appreciative, and asked me [Graham] to read them twice.'" Ambrose, *Nixon (Volume Two)*, 183-184.

[19] During Billy Graham's meeting with LBJ, held at the behest of Nixon, after Graham read Nixon's talking points of support to LBJ, Johnson told Graham that he was obliged to support Humphrey for the presidency, "but if Mr. Nixon becomes the president-elect, I will do all in my power to cooperate with him." Ambrose, *Nixon (Volume Two)*, 183-184.

[20] After Nixon's meeting with LBJ, Bryce Harlow (a key Nixon campaign staffer) warned Nixon that LBJ might pull the rug out from under the Nixon campaign. Nixon refused to believe it, insisting that LBJ gave him his word he would not use Vietnam as a campaign ploy to help Humphrey. See Dallek, *Flawed Giant*, 583, 585.

[21] When Nixon learned of LBJ's decision to order a late-October 1968 bombing halt over North Vietnam, he fumed privately: "I remembered how categorical Johnson had been at our briefing earlier that summer. Then he had been contemptuous of those who wanted a bombing halt... [and] he was not going to let one ammunition truck pass freely into South Vietnam carrying the weapons to kill American boys." Nixon, *RN*, 323.

[22] At the end of Nixon's visit with LBJ at the president's Texas ranch after Nixon won the GOP presidential nomination, "As Nixon climbed aboard the helicopter, Johnson's dog Yuki darted between his legs and into the cabin. Johnson shouted, 'Dick, here you've got my helicopter, you're after my job, and now you're gonna take my dog.' [¶] Nixon laughed and replied that Johnson could have the dog back, as two out of three was enough." Ambrose, *Nixon (Volume Two)*, 178.

[23] Decades later, in reflecting on the closing days of the 1968 Nixon presidential campaign, Pat Buchanan wrote, "We were like a basketball team sitting on a lead, taking no risks, freezing the ball, running out the clock, as our floundering opponent remained so far behind he could never catch up. But what if Hubert got it together?" Buchanan, *The Greatest Comeback*, 340.

[24]   During the closing days of the 1968 campaign, Nixon speechwriter Ray Price said that there were four things that would lose the election for Nixon: 1) a critical campaign error; 2) a truce of hostilities in Vietnam; 3) the White House announcing a peace summit meeting between Johnson and the Soviets; and 4) the inherent loyalty of Democrats to their Party. See White, *The Making of the President 1968*, 333-334.

"The only thing Nixon had to fear [in the closing days of the 1968 presidential election] was a dramatic move toward peace by Johnson. That had always been a great danger[.]" Ambrose, *Nixon (Volume Two)*, 199-200.

[25]   In the final weeks leading up to Election Day, "Nixon had been anticipating [LBJ declaring] a bombing halt. He both feared and welcomed it. Much depended on the timing; even more depended on the immediate reaction in the two Vietnams. [¶] This was high-stakes politics. If Johnson could pull off a bombing halt, get Hanoi to the peace table with promises to behave, bring [South Vietnam] into the talks, make it appear that a coalition government was about to be formed, and be able to claim that peace and reconciliation were just around the corner, why then Humphrey, already closing fast, would be a sure winner. But if anything slipped, if the [South Vietnamese] refused to sit down with the communists, or if Hanoi took advantage of a bombing halt to send more men and weapons across the [demilitarized zone into South Vietnam], it would appear that LBJ was playing politics with peace, and then it was Nixon who would be an almost certain winner." Ambrose, *Nixon (Volume Two)*, 207.

[26]   In discussing his theory of leadership, Nixon told aide Monica Crowley that, "[A]ny effective leader has got to be a son-of-a-bitch." Crowley, *Nixon Off the Record*, 4-5, 51.

[27]   In reflecting on Humphrey's post-convention slump in the polls, *New York Times* writer Tom Wicker wrote, "No Republican, as has often been said, unites the Democrats the way Nixon does." Nixon, *RN*, 317-318.

CHAPTER 44

[1] "Two major points stalled the [Vietnam War peace] negotiations. The first was the North Vietnamese demand for an unconditional stop to the bombing. The second was whether or not the talks could be described as a 'four–power' conference if, as planned, the National Liberation Front (Vietcong) took part. This would imply that the NLF [*National Liberation Front*—also known as the Vietcong—an armed band of South Vietnamese guerilla insurgents fighting for the communist North] was the equal of [South Vietnam]." See "The Bomb Halt Decision," *Life*, November 15, 1968, 87.

Between May-October 1968, "the American and North Vietnamese negotiators at the Majestic Hotel in Paris had been, in [Secretary of State] Dean Rusk's phrase, 'talking past each other.' The peace negotiations were getting nowhere. But on October 9 the atmosphere changed dramatically. The North Vietnamese suddenly began to focus on points the administration regarded as crucial. The U.S. wanted three assurances: first, that the DMZ [demilitarized zone] would be truly demilitarized; second, that attacks on South Vietnamese population centers would stop; and third, that 'meaningful' discussions would begin promptly after a bombing halt. The U.S. insisted that South Vietnam be a participant. Two days later the North Vietnamese went so far as to ask whether an 'unconditional' bombing halt would follow an agreement permitting South Vietnam to take part. The American negotiators in Paris, Averill Harriman and Cyrus Vance, could not promise an unconditional cessation. But they did promptly advise Washington of the optimistic turn the talks had taken." See "The Bomb Halt Decision," *Life*, 84B.

On October 9, 1968, North Vietnam first indicated an interest in striking a bargain to begin peace negotiations with South Vietnam. "The Bomb Halt Decision," *Life*, 84A.

On October 9-11, 1968, North Vietnam signaled to U.S. representatives at the Paris peace talks that it was ready to negotiate in good faith and wanted to know if the U.S. would halt the bombing of the North if they accepted the South Vietnamese government at the negotiations. Dallek, *Flawed Giant*, 582.

[2] On October 11, 1968, LBJ and Secretary of State Dean Rusk "met in the White House Cabinet Room to decide how to pry the door farther open. Reports from the Paris negotiators lay on the table. After the meeting, Rusk and presidential advisor Walt Rostow cabled Saigon to get the reactions of Ambassador Ellsworth Bunker and General Creighton Abrams.... They informed South Vietnamese President Nguyen Van Thieu who agreed to a cessation but set three conditions of his own: 1) the bombing of North Vietnamese infiltration routes in Laos must continue; 2) the war... must be pressed vigorously; and 3) the security of the DMZ [demilitarized zone] and South Vietnamese cities must be guaranteed. [¶] On October 14 the five Allied nations with troops in Vietnam—South Korea, the Philippines, New Zealand, Thailand and Australia—had assented. The president assembled the Joint Chiefs of Staff, Secretary Rusk and other top-level advisors and polled them individually. All concurred. The feeling that the U.S. should go ahead with the [bombing] halt, if the conditions were met, was unanimous.... When the major players in the Vietnam peace discussions reached a consensus, "'We all felt a sense of exhilaration,' one participant in the meetings said. But by the afternoon of [October] 29th, the exhilaration had fled—'We knew we were in trouble [with South Vietnam].' The Thieu government, unhappy with the prospect of sitting down with the [Vietcong] and concerned about the outcome of the U.S. election, was balking, even though it had approved of the plan as late as the day before. Urgent attempts to 'bring Saigon around' were made on the 30th. These efforts were to continue.... On Halloween night came the dénouement to three weeks of consultation and diplomatic tugging. The president's speech lay taped and ready, and although [South Vietnam] had still not come back in line, the weight of opinion in the White House councils favored going ahead." See "The

Bomb Halt Decision," *Life*, 84B, 92-93, 96-97.

"In Paris the parts—and the parties—seemed to be falling together. The North Vietnamese were willing to accept the [South Vietnamese] government at the negotiating table. In return, the Vietcong would be present, although the U.S. would not agree to recognize [them] as an 'independent entity.' 'Each side,' commented a participant with an acute sense of reality, 'will have its own mythology.'" See "The Bomb Halt Decision," *Life*, 88.

[3] On October 27, 1968, North Vietnam and U.S. negotiators agreed that LBJ would announce a bombing halt on October 31. Dallek, *Flawed Giant*, 584.

Contrary to popular belief, LBJ's October 31, 1968 "Bombing Halt" speech was not broadcast live. LBJ recorded the speech on October 30, 1968 in the White House's Family Theater for broadcast over nationwide radio and television at 8:00 p.m. on October 31. See *Public Papers of the Presidents of the United States: Lyndon B. Johnson*, 1968-69. (Washington: Government Printing Office, 1970), Volume II, entry 572, 1099-1103.

[4] On the afternoon of October 31, 1968, LBJ "then turned to the next task: notifying the three presidential candidates—simultaneously on the White House speaker-phone—that the decision to stop the bombing had been made. There was a pause while the president considered an answer to a question from Richard Nixon. Then each of the three candidates said he would back the decision." See "The Bomb Halt Decision," *Life*, 95.

On October 31, 1968, a few hours before his nationwide address aired on television, LBJ called the three major presidential candidates and told them of his upcoming bombing halt decision. See Nixon, *RN*, 323.

After his conference call with the three presidential candidates, LBJ returned to final meetings with his staff before the 8:00 p.m. bombing halt speech broadcast. "Their meeting was brief, and at its conclusion each man shook the president's hand and reaffirmed his support. Meanwhile, General Earle Wheeler had moved to a small room off the Oval Office to call the Pentagon. He ordered Lieutenant General John Meyer, chief of operations for the Joint Chiefs, to relay word to Saigon, Honolulu and other U.S. command centers in the Pacific. At 8:00 a.m. on Friday, November 1, the message ran: all air, land and naval bombardment of

North Vietnam was to cease." See "The Bomb Halt Decision," *Life*, 95.

⁵   Clark Clifford, an adviser and confidant to Democratic presidents from Truman to Clinton and LBJ's Secretary of Defense, knew FBI Director J. Edgar Hoover since their days in the Truman Administration. In his later years, Clifford recalled that in January 1966, Hoover showed Clifford a film of the late actress Marilyn Monroe performing fellatio on a man whose face was out of camera range. Hoover then told Clifford that RFK was the man in the film. "Hoover explained that the film had been taken with a hidden camera planted in the actress' bedroom during the period shortly before her death when she was consorting with Bobby Kennedy…. The Bureau had been given the film in 1965 by a former aide to Teamster union boss Jimmy Hoffa, RFK's number one target during his term as Attorney General." Hoover suggested that Clifford tell Lyndon Johnson about the film since LBJ had his own grievances against RFK. "Clifford surmised that the FBI director hoped to use the film to ruin RFK politically—and he hoped to accomplish this feat at the highest possible level." At a later dinner party, Jackie Kennedy encountered Clifford and asked if he had any knowledge of a "certain film" involving Monroe and RFK engaging in a sexual act. Clifford denied knowledge of the film to avoid getting involved, and Jackie dropped the matter with him. Heymann, *Bobby and Jackie*, 101-103.

Did RFK have a sexual relationship with Marilyn Monroe? According to RFK's and J. Edgar Hoover's biographer, Burton Hersh, the evidence is compelling. In his book, *Bobby and J. Edgar: The Historic Face-Off Between the Kennedys and J. Edgar Hoover That Transformed America* (New York: Carroll & Graf Publishers, 2007), Hersh cites evidence from two of RFK's brothers-in-law, among others:

- Actor Peter Lawford, RFK's brother in law, shared a story of RFK "stopping by Monroe's dressing room in Madison Square Garden for a quickie before her couturier, Jean Louis, stitched the tipsy star into the legendary 'skin and beads' creation… and she wobbled onstage to croon 'Happy Birthday' to JFK before millions." JFK had told RFK to meet Marilyn and tell her that JFK was ending his affair with her. Lawford recounted that RFK tried to reassure the depressed star about his brother, and then he himself succumbed to her charms. "'It wasn't Bobby's intention,' Lawford reported, 'but they became lovers and spent the night in our guest bedroom. Almost immediately the affair got heavy.... It was as if she could no longer tell the difference between Bobby and Jack.'" Hersh, *Bobby and J. Edgar,* 321-322.

- In a phone call with his brother-in-law and former Harvard roommate, George Terrien, RFK "cackled" that another RFK brother-in-law George Skakel "would keel over if he knew who I was screwing.... Just tell George I've had Marilyn's pussy.... You know, the woman Jack used to jack off over." Hersh, *Bobby and J. Edgar,* 322.

- Marilyn Monroe's neighbor at her Hollywood apartment, actress Jeanne Carmen, "remember[ed] answering Marilyn's door to confront an astonished Robert Kennedy. Suddenly, Marilyn 'came out of the bathroom with her robe on and her hair wrapped in a towel and she jumped into his arms and they kissed... they were like two kids in love.'" Hersh, *Bobby and J. Edgar,* 322-323.

- On July 30, 1962, Marilyn Monroe placed her last telephone call to RFK in Washington. "She evidently did not get a lot of satisfaction, because Peter Lawford passed along her ultimatum that unless Bobby Kennedy 'explain to her face-to-face why their relationship was over, she would hold a press conference and reveal their affair....' When Kennedy did appear around three in the afternoon... the actress had been drinking most of the day and again threatened a press conference during which she would ventilate everything she knew about both Kennedy brothers. 'Marilyn presently lost it,' Peter Lawford told C. David Heymann, 'screaming obscenities and flailing away at Bobby with her fists.'" Hersh, *Bobby and J. Edgar,* 327.

- "When Fred Otash, the best-known of the Hollywood private investigators, got commissioned to wire up Peter Lawford's home, purportedly at the behest of Joe DiMaggio, he discovered a working bug already in place, courtesy of Howard Hughes, who had no scruples when it came to helping out Nixon. The ever-accommodating Otash had already been hired by Marilyn Monroe to install electronic surveillance in her own apartment so she would have plenty of documentation should she need it later to deal with the Kennedys. Meanwhile, [Teamster leader James] Hoffa's highly regarded wireman, Bernard Spindel, had infiltrated both of Marilyn's residences in California as well as her New York apartment on East Fifty-Seventh, along with the Lawford properties, and set in place a galaxy of hidden microphones, reportedly on a contract that originated with the FBI." Hersh, *Bobby and J. Edgar,* 324.

• The FBI knew about the Monroe-RFK affair. J. Edgar Hoover had ordered surreptitious listening devices placed in the homes of JFK's brother-in-law Peter Lawford and actress Marilyn Monroe to capture evidence of the relationship. Hersh, *Bobby and J. Edgar,* 322.

• "An outside technician who knew Hoover entrusted to [help bug Marilyn Monroe's] Brentwood house and the Lawford estate would remember [Hoover] 'sitting alone in a car,' rasping out 'This needs to be done. Could you get this done? If you could do it, it would be greatly appreciated. I will not be obligated. I will owe you no favors. But I will remember.'" Hersh, *Bobby and J. Edgar,* 325.

• The surviving FBI dossier on Marilyn Monroe includes files kept by J. Edgar Hoover. "One, which is evidently intended to summarize the Bureau's findings of recent years, refers to papers found in a taxi which tied RFK to 'sex parties' in [JFK's] penthouse suite at the Carlyle Hotel which included the Kennedy brothers and Marilyn Monroe." Hersh, *Bobby and J. Edgar,* 325.

CHAPTER 45

[1]   On October 31, 1968, when LBJ announced that North Vietnam would join the peace talks, "A giant wave of relief swept across the nation. Finally, at last, after all those years, there was an end [to the Vietnam War] in sight. Polls taken the next day showed a 55-28 approval for the bombing halt. Humphrey, according to the *Washington Post*, made 'clear in public and private his belief that an enormous burden had now been lifted from his candidacy.'" Ambrose, *Nixon (Volume Two)*, 211.

[2]   After the 1968 Democratic National Convention, instead of endorsing Humphrey and campaigning for him that fall, McCarthy took an extended vacation on the French Riviera. When reporters greeted him upon his return, he told them he was not now endorsing Humphrey and would say nothing else on the matter until at least mid-October. Finally, McCarthy gave Humphrey an anemic endorsement on October 29, 1968, only a week before the election: "I'm voting for Humphrey," he said publicly, "and I think you should suffer with me." Chester, Hodgson, Page, *An American Melodrama*, 645, 740, 744-745.

Why didn't McCarthy endorse Humphrey until the very end of the campaign? Reporter and historian Theodore H. White, who covered the campaign, gave his opinion: "A man of McCarthy's morality could not accept the sight of blood [from the Chicago convention riots], the beating of his own students, and then go on to support a ticket which had not condemned this brutality. It would, he felt, be breaking faith with those he had called to follow him." White, *The Making of the President 1968*, 311.

McCarthy campaign aide Ben Stavis said the blame for McCarthy's failure to endorse the Democratic nominee belonged to Humphrey: "The blame should properly be placed at Hubert Humphrey's doorstep. His consistent, energetic support of Johnson's war policy made it hard for the McCarthy workers to accept him.... I do not think McCarthy himself was to blame for this failure to help Humphrey; nor could he have reversed the attitudes of his supporters. Had he backed Humphrey earlier rather than half-heartedly endorsing him during the last week of the campaign, most of his young supporters would have been furious and would have ignored such leadership." Stavis, *We Were the Campaign*, 201-202.

[3]   At Nixon's Madison Square Garden rally on October 31, 1968 (the same night of LBJ's bombing halt speech), it was Nixon advance man Ed Morgan who devised an elaborate scheme to keep out protesters and Democrat troublemakers: "[A]s the thousands of general ticket holders arrived at the Garden they passed through a couple of roped-off, one way chutes manned by Morgan's men. Anyone who looked like the potential troublemaker was directed to a door on the right, while putative good guys went left. The right-hand door led to a one-way hall, then down a flight of stairs into a corridor, which brought them to another door. Out the door was truly out; the traveler who was carrying a megaphone, a hostile sign or a McGovern haircut found himself on the street. [¶] If the ticket holder returned to the entrance and complained, he was profusely apologized to, his ticket was reexamined and he was directed to an office in a nearby building. Apparently, he was told, there was a problem with his ticket. At the office he was courteously requested to wait in the reception room until someone in charge could help him. After the Garden was completely filled, Morgan phoned the office to close the operation down. Those still in the reception room were told to return to the Garden. There they were informed by fire marshals that all seats were taken and they could not be admitted." Ehrlichman, *Witness to Power*, 51.

The Nixon campaign had an effective technique to screen hecklers from their rallies. "Ten times as many tickets as seats were handed out, to ensure an overflow audience. There were Nixon aides at every entrance to make certain it was a sympathetic audience. The aides would send longhaired youngsters off to the left, down a hallway to an exit door that led back out to the street, while sending clean-cut youngsters to the right, down to the front-row seats. Or they would simply turn away long-haired ticket holders, telling them the tickets were counterfeit." Ambrose, *Nixon (Volume Two)*, 186.

⁴   Nixon knew that LBJ planned to announce an election-eve bombing halt designed to kneecap Nixon's campaign in the closing days. On October 22, 1968, Bryce Harlow, one of Nixon's closest aides, passed along in a memorandum information he had received from a "mole," that is, a Nixon sympathizer, on LBJ's White House staff. "'The president is driving exceedingly hard for a deal with North Vietnam,' Harlow reported. 'He is becoming almost pathologically eager for an excuse to order a bombing halt.' [¶] Harlow added that… the Johnson people [were] pushing hardest for the halt, and that careful plans were being made 'to help Humphrey exploit whatever happens…. White Housers still think they can pull the election out for Humphrey with this ploy; that's what is being attempted.' [¶] In a poker analogy, Nixon and Humphrey, Johnson and [South Vietnamese President] Thieu, and the North Vietnamese were playing the last and biggest hand of the evening, placing and calling bets recklessly, under intense pressure." On October 24, Harlow reported "his source said that an agreement had been reached with Hanoi (which was not true). Nixon 'immediately decided,' as he wrote in his memoirs, 'that the only way to prevent Johnson from totally undercutting my candidacy at the eleventh hour was for me to make public the fact that a bombing halt was imminent.' [¶] In other words, after having gone seven months without comment on Vietnam, using the excuse that he did not want to undercut the president, Nixon decided to undercut the president. In his own words, 'I wanted to plant the impression… that [Johnson's] motives and his timing were political.'" On October 26, after divulging publicly that he believed LBJ was about to order a bombing halt, Nixon stated, "I am also told that this spurt of activity is a cynical, last-minute attempt by President Johnson to salvage the candidacy of Mr. Humphrey. This I do not believe." On October 27, LBJ responded to Nixon's comments: he "portrayed Nixon as the shallow and deceitful man the Democrats had always said he was. Johnson charged that Nixon's statement contained 'ugly and unfair charges,' and he called Nixon 'a man who distorts the history of his time.'" Ambrose, *Nixon (Volume Two)*, 208-210.

When it became apparent that a bombing halt "October Surprise" was in the offing, the Nixon team realized it could have catastrophic results in the election. See Dallek, *Flawed Giant*, 583, 585.

"In his oral interview with the Miller Center at the University of Virginia, [1968 Nixon campaign aide Bryce] Harlow said he 'had a double agent working in the White House. I knew about every meeting they held. I knew who attended the meetings. I knew what their next move was going to be." Harlow said he told Nixon, 'Boss, [Johnson's] going to dump on you,' to which Nixon replied, 'He promised me he would not. He has sworn he would not.' [¶] 'They're having a hell of a time with the Joint Chiefs,' Harlow said he told Nixon. 'Lyndon is bringing them around. He's twisting and turning it so that they'll go with it. He's forcing them to go with it. He can't have them repudiate it. That's where it is right now, the chiefs. As soon as he gets them over, and the time is right, he's going to dump. That's the plan.' [¶] Harlow tried to preempt Johnson by leaking the president's plan to Merriman Smith, the White House correspondent for United Press International. Smith discounted Harlow, saying Johnson had personally assured him he would keep foreign policy out of the election. [¶] After Johnson announced the bombing halt on October 31, Smith telephoned Harlow at two in the morning 'drunk as a hoot owl.' He had that problem. He said, 'I just want to apologize. The son-of-a-bitch lied to me; he lied to you; he lied to Nixon. He did exactly what you said, and I apologize from the bottom of my heart.'" Jack Torry, "Don't Blame Nixon for Scuttled Peace Overture," Real Clear Politics, August 9, 2015, http://www.realclearpolitics.com/articles/2015/08/09/dont_blame_nixon_for_scuttled_peace_overture_127667.html

After LBJ's October 31, 1968, bombing halt speech, Nixon fumed privately: "I remembered how categorical Johnson had been at our briefing earlier that summer. Then he had been contemptuous of those who wanted a bombing halt... [and he said] he was not going to let one ammunition truck pass freely into South Vietnam carrying the weapons to kill American boys." Nixon, *RN*, 323.

In later years, Nixon claimed that "Johnson called the bombing halt [on October 31, 1968] to swing the vote for [Vice President Hubert] Humphrey. The Russians were terrified that I'd get elected, so they stepped in to bring the North Vietnamese to the [peace negotiating] table. [Johnson] was a schemer, boy, but a pretty good one." Crowley, *Nixon Off the Record*, 17.

[5]   After LBJ's October 31, 1968 bombing halt announcement, "Nixon let the euphoria build. Even as Humphrey passed him in the polls, he kept quiet. On November 2, Humphrey went ahead of Nixon in the Lou Harris poll, 43 percent to 40 percent, with Wallace down to 13 percent and 4 percent undecided." Ambrose, *Nixon (Volume Two)*, 212.

[6]   On October 31, 1968, when LBJ announced that South Vietnam would join the peace talks with North Vietnam, "Nixon believed Johnson was bluffing, that he could not deliver [South Vietnam President] Thieu, that Thieu would call the bluff, and that the Democrats would then lose[.]" Ambrose, *Nixon (Volume Two)*, 212.

CHAPTER 46

¹ In the closing days of the campaign, Nixon irritated LBJ with a series of fall television campaign commercials that depicted destroyed Vietnamese cities and closed with a calm Nixon voiceover promising to end the "mistakes" of those leaders who got America into this war. See Dallek, *Flawed Giant*, 577-578.

On Sunday, November 2, 1968, Nixon appeared on the NBC News show *Meet the Press*. Reporter Herbert Kaplow asked, "Mr. Nixon, some of your close aides have been trying to spread the word that President Johnson timed the Vietnam bombing halt to help Vice President Humphrey in Tuesday's election. Do you agree with them?" Nixon replied cagily, "No, I don't make that charge. I must say that many of my aides and many of the people supporting my candidacy around the country seem to share that view. They share it, I suppose, because the pause came at that time so late in the campaign. But President Johnson has been very candid with me throughout these discussions, and I do not make such a charge." See Ambrose, *Nixon (Volume Two)*, 212-213.

² On Saturday, November 2, 1968, South Vietnamese President Thieu announced in a public speech that his country would not participate in the negotiations set to begin the day after the U.S. presidential election. Dallek, *Flawed Giant*, 588.

"With Thieu's [November 2, 1968] announcement the air started to leak out of the balloon. Suddenly peace seemed not so much at hand as more elusive than ever." Ambrose, *Nixon (Volume Two)*, 212.

³ "From NSA-intercepted cable traffic and CIA reports (the agency had [South Vietnamese President Nguyen Van] Thieu's office bugged),

Johnson learned that Thieu was attempting to sabotage the talks in the hope that if Nixon was elected he would demand much tougher terms. Johnson, not too surprisingly, suspected that Nixon's people were orchestrating the stall." Gentry, *J. Edgar Hoover*, 608-609.

[4]   U.S. intelligence intercepted South Vietnamese cables indicating that a key Nixon supporter, Mrs. Anna Chennault, asked South Vietnamese President Thieu to halt or cripple the proposed negotiations by refusing to participate. See Dallek, *Flawed Giant*, 587.

LBJ believed Nixon was involved personally in the back-channel effort to get South Vietnam to pull out of the peace talks. To aides, he accused Nixon of "treason." With LBJ's rage increasing against Nixon over the Anna Chennault episode, word got back to Nixon from his and LBJ's mutual friend, Florida Senator George Smathers, that LBJ was prepared to accuse Nixon of interfering with the peace talks for political gain. On November 3, Nixon called LBJ personally and insisted neither he nor his staff had anything to do with Mrs. Chennault and any contacts she might have made with South Vietnam. During the lengthy conversation, Nixon succeeded in cooling down LBJ and his threats, although LBJ didn't believe Nixon's denials. See Dallek, *Flawed Giant*, 589-591; see also Chester, Hodgson, Page, *An American Melodrama*, 732-735.

[5]   "At the end of October, with Johnson apparently ready to call a bombing halt, Nixon had [campaign manager John] Mitchell call Mrs. [Anna] Chennault. [¶] 'Anna,' Mitchell said, 'I'm speaking on behalf of Mr. Nixon. It's very important that our Vietnamese friends understand our Republican position and I hope you have made that clear to them.' He said that if Mrs. Chennault could persuade them to refuse to go to the peace table, Johnson's bombing halt would look unwise at best, cynical at worst, and would therefore backfire on the Democrats. Mitchell used guarded language to convey this message, because he knew that Mrs. Chennault's telephone was tapped by the FBI and that J. Edgar Hoover would make sure that Johnson heard about the Chennault-Mitchell conversation." Ambrose, *Nixon (Volume Two)*, 208.

When the South Vietnamese government refused to join the peace talks in early November 1968, Johnson was in a quandary. "[T]o denounce Nixon publicly for interfering with the peace process was to admit that the FBI had been tapping Mrs. Chennault's telephone, so nothing was done." Ambrose, *Nixon (Volume Two)*, 210-216.

In October 1968, Mrs. Anna Chennault was dating longtime Washington lobbyist, FDR aide, and Democratic Party insider Thomas "Tommy the Cork" Corcoran. According to Corcoran's biographer, David McKean, on the night LBJ announced the bombing halt of North Vietnam [incorrectly reported in McKean's book as July 31, 1968], Mrs. Chennault and Corcoran were attending a party in Washington. During the party, "Chennault was called to the telephone. It was [Nixon's campaign manager] John Mitchell. He asked her to call him back from a more private phone.... [W]ith Tommy listening in on a phone in an adjacent room and taking notes, Chennault returned Mitchell's call. 'Anna,' Mitchell said in a gravely serious tone, 'I'm speaking on behalf of Mr. Nixon. It's very important that our South Vietnamese friends understand our Republican position and I hope you have made this clear to them.' Chennault knew exactly what Mitchell was talking about: the South Vietnamese should continue to resist peace negotiations. Chennault later claimed that she responded: 'Look John, all I've done is to relay messages. If you are talking about direct influence, I have to tell you it isn't wise for us to try to influence the South Vietnamese. Their actions have to follow their own national interests, and I'm sure that is what will dictate [South Vietnamese President] Thieu's decision.'" When LBJ learned of Mrs. Chennault's contacts with the South Vietnamese, he ordered the FBI to conduct physical and electronic surveillance on her. In later years, Mrs. Chennault offered this explanation of how she ended up on the surveillance radar of LBJ and his advisers: "Tommy told them." Corcoran's friendship with LBJ dated back to when the Texan was a young rookie congressman, and Corcoran was one of FDR's most powerful White House aides. See McKean, *Tommy the Cork*, 95-96, 290-293.

"Johnson requested that Madame Chennault, Bui Diem, and the embassy of Vietnam be placed under physical and electronic surveillance." At LBJ's insistence, "around-the-clock surveillances were approved.... [A]lthough LBJ strongly suspected that the Republicans had delayed the end of the war for purely political reasons, he couldn't prove it and reluctantly dropped the matter. [¶] This left Hoover on the spot. Were Nixon to win—as Hoover fervently hoped he would—the Chennault... investigation would indeed place the FBI in 'a most untenable and embarrassing position.' But the wily FBI director had already devised an out: if Nixon won, he'd tell him about the investigation, and put the blame on LBJ." Curt Gentry, *J. Edgar Hoover*, 608-609.

After LBJ learned of Mrs. Chennault's alleged involvement in contacting South Vietnam on Nixon's behalf, LBJ ordered FBI agents "to put Mrs. Chennault and the South Vietnamese Embassy under physical surveillance and to put wiretaps on their telephones, which we did." Sullivan and Brown, *The Bureau*, 77-78.

[6] "Mrs. Anna Chan Chennault, the Chinese widow of the wartime hero General Claire Chennault… had close ties with… Nixon and his friends in the China Lobby. She was co-chair of the Republican Women for Nixon… and had raised $250,000 for Nixon's campaign. Most important of all, she was close to President Thieu and his aides." Ambrose, *Nixon (Volume Two)*, 207-208.

"Suspicion [for getting South Vietnam President Thieu to back out of the peace talks] focused on 'the Dragon Lady,' Madame Anna Chennault…. A leader in the Republican Party, and head of a group called Concerned Asians for Nixon, Madame Chennault was known to be a close confidante of the South Vietnamese Ambassador Bui Diem." Gentry, *J. Edgar Hoover*, 608-609.

[7] "On Friday morning [November 1, 1968], Americans were convinced that peace was at hand; on Saturday, Saigon's repudiation of peace upset them; by Sunday, nobody knew what was happening, and every dial and index of public opinion sampling was spinning." White, *The Making of the President 1968*, 382.

"Johnson had changed the debate five days before the election and shoved his whole stack in for Humphrey. If the country believed what appeared to be true—a deal to end the war might be at hand—this could swing it. But the White House did not have all its ducks in a row. Twenty-four hours later, headlines about a bombing halt had been replaced. In the *New York Times*, the new headline read 'Saigon Opposes Paris Talk Plans, Says It Cannot Attend Next Week.'" Buchanan, *The Greatest Comeback*, 357.

After the 1968 election, FBI Director J. Edgar Hoover told President

Nixon that LBJ ordered surveillance on both the Republican presidential and vice presidential nominees in the closing days of the campaign to see if they had any hand in the South Vietnamese pulling out of the peace negotiations. See Witcover, *Very Strange Bedfellows*, 52.

In late 1968 President-elect Nixon met with FBI Director J. Edgar Hoover in the transition office. Hoover told Nixon "that Johnson had ordered the FBI to wiretap Nixon during the campaign and that the FBI had successfully planted a bug on Nixon's campaign airplane. He said the FBI had wiretapped Mrs. Chennault's telephone, something Nixon already knew." Ambrose, *Nixon (Volume Two)*, 235.

8   "Johnson's suspicions were confirmed on November 2 [1968] when the FBI intercepted the call from Madame Chennault to the [South Vietnamese] embassy in which she urged Saigon to stay firm: they'd get a better deal with Nixon, she said. When the embassy official asked if Nixon knew about the call, Madame Chennault replied, 'No, but our friend in New Mexico does.' The [Republican vice presidential candidate's] campaign plane had stopped briefly in Albuquerque, New Mexico, that day, and Johnson had the FBI check telephone toll records to see if [the Republican vice presidential candidate] or his staff had called Chennault. No such call was found[.]" Gentry, *J. Edgar Hoover*, 608-609.

"Just a few days before the 1968 presidential election between Nixon and Humphrey, Johnson decided he wanted us to check on the phone calls made from [the Republican vice presidential candidate's] campaign plane during a stopover in Albuquerque, New Mexico. Johnson believed that the Republicans were in contact with the South Vietnamese government, and that they were trying to keep the South Vietnamese away from the conference table in an effort to sabotage Johnson's Paris peace talks. LBJ suspected that Mrs. Anna Chennault, an influential and wealthy Washington widow who also headed a group called 'Concerned Asians for Nixon,' was carrying messages between [the Republican vice presidential candidate] and the South Vietnamese embassy. The president's orders to the FBI... were for the Albuquerque office to conduct a careful check of all outgoing phone calls made by the then vice presidential candidate... on the date of 2 November 1968, at the time he was in Albuquerque.... We never came up with any damaging evidence against [the Republican vice presidential candidate] or Mrs. Chennault[.]" Sullivan and Brown, *The Bureau*, 77-78.

On her wiretapped conversation with a South Vietnamese official, Mrs. Chennault was asked if Nixon knew of her role in getting the South to back out of the peace talks. She answered no, but then suggested that Nixon's running mate might know. See Witcover, *Very Strange Bedfellows*, 52.

[9] After learning that Thieu had backed out of the peace talks, "Johnson sent word to the American ambassador in Saigon, Ellsworth Bunker, to put every pressure he could on Thieu to cooperate.... If Thieu refused to go along with Johnson and Humphrey won [the election] anyway, he would be in big trouble with the new president. Nevertheless, Thieu refused to go to [the peace talks], whatever Johnson did." Ambrose, *Nixon (Volume Two)*, 210-211.

LBJ's fury over the Chennault episode helped nudge LBJ into campaigning actively for Humphrey. See Dallek, *Flawed Giant*, 589.

[10] Did Nixon sabotage the Vietnam peace talks in 1968 on the eve of the election?

- Writing almost 50 years after the 1968 election, reporter Jack Torry concluded, "Nixon did not sabotage a peace agreement in 1968 for one simple reason: There was no chance for peace in 1968 on any terms that would have been acceptable to any American president, be it Johnson, Nixon, or Humphrey. [¶] Nor was there even a remote possibility Le Duan, the general secretary of the Communist Party in North Vietnam and the real power in Hanoi, would have accepted anything less in 1968 than a unilateral American withdrawal from Vietnam and a promise to topple the Saigon regime. The whole purpose behind the commitment to South Vietnam by Presidents Dwight Eisenhower, John F. Kennedy, and Johnson was to preserve a non-communist government in Saigon.... In reality, there never was any chance Thieu would participate in the talks in November of 1968—no matter what Nixon did or did not tell him. The declassified transcripts of Thieu's meetings with his top advisers throughout October make clear that he would not agree to four-way talks in Paris with the NLF [Vietcong] as "a separate entity." That was not just some procedural objection on Saigon's part. By recognizing the NLF as a legitimate government, Thieu was acknowledging it as a potential coalition partner, a stance Saigon consistently rejected throughout the war. [¶] It is true Nixon's people urged Thieu to stand firm and resist Johnson's pressure to join the proposed talks in Paris. But that is because they saw Johnson's bombing halt not as a serious peace plan but as a cynical eleventh-hour move to tip the election to Humphrey.... Those contacts, while improper, were hardly treason and not much different than George McGovern secretly sending Pierre Salinger to Paris in 1972 to meet with Hanoi's negotiators at a time when Nixon and White House National Security Adviser Henry Kissinger were trying to negotiate an end to the war with Hanoi.... In a prescient cable sent to the State Department on October 12, 1968, [U.S. Ambassador to South Vietnam Ellsworth] Bunker made clear his belief that Hanoi 'assumes that if it can get the bombing stopped and keep it stopped until [Inauguration Day 1969], the next president will find it very difficult to resume the bombing. Meanwhile it will have time to rest and resupply and prepare for a renewed struggle in the spring.' That is precisely what happened.... As for Anna Chennault, her role [in scuttling the North-South Vietnam peace talks in November 1968] has been grossly exaggerated. Nixon denied ever telling her to contact Thieu to boycott the proposed peace talks, but any Nixon denial needs to be treated with deep skepticism. Yet Nguyen Phu Duc, who served as special assistant to foreign affairs to Thieu, later wrote he never received any message from Chennault and never heard either Thieu or the South Vietnamese foreign minister mention 'any message from Mrs. Chennault via Bui Diem.'" See Torry, "Don't Blame Nixon for Scuttled Peace Overture."

- Award-winning historian Stephen Ambrose analyzed the accusation that Nixon used back-door channels to scuttle a Vietnam peace agreement on the eve of the November 1968 presidential election. He determined that the accusation was false. Ambrose, *Nixon (Volume Two)*, 210-211; 214-216.

- According to LBJ biographer and historian Robert Dallek, in 1997 Anna Chennault claimed both Nixon and his campaign manager John Mitchell knew of her intercession with the South Vietnamese government to torpedo the peace negotiations. See Dallek, *Flawed Giant*, 591.

- In early November 1968, when LBJ briefed Humphrey on Anna Chennault's contacts with South Vietnamese government officials, Humphrey concluded he could not make the accusation public without direct evidence of Nixon's personal involvement. Humphrey later told aides that if he did publicize it, it would be "difficult to explain how we knew about what she had done." When he learned that South Vietnam backed out of the peace negotiations, he exploded. Pounding his fist on the table, he shouted, "I'll be damned if I'm going to let the China Lobby of all people steal the election from me." In his anger, Humphrey dictated a press release stating that, as president, he will sever all ties with the South Vietnamese government "and leave them on their own." Then, after cooling off, he modified the release and put out to the press he would continue negotiations with or without the cooperation of the South Vietnamese government. See Dallek, *Flawed Giant*, 591.

- Humphrey remained bothered by his inability to pin the Chennault episode on Nixon personally. In his diary that made during the campaign's final weekend, he wrote, "I wonder if I should have blown the whistle on Anna Chennault and Nixon? He must have known about her call to [South Vietnam President] Thieu. I wish I could have been sure. Damn Thieu. Dragging his feet this past weekend hurt us. I wonder if that call did it. If Nixon knew. Maybe I should have blasted him anyway." Humphrey, *The Education of a Public Man*, 8-9.

[11] In a memoir published after his death, former Texas Governor John B. Connally wrote that in 1968, "Contrary to other published accounts, I did not support [Nixon], did not raise money for him, did not vote for him against Hubert Humphrey[.]" Connally and Herskowitz, *In History's Shadow*, 232.

[12]   LBJ's quoted speech at the Humphrey campaign rally at the Houston Astrodome on November 3, 1968, is adapted from his actual remarks made at that event. See "Lyndon B. Johnson, Remarks at the Astrodome at a Democratic Party Rally," *The American Presidency Project*, November 3, 1968, http://www.presidency.ucsb.edu/ws/?pid=29221.

[13]   In later years, Humphrey remembered LBJ appearing for him at the November 3, 1968 Houston Astrodome rally: "And there on that day was an uncomplicated, giving, supporting Lyndon Johnson, my friend and president of the United States.... No ambiguity about Lyndon Johnson that day. He strongly supported me, and his message got across to the Texans. That afternoon, at least, we seemed to have resolved whatever difficulties we had." Humphrey, *The Education of a Public Man*, 405.

After freezing out Hubert Humphrey throughout most of the 1968 presidential campaign, why did Lyndon Johnson embrace his vice president in the closing days of the race? LBJ knew that if Humphrey lost the presidency to Nixon, Democrats would blame the loss on him. Further, world leaders—and future historians—would interpret a Humphrey loss as a complete repudiation of the Johnson Administration. See Dallek, *Flawed Giant*, 576.

[14]   In a 1971 interview with historian Doris Kearns Goodwin, during the second year of the Nixon Administration, LBJ lamented, "I figured when my legislative program passed the Congress that the Great Society had a real chance to grow into a beautiful woman [and become] a permanent part of American life, more permanent even than the New Deal. [¶] But now Nixon has come along and everything I've worked for is ruined. There's a story in the paper every day about him slashing another one of my Great Society programs. I can just see him waking up in the morning, making that victory sign of his and deciding which program to kill. It's a terrible thing for me to sit by and watch someone else starve my Great Society to death. She's getting thinner and thinner and uglier and uglier all the time.... Soon she'll be so ugly that the American people will refuse to look at her; they'll stick her in a closet to hide her away and there she'll die. And when she dies, I, too, will die." Kearns Goodwin, *Lyndon Johnson and the American Dream*, 286-287.

[15] Historian Stephen Ambrose wrote: "Johnson would not let Humphrey break the story because he would have had to reveal the illegal telephone tap on Mrs. Chennault. Further, according to an unnamed official in the Johnson White House interviewed by Seymore Hersh, Johnson was angry at Humphrey for breaking with him on the war, and thus 'had no interest in defeating Nixon. He wasn't going to do anything for the purpose of seeing Nixon discredited.'" Ambrose, *Nixon (Volume Two)*, 210-216.

[16] 4936 Thirtieth Place NW, Washington, DC, was the home of FBI Director J. Edgar Hoover. See Gentry, *J. Edgar Hoover*, 30-31, 50-52.

[17] Why did FBI Director J. Edgar Hoover seek to torpedo the Democrats in 1968?

- "Richard Nixon and J. Edgar Hoover had been political allies since Nixon served in the House of Representatives.... Over the years, Hoover and Nixon grew to be personal friends. Nixon frequently had dinner at Hoover's house, and Hoover was a regular dinner guest of the Nixons at the White House. Of course, Hoover liked to claim to be a personal friend of whichever president was in office, but in Nixon's case it seemed to be true." Sullivan and Brown, *The Bureau*, 196.

- "Because of the possibility that the Democrats might win [in 1968], Hoover's aid and comfort to the Republican presidential candidate, Richard Nixon, had to be covert.... [Former FBI agent and Hoover close aide] Lou Nichols was in charge of the former vice president's campaign security. [Nichols] mounted 'Operation Eagle Eye,' a nationwide network of ex-FBI agents and attorneys given the task of making sure the theft of 1960 was not repeated. The FBI director could just sit back, feed helpful information to Nichols, and feign uninvolvement." Gentry, *J. Edgar Hoover*, 608.

- "During the [1960 presidential] campaign, Hoover did his best to keep the press supplied with anti-Kennedy stories.... Hoover, a staunch Republican... was trying to sabotage Jack Kennedy's campaign, he was quietly helping Richard Nixon." Sullivan and Brown, *The Bureau*, 48-49.

CHAPTER 47

[1] "Founded by Drew Pearson, *Washington Merry-Go-Round* began as a syndicated column in 1932. The provocative and often controversial column broke the story of Lt. Gen. George S. Patton and the soldier he slapped in 1943. Pearson later brought about the downfall of Secretary of Defense James V. Forrestal, an ideological foe, and he denounced the witch-hunt agenda of Sen. Joseph McCarthy, R-Wisc." *Washington Merry-Go-Round*, History of the Column, http://washingtonmerrygoround.com/history-of-column.

[2] After commissioning a poll, *Time* magazine named Drew Pearson as America's best-known newspaper columnist. See "The Tenacious Muck-raker," *Time*, September 12, 1969.

[3] President Franklin Roosevelt called Drew Pearson "a chronic liar." Pearson and Hannaford, *Washington Merry-Go-Round*, x.

Columnist Drew Pearson revealed on his radio program during World War II that General George S. Patton slapped an enlisted soldier, which caused a public outrage. As a result, Patton lost his battle command and did not regain another for 11 months. Alan Axelrod, *Patton: A Biography* (New York: St. Martin's Press, 2009), 115-122.

General Douglas MacArthur sued Drew Pearson for defamation, but he later dropped the suit when Pearson threatened to publish MacArthur's love letters to his mistress. Pearson and Hannaford, *Washington Merry-Go-Round*, xi.

"People are repeating the charge that I killed [former U.S. Secretary of Defense James Forrestal, who committed suicide by leaping from a window at Bethesda Naval Hospital on May 22, 1949] to the extent that

I am almost beginning to lie awake nights wondering whether I did. Certainly a lot of people have convinced themselves that it is true." Pearson and Abell, *Diaries 1949-1959*, 52.

Pearson's "protégé and eventual successor, Jack Anderson, blamed Pearson for hounding Secretary of Defense James Forrestal into leaping to his death from the sixteenth floor of Bethesda Naval Hospital." Pearson and Hannaford, *Washington Merry-Go-Round*, x.

"The truth is that my exposé of [U.S. Senator John H. Bankhead II's (1872-1946)] speculation on the cotton market probably did kill him. The Alabama Democrat had a stroke a few days thereafter and died. I was always afraid I might be accused of his death, and in his case I undoubtedly would have been guilty." Pearson, Abell, *Diaries 1949-1959*, 52.

In 1950, after Drew Pearson published an attack on Senator Joseph McCarthy, the senator "encountered Pearson and his wife, Luvie, at Washington's posh Sulgrave Club. 'How long are they going to let you stay out of jail?' Pearson goaded McCarthy, who did his talking with his knee, swiftly planted in Pearson's groin. For good measure he slapped the columnist to the ground." Pearson later sued McCarthy, who retaliated by calling for a boycott of Pearson's radio sponsor and denounced the writer as the "sugar-coated voice of Russia." Pearson and Hannaford, *Washington Merry-Go-Round*, ix-x.

For details on Drew Pearson's allegation that JFK's Pulitzer Prize-winning bestselling book, *Profiles in Courage*, was ghostwritten, see Clifford, *Counsel to the President*, 306-310; Pearson and Hannaford, *Washington Merry-Go-Round*, x; Sorensen, *Counselor*, 148-150.

[4] According to Pearson's protégé and longtime *Washington Merry-Go-Round* co-author Jack Anderson, "[T]ruth for Drew Pearson 'was often a subjective matter.' When forced to choose between publishing a story that was accurate and one that damaged [his subject], Pearson did not hesitate" to publish it. See Herman, *Joseph McCarthy*, 233.

[5] According to Jack Anderson, Pearson's protégé and longtime *Washington Merry-Go-Round* co-author, "[U]nderneath Pearson's aristocratic demeanor was a Machiavellian toughness that did not shrink at using blackmail and bribery to further his goals. He put eavesdropping waiters and chauffeurs on his payroll, bribed a Navy clerk to leak classified docu-

ments, and ordered an assistant to break into the desk of a prominent Washington attorney to search for incriminating financial records. He stymied World War II censors, foiled government eavesdroppers, and outwitted federal agents who tailed him.... [He was] gentle in private but ferocious in public; a pacifist who waged unconditional war on his enemies[.]" Mark Feldstein, *Poisoning the Press: Richard Nixon, Jack Anderson, and the Rise of Washington's Scandal Culture* (New York: Picador, 2010), 36.

[6]   Drew Pearson revealed embarrassing sexual behavior of his subjects if he felt the disclosure newsworthy. See, e.g., Pearson and Hannaford, *Washington Merry-Go-Round*, 505-509, 511, 516-517 (Pearson broke the 1967 scandal regarding homosexuals on Governor Ronald Reagan's Sacramento staff).

[7]   After RFK's assassination, when former First Lady Jacqueline Kennedy moved with her children to Greece, she shared with a friend her fears about America: "I hate this country! I don't want my children to live here anymore. If they're killing Kennedys, my kids are number-one targets." Heymann, *RFK*, 511.

[8]   After columnist Drew Pearson launched an unrelated attack against RFK four days before the 1968 California presidential primary, William H. Orrick Jr. of RFK's Northern California campaign issued a press release stating, "This misrepresentation is another example of the lengths to which Drew Pearson will go in his current efforts to vilify and defeat Senator Kennedy." William H. Orrick Jr., Kennedy Campaign Press Release, Northern California Headquarters, 1499 Market Street, San Francisco, May 31, 1968 (Author's collection).

[9]   In an exhaustively researched book, investigative reporter and RFK biographer C. David Heymann concluded, "Too often in earlier biographies, Robert Kennedy was depicted as something of a choirboy when, in fact, he enjoyed the same proclivity for extramarital affairs as his brothers, Jack and Ted Kennedy." Heymann, *Bobby and Jackie*, viii. According to Heymann, RFK's sexual partners included:

- Socialite and Kennedy family friend Joan Braden. One night, on a visit to her home after JFK's assassination, RFK invited Joan to her bedroom. After kissing her and removing his tie, he asked to have sex with her. "I couldn't go through with it," she said. "He was hurt, silent, and angry. He left in a huff. I watched through the window as he walked under the streetlights toward his car." Heymann, *Bobby and Jackie*, 63.

- A 26 year-old 1964 Senate campaign aide: According to Kenneth P. O'Donnell, one of JFK's closest aides, Kennedy's brother-in-law Steve Smith (who managed RFK's 1964 Senate campaign) worried that if RFK's affair with his young aide became public, "it would impact on RFK's political future." Heymann, *Bobby and Jackie*, 74.

- Barbara Marx (Frank Sinatra's future wife) and her friend Mary Harrington. In 1959, RFK met Barbara and her friend Mary Harrington, a Southern socialite, at a Las Vegas nightclub. As Ms. Harrington recalled, "'Bobby and Barbara took one look at each other, and the next thing I knew, they were off and running. They weren't heard from again until the next morning. Although Barbara always publicly denied having had an affair with Bobby, I can vouch for the fact that it happened. The affair lasted about three or four months. Frank Sinatra always hated Bobby for it—he couldn't stand it that RFK had been there before him.' [¶] Whenever Bobby and Barbara saw each other, Mary Harrington accompanied them as a kind of female beard. But before too long, Bobby came to regard Mary as more than just a convenient camouflage. She had an apartment at the Carlyle in New York, and whenever Bobby came to town, he would call her up and they would have a drink. 'I wasn't attracted to him at first,' she continued, 'but he gradually grew on me....' [¶] By early 1960, RFK began calling Mary more often, saying he could no longer see Barbara Marx because she was becoming so emotional. Then, in March, Harrington came down with phlebitis and wound up in New York Hospital. Bobby sent a note up to her room along with flowers and a gold bracelet from Cartier.... [During one late night visit, he] told Mary he thought he was falling in love with her. Their affair began then and there,

Bobby crawling into Mary's hospital bed. Following her recovery a week later, they saw each other an average of twice a week.... After a while, he became deeply involved in his brother's presidential campaign, and they saw less of each other. They remained close friends, and the friendship endured until the end of his life." Heymann, *Bobby and Jackie*, 81-82.

- Columnist Carole Bjorkman. Peter Jay Sharpe, a longtime JFK and RFK friend who owned New York's Carlyle Hotel (where the Kennedys maintained a penthouse suite), recalled one day during JFK's presidency that he went up to the Kennedy suite and found a Secret Service agent posted at the front door. "He ushered me inside, and there I found Jack in bed with a blonde and Bobby on the living room floor with a brunette. I was really looking for Teddy, but Bobby told me he was in the bathroom with another girl. I didn't want to bother Ted, so as I was leaving, I asked Bobby to have his younger brother call me that evening. Bobby carried on a conversation with me without missing a beat. Caught up in the moment, his companion barely noticed me." According to Sharpe, the woman with RFK was Carole Bjorkman, a columnist for *Women's Wear Daily*, whom RFK met earlier at a cocktail party. Heymann, *Bobby and Jackie*, 31-32.

- Polly Bissell, a recent college graduate working in RFK's Senate office. NBC News political reporter Douglas Kiker, a guest at a 1965 barbeque at RFK's Hickory Hill home, recalled that RFK and Ms. Bissell took off on a motorcycle, clad only in bathing suits, to a nearby wooded area. According to an official police report, a few minutes later a McLean police car pulled up to the area and found a man and woman copulating. The report (filed May 25, 1965) reveals that as the police arrived, the man spotted the two officers, pulled up his swim trunks, and fled into the woods, leaving the young woman and motorcycle behind. Once Miss Bissell identified herself as a guest of the Kennedys, they escorted her back to Hickory Hill. The police report stated that the man seen with her was not identified. RFK emerged home later after making his way back to the party. Heymann, *Bobby and Jackie*, 92-93.

- Mary Jo Kopechne: The pretty 27 year-old, blue-eyed blonde went to work as a secretary for a longtime Kennedy family friend, U.S. Senator George Smathers of Florida, who later introduced her to the Kennedys. "When Bobby became a senator, she transferred to his secretarial pool, sharing a Georgetown townhouse with four other women her age, all of them members of Bobby's staff. During his run for the presidency, this enclave became known as the Boiler Room Girls. [¶] 'Although she no longer worked for me,' said George Smathers, 'Mary Jo and I stayed in touch. I'd become her father confessor, so to speak. She was young, sweet, and impressionable. When she informed me that Bobby had invited her to join him as a secretary on the presidential campaign plane, I warned her against it. I knew Bobby, and I knew that he would take advantage of the situation. And that's precisely what happened. It didn't matter to him whether Ethel was also on the plane. They'd check into hotels at night, and Mary Jo would be given her own room. It didn't take much for Bobby to excuse himself from a strategy meeting for a few minutes and go visit Mary Jo in her room. Nobody was the wiser for it. It reminded me a little of Jack when he campaigned for the presidency in 1960, except that Jackie wasn't around most of the time.'" Heymann, *RFK*, 152-153.

- A prominent young actress: Jack Valenti, president of the Motion Picture Association of America, confided to reporter Drew Pearson in 1967 the following story about RFK and the actress: "Valenti told me an interesting story about Bobby Kennedy, who has been preaching morality around the White House but is not exactly a paragon of virtue himself. When Bobby went to France for the visit with [French President Charles] de Gaulle, Valenti happened to be there, and one of the motion picture companies, which was shooting in Paris, complained that their star… had disappeared from the set for four days. They finally traced her to a hotel on the East Bank where Bobby was staying. They tried to get her to come back to work, but she refused. In fact, she did not go back to work until after Bobby had left Paris. The hotel's majordomo said they were shacking up. Jack said that at the birthday dinner

Bobby gave for Averell Harriman, [the actress] sat on Bobby's left, Marie Harriman on his right." The day after RFK died (June 7, 1968), Pearson wrote in his diary that RFK was "almost as flagrant as his brother in his infidelity. There was no question that he did have an affair with Marilyn Monroe.... He also had that famous case in Paris with [the actress identified earlier by Jack Valenti]." Pearson and Hannaford, *Washington Merry-Go-Round* 584.

- For additional reports of RFK's marital infidelity: see generally Heymann, *Bobby and Jackie*, 32-33, 88-89, 90-92; see also Pearson and Hannaford, *Washington Merry-Go-Round*, 524.

- For details of RFK's affair with actress Marilyn Monroe, see Chapter 44 endnotes, *supra*.

In 1966, reporter Drew Pearson recorded in his diary that Teamster President James Hoffa told him that the Teamsters had surveilled RFK's philandering ways. Hoffa told Pearson "that the Teamsters made it a point to check on Bobby's activities and had found that whenever he went to Los Angeles, one of his girlfriends registered at the hotel one day in advance. When he went to Chicago, another girlfriend joined him, and altogether he had four girls scattered around the country. 'I would have the FBI bring in the facts on these women,' said Hoffa. 'They are crossing state boundaries, which is against the law, and it's about time Bobby was put in his place.'" Two years later, Pearson recorded in his diary (April 6, 1968) a discussion he had with Edward Morgan, a former FBI agent who later became counsel to the Senate Foreign Relations Committee: "Ed did [RFK] a great favor, which Bobby obviously did not appreciate. A friend of Ed's lived on one side of Bobby Kennedy's mistress. [RFK] used to park his Justice Department car, with a Cabinet tag, in front of her house in Georgetown while he went in and laid her. He was so indiscreet that he never pulled down the blinds. On the other side of the house lived Harold Gibbons, a vice president of the Teamsters. I had heard the story previously from Gibbons. Ed said that he tipped off Bobby and he discontinued his noonday visits." Pearson and Hannaford, *Washington Merry-Go-Round*, 423, 564.

[10] Investigative reporter and RFK biographer C. David Heymann reported that Lawrence F. O'Brien, JFK's Postmaster General and later chairman of the Democratic National Committee, said that his friend JFK always suspected Jackie of having an affair with Greek shipping magnate Aristotle Onassis (whom JFK called derisively "the pirate"). JFK told O'Brien, "She tired of my screwing around, so she's stepping out on me with the pirate." When Drew Pearson found out about Jackie's visits to Onassis, he "wrote a scathing article insinuating that Onassis was sleeping with both [Jackie and her sister] at the same time." Heymann's investigations revealed that Jacqueline Kennedy had other paramours: San Francisco architect John Carl Warnecke, financier Andre Meyer, actor Marlon Brando, and JFK's Under Secretary of the Air Force and Deputy Secretary of Defense Roswell Gilpatric. Heymann, *RFK*, 54-56, 74, 84-85, 144-145, 511-512.

Did Ethel Kennedy believe that her husband, RFK, had an affair with Jacqueline Kennedy?

- Kenneth O'Donnell, RFK's college roommate and one of JFK's longest serving and closest aides, said that despite the Jacqueline Kennedy-RFK romance, "The possibility of a divorce never entered Ethel's mind... but you can well imagine how much the thought of Bobby's affair with Jackie must have bothered her." Heymann, *Bobby and Jackie*, 135, 142.

- Coates Redmon, a close friend of Ethel Kennedy, said Ethel remained reluctant to play a larger part in RFK's 1964 Senate campaign due to her suspicions about Jacqueline Kennedy: "I'm certain her reluctance had something to do with her suspicion that Bobby and Jackie had initiated a sexual relationship.... Her suspicions were well-founded.... I'm sure Ethel had caught on at some point." Heymann, *Bobby and Jackie*, 75.

- Merribell Moore, another friend of Ethel Kennedy's family, said Ethel would call her brother Frank "all the time to discuss the situation. She couldn't understand what Bobby saw in Jackie. She wanted Frank to tell Bobby to stop sleeping with Jackie. But Frank had no intention of getting involved. He told Ethel what she needed to do was find a marriage counselor to help heal her marriage." Heymann, *Bobby and Jackie*, 75-76.

- Ethel disliked Jacqueline Kennedy instantly because of her husband's admiration for her. The dislike intensified after JFK's death, when RFK insisted that he and Ethel assist Jacqueline Kennedy financially by contributing $50,000 a year to her. "The free-spending Ethel... started to bellyache openly about the 'situation' involving her husband and Jackie." Hersh, *Bobby and J. Edgar*, 140, 453.

Despite Ethel Kennedy's suspicions, did RFK and Jacqueline Kennedy really have an affair? When *Newsweek*'s Evan Thomas published his biography of RFK in 2000, he addressed this persistent rumor and concluded the question remained unresolved: "It is impossible to know the intimate nature of the relationship between Robert and his brother's widow. There can be no doubt they shared a deep affection and emotional bond. In their grief and yearning for solace, they may have shared more.... [N]o evidence has emerged that would prove a physical relationship." See Thomas, *Robert Kennedy*, 285.

Nine years after the publication of Evan Thomas' book, investigative reporter and RFK biographer C. David Heymann published his interviews with unimpeachable sources who spoke candidly on the subject after Jacqueline Kennedy's death:

- Secretary of Defense Clark Clifford: In May 1967, when the wife of Lord Harlech was killed in a traffic collision, RFK, Jacqueline Kennedy, and Clifford (a longtime Kennedy family friend and adviser) flew to England to attend the funeral. "All three of us stayed at the Dorchester Hotel in London," recalled Clifford. "We booked three junior suites. It soon emerged that the two of them were sharing her boudoir; his served only as a decoy. I can't say it bothered me that they were shacking up together, though it seemed a bit odd that they would do so under such a somber occasion." Heymann, *Bobby and Jackie*, 133.

- Kenneth O'Donnell, RFK's college roommate and one of JFK's longest serving and closest aides: "I think he [RFK] loved [Jacqueline Kennedy], but he understood and accepted the limitations of their romance. They couldn't marry, so eventually she would marry somebody else. He also understood that she was super-high maintenance. She could marry virtually anyone, but there weren't many men around who could afford to take her on.... The possibility of a divorce never entered Ethel's mind... but you can well imagine how much the thought of Bobby's affair with Jackie must have bothered her." Heymann, *Bobby and Jackie*, 135, 142.

- Arthur M. Schlesinger Jr., a close friend and later RFK biographer: "I knew Bobby and Jackie had grown close.... What I didn't know is that there was apparently more to their relationship than I originally thought." Schlesinger recalled that after JFK's assassination, aboard a private dinner cruise on the presidential yacht Sequoia, RFK and Jackie disappeared below deck for ten minutes. "I have no idea what transpired between them," said Schlesinger, "but when they returned, they looked as chummy and relaxed as a pair of Cheshire cats." Heymann, *Bobby and Jackie*, 61.

- After JFK's assassination, Maud Shaw, Jacqueline Kennedy's longtime nanny to her two children, complained in a letter to JFK's personal secretary Evelyn Lincoln that while she, Mrs. Kennedy, and the Kennedy children visited the estate of socialite Audrey Zauderer in Jamaica, RFK arrived and also stayed there. She wrote that even though Jackie and RFK had separate bedrooms on the estate, "they kept dodging in and out of each other's boudoir, making no secret of their dalliance. I have seen this happen in the privacy of Mrs. Kennedy's New York residence, but I was shocked they were so blatant in front of Mrs. Zauderer." Heymann, *Bobby and Jackie*, 86-88.

- Another guest staying at a nearby resort during RFK's and Jacqueline Kennedy's visit to the Zauderer's Jamaica estate, screenwriter Bernard Hayworth, reclined on the beach when RFK and Jackie arrived. After Jackie took a swim, she "dried herself off, and lay face down on the blanket next to Bobby. He began massaging her back and kissing her neck. I felt like an intruder, so I stood up to leave, and that's when he saw me. He froze, and so did I.

After what seemed an eternity, he started massaging Jackie again. I departed." Heymann, *Bobby and Jackie,* 86-88.

• Pierre Salinger, JFK's press secretary and a former U.S. Senator, said that sometime after JFK's death, Jacqueline Kennedy declined further Secret Service protection for herself because it meant she could come and go from RFK's apartment without having to log in with the Secret Service each time. Heymann, *Bobby and Jackie,* 76.

• Franklin D. Roosevelt Jr., son of the president and a close friend of both JFK and RFK: "Everybody knew about the [RFK-Jacqueline Kennedy] affair. The two of them carried on like a pair of lovesick teenagers. People used to see them at Le Club, their torsos stuck together as they danced the night away. I suspect Bobby would've liked to dump Ethel and marry Jackie, but of course that wasn't possible. Among other things, I doubt Jackie ever intended to remarry. For all the hope and optimism he engendered among his fellow citizens while he served as president, JFK had been nothing but trouble as a husband—daily assignations and a lifetime of serious venereal diseases. Jackie had no intention of repeating the exercise—not now, at any rate." Heymann, *Bobby and Jackie,* 77.

• Kenneth McKnight, the former chief administrator of the U.S. Department of Commerce who knew President and Mrs. Kennedy, was invited to join RFK's Senate staff. He arrived at RFK's Washington office one evening to discuss the position with RFK. "[When I arrived] the place was empty. I wandered down a corridor past cubicles and closed office doors to Bobby's personal suite at the far end. The door was ajar. I peeked in and there, on a sofa, sat Bobby Kennedy, and straddling his lap, her arms around his neck, was Jackie Kennedy. When they saw me, they disengaged and stood. I apologized for barging in on them. Jackie smiled. To my surprise, she remembered my name. 'How are you, Ken?' she asked. 'How have you been?' She introduced me to the senator and left the room." At the end of their hour-long meeting, as McKnight was leaving, RFK extended his hand and said, "By the way, Ken, nothing you saw or heard tonight leaves this office. Is that understood?" Heymann, *Bobby and Jackie*, 121-122.

- C. Douglas Dillon, JFK's Secretary of the Treasury and a Kennedy family friend who sponsored Jacqueline Kennedy's membership in the Essex Fox Hounds, arrived unannounced one day at the former first lady's home. Dillon later recalled that he was shocked to find her "smooching" with RFK in the backyard. "It never dawned on me that they were anything but devoted friends, brought closer by the death of John F. Kennedy. But when I saw them together that day at Jackie's weekend retreat, everything suddenly began to make sense." Heymann, *Bobby and Jackie*, 100.

- Mary Harrington: The Southern socialite, longtime friend of RFK (as well as his mistress), recalled that during her 1964 Christmas vacation she stayed in a house next door to the Kennedy home in Palm Beach, Florida. "'It was purely coincidental,' she said. One morning she peered out her bedroom window on the third floor, overlooking the Kennedy property, and there, sunbathing in the grass next to the house, was Jacqueline Kennedy, wearing a black bikini bottom and no top. A door opened and out walked Bobby Kennedy in a white swimsuit. He approached Jackie and knelt by her side. 'As they began to kiss,' said Harrington, 'he placed one hand on her breast and the other inside of her bikini bottom. After a minute or so, she stood up, wrapped a towel around her breasts and shoulders, and walked toward the house. Bobby followed. I was shocked. It was clear that Bobby was sleeping with his sister-in-law.' [¶] The next time Mary Harrington and Bobby spoke on the phone, she chided him for his public display of affection. [¶] 'You mean you were watching?' he asked. [¶] 'It was inadvertent,' she responded. 'I happened to look out the guest bedroom window. I wasn't spying on you.' [¶] Bobby proceeded to tell Harrington all about Jackie and their relationship—how, as a senator, he divided his time between Jackie in New York and Ethel in McLean, Virginia. It was as though he had two families and two homes. He loved Ethel, he told Mary, but he felt just as strongly about Jackie." Heymann, *Bobby and Jackie*, 82-83; see also Hersh, *Bobby and J. Edgar*, 453 ("A visitor to a house overlooking the [Kennedy home in Palm Beach] reported watching Jackie sunbathing on the grass with her halter off as Bobby traipsed over to kneel beside her as they kissed, one hand above and the other below.").

- During the 1964 Democratic National Convention, LBJ asked FBI Director J. Edgar Hoover to monitor RFK's activities in Atlantic City. "Hoover assigned a team of FBI agents to spy on Bobby for the duration of the convention. The only internal memorandum of interest received by Hoover had it that 'the subject [RFK] seems to spend all his free time with Mrs. John F. Kennedy. Although it can't be confirmed at this time, they appear to be sharing the same hotel suite.'" Heymann, *Bobby and Jackie*, 68.

- One Secret Service file, dated October 18, 1964, reveals that RFK and Jacqueline Kennedy shared a bedroom on at least one location in the New York apartment of Steve and Jean Kennedy Smith. Another undated file stated that they shared a bedroom in the suite occupied by RFK's former brother-in-law Peter Lawford at the Sherry-Netherland Hotel in New York City. Heymann, *Bobby and Jackie*, 76-77.

- Bruce Balding, the Glen Cove stable owner, walked in on RFK and Jacqueline Kennedy "as they embraced and kissed in the barn after their ride. Although they quickly separated, Balding had virtually caught them in the act." Heymann, *Bobby and Jackie*, 67-68.

- RFK's chauffer, Jim Fitzgerald, described how on evenings around midnight he regularly dropped off RFK in front of Jacqueline Kennedy's Fifth Avenue apartment building, retrieving him again the following morning. "He'd stride out of the building with a grin on his face and a twinkle in his eye," claimed Fitzgerald, suggesting the obvious inference. Heymann, *Bobby and Jackie*, 70.

- Sam Murphy, the doorman at Mrs. Kennedy's 1040 Fifth Avenue apartment during the spring and summer of 1966, saw RFK at her apartment on a regular basis. "I worked the overnight shift for most of those six months—11:00 p.m. to 7:00 a.m.—and I'd see Senator Kennedy an average of three times a week; that is, when Mrs. Kennedy and her children were in town. The senator usually arrived late at night and left early the next morning." Heymann, *Bobby and Jackie*, 120-121.

- Barbara Deutsch, Jacqueline Kennedy's neighbor at her 1040 Fifth Avenue apartment building, reported that "About three or four times a week, a black Town Car drove up and dropped off Bobby Kennedy in front of the building. He'd always… continue into the building and take the passenger elevator up to Jackie's apartment. I'd often see him again in the morning, climbing back into the car." Heymann, *Bobby and Jackie*, 70.

- Chuck Spaulding, a longtime JFK and Kennedy family friend: After JFK's assassination, RFK confided to him that, "Without Jackie, I don't think I'd have made it. When Jack's life ended, my hell began. I couldn't eat, sleep, or function. Jackie kept me going in a way nobody else could, not even Ethel." Spaulding confirmed that RFK and Jacqueline Kennedy had an affair. Also confirming it were former U.S. Senator George Smathers (a longtime friend of and fellow skirt-chaser with JFK), and author Truman Capote. Heymann, *Bobby and Jackie*, 113-118, 185.

CHAPTER 48

1   During World War II, Sergeant George Wallace served as a member of a lowly B-29 bomber crew under the overall theater command of General Curtis LeMay. Lesher, *George Wallace*, 55.

"Wallace had not been overly keen on LeMay [as a running mate]... there may also have been traces of shyness at the idea of a former sergeant in the 20th Air Force giving orders to his former commanding general." Chester, Hodgson, Page, *An American Melodrama*, 696.

2   "In his book *Mission with LeMay*, published by Doubleday in 1965, [LeMay] wrote of the North Vietnamese, 'My solution to the problem would be to tell them frankly that they've got to draw in their horns and stop their aggression or we're going to bomb them back into the Stone Ages.'" Alfonso A. Narvaez, "Gen. Curtis LeMay, an Architect Of Strategic Air Power, Dies at 83," *New York Times*, October 2, 1990, http://www.nytimes.com/1990/10/02/obituaries/gen-curtis-lemay-an-architect-of-strategic-air-power-dies-at-83.html. [Author's note: In an interview with the *Washington Post* in 1968, LeMay later disputed the accuracy of the quotation in his book, saying, "I never said we should bomb them back to the Stone Age. I said we had the capability to do it. I want to save lives on both sides." See the *Washington Post*, October 4, 1968, A8, cited in James H. Billington, *Respectfully Quoted: A Dictionary of Quotations* (Mineola: Dover Publications, 2010), 28-29.]

3   Wallace, "who had repeatedly told interviewers he would not use nuclear weapons in Vietnam, anticipated that the media would press LeMay on that question.... Wallace tried to prepare LeMay for what he was certain would be the principal thrust of the reporters' questions: 'Gen-

eral… we are out here among a bunch of hungry media wolves and they want to trap you into saying you would drop nuclear bombs.'" He then warned his running mate that when a reporter asked if he was willing to use a nuclear bomb if America faced annihilation, LeMay must not take the bait. "The answer you give is this: 'Listen, my friend, you are asking a purely hypothetical question… that would never have to be decided because we are going to be so strong under President Wallace that… no nuclear bomb will ever have to be dropped in our administration.'" Lesher, *George Wallace*, 425.

4   "Thursday, October 3, [1968,] at a little after ten-thirty in the morning, in the number three ballroom of the Pittsburgh Hilton Hotel, [Wallace] dropped the big one…. 'I am extremely pleased,' said George Wallace, looking pleased with himself, 'to present to you and commend to the people of the United States the very capable gentleman whom I have selected as my vice presidential running mate, General Curtis Emerson LeMay.'" Chester, Hodgson, Page, *An American Melodrama*, 692-693.

The press conference introducing General LeMay as Wallace's running mate, and the political damage inflicted on the Wallace campaign "was all over in seven minutes flat. One reporter was so stunned [by LeMay's discourse on using nuclear weapons] that he forgot to switch on his tape recorder. A CBS reporter, broadcasting live, had to take a grip on himself not to shake his head with sheer astonishment as he listened." Chester, Hodgson, Page, *An American Melodrama*, 699.

5   In his rollout press conference as a vice presidential candidate, General LeMay volunteered, much to Wallace's horror, "We seem to have a phobia about nuclear weapons…. I think there are many times when it would be more efficient to use nuclear weapons. However, the public opinion in this country and throughout the world throw up their hands in horror when you mention nuclear weapons, just because of the propaganda that's been fed to them. I don't believe the world would end if we exploded a nuclear weapon." LeMay then told of watching a film on Bikini Atoll, where the government conducted over 20 nuclear tests [in the 1940s and 1950s]. Today, he said, "[t]he fish are all back in the lagoons; the coconut trees are growing coconuts; the guava bushes have fruit on them; the birds are back. As a matter of fact, everything is about

the same except the land crabs. They get minerals from the soil, I guess, through their shells, and the land crabs were a little bit 'hot,' and there's a little question about whether you should eat a land crab or not." However, he reassured the press, "'The rats are bigger, fatter, and healthier than they ever were before....' By this time, Wallace was in anguish. 'General LeMay hasn't advocated the use of nuclear weapons, not at all,' he said desperately. 'He discussed nuclear weapons with you. He's against the use of nuclear weapons, and I am too.' [¶] But LeMay would not leave well enough alone. 'I gave you a discussion on the phobia that we have in this country about the use of nuclear weapons. I prefer not to use them. I prefer not to use any weapons at all.' [¶] 'If you found it necessary to end the war,' someone insisted, 'you would use them, wouldn't you?' [¶] 'If I found it necessary, I would use anything... including nuclear weapons, if it was necessary.' [¶] Wallace decided the time had come for a preemptive strike of his own. 'All General LeMay has said... [is that] if the security of the country depended on the use of any weapon in the future he would use it. But he has said he prefers not to use any weapon. He prefers to negotiate. I believe we must defend our country, but I've always said we can win and defend in Vietnam without the use of nuclear weapons. And General LeMay hasn't said anything about the use of nuclear weapons.' [¶] Still LeMay wouldn't let it alone. 'Let me make sure you've got this straight. I know I'm going to come out with a lot of misquotes from this campaign. I have in the past. And I'll be damned lucky if I don't appear as a drooling idiot whose only solution to any problem is to drop atomic bombs all over the world. I assure you I'm not.'" Chester, Hodgson, Page, *An American Melodrama*, 699-700.

On October 3, 1968, "Wallace announced that he had chosen General Curtis LeMay as his running mate, and LeMay, in his first press conference, said he would use nuclear weapons immediately in Vietnam." See Ambrose, *Nixon (Volume Two)*, 193.

"When Mr. Wallace introduced him as his running mate in 1968 on the American Independent Party ticket, General LeMay called for use of any available means, including nuclear weapons, to end the [Vietnam] war." See Narvaez, "Gen. Curtis LeMay."

"Wallace's choice of LeMay is a disaster. Many voters perceive LeMay, a retired Air Force general, as a loose cannon because of his apparent support for nuclear bombs. At his first official press conference he tells reporters, 'I don't believe the world will end if we explode a nuclear weapon.' Support for Wallace begins to decline once LeMay is added to the ticket." Stephen Smith and Kate Ellis, "Campaign '68: Timeline of the 1968 Campaign," *American RadioWorks*, American Public Media, http://americanradioworks.publicradio.org/features/campaign68/timeline.html.

The *Los Angeles Times* offered this contemporary account of LeMay's October 3, 1968 maiden campaign press conference: "LeMay, joining Wallace's campaign in Pittsburgh, said the world had a 'phobia about nuclear weapons' destroying the world. To support his statement minimizing the effects of nuclear contamination, he talked extensively about a film made in Bikini [a U.S. nuclear testing site before the Test Ban Treaty] in 1964 by a University of Washington expedition. LeMay said the film showed that except for land crabs which were 'still a little bit hot' and rats that were 'bigger, fatter and healthier than before,' conditions had returned to 'about the same' on the ring of coral islands that were battered by 23 nuclear test explosions during the late 1940s and 1950s." A horrified Wallace tried to interrupt LeMay, but the general refused to yield until he expressed his support for tactical nuclear weapons. Ed Kilgore, "The Ghost of Curtis LeMay," *Washington Monthly*, December 4, 2013, http://washingtonmonthly.com/2013/12/04/the-ghost-of-curtis-lemay/.

[6]   Wallace's increasing national support began collapsing in the aftermath of the LeMay press conference. "But from the first week in October and the choice of Curtis Lemay, every poll, every sampling, even the very spirit of the Wallace campaign appeared to change. Down he went, gurgling, first in the Harris poll, then in the Gallup poll, followed by every other index[.]" White, *The Making of the President 1968*, 368.

[7]   Ja-Neen Welch (true name Geneva Ruth Elkins, 1927-2008) was a sometimes-actress, model, singer, and songwriter. In later years, she opened an antique store, raised five children, and lived to be a grandmother and great-grandmother. She died in Indiana at age 81 in 2008. See Conkle Funeral Homes, November 19, 2008, https://www.meaningfulfunerals.net/home/index.cfm/obituaries/view/fh_id/11820/id/2687553

A 1968 Wallace campaign aide, Dick Smith, "was persuaded by a shapely, fortyish model named Ja-Neen Welch that she was the original

Miss Dodge Rebellion (of a recent and successful series of television commercials) and that she would add some glamour to the Wallace rallies. Dressed in skin-tight cowgirl outfits of gold lamé, she would rush to the microphone and, after Smith had implored the faithful to fill up the plastic money buckets, coo suggestively, 'The Wallace rebellion wants you!' Smith started souring on Welch within a month when he was told by reporters that the Dodge public relations office had never heard of her; apparently, Welch had made some commercials for local Dodge dealers in which she impersonated the model in the network ads.... Wallace at first had thought that having the Dodge Rebellion girl in his entourage was a coup (even though, after meeting her up close, he allowed to a security guard, 'I reckon television makes you look younger than you really are,' to which the guard replied, without gallantry, 'She must have been Miss Dodge Rebellion of 1928.')." Lesher, *George Wallace*, 418.

8   One Wallace campaign staffer remembered Ja-Neen Welch: "Hell, she was sexy looking... She had those damn boobs out there." Campaign manager Seymore Trammell noted that she "had more looks than brains." Without embarrassment, she explained to Trammell her contribution to the campaign: "'I go in there'—nodding toward Wallace's suite—'every night... for a few hours... and make love.'" She then told Trammell about her concerns for Wallace's mental state. "He's very nervous, and sometimes he won't even take his coat off when we're making love, he's in such a hurry. If I was just married to him, if I was his wife, I could calm him down and... make him the best lover you ever saw." Dan T. Carter, *The Politics of Rage: George Wallace, the Origins of the New Conservatism, and the Transformation of American Politics* (Baton Rouge: LSU Press Paperback Edition, 2000), 353-354.

9   During the closing days of Wallace's 1968 presidential campaign, Ja-Neen Welch "called a news conference to announce her impending marriage to [Wallace]. Fortunately for Wallace, no one in the press corps took her seriously[.]" Lesher, *George Wallace*, 418.

10   After Ja-Neen Welch told reporters about her impending marriage to Wallace, "Wallace instructed his staff and Secret Service agents to keep her far away from him, and Welch, seemingly satisfied with her fifteen

minutes of fame, finally gave up." Lesher, *George Wallace*, 418.

"Before peephole journalism became the order of the day, there was little danger that newsmen would report on the former governor's after-hours diversions. The real problem was that Ja-Neen Welch had become fixated on becoming the second Mrs. Wallace. [She shared with the press] that she and Wallace were in love and were 'going to get married....' In one of his famous 'not for attribution' interviews with reporters, Wallace explained that Ms. Welch had been separated from her 'limited role' in the campaign because her 'erratic behavior caused our security to have serious skepticism about her....' But reporters let her—and the story—drift into obscurity." Carter, *The Politics of Rage*, 353-354.

CHAPTER 49

¹ After telling writer Truman Capote that she might marry shipping magnate Aristotle Onassis, Capote told Jacqueline Kennedy, "If you marry that man, you'll fall off your pedestal." She replied, "Better to fall off than to be frozen there." Heyman, *RFK*, 511.

² At Humphrey's two-hour 1968 election eve telethon, broadcast from a television studio in Los Angeles, "Humphrey had [his vice-presidential running mate] by his side." Ambrose, *Nixon (Volume Two)*, 218.

³ By Election Day 1968, the final polls were close: Gallup had it Nixon 44 percent, Humphrey 43 percent; Harris had it reversed: Humphrey 44 percent, Nixon 43 percent. The Sindlinger daily tracking poll showed the race neck-and-neck, with Humphrey coming on strong. Humphrey, *The Education of a Public Man*, 406.

On October 21, 1968, two weeks before the election, Nixon led Humphrey by eight points in the Gallup Poll (44 percent to 36 percent). On Saturday, November 2, two days after LBJ's bombing halt speech, Gallup gave Nixon a lead of only two points (42 percent to 40 percent). By Sunday, Nixon's Gallup lead was down to one point. On Monday— election eve—the Harris Poll showed Humphrey defeating Nixon 43 percent to 40 percent. See White, *The Making of the President 1968*, 382.

⁴ Humphrey campaign aide Ted Van Dyk recalled the night in 1968 as Election Day neared: "Humphrey and Richard Nixon addressed the annual Al Smith dinner in New York, a forum traditionally addressed by both major party candidates. After the black-tie dinner, private receptions were held for friends of both candidates.... [At the Humphrey reception] were former New York Governor Tom Dewey and Nelson Rockefeller and

his wife Happy—people not usually on the guest list at parties honoring Democratic presidential candidates, especially when the Republican candidate was being fêted just down the hall. [¶] Happy Rockefeller walked directly over to me. 'Are you the vice president's assistant?' she asked. I told her I was. 'How is the campaign going?' she inquired. I told her things were looking better. 'How are you fixed for money?' I told her we needed it. [¶] 'Nelson and I think Nixon is a real shit,' she said. 'I'll talk to Nelson and see if we can't get you some real money....' Later, as the Rockefellers left the party, she waved to me and pointed to her purse. The following week the [Humphrey] campaign began making television buys it had previously been unable to make. I asked... the campaign treasurer where the money was coming from. 'You know where it is coming from,' he said. I presume that the Rockefellers were, in fact, the source of the money, which in those days could be contributed in unlimited amounts and without today's reporting requirements. Our television advertising spending probably equaled Nixon's during the last two weeks of the campaign." Van Dyk, *Heroes, Hacks & Fools*, 103-104.

The notion of Rockefeller donating secretly to Humphrey's campaign isn't the first unorthodox connection between the two presidential contenders from rival political parties in 1968. Behind the scenes at the 1968 Democratic National Convention in Chicago, Humphrey gave brief consideration to selecting Rockefeller as his running mate—and Rockefeller showed at least a passing interest in the bipartisan idea. Longtime Humphrey friend and senior adviser, Ambassador Max M. Kampelman, recalled in his memoir, "I urged Humphrey to break new ground and dramatically announce at the [1968 Democratic] convention that Nelson Rockefeller was his choice for vice president.... Humphrey was skeptical that it would work, but he was intrigued by the idea of making a healing gesture to the nation. He talked to Dwayne Andreas, a close friend of Nelson's as he was of Hubert's, about the idea, hoping, I think, that Dwayne might discover whether Rockefeller found the possibility attractive.... [Just before the convention, Rockefeller] 'wanted to know whether Hubert is serious.' Humphrey was serious, but ultimately neither Humphrey nor Rockefeller was willing to take the chance. Rockefeller finally said no, and Humphrey never had to make the decision." Kampelman, *Entering New Worlds*, 167.

[5] On election night 1968, Humphrey wondered whether he would reap the harvest of his last-minute surge of support, or would he come up short—excruciatingly short. Writing in his diary that night, he noted, "That top rung is never going to be mine. My fingernails are scraping it, but I don't have a grip. Yet maybe we can make it. It's so damn close. I am so tired." Humphrey, *The Education of a Public Man*, 4, 406.

[6] On election night 1968, in Humphrey's suite at the Leamington Hotel in Minneapolis, "[s]hut away in a phone–filled room, campaign manager Larry O'Brien and his staff were doing vote analyses and projections. About 1 a.m. Max Kampelman, a lifelong [Humphrey] friend and former aide, came from that room and intercepted Humphrey in the hall. Face to face, not a muscle moving, eyes on Kampelman's, unwavering, Humphrey listened. He was hearing why he would not win unless he took Ohio, Illinois and California. Finally, as though saying 'comme ci, comme ca,' Kampelman rocked his hand from side to side. Humphrey looked ruefully at the ceiling and said, 'Oh, Jesus.'" Thomas Griffin, "The Nixon Era Begins: What the Election Wasn't About," *Life,* November 15, 1968, 42.

[7] Just before Humphrey's election eve live telethon aired, McCarthy called and asked if he could appear on camera to give Humphrey his endorsement. By then it was too late to schedule an in-person appearance, so McCarthy called into the program and endorsed Humphrey. Van Dyk, *Heroes, Hacks & Fools*, 92, 99.

Had McCarthy come out and endorsed Humphrey earlier—and heartily—Humphrey believed that he would have won several states where McCarthy enjoyed strong support: New Jersey, Ohio, Illinois, and California. Instead, he lost them all to Nixon. "Particularly in California, had McCarthy campaigned early and hard for me and the Democratic Party, he might have turned it." In his diary on election night, Humphrey wrote, "I can carry California. I've got to or I'm dead. Gene McCarthy could have helped. I thought we had an understanding, but he didn't deliver. Maybe he couldn't. God knows the pressure would have been great not to. And when he did speak out, it was late and half-hearted." Humphrey, *The Education of a Public Man*, 5, 377.

McCarthy polled strongly in the primary states he won: Oregon and Wisconsin, and he also had strong support in California. (Nixon ended up winning these states in 1968). McCarthy's last-minute endorsement of Humphrey may or may not have had much effect. Some McCarthy supporters had already moved into Humphrey's camp, albeit reluctantly. Others viewed McCarthy's eleventh-hour finding of Humphrey's presidential suitability as a betrayal of principle. Chester, Hodgson, Page, *An American Melodrama*, 737-738.

Reporter Drew Pearson reflected on McCarthy's failure to endorse Humphrey until almost the end of the general election campaign. In his diary entry the day after the election (November 6, 1968), Pearson wrote, "If McCarthy had come out two weeks earlier for Hubert instead of the night before the election, I think [Humphrey] would have won." Pearson and Hannaford, *Washington Merry-Go-Round*, 629-630.

8   In November 1968, had Humphrey won California instead of Nixon, Nixon would have lost his Electoral College majority and the House of Representatives would have been called upon to decide the next president.

9   On election eve 1968, "Nixon wrapped up his final telethon in Los Angeles. His last answer of the show ended the 1968 campaign.... We drove back to the Beverly Wilshire Hotel, slightly numb but exhilarated and thirsty." Garment, *Crazy Rhythm*, 139.

"On Monday night [election eve], from Los Angeles television studios, Nixon and Humphrey staged telethons, two hours for Humphrey, four for Nixon.... Both presidential candidates answered call-in questions, which came in at an astounding rate of 130,000 per hour." Ambrose, *Nixon (Volume Two)*, 218.

10   During the final days of the 1968 campaign, Nixon often called law partner Leonard Garment late at night. "Nixon would usually apologize for the late hour, ask after my family and the morale of the New York staff... some such thing. Then [he] began what was less a conversation than a monologue, centered on his anxieties of the day. These were mostly about his narrowing margin over Humphrey and the impact of an expected bombing halt in Vietnam. [¶] The Democrats are going home, Len, he would say. The Wallace vote is hurting us. Watch for an L.B.J. stunt right before the election. Don't let your people panic. I would offer an occasional opinion, but he didn't need that from me. What he wanted was reassurance." Garment, *Crazy Rhythm*, 143-144.

[11]   Nixon voted in the 1968 presidential election by absentee ballot. After his last campaign appearance on election eve night, his entourage left Los Angeles International Airport at 10:00 p.m. and flew to Newark Airport, arriving just after 6:00 a.m. on Election Day. Nixon, *RN,* 331-333.

[12]   On the plane ride back east in the early hours of Election Day morning, "Nixon seemed relaxed, confident, fatalistic about the outcome." Buchanan, *The Greatest Comeback,* 363.

Aboard his campaign jet, Nixon "settled down in his private compartment, as he had done all through the campaign, and summoned people forward. He thanked his speechwriters, thanked the advance men, thanked the managers. He told his family he expected to win, but it was quite possible that he would lose because of the bombing halt, which he estimated had cost him from three to five million votes." Ambrose, *Nixon (Volume Two),* 218-219.

In the early morning hours of Election Day 1968, Nixon and his staff "boarded the Tricia, Nixon's big jet, for the flight back to New York. Floating high over the country, the entire campaign family was together for the first time, sealed off from the voters five miles below in an airborne metaphor of the separation that takes place on Election Day between the candidate and the country. For the first time that year, we were merely observers; the process was on its own. [¶] After some booze and nervous babble, the functional staff group—writers, media, advance men, secretaries— trooped forward to Nixon's compartment for thanks and, for us media advisers, a not-unhappy farewell. Then we gradually settled into our own private thoughts, drawing apart, thumbing through magazines and newspapers. A TV set in the staff compartment began giving fuzzy accounts of voting turnout in places like Kansas and New Hampshire." Garment, *Crazy Rhythm,* 140-142.

[13]   In 1968, shortly after winning the presidency, Nixon asked McCarthy to be his ambassador to the United Nations. In this book, the author suggested—for dramatic purposes only—that Nixon offered McCarthy the position before Election Day as an incentive to withhold his endorsement of Humphrey until the last minute. This was fiction. Nixon did offer McCarthy the U.N. ambassadorship, but the offer came after Nixon won the 1968 election. Recalling Nixon's unexpected offer of the U.N.

ambassadorship two decades later, McCarthy wrote, "I wanted to take the office, since I saw an opportunity to return the office to what it had been conceived to be and to what it was [previously]." The plan fell through, however, when the Republican governor of Minnesota refused to accede to McCarthy's condition precedent: that the governor appoint a Democrat to fill McCarthy's Senate vacancy if McCarthy joined the Nixon Administration. "Having been elected by the Democratic Farmer Labor Party," McCarthy concluded, "I did not feel I had the right to give up the office to a Republican... so I rejected the offer." McCarthy, *Up 'Til Now*, 115-117.

On December 18, 1968, when Nixon was president-elect, aide Pat Buchanan learned that Nixon was about to offer McCarthy the post of ambassador to the United Nations. Buchanan wrote a protest memo to Nixon, calling McCarthy "an arrogant mystic with a messianic streak, who left his good friend [Humphrey] dangling on a hook for months and perhaps cost him the election, merely because Humphrey caviled over a few words in a party platform.... If he had no loyalty to his old friend Humphrey, what kind of loyalty would he have to RN?" Patrick J. Buchanan, *Nixon's White House Wars* (New York: Crown Forum, 2017), 16.

McCarthy was willing to serve as Nixon's United Nations ambassador. Herzog, *McCarthy for President*, 292.

Eugene McCarthy wasn't the only 1968 presidential candidate to whom Nixon offered the position of United States Ambassador to the United Nations. After winning the 1968 election, he also tried recruiting Hubert Humphrey for the post when they met after the election. Humphrey, *The Education of a Public Man*, 432-433.

After the 1968 election, "[w]hen Humphrey landed at Opa Locka airport just north of Miami, there stood Nixon. With little pause or ceremony, Nixon said, 'I want you to be my ambassador to the United Nations.' If Humphrey would do that, Nixon would also let him clear any appointment to a regulatory agency that required a Democrat. To top it off, Nixon said, 'If I have to lose to a Democrat in 1972, I'd like it to be you.' Humphrey turned down the offer." Sherman, *From Nowhere to Somewhere*, 202.

[14]   On Election Day, upon their return to New York, the Nixon party settled into their suites on the 35th floor of the Waldorf Towers in New York City to await the returns. Nixon, *RN*, 331-333.

At the Waldorf-Astoria Hotel in New York City on Election Day, Nixon occupied Suite 35H. White, *The Making of the President 1968*, 392 et seq.

On Election Day, once Nixon arrived at his hotel suite in the Waldorf Towers, "He took a hot bath, tried to nap, failed, and by 8:20 p.m. was drinking coffee and watching the early returns." Ambrose, *Nixon (Volume Two)*, 218-219.

On Election Day, "[r]eturning to New York exhausted but excited, the staff piled aboard a waiting bus that took us to our election-night headquarters at the Waldorf-Astoria... where thousands of supporters milled about, and were in the ballroom and adjacent public rooms of the Waldorf proper. But the inner circle gathered on the thirty-fifth floor of the Waldorf Towers, where the Nixons had their own suite. Scattered through the other rooms on the floor were television sets and refreshments and, of course, telephones." Price, *With Nixon*, 36.

"We landed at Newark Airport [on Election Day] in a blaze of excitement and television lights.... We voted, then went to the thirty-fifth floor of the Waldorf-Astoria to watch the returns. Tonight the future had arrived, and stopped.... [¶] [I]t was going to be close. For the next few hours I watched the returns with Frank Shakespeare in a hospitality suite down the hall from Nixon. Rockefeller, Jacob Javits, Strom Thurmond, and other political figures came and went, but Nixon was not ready to see anyone. Bob Haldeman, John Ehrlichman, and campaign aide Dwight Chapin monitored the television next door to Nixon's suite." Garment, *Crazy Rhythm*, 140-142.

[15]   On election night 1968, in the Nixon camp at the Waldorf, "[w]e circulated from one room to another, keeping tabs on the results, the tension mounting as the count dragged on. Through most of the evening Nixon clung to a thin but precarious lead. Around midnight Humphrey appeared to be surging forward, and for the first time my own characteristic optimism turned to a queasy pessimism. By 2:00, as more returns trickled in, it looked again as though we were winning. Shortly after 3:00,

the man we thought was the president-elect invited a dozen of us to wait out the results with him in his suite. The banter was light, the campaign reminiscences good-natured, but there was a heavy tension in the air. Every once in a while, in a flash of impatient irritation, Nixon sent Mitchell or Haldeman or another aide to the next room to call headquarters in one of the states that had still not reported, and to try to get some sort of reading that might cut through the clouds of uncertainty. But by then there was little to report. Most had shut down their counting operations until morning. Texas reported before midnight that 'mechanical problems' would delay the totals until morning—a report which sounded ominous to those with memories of 1960." Price, *With Nixon*, 36.

[16] "The key results came down to California, Ohio, and Illinois…. If Humphrey… carried all three of these states, he would have won the election. [If he] won just two of them—or even just California—Wallace would [succeed] in his quest to prevent an electoral majority. The race would [go] to the Democrat-controlled House of Representatives, dashing Nixon's hopes again." Stone, *Nixon's Secrets*, 377.

[17] By election night, "Illinois was even more ominous: Mayor Richard Daley was up to his traditional trick, withholding votes from his Chicago vote cache until the downstate results revealed the deficit, which would then be made up by hook or, more likely, by crook. This could be a stomach-turning reprise of 1960…. [¶] Mitchell's strategy to counter Daley had been to arrange the withholding of a large cache of Republican-controlled votes in downstate Illinois. So, hour after hour, John Mitchell and Richard Daley dueled, each withholding his ultimate weapon as the sun rose over a still-sleeping America. [¶] About 8:00 a.m., Nixon, out of patience, told Mitchell to place a call to Mike Wallace, who was live on CBS television, and challenge Daley to release his votes. We watched the TV screen as Mike took Mitchell's call and put Mitchell's challenge to Daley. The Illinois votes were released, the state went to Nixon, and, around noon, Humphrey conceded." Garment, *Crazy Rhythm*, 140-142.

"Another of the holdout states was Illinois. There, Mayor Richard J Daley was up to his traditional trick of holding back the results from key Chicago areas until the count was in from downstate. That way, if the results were close and a few thousand extra votes were needed to tip the state into the Democratic column, the Daley machine could usually manage to find those 'votes.' But this time, the Nixon campaign organization was prepared. Instructions had gone out to several Republican-controlled jurisdictions not to release their totals until Daley had released his. Demands did no good; Daley stubbornly sat on his vote counts. Then, at about 8:00 a.m., as we sat together in front of the television set, campaign manager John Mitchell put in a call to Mike Wallace of CBS. We watched the screen as Wallace, who was on the air, took the call. Mitchell prodded Wallace to challenge Daley—on television. Wallace did, and shortly thereafter the Illinois totals were released. Illinois fell into the Nixon column." Price, *With Nixon*, 36.

CHAPTER 50

1   "When we started the third party, we had no organization and no established sources of funds. Our income came principally from the 'little man' all over the nation. By his contributions, we raised the money to gain ballot position and to finance the campaign. We did not have purse power, but we did have people power." Wallace, *Stand Up for America*, 123.

   During his presidential campaign, Wallace said that "Washington had been taken over by 'pure, brute, naked federal force' and that because of the Supreme Court, schoolchildren could not 'even sing America because it has the word God in it.'" Lesher, *George Wallace*, 307.

2   In the closing days of the 1968 presidential campaign, the two major presidential candidates began copying from Wallace's playbook. "As the election drew closer, however, Nixon decided to make the law-and-order theme central to his campaign in an overt quest to appropriate the issue from Wallace; he would succeed, he thought, because voters would soon realize that Wallace could not be elected and would switch to Nixon as the electable law-and-order candidate." One reporter covering the race wrote that Wallace had "made law and order the controlling issue—one that Nixon latched onto with gusto by making it the centerpiece of his national television commercial blitz.... And Humphrey, even after renouncing his president's Vietnam policies, condemned 'anarchists' for domestic disruptions." Lesher, *George Wallace*, 414, 422.

   "Rising taxes and inflation were the scourge of the middle class, who carried on their backs the non-producers and welfare loafers.... My platform in 1968 was neither revolutionary nor extreme. It called for equity: curtailment of foreign aid to our enemies even if it meant loss of profits, reform of our welfare program to eliminate abuses, an end to the federal government's encroachment in areas belonging to the states, an end to busing of little children to achieve racial quotas, and an end to judicial usurpation." Wallace, *Stand Up for America*, 122.

[3] In the 1968 presidential election, a shift of 112,000 votes (out of almost 7 million cast) in California from Nixon to Humphrey would have left Nixon with 261 electoral votes, nine short of an Electoral College majority. Buchanan, *The Greatest Comeback*, 1.

[4] The Wallace campaign transported from rally to rally an 800-pound bulletproof lectern to deflect the barrage of rocks, oranges, tomatoes, and other missiles thrown at Wallace routinely during public appearances. See Lesher, *George Wallace*, 480.

[5] "Some elements of the Electoral College, such as the indirect vote through intermediaries, were hotly debated at the 1787 Constitutional Convention. It was eventually justified in part as a stopgap to potentially reverse the vote if the people elected a criminal, traitor, or similar kind of heinous person…. Alexander Hamilton defended the Electoral College in *Federalist 68*. He argued that it was important for the people as a whole to have a great deal of power in choosing their president, but it was also 'desirable' that 'the immediate election should be made by men most capable of analyzing the qualities adapted to the station, and acting under circumstances favorable to deliberation, and to a judicious combination of all the reasons and inducements which were proper to govern their choice.'" Jarrett Stepman, "Why We Use Electoral College, Not Popular Vote," *The Daily Signal*, November 7, 2016, http://dailysignal.com/2016/11/07/why-the-founders-created-the-electoral-college/.

[6] After the 1968 election, Wallace shattered the notion that he was a "sectional candidate." Although he received a huge share of his votes from the South, 40 percent of his total popular vote came from labor votes in the North and West. "Despite all the influences of the media, all the pressure of their labor unions, all the blunders and incompetence of the Wallace campaign," wrote Theodore H. White, they voted for Wallace. [Author's note: Muddying his otherwise competent analysis of the Wallace

vote, Mr. White—unfairly—concluded that Wallace's ten million voters all cast their ballots because "they had voted racist." White, *The Making of the President 1968*, 369.]

During the 1968 presidential campaign, the AFL-CIO viewed Wallace's candidacy as a major threat. With the populist governor pulling 25 percent to 35 percent of labor voters in key industrial states, the union bosses determined to dirty him up. In conjunction with a full-fledged assault against Wallace in the mainstream press, both forces attacked him incessantly. The AFL-CIO dropped over 20 million pamphlets in the industrial Northern states and 100 million pamphlets nationwide blasting Wallace as a union-busting racist. The AFL-CIO attacks on Wallace had a major impact. After their blitzkrieg against him, a Gallup poll showed the number of people who believed Wallace was a racist jumped 27 points from September to October. When asked about such polls, the average Wallace voter shrugged. "I don't know who they're asking," was a frequent reply. "They never asked my opinion." See White, *The Making of the President 1968*, 363-364.

CHAPTER 51

[1]   Chris' Hot Dog Stand, 138 Dexter Avenue, Montgomery, Alabama: "Founded in 1917, Chris' Hot Dogs [has] had customers from every state in the Union, and countless guests from other countries. Some of our more notable patrons include Franklin D. Roosevelt (who would frequently ask for a box of the world famous hot dogs as his train stopped in the Montgomery train station), Harry Truman, Dr. Martin Luther King, Jr., Presidents Bush 41 & 43, Jimmy Stewart, Elvis Presley, Hank Williams, Clark Gable.... Since our opening in 1917, every Alabama governor has eaten at Chris'." https://www.facebook.com/ChrisHotDogs/about/.

[2]   In the event no candidate receives the majority of the votes cast by the Electoral College, a "contingent election" is held by the House of Representatives. Each state delegation casts one vote for one of the top three contenders to determine a winner. "Electoral College Fast Facts," United States House of Representatives, Office of Art and Archives, http://history.house.gov/Institution/Electoral-College/Electoral-College/.

[3]   In a speech to union workers at a Detroit rally in late 1968, Humphrey blasted Wallace: "Let's lay it on the line—George Wallace's pitch is racism. If you want to feel damn mean and ornery, find some other way to do it, but don't sacrifice your country. George Wallace has been engaged in union-busting whenever he's had the chance.... And any union man who votes for him is not a good union man." White, *The Making of the President 1968*, 363.

Humphrey called Wallace "the 'know-nothing' candidate of our period, a canny and shrewd politician who captured the votes of those whose fears and hates and alienation he articulated." He claimed that Wallace "demagogued his way into the hearts and minds of those who wanted simplistic answers to difficult problems[,]" and he alleged that Wallace tied "crime" and "black" together, so that every threat to a voter's person or property appeared to be a black threat. Regarding Wallace's campaign slogan, "Send them a message," Humphrey wrote: "Some of the 'message' was racist, some illogical and absurd.... Wallace personally was a threat to what I considered the essence of the American experiment: goodwill, conciliation, justice for all. We had his message. We simply did not need his presidency." Humphrey, *The Education of a Public Man*, 373, 379, 434.

4   In 2016, a senior 1968 Wallace campaign aide (who later served as national director of Wallace's 1972 and 1976 presidential campaigns), Charles Snider, told the author that Wallace wanted Nixon, not Humphrey, to win in 1968: "We were on the Nixon side. George [Wallace] stated on several occasions [that] if he did nothing else in [running for president in 1968] it was to keep Humphrey from becoming president." Charles Snyder, text message to the author, December 2, 2016.

5   If neither major party candidate had won an outright Electoral College majority in 1968, would either Nixon or Humphrey—or both of them—have been willing to make a deal with Wallace? History leaves that question unanswered. We do know that each side feared that the other would strike a deal with Wallace if needed:

- "As the [1968] campaign wore on, Nixon told reporters he was sure that neither he nor Hubert Humphrey would ever make a deal with Wallace. Humphrey, whose famous speech on civil rights at the 1948 Democratic Convention had provoked Wallace and the Alabama delegation to walk out of that convention, insisted that he would never bargain with Wallace, saying: 'If there's any office in this country that ought to be above any kind of deal with Mr. Wallace... it's the presidency. I'm a no-deal man.' On October 14, 1968, Humphrey's campaign manager, Lawrence O'Brien, suggested that 'secret negotiations' had already begun between Nixon and Wallace. Two days later, it was reported that emissaries of Nixon and Wallace were negotiating in New York—and that Nixon campaign manager John Mitchell was pushing the strategy. But because Nixon won decisively in the Electoral College, he never had to pay Wallace for the presidency." Laurence H. Tribe and Thomas M. Rollins, "Deadlock," *The Atlantic Monthly*, October 1980, http://www.theatlantic.com/past/docs/issues/80oct/deadlock.htm.

- If the election deadlocked in the Electoral College, and the selection of a president went to the House of Representatives, Nixon feared it was Humphrey who would make a deal with Wallace. Since the Democrats dominated the House, this would guarantee Humphrey's election. To combat that scenario, before Election Day, Nixon challenged Humphrey to agree that the loser of the popular vote would support the winner if the election went to the House. Humphrey refused to agree. Nixon, *RN*, 320.

- 1968 Humphrey senior campaign aide Ted Van Dyk recalled that one week before the 1968 election, Bill Welsh, another senior Humphrey aide, delivered to him "a document prepared by campaign analysts and attorneys. It suggested that neither Humphrey nor Nixon might win outright on election night. Humphrey might need to bargain with Wallace in order to win an Electoral College victory. Humphrey had wasted few words on Wallace during the campaign. He viewed him with distaste and believed he had traded on racial fears to sustain his third party candidacy. Humphrey had not been asked what he would do if Wallace held the balance of power in deciding the election. I had told reporters on several occasions that [Humphrey] would not compromise with George Wallace in any circumstance. Welsh urged me to withhold further such statements and to caution Humphrey against them as well. I acknowledged the information but thought it highly unlikely that Humphrey would want to negotiate with Wallace, whereas I was sure that Nixon would." Van Dyk, *Heroes, Hacks & Fools*, 95.

[6] Regarding the animosity between Nixon and Chief Justice Earl Warren: "On June 21 [1968], it was revealed that Chief Justice Earl Warren had submitted his resignation to President Johnson. [¶] Warren [governor of California from 1943-1953] had never much liked Nixon.

Warren thought, with reason, that in 1952 Nixon had stolen the California delegation to the Republican Convention from him, thereby giving the nomination to Ike and depriving Warren of his chance. [¶] By 1968, Nixon had become almost as critical of the Warren Court as he was of the Johnson Administration. He was promising, as president, to appoint judges who would reverse some of the basic decisions of the past fifteen years. When Warren resigned, reports spread quickly that he had chosen this moment to do so because he feared that Nixon would win in November and eventually have the opportunity to appoint Warren's successor. Nixon... looked on Warren's timing as being vindictive because of the chief justice's known dislike for him.... The two men had been hostile toward each other since the 1952 campaign for the Republican nomination, and Nixon had been sharply, even cruelly critical of the Warren Court during the 1968 campaign[.]" Ambrose, *Nixon (Volume Two)*, 159, 274.

CHAPTER 52

1   "The Electoral College, which has no campus, no facility, no student body... holds its quadrennial meeting [today].... The 538 participants, called electors, will gather in state capitals to pick [the next president and vice president]. Frank Eleazer, United Press International, "Possibly Last Electoral College Meets to Formally Elect Nixon," *The Technician,* North Carolina State University at Raleigh, December 16, 1968.

2   Since the mid-20th century, on January 6 at 1:00 p.m., congressional tellers count the ballots cast by the Electoral College before a joint session of Congress. See "Electoral College Fast Facts."

3   Writing about his presidential election defeat in his diary, Humphrey recalled thinking during his concession call to Nixon, "He's gracious. That's about it. Losing to Nixon—Ye gods! No warmth, no strength, no emotion, no spirit. No heart. Politics of the computer. Probably if I had more of it, I'd be president. This is the worst moment of my life." Before going downstairs to the Hall of States at the Leamington Hotel in Minneapolis to deliver his concession speech, Humphrey pondered all the people who could have helped—should have helped—but didn't. "I've got to hide the bitterness," he told himself. "We'll carry this off with dignity. No crybaby act. No complaining." When it was over, he had only one desire: go home to Waverly. "I need to get away," he recorded in his diary later that day. "I'm numb—and heartbroken.... I was ready. I'd really trained for the presidency.... We could have changed things. Damn it, I love this country. We could have done so much good." The day after the election, instead of a testimonial feting him as the new president-elect, the outgoing vice president ate a corned beef sandwich in a Jewish deli with an old Minnesota pal. See Humphrey, *The Education of a Public Man,* 13-14.

[4]   After the tabulation of electoral votes before a joint session of Congress, sitting Vice Presidents Richard Nixon (1961), Hubert Humphrey (1969), and Al Gore (2001) each announced that they had lost their own bid for the presidency. See "Electoral College Fast Facts."

[5]   When the author served as United States Under Secretary of Commerce for Intellectual Property and Director of the United States Patent and Trademark Office (2001-2004), Wayne Paugh was his chief of staff. Once, on an overseas flight, the author noticed Wayne working diligently on a document. When asked what he was doing, Wayne replied that the Commerce Department's personnel office told him that there was no job description for the position of chief of staff. "I'm drafting one for them," he said. "Let me see what you've got so far," the author replied. Taking the document from him, the author began scribbling his own edits onto Wayne's work product. After handing it back, Wayne read the author's contribution to the chief of staff job description. "Do you really want me to turn this in?" Wayne asked. The author instructed him to do so, and he followed orders. When Wayne delivered the document to the Commerce Department personnel director, she read it and then asked if this was a joke. "Do you recognize the handwriting on that document?" he asked her. She processed it. As far as the author knows, to this day the official responsibilities listed for the USPTO chief of staff is *Job Description Number Seven*: "Espouse willing, effective, and sincere acceptance of random assignments of blame, irrespective of merit or fairness, and preferably in advance of any error occurring." During the author's tenure as Under Secretary of Commerce, his senior staff called this *The Wayne Rule*.

[6]   Abe Fortas (1910-1982), a longtime political crony of LBJ's, served as an associate justice of the United States Supreme Court. Originally appointed to the court by LBJ in 1965, when Earl Warren announced his plan to retire as chief justice in 1968, LBJ nominated Fortas to replace him. The nomination received strenuous opposition from Republicans and Southern Democrats angry over Fortas' contribution to the liberal Warren-court rulings. Later, when senators learned that Fortas continued advising LBJ on political matters while a sitting justice, the revelation forced Fortas to ask LBJ to withdraw his nomination. The following year,

the press revealed that Fortas accepted a $20,000 annual payment for life from a Wall Street financier seeking a presidential pardon from LBJ for a criminal conviction. The resulting scandal drove Fortas to resign from the Court in disgrace on May 14, 1969. See Ambrose, *Nixon (Volume Two)*, 199, 275.

[7] Chief Justice Earl Warren agreed to defer his retirement (announced in mid-1968) until the Senate confirmed his successor. A few months after assuming the presidency, Nixon nominated Judge Warren E. Burger for the position. While the Burger nomination was pending, the unexpected resignation of Associate Justice Abe Fortas gave Nixon his second Supreme Court vacancy to fill within the first few months of his administration.

[8] Following the resignation of Justice Abe Fortas, President Nixon nominated Judge Clement F. Haynsworth of South Carolina to the United States Supreme Court. "Haynsworth had a segregationist background, as did virtually every Southerner of that time; he belonged to exclusive clubs; he was a wealthy man. [¶] When the Senate went into session in September [1969 to consider the nomination], Birch Bayh (D-IN) unleashed a barrage of charges against Haynsworth, centering on an allegation that he had adjudicated cases in which he had a financial interest. The *Washington Post* and the television news programs added innuendo and rumor of their own. Nixon complained, with some justification, that no rich man would ever be able to meet the standards demanded of Haynsworth. But by the end of September, [White House aide Bryce] Harlow knew Haynsworth could not make it.... The liberals in the Senate [went] after Judge Haynsworth with a vengeance. Nixon told newsmen that 'a vicious character assassination' was underway, and reaffirmed his support.... The real objection was Haynsworth's conservative philosophy, and beyond that the Democrats desire to have some revenge [for Fortas].... On November 21, [1969] the Senate voted 55-45 to reject Haynsworth's nomination.... In a statement saying that he deeply regretted the Senate action and deplored the nature of the attacks made upon Haynsworth, Nixon promised to appoint [another] conservative. His next nomination, he said, would be made on the same criteria he applied to Haynsworth." Ambrose, *Nixon (Volume Two)*, 295-296, 315-316.

On January 19, 1970, Nixon nominated Judge G. Harrold Carswell of Georgia for the same U.S. Supreme Court seat for which the Senate had rejected his earlier nominee, Clement Haynsworth. "Carswell had everything going against him. As a candidate for the Georgia legislature in 1948, he had said, 'Segregation of the races is proper and the only practical and correct way of life.... I have always so believed and I shall always so act.' His rulings, as a circuit judge in Florida, had reflected those views (although he renounced the statement itself). Further, his qualifications for the high court were simply nonexistent. [Nixon White House aide] Bryce Harlow, always one to tell the truth, informed Nixon that the senators 'think Carswell's a boob, a dummy. And what counter is there to that? He is.' [¶] Senator Roman Hruska (R-NE) nevertheless tried to counter. In a TV interview, Hruska declared that there were millions of mediocre people in America and they too deserved representation on the Supreme Court." In April, when the Carswell nomination came before the Senate, they rejected him by a vote of 51-45. Ambrose, *Nixon (Volume Two)*, 330, 337.

Angry over the Senate's refusal to confirm two consecutive Supreme Court nominees (both of whom were Southerners), Nixon called a press conference and "used the occasion to issue a verbal blast unprecedented in the history of rejected Supreme Court nominations. [¶] 'I have reluctantly concluded that it is not possible to get a confirmation for a judge on the Supreme Court of any man who believes in the strict construction of the Constitution,' he said, 'if he happens to come from the South.' Referring back to Haynsworth, he went on, 'When you strip away all the hypocrisy, the real reason for their rejection [of Haynsworth and Carswell] was their legal philosophy... and also the accident of their birth, the fact that they were born in the South.' He said that so long as the Senate 'is constituted the way it is today, I will not nominate another Southerner and let him be subjected to the kind of malicious character assassination accorded both Judges Haynsworth and Carswell.'" Ambrose, *Nixon (Volume Two)*, 337-338.

CHAPTER 53

1   RFK found life in the Senate boring. "[H]e wasn't exactly wild about the place," wrote former senator and RFK's 1968 campaign senior aide Pierre Salinger. "For him, it was too archaic, too slow and inactive, and he was soon rather restless." Salinger, *P.S.*, 188.

   Political analyst and columnist Joseph Kraft remembered that RFK "was not awfully happy in the Senate, that he felt it was a talking place rather than a doing place. He would frequently talk about how little it was his style. He referred, often contemptuously, to things that were going on as 'five or six old men sitting around.'" Heyman, *RFK*, 400.

2   There is substantial evidence that Mary Jo Kopechne was RFK's mistress. Former U.S. Senator George Smathers, a very close friend of John and Robert Kennedy, said that Kopechne came to work for him as a secretary in his office. He introduced her to the Kennedys. Smathers later recalled, "When Bobby became a senator, [Kopechne] transferred to his secretarial pool, sharing a Georgetown townhouse with four other women her age, all of them members of Bobby's staff. During his run for the presidency, this enclave became known as the Boiler Room Girls. [¶] 'Although she no longer worked for me, Mary Jo and I stayed in touch. I'd become her father confessor, so to speak. She was young, sweet, and impressionable. When she informed me that Bobby had invited her to join him as a secretary on the presidential campaign plane, I warned her against it. I knew Bobby, and I knew that he would take advantage of the situation. And that's precisely what happened. It didn't matter to him whether Ethel was also on the plane. They'd check into hotels at night, and Mary Jo would be given her own room. It didn't take much for Bobby to excuse himself from a strategy meeting for a few minutes and go visit

Mary Jo in her room. Nobody was the wiser for it. It reminded me a little of Jack when he campaigned for the presidency in 1960, except that Jackie wasn't around most of the time.'" Heyman, *RFK*, 152-153.

Another close friend of Mary Jo Kopechne said that Mary Jo never had an affair with Senator Edward Kennedy as many suspected. She had an affair with his brother, Robert F. Kennedy. Heyman, *RFK*, 419.

Doris Lilly, Mary Jo Kopechne's friend since 1965, said that after RFK's assassination, she and Mary Jo together began writing an article on him. "She admitted that she'd been in love with him and that they'd had an affair during the early months of 1968. This didn't surprise me. Bobby wasn't exactly the choirboy that everybody thought he was. He had dozens of affairs, some longer-lived, some shorter. And Mary Jo had all the prerequisites: youth, vibrancy, intelligence. She was a sweet, sweet child. She deserved far better than to end up a passenger in the hands of somebody like Ted Kennedy. I wouldn't trust that man to walk my dog in the park." Heyman, *RFK*, 516.

"Friends scoffed at the idea that there had been anything between [Mary Jo] and [Edward Kennedy]; it was Bobby she revered and Bobby whose death so disturbed her." See "Ted Kennedy Car Accident in Chappaquiddick," *Newsweek*, August 3, 1969.

[3]   "The circumstances of the accident, however innocent they may have been in fact, were bad enough on their face for any politician: Teddy and Mary Jo, 28, had just left four other married men and five other single girls at a party at 11:15 p.m. and were headed down a lonely dirt road to nowhere when the car went off the bridge." See "Ted Kennedy Car Accident in Chappaquiddick," *Newsweek*.

[4]   Another of RFK's "Boiler Room Girls," Susan Tannenbaum, said the girls "began urging some of the Kennedy men—Teddy [Kennedy] and [Joe] Gargan included—to 'take us sailing again,' as they had done [previously]. They settled on the regatta weekend because the girls wanted to cheer Teddy on (he finished ninth), and Gargan made the arrangements, signing an eight-day lease on the cottage [at Chappaquiddick] for $200 and booking the girls into an Edgartown motel." See "Ted Kennedy Car Accident in Chappaquiddick," *Newsweek*.

⁵   In his 1988 book, *Senatorial Privilege*, author Leo Damore interviewed Edward Kennedy's cousin (and fellow Chappaquiddick party host) Joe Gargan, who told Damore that after Kopechne's death at Chappaquiddick, Edward Kennedy attempted to establish an alibi by claiming she was the sole driver and occupant of the car. "It was Gargan whom Kennedy first summoned for help when he stumbled in exhaustion back to the cottage after failing to rescue Kopechne. It was Gargan and another Kennedy friend, Paul Markham, who returned to the bridge with the senator and dove into tideswept Poucha Pond in another unsuccessful effort to reach the 28 year-old woman. And it was Gargan who said they kept telling Kennedy to call the police as they drove over to the ferry landing on Kennedy's instructions.... Kennedy suggested [to Gargan] making Kopechne the driver and lone occupant of the car, in an accident that Gargan could 'discover' after Kennedy had returned to Edgartown." George Lardner Jr., "Chappaquiddick, 1989," *Washington Post*, July 16, 1989, https://www. washingtonpost.com/archive/opinions/1989/07/16/chappaquiddick-1989/28d50758-314b-49e1-90bd-78eb8fddf64f/.

About two hours after the Chappaquiddick accident, Edward Kennedy appears to have attempted to establish a second alibi with his hotel clerk. Russell E. Peachey, one of the owners of the Shiretown Inn (Edward Kennedy's hotel), said that on the night of the accident, at about 2:00 a.m., Edward Kennedy "was standing just outside the office window... fully dressed, standing some forty to fifty feet away, in the shadows near the foot of the stairs that led to his quarters. [¶] 'May I help you in any way?' Peachey inquired. [¶] He said Kennedy replied, 'I've been disturbed by the noise coming from the party next door. I've looked for my watch and seem to have misplaced it. What time is it?' [¶] Peachey said he looked through the office window at a clock inside and answered, 'It's exactly 2:25. Is there anything else I can do to help you?' [¶] 'No, thank you,' said Teddy. Then, Peachey said, the senator turned and went up the stairs to his quarters." See "Ted Kennedy Car Accident in Chappaquiddick," *Newsweek*.

⁶   Following Mary Jo Kopechne's death, and after Edward Kennedy advised cousin Joe Gargan of the accident, Kennedy "told Gargan and [Paul Markham, who also attended the party on the island] not to 'alarm Mary Jo's friends' with the news that night, then had them drive him to

the ferry landing on the Chappaquiddick side of the 500-foot channel. They found the ferry closed for the night. 'I suddenly jumped into the water and impulsively swam across, nearly drowning once again in the effort,' said Kennedy. '[I] returned to my hotel about 2 a.m. and collapsed in my room.' Not till the next morning, 'with my mind somewhat more lucid,' did he try first to reach family lawyer Burke Marshall and then finally, at about 10 a.m., report the accident at the police station." See "Ted Kennedy Car Accident in Chappaquiddick," *Newsweek.*

[7] Edward Kennedy reported the Chappaquiddick accident to Edgartown, Massachusetts, Police Chief Dominic J. Arena. See "Ted Kennedy Car Accident in Chappaquiddick," *Newsweek.*

[8] For a summary of the July 1969 car accident in which Mary Jo Kopechne died while a passenger in Edward Kennedy's car, and an analysis of the troubling inconsistencies emanating from the official investigation of the tragedy, see Lardner Jr., "Chappaquiddick, 1989."

Biographical Sketches of the Presidential Candidates (As of 1968)

THE DEMOCRATS

LYNDON B. JOHNSON: president of the United States. First elected to Congress in 1937, Johnson later served as U.S. Senate majority leader and vice president under John F. Kennedy. He succeeded to the presidency upon Kennedy's assassination in 1963. The following year, LBJ won a landslide election by beating his conservative Republican opponent Barry Goldwater in a 44-state rout. Soon thereafter, Johnson ordered U.S. combat forces into Vietnam in an effort to halt the spread of Soviet and Red Chinese-backed communists. By 1968, over 20,000 U.S. troops had died fighting there, and with no end in sight. As the war's unpopularity grew, finding a satisfactory resolution bedeviled the incumbent president as he prepared for his 1968 reelection race.

HUBERT H. HUMPHREY: vice president of the United States. A former mayor of Minneapolis, Humphrey won election to the U.S. Senate in 1948. One of the leading liberals in Congress throughout the 1950s and 1960s, he sponsored landmark legislation such as Medicare, the 1964 Civil Rights Act, the Peace Corps, and nuclear disarmament. When President Kennedy signed the 1963 Nuclear Test Ban Treaty, he gave Humphrey the pen as a souvenir and told him, "Hubert, this is your treaty. It had better work." Chosen by Johnson as his 1964 running mate, Humphrey remained a loyal vice president, but by 1968, he felt conflicted between private concerns over LBJ's Vietnam policies and personal loyalty to his leader.

ROBERT F. KENNEDY: U.S. senator from New York and younger brother of President John F. Kennedy. RFK served as Attorney General in JFK's administration. Despite a lengthy feud with, and a hatred for, Lyndon Johnson, in 1964 Kennedy hoped to maneuver himself onto the ticket as LBJ's running mate. After Johnson scotched that desire, Kennedy resigned from the Cabinet and won a U.S. Senate seat later that year. Although supportive of America's incursion into Vietnam initially, by 1968 RFK had adopted increasingly critical views of the war. Appealing to young and minority voters, and inheriting the large remnant of so-called "Camelot" sentimentalists, RFK stood as a potentially formidable challenger to Johnson's 1968 reelection.

EUGENE J. MCCARTHY: U.S. senator from Minnesota. A 20-year congressional veteran, McCarthy was more at home writing and reading poetry than engaging in the arcane rituals of lawmaking. Like almost every senator, McCarthy supported military action in Vietnam initially, but he soon became a vocal opponent. In late 1967, McCarthy tried to recruit a "peace" challenger to Johnson's expected 1968 Democratic presidential renomination campaign. When none materialized, he took upon himself the longshot effort.

THE REPUBLICANS

RICHARD NIXON: former vice president of the United States. Elected to the House of Representatives in 1946, Nixon gained national fame for exposing Alger Hiss, a high-ranking State Department official in the Roosevelt and Truman Administrations, as a Soviet agent. Winning a U.S. Senate seat in 1950, two years later Dwight D. Eisenhower tapped him (at age 39) as his running mate. After eight years as Ike's vice president, he lost the 1960 presidential election to John F. Kennedy by a whisker. Two years later, Nixon ran unsuccessfully for California governor. In a legendary concession speech, he announced the end of his political career by lashing out at the press and telling the assembled reporters, "You won't have Nixon to kick around anymore, because, gentlemen, this is my last press conference." Leaving California for New York and joining a white-shoe law firm, he traveled the world, wrote articles, and eased back into political life from his new East Coast base. In 1964, when many Republican leaders avoided campaigning with Barry Goldwater, Nixon stumped the country for the GOP nominee, covering 36 states and making more than 150 appearances on behalf of Republican candidates.[a] After Goldwater's overwhelming defeat, the Republican Party teetered on the verge of permanent minority status. However, during the 1966 midterm election campaign, Nixon became America's most peripatetic campaigner. He traveled 127,000 miles, visited 40 states, and delivered over 400 speeches for GOP candidates and Party organizations.[b] Republicans won stunning gains that November, picking up 47 House seats, three U.S. Senate seats, eight governorships, and 557 state legislative seats. Around the country, scores of winning and losing candidates credited Nixon for helping them when nobody else would. Not surprisingly, a large number of them would be delegates to the next Republican National Convention. As

---

a   Steven E. Ambrose, *Nixon* (Volume Two): The Triumph of a Politician 1962-1972 (1989), 56. See also Buchanan, *The Greatest Comeback*, 18.

b   Buchanan, *The Greatest Comeback*, 56, 96; Chester et al., *An American Melodrama,* 185; Richard Nixon, *RN: The Memoirs of Richard Nixon* (1978), 272; Ambrose, *Nixon* (Volume Two), 60.

1968 approached, Nixon remained popular with both establishment and rank-and-file Republicans. However, these same Party regulars also worried that he could not shed his loser image to stage a successful comeback.

NELSON A. ROCKEFELLER: elected to three terms as governor of New York,[c] heir to one of America's greatest fortunes, and the leader of the GOP's Eastern liberal wing. Rockefeller's public service dated back to the Franklin Roosevelt Administration. FDR tried to recruit "Rocky" to the Democratic Party unsuccessfully. In 1960, Rocky aborted his brief challenge to Nixon for the presidential nomination. In 1964, he sought the nomination again and battled Barry Goldwater in a nasty primary fight. After Goldwater defeated Rocky, the bitterness between the rival camps persisted. When Rocky tried to address the 1964 GOP convention, he suffered 16 minutes of booing. In the general election, Rocky endorsed "the entire Republican ticket," but he refused to endorse Goldwater specifically. LBJ massacred Goldwater, and furious conservative activists blamed Rockefeller for the stinging defeat. They never forgave him. However, by late 1967, many rank-and-file Republicans started giving Rocky a second look. After the Democrats trounced the 1964 GOP ticket, Republicans wanted a winner next time. With nagging concerns that Nixon was a perennial loser, and polls showing Rocky beating LBJ in head-to-head match-ups, 1968 looked like it could be his time.

RONALD REAGAN: newly elected governor of California. Although only in office since January 1967, Reagan was no stranger to voters. After a decades-long Hollywood career coupled with his ongoing political activism—first as an FDR Democrat, and later as a corporate spokesman for General Electric, Reagan gained political stardom for his 1964 nationally televised speech supporting Barry Goldwater. California Republicans recruited the former actor to challenge Democratic Governor Pat Brown, the man who beat Richard Nixon four years earlier. In 1966, Reagan trounced Brown for the California governorship by a million votes. Almost immediately after taking office in Sacramento, conservatives saw

---

c   Nelson Rockefeller won his fourth and final term as governor of New York in 1970.

the charismatic Reagan as an electable ideological heir to Goldwater. In 1968, with Rockefeller's Eastern support matching Reagan's phenomenal popularity in the South, Nixon feared a Rocky-Reagan cabal could stop his drive for the nomination. If that happened, it would set the stage for a California-New York convention duel for control of the Republican Party.

GEORGE ROMNEY: governor of Michigan. Romney embodied the Horatio Alger spirit: a devout Mormon missionary from a poor family who never finished college. As a young man, he took an entry-level job in the automobile industry. Later moving into management, he worked his way up the corporate ladder and became chairman of American Motors. In 1962, he won the first of three two-year terms as Michigan governor, and he was the only Republican statewide candidate that year to win in the heavily Democratic state. His overwhelming reelection victory in 1966 made him the early frontrunner for the GOP presidential nomination in 1968. Enjoying strong support with civil rights groups and union leaders, the moderate Romney had crossover appeal with independents and blue-collar Democrats.

THE WILD CARD

GEORGE C. WALLACE: former governor of Alabama. The poor farm boy from Clio, Alabama, won two state boxing titles while in high school. After working his way through college and law school, he entered the Army Air Corps and saw combat in World War II before returning home and becoming a prosecutor, a state legislator, and a circuit court judge. During an unsuccessful run for governor in 1958, Wallace's comparatively moderate views earned him the endorsement of the NAACP, while the Ku Klux Klan supported his opponent. Four years later, with federal court decisions ordering desegregation in the Deep South, Wallace ran again and challenged the U.S. Supreme Court's legal right to force its unelected will upon the states. Wallace campaigned in 1962 on a platform of preserving racial segregation and destroying the bloated and increasingly intrusive Washington bureaucracy. A *Saturday Evening Post* story related that Wallace "campaigned like a one-man army at war with the federal government."[d] Winning 96 percent of the vote (no Republican filed against him), Wallace proclaimed in his inaugural address, "I draw the line in the dust and toss the gauntlet before the feet of tyranny, and I say segregation now, segregation tomorrow, segregation forever." Early in his term, Wallace made his point defiantly: when Robert Kennedy's Justice Department sought to integrate the University of Alabama with federal troops, Wallace stood in front of the college's door and confronted Kennedy's deputy as cameras recorded the temporary standoff.[e] In 1964, Wallace entered three Democratic presidential primaries to test his populist message outside the South. Hammering away on states rights, a strong national defense, and law and order to combat violent racial and campus protests, Wallace showed surprising strength. Primary voters in Indiana, Wisconsin, and Maryland gave him 34 percent, 30 percent, and 43 percent, respectively. As 1968 approached, Wallace prepared another presidential run, this time as a third-party candidate leading his newly

d   Richard Pearson, "Former Ala. Gov. George C. Wallace Dies," *Washington Post*, September 14, 1998, A1, https://www.washingtonpost.com/wp-srv/politics/daily/sept98/wallace.htm (quoting the *Saturday Evening Post* story that Wallace "campaigned like a one-man army at war with the Federal government").

e   Wallace always maintained that his stand in the schoolhouse door at the University of Alabama was not based on racism, but rather to raise a constitutional sovereignty objection to federal encroachment over states rights. "I stirred the people up about the court system, not against black folks," Wallace said. "I said that the white and black people of Alabama can work these problems out themselves. We don't need the Justice Department to tell us everything to do and what time frame to use. We can do that ourselves in Alabama." Wallace's first press secretary, Bill Jones, said Wallace "knew that integration was coming.... He felt that the way to keep violence down and prepare the people to accept what they were going to have to accept was to say repeatedly—repeatedly: 'Let me do it, let me stand for you'—not only in the schoolhouse door, but in every way, such as in the courts and everything. He realized that he could be a catalyst for getting the thing accepted finally that he knew was going to be forced down the South's throat, whether they wanted it or not." In any event, Wallace later came to regret his "schoolhouse door" defiance, saying, "I made a very bad mistake in saying 'segregation forever'—[and] that day at the University of Alabama, carried nationwide [on radio and television], gave me a bad image and was not good for the state's image.... If I had it to do over, I would not have stood in the schoolhouse door at all; I would have prevented violence on campus in some other manner." As his biographer noted, "the irony of ironies—that within a year [of the schoolhouse door incident], Wallace's Alabama was integrating at the rate as fast as or faster than most other states in the Union, much less the South." Lesher, *George Wallace*, 167, 238, 240.

formed American Independent Party. The specter of an independent Wallace campaign worried both Republican and Democratic leaders. The GOP feared Wallace would siphon conservative votes from the South, while Democrats feared a hemorrhage of union and blue-collar voters from all regions to "Alabama's Fightin' Governor."

Chronology of the 1968 Presidential Campaign

1960   John F. Kennedy defeats Richard Nixon for the presidency.

1962   Nixon loses his race for California governor. He quits politics in a bitter farewell press conference.

1963   Lee Harvey Oswald assassinates Kennedy; Vice President Lyndon Johnson becomes president.

1964

July 15   Conservative U.S. Senator Barry Goldwater defeats liberal New York Governor Nelson Rockefeller for the Republican presidential nomination. Rockefeller refuses to endorse Goldwater publicly in the general election.

August 2   North Vietnamese gunboats fire on the USS Maddox in the Gulf of Tonkin. Two days later, the Maddox and the USS Turner Joy report coming under fire. Six days later, Congress passes the Tonkin Gulf Resolution, giving President Johnson authority to order an armed response to protect American forces in Vietnam. The Senate passes the resolution 88-2; the House passes it unanimously.

November 3   Johnson trounces Goldwater in the general election. Conservative Republicans blame Rockefeller for Goldwater's loss.

1965   Johnson begins escalating American military involvement in Vietnam, citing the Tonkin Gulf Resolution as his authority. He enjoys widespread public support.

1966   During a tough campaign for a third term as New York governor, Rockefeller promises the voters that if they reelected him, he will not run for president in 1968. He wins reelection in November.

Nixon stumps tirelessly for Republican candidates in the national midterm elections. When the GOP win significant gains on Election Day, Nixon gets credit for many of the unanticipated victories.

1967

November 18   Michigan Governor George Romney announces his candidacy for the Republican presidential nomination; Nelson Rockefeller endorses Romney and becomes his de facto campaign director.

November 30   Senator Eugene McCarthy announces he will enter the Democratic primaries and challenge President Johnson for the nomination.

1968

January 31   "The Tet Offensive": North Vietnam violates the Vietnamese New Year ("Tet") cease-fire and launches 70,000 troops against over 100 South Vietnamese cities, including the U.S. Embassy in Saigon. Although the offensive is repelled with relative ease, it takes several weeks to push back the enemy. Because of Tet, American public support for continued U.S. intervention in Vietnam begins to slide. Polls show an increasing disbelief in Pentagon and White House assurances about Vietnam. Two weeks after Tet, the Gallup Poll reports that 50 percent now disapprove of Johnson's handling of the war.

On that same day, at an off-the-record breakfast at the National Press Club in Washington, Senator Robert F. Kennedy says there are no "conceivable circumstances" under which he would challenge President Johnson for renomination. At the frantic urging of his press secretary, Kennedy changes the word "conceivable" to "foreseeable" before releasing the statement officially.

February 1   Richard Nixon announces his candidacy for the Republican presidential nomination and enters the New Hampshire primary.

February 8   Former Alabama Governor George Wallace announces his presidential candidacy under his newly created American Independent Party.

February 24   After endorsing Romney, Rockefeller mentions casually to a reporter he would accept a convention draft. The comment angers Romney, whose support continues to evaporate as his gaffe-plagued campaign limps along.

March 9   Faced with collapsing poll numbers, Romney withdraws from the presidential campaign three days before the New Hampshire primary.

March 10   Rockefeller (reconsidering his decision not to run for president) meets privately with key leaders and advisers.

March 12   The New Hampshire primary: thanks to thousands of college students invading the state as part of a grassroots effort, McCarthy stuns the political world by nearly defeating Johnson (LBJ was not on the ballot, but he won with write-in votes). Johnson's humiliating showing signals that his reelection effort may be jeopardized.

In the New Hampshire Republican primary, with Romney's withdrawal three days earlier, Nixon wins almost 78 percent of the GOP vote there.

March 13   The day after McCarthy's unexpectedly strong performance in New Hampshire, Robert Kennedy announces he is "reassessing" his decision not to run for president.

March 16   Kennedy announces his candidacy for the Democratic presidential nomination. His late entry infuriates McCarthy's antiwar supporters. They view Kennedy as an opportunist, a nakedly ambitious politician exploiting McCarthy's efforts, and one whose selfishness threatens to split the Democratic "peace vote."

March 21   Despite widespread speculation that he would enter the campaign, Rockefeller again announces he will not seek the Republican presidential nomination.

March 31   In a nationwide address, Johnson astonishes the nation by announcing that he will not seek reelection. This opens the way for Vice President Hubert Humphrey's entry into the race.

April 2   The Wisconsin primary: McCarthy sweeps the state with 56 percent of the Democratic vote.

April 4   James Earl Ray assassinates Dr. Martin Luther King Jr. in Memphis; riots break out in over 100 cities. Police arrest tens of thousands of rioters and looters, and scores of people die in the violence.

April 27   Humphrey announces his candidacy for the Democratic presidential nomination. His entry is too late to file for any primaries.

April 30   Changing his mind again, Rockefeller announces he will seek the Republican presidential nomination. His entry is too late to file for any primaries.

May 1   The day after he announces his candidacy (and without appearing on the ballot), Rockefeller wins all 34 convention delegates in the Massachusetts primary; Nixon and Massachusetts Governor John Volpe (running as a favorite son) receive zero delegates.

May 3   United States and North Vietnam agree to peace discussions in Paris beginning May 10.

May 14   Kennedy defeats McCarthy in the Nebraska primary; Nixon wins the GOP primary, beating both Ronald Reagan (whose name appeared on the ballot, although he had not declared his candidacy) and a Rockefeller write-in effort.

May 28   McCarthy beats Kennedy in the Oregon primary, making RFK the first Kennedy ever to lose an election. Kennedy tells friends he will withdraw from the race if he does not beat McCarthy in the upcoming California primary. Nixon wins the Oregon primary easily.

June 1   Seeking to shore up Southern delegates (and block any right-flank assault by a potential Reagan candidacy), Nixon meets with Senator Strom Thurmond of South Carolina, who endorses Nixon after the meeting. This support will have tremendous influence on Southern delegates to the GOP convention, as well as with Southern voters in the general election.

June 4-5   The California primary: shortly after midnight, Kennedy addresses supporters at the Ambassador Hotel in Los Angeles and claims victory over McCarthy. After his speech, Kennedy exits the stage; moments later, Sirhan Sirhan shoots him.

June 6   Kennedy dies.

August 5   The Republican National Convention opens in Miami. On that same day, Reagan announces he will seek the presidential nomination.

August 7   Nixon wins the Republican presidential nomination over rivals Rockefeller and Reagan; his margin of victory is a mere 25 votes. Nixon selects Maryland Governor Spiro Agnew as his running mate.

August 20   After several months of the Czechoslovakian "Prague Spring" and its growing democratic movement, the Soviet Union invades Czechoslovakia and crushes the revolt with over 200,000 Warsaw Pact troops.

August 26   The Democratic National Convention opens in Chicago. During the week, bloody riots and antiwar protests erupt. Americans watch on live television as the Chicago police put down the riots with nightsticks and tear gas. The violent confrontations shock America and cast a pall over the proceedings.

August 28   Humphrey wins the presidential nomination on the first ballot and selects Senator Edmund Muskie as his running mate.

September 30   After months of lagging poll numbers, Humphrey breaks with Johnson on Vietnam. In a speech at Salt Lake City, Humphrey announces that if elected, he will halt bombing North Vietnam to aid the peace process. Following this speech, many previously disaffected RFK and McCarthy voters return to the fold and support Humphrey.

October 3   George Wallace selects retired Air Force General Curtis LeMay as his running mate.

October 20   Former First Lady Jacqueline Kennedy (age 39), the widow of the slain president, shocks the world by marrying 62 year-old Aristotle Onassis, a Greek shipping magnate. She and her children move to Greece amid negative public opinion surrounding her remarriage.

October 31   As the presidential race between Nixon and Humphrey tightens, and with only five days until the election, President Johnson delivers a nationwide address and announces a bombing halt in North Vietnam, coupled with a major peace overture. This speech signals a possible end of the Vietnam War. After the speech, Humphrey pulls ahead of Nixon in the polls for the first time.

November 1   A few hours after Johnson's speech, South Vietnam announces it will not participate in the peace talks. This halts Humphrey's momentum amid confusion as to whether a peace settlement is imminent. LBJ privately blames Nixon and his campaign for interceding secretly with the South Vietnamese government to get them to boycott the peace negotiations.

November 5   In one of America's closest elections, Nixon defeats Humphrey by less than 500,000 votes out of 73 million cast. Third-party candidate Wallace wins five states and receives almost 14 million votes.

November 26   South Vietnam announces it will join the peace negotiations.

1969

January 20   Richard Nixon and Spiro Agnew become president and vice president of the United States.

1972

November 7   Despite a brewing scandal surrounding an attempted burglary in the offices of the Democratic National Committee at Washington, D.C.'s Watergate office complex, Nixon and Agnew win reelection in one of the largest landslides in history. The Republican ticket carries 49 states.

1973

October 10   Facing an indictment for tax fraud, bribery, and other felonies dating back to his years in Maryland politics, Vice President Agnew resigns. He pleads no contest to one count of failing to report income. Pursuant to a plea bargain, Agnew receives probation, a fine, and no jail time.

October 12   President Nixon nominates Congressman Gerald Ford as his new vice president. Both houses of Congress confirm Ford, who takes office on December 6.

1974   As a result of the Watergate scandal, and facing almost certain impeachment, Nixon resigns the presidency on August 9; Ford becomes president.

1976   Former California Governor Ronald Reagan challenges Ford for the 1976 GOP presidential nomination. In their convention showdown, Ford beats Reagan narrowly. In November, Ford loses the election in a close race to former Georgia Governor Jimmy Carter.

1980   Reagan wins the 1980 GOP presidential nomination; in November, he beats President Carter in a landslide.

Background on U.S. Military Involvement in Vietnam

Almost 50 years after U.S. involvement there ended, most Americans (when asked) still believe that Vietnam was a "bad" war, but they don't know why. Tell them the U.S. went in to stop the spread of communism and to blunt Soviet and Red Chinese domination in the region, and they blink in confusion. They don't know about the Soviet Union because that totalitarian empire crumbled 30 years ago. "Red" China? Is that like today's "red state-blue state" political distinctions?" Try explaining the "Domino Theory" (if South Vietnam fell to the communists, then surrounding countries might fall like a row of dominos) to a generation that never played dominos—or any other game not accessible on a video screen. To the "bad war" crowd, Vietnam was just bad and everyone knows it. What's your next question?

This simplistic approach is unsatisfactory because to understand the 1968 election and its continuing impact, a few paragraphs explaining why America fought in Vietnam will help since the battle for the presidency that year was in many ways a battle over Vietnam policy.

After a century of occupation by various countries, after World War II a peace agreement divided Vietnam into two states: the communist North and the democratic South. Later, the North attacked the South to force reunification under communist domination. The Soviet Union and Red China (so called in those days to distinguish it from the non-communist Republic of China, which the communists drove onto the island of Taiwan during their civil war in 1949) supported their fellow communists in the North. Since the South was ill equipped to defend itself against this troika, America faced two choices: let South Vietnam fall to the communists and risk the spread of totalitarianism in the region, or help.

America chose to help.

In the 1950s, President Eisenhower sent advisers. President Kennedy sent military personnel in the guise of more advisers. Combat operations began in 1964 under President Lyndon Johnson. After Northern communist guerillas reportedly firing on two U.S. ships, Congress voted for the Tonkin Gulf Resolution to authorize a limited armed response to aggression. During the next four years, Johnson treated it as a de facto declaration of war.

From 1965 until the end of his presidency, Johnson ordered his generals to attack the North, but to limit U.S. engagement with the communists to avoid provoking a military response from Red China (as happened in Korea in 1950). Johnson's policy was to squeeze the North into seeking peace, not to destroy them.

Vice President Humphrey recalled the night in 1966 when Johnson told neutralist Burmese President Ne Win that Johnson was doing everything he could for peace, and then LBJ asked why that goal continued to elude him. Win told LBJ, "What you are doing wrong is asking for peace. The North Vietnamese view that as a sign of weakness." Johnson insisted that, as president, he must do everything possible for peace. Win replied, "The North Vietnamese do not hear your peace overtures as an honest, legitimate desire for peace, but as weakness. You must make them believe there will be no peace until they are defeated. When they understand you are going to destroy them, then there will be peace."

Johnson shook his head: "I can't do that," he replied.[a] Thus, Lyndon Johnson's war of attrition doomed America's prospect for military success in the region.

Throughout most of his presidency, Johnson continued his Vietnam military policies with solid bipartisan congressional support. The first Democratic intraparty fissure occurred in the U.S. Senate on March 1, 1966, when Wayne Morse (D-OR) offered an amendment to repeal the Gulf of Tonkin Resolution. The Senate defeated the Morse amendment 92-5. Eugene McCarthy supported the amendment; Robert F. Kennedy voted to continue the war.[b] Even into late 1967, with Johnson expanding the war, the antiwar forces mustered a meager five votes in the Senate to end American involvement.

It was then that Eugene McCarthy challenged Johnson for the presidency on the platform of ending U.S. military action in Vietnam. When the Minnesota senator announced his candidacy in late November 1967, he trod a lonely road.

And then came 1968. . . .

a   Humphrey, *The Education of a Public Man*, 346.

b   Eugene McCarthy, *Up 'Til Now* (1987), 184.

BIBLIOGRAPHY

1968 Republican National Convention Telephone Directory and Guide. Miami: Systems Programing Services, Inc., 1968.

Abramson, Rudy. *Spanning the Century: The Life of W. Averell Harriman 1891-1986*. New York: William Morrow and Co., 1982.

Agnew, Spiro T. *Go Quietly... or Else*. New York: William Morrow and Co., 1980.

Alsop, Stewart. "Hubert Horatio Humphrey." *Saturday Evening Post*, August 24, 1968.

Ambrose, Stephen E. *Eisenhower: Soldier and President*. New York: Simon and Schuster Paperbacks, 1990.

Ambrose, Stephen E. *Nixon (Volume Two): The Triumph of a Politician* 1962-1972. New York: Simon and Schuster, 1989.

American Heritage New Dictionary of Cultural Literacy (Third Edition). Boston: Houghton Mifflin Company, 2005.

American Presidency Project, Papers of Lyndon B. Johnson. "Remarks at a Dinner of the Veterans of Foreign Wars." March 12, 1968. http://www.presidency.ucsb.edu/lyndon_johnson.php.

American Presidency Project, Papers of Lyndon B. Johnson. "Remarks at the Astrodome at a Democratic Party Rally." November 3, 1968. http://www.presidency.ucsb.edu/ws/?pid=29221.

Associated Press. "California Delegation's Resolution Forced His Hand, Reagan Claims." *Santa Cruz Sentinel*, Santa Cruz, California, August 6, 1968.

Associated Press. "Clark to Head McCarthy Bid for President." Fitchburg, Mass., *Sentinel*, December 13, 1967.

Associated Press. "Disappointed Md. Gov. Agnew to Review Draft Rocky Drive." *Cumberland News*, Cumberland, Maryland, March 22, 1968.

Associated Press. "Election Results Hint at Realignment." *North Adams Massachusetts Transcript*, May 2, 1968.

Associated Press. "Like a Space Shot, Pat [Nixon] Says." *Florence Morning News*, Florence, South Carolina, August 8, 1968.

Associated Press. "M'Carthy Urges LBJ to Campaign." *Bridgeport Post*, Bridgeport, Connecticut, March 13, 1968.

Associated Press. "Nixon Calls it 'Smashing Win.'" *Bridgeport Post*, Bridgeport, Connecticut, March 13, 1968.

Associated Press. "Nixon Holding Lead as Balloting Begins: Tabulation Shows Top Commitment." *Florence Morning News*, Florence, South Carolina, August 8, 1968.

Associated Press. "Reagan Will Run: Candidacy is Official." *The Lincoln Star*, Lincoln, Nebraska, August 6, 1968.

Associated Press. "Rockefeller Won't Seek Nomination: N.Y. Governor Leaves Door Open to Draft." *Cumberland News*, Cumberland, Maryland, March 22, 1968.

Associated Press. "Rocky Entry Sparks GOP Enthusiasm." *Salt Lake Tribune*, May 1, 1968.

Bibliography

Associated Press. "Rocky Still Backs Romney." *Independent*, Long Beach, California, February 2, 1968.

Associated Press. "Senator Gets 42% of Vote; President 48%." *Bridgeport Post*, Bridgeport, Connecticut, March 13, 1968.

Associated Press. "What They Said." *Post Crescent*, Appleton, Wisconsin, March 13, 1968.

Axelrod, Alan. *Patton: A Biography*. New York: St. Martin's Press, 2009.

Azbell, David. Facebook post, American Political Items Collectors page, July 18, 2014. https://www.facebook.com/groups/apicusa/search/?query=azbell%20wallace%20cigar.

Bass, Jack, and Marilyn W. Thompson. *Strom: The Complicated Personal and Political Life of Strom Thurmond*. New York: Public Affairs, 2005.

Bell, Jack, Associated Press. "LBJ Can Expect Rise in Fury of Criticism." *Bridgeport Post*, Bridgeport, Connecticut, March 13, 1968.

Bennett, Jim. "I Covered George Wallace's Presidential Races in the 60s." *Alabama Media Group*, March 16, 2016. http://www.al.com/opinion/index.ssf/2016/03/i_covered_george_wallaces_pres.html.

Billington, James H. *Respectfully Quoted: A Dictionary of Quotations*. Mineola, New York: Dover Publications, 2010.

Buchanan, Patrick J. *Nixon's White House Wars*. New York: Crown Forum, 2017.

Buchanan, Patrick J. *The Greatest Comeback: How Richard Nixon Rose from Defeat to Create the New Majority*. New York: Crown Forum, 2014.

Buckley, William F. Jr. *The Reagan I Knew*. New York: Basic Books, 2008.

Burka, Paul. "Presidential Hopefuls Juggle Appealing to the Common Man While Benefiting from Their Sizable Bank Accounts." *Los Angeles Times*, July 25, 2004.

Burke, Cathy. "Bobby Kennedy: Was Ronald Reagan's 'Supreme Villain.'" *Newsmax*, October 7, 2015. http://www.newsmax.com/Politics/Robert-Kennedy-Ronald-Reagan/2014/12/05/id/611395/.

Busby, Horace. *The Thirty-First of March: An Intimate Portrait of Lyndon Johnson's Final Days in Office*. New York: Farrar, Straus and Girioux, 2005.

Boyd, Joseph H. Jr., and Charles R. Holcomb. *Oreos & Dubonnet: Remembering Governor Nelson A. Rockefeller*. Albany: Excelsior Editions, 2012.

Cannon, Lou. "Actor, Governor, President, Icon." *Washington Post*, June 6, 2004. http://www.washingtonpost.com/wp-dyn/articles/A18329-2004Jun5.html.

Cannon, Lou. *Governor Reagan: His Rise to Power*. New York: Public Affairs, 2003.

Cannon, Lou. *Ronnie & Jesse: A Political Odyssey*. Garden City: Doubleday & Company, 1969.

Caro, Robert A. *The Years of Lyndon Johnson: The Passage of Power*. New York: Alfred A. Knopf, 2012.

Carter, Dan T. *The Politics of Rage: George Wallace, the Origins of the New Conservatism, and the Transformation of American Politics*. Baton Rouge. LSU Press Paperback Edition, 2000.

Chafets, Zev. *Roger Ailes Off Camera*. New York: Sentinel, 2013.

Chester, Lewis, Godfrey Hodgson, and Bruce Page. *An American Melodrama: The Presidential Campaign of 1968*. New York: Viking Press, 1969.

Chicago Tribune. "A Diary of Convention's Triumphs and Tragedies." September 8, 1968.

Chris' Hot Dog Stand. Facebook. https://www.facebook.com/ChrisHotDogs/about/.

Clarke, Thurston, *The Last Campaign: Robert F. Kennedy and the 82 Days that Inspired America*. New York: Henry Holt and Company, 2008.

Clifford, Clark. *Counsel to the President: A Memoir*. New York: Random House, 1991.

Cohodas, Nadine. *Strom Thurmond & The Politics of Southern Change*. New York: Simon & Schuster, 1993.

Bibliography

Conklin, Ellis. "Hospital Where Robert Kennedy Died Rich in Other History." UPI Archives, May 29, 1985. http://www.upi.com/Archives/1985/05/29/Hospital-where-Robert-Kennedy-died-rich-inother-history/4136486187200/.

Connally, John B., with Mickey Herskowitz. *In History's Shadow: An American Odyssey*. New York: Hyperion, 1993.

Cross, James U. *Around the World with LBJ: My Wild Ride as Air Force One Pilot, White House Aide, and Personal Confidant*. Austin: University of Texas Press, 2009.

Crowley, Monica. *Nixon Off the Record: His Candid Commentaries on People and Politics*. New York: Random House, 1996.

Dallek, Robert. *Flawed Giant: Lyndon Johnson and His Times 1961-1973*. New York: Oxford University Press, 1998.

David, Mark. "Rock It Like a Rockefeller." *Variety*, February 27, 2008. http://variety.com/2008/more/ real-estalker/rock-it-like-a-rockefeller-1201227746/.

Deaver, Michael K. *A Different Drummer: My Thirty Years with Ronald Reagan*. New York: HarperCollins, 2001.

DeFrank, Thomas M. *Write It When I'm Gone: Remarkable Off-the-Record Conversations with Gerald R. Ford*. New York: The Berkley Publishing Co., 2007.

de Toledano, Ralph. *R.F.K. The Man Who Would Be President*. New York: G.P. Putnam's Sons, 1967.

Dorley, Edward. United Press International. "Nixon Begins His Presidency Fight," *The Times*, San Mateo, California, February 2, 1968.

Duncan, David Douglas. *Self-Portrait U.S.A.* New York: Harry N. Abrams, Inc., 1969.

Dunlap, David W. "New York Says Farewell to American Bible Society, and Its Building." *New York Times*, October 21, 2015. http://www.nytimes.com/2015/10/22/nyregion/new-york-says-farewellto-american-bible-society-and-its-building.html.

Ehrlichman, John. *Witness to Power: The Nixon Years*. New York: Simon and Schuster, 1982.

Eleazer, Frank. United Press International. "Possibly Last Electoral College Meets to Formally Elect Nixon." *The Technician*, North Carolina State University at Raleigh, December 16, 1968.

Elmer, John, and William Fulton. "Rockefeller Begins Campaign in Miami." *Chicago Tribune*, August 4, 1968.

Encyclopedia of Television. "Kennedy-Nixon Presidential Debates, 1960." http://www.museum. tv/eotv/ kennedy-nixon.htm.

Eskew, Glenn T. "Lurleen B. Wallace (1967-1968)." Encyclopedia of Alabama, updated September 30, 2014. http://www.encyclopediaofalabama.org/article/h-1662.

Feldstein, Mark. *Poisoning the Press: Richard Nixon, Jack Anderson, and the Rise of Washington's Scandal Culture*. New York: Picador, 2010.

Frank, Jeffrey. *Ike and Dick: Portrait of a Strange Political Marriage*. New York: Simon and Schuster Paperbacks, 2013.

Freeburg, Russell. "Bartlett Withdraws, Indorses Nixon." *Chicago Tribune*, August 4, 1968.

Freeburg, Russell. "Rocky's 'Halt Nixon' Plan—Secret Hot Line to Reagan Camp Set Up at Parley: Staff Ordered to Shadow Leading GOP Figures." *Chicago Tribune*, August 4, 1968.

Garment, Leonard. *Crazy Rhythm: My Journey from Brooklyn, Jazz, and Wall Street to Nixon's White House, Watergate, and Beyond...* New York: Time Books, 1997.

Gentry, Curt. *J. Edgar Hoover: The Man and the Secrets*. New York: W.W. Norton & Company, 1991.

Goodwin, Richard N. *Remembering America: A Voice from the Sixties*. Boston: Little Brown and Company, 1988.

Griffin, Thomas. "The Nixon Era Begins: What the Election Wasn't About." *Life*, November 15, 1968.

Bibliography

Guthman, Edwin O., and Jeffrey Shulman, eds. *Robert Kennedy in His Own Words: The Unpublished Recollections of the Kennedy Years*. New York: Bantam Press, 1988.

Halberstam, David. *The Unfinished Odyssey of Robert Kennedy*. New York: Random House, 1969.
Healy, Patrick. "An Exclusive Club Gets Included." *New York Times*, July 27, 2008. http://www.nytimes.com/2008/07/27/weekinreview/27healy.html.
Herman, Arthur. *Joseph McCarthy: Re-Examining the Life and Legacy of America's Most Hated Senator*. New York: The Free Press, 2000.
Hersh, Burton. *Bobby and J. Edgar: The Historic Face-Off Between the Kennedys and J. Edgar Hoover That Transformed America*. New York: Carroll & Graf Publishers, 2007.
Herzog, Arthur. *McCarthy for President*. New York: Viking Press, 1969.
Hewitt, Hugh. *A Mormon in the White House? 10 Things Every American Should Know About Mitt Romney*. Washington: Regnery Publishing, Inc., 2007.
Heymann, C. David. *Bobby and Jackie: A Love Story*. New York: Atria Paperback, 2009.
Heymann, C. David. *RFK: A Candid Biography of Robert F. Kennedy*. New York: Dutton, 1998.
Hoeh, David C. *1968 • McCarthy • New Hampshire: "I Hear America Singing."* Rochester: Lone Oak Press, 1994.
Humphrey, Hubert H. *The Education of a Public Man: My Life and Politics*. New York: Doubleday & Co., Inc., 1976.

Janis, Ronald H. "Stop the Bombing Says Humphrey." *Harvard Crimson*, October 1, 1968. http://www.thecrimson.com/article/1968/10/1/stop-the-bombing-says-humphrey-pvice-president
Johnson, Lyndon B. *The Vantage Point: Perspectives of the Presidency 1963-1969*. New York: Holt, Rinehart and Winston, 1971.
Johnson, Sam Houston. *My Brother Lyndon*. New York: Cowles Book Company, 1970.
Jordan, Winthrop. *The Americans*. Boston: McDougal Littel, 1996.

Kampelman, Max M. *Entering New Worlds*. Norwalk: The Easton Press, 1991.
Kearns Goodwin, Doris. *Lyndon Johnson and the American Dream*. New York: Harper & Row, 1976.
Kengor, Paul. "The Great Forgotten Debate." *National Review*, May 22, 2007. http://www.nationalreview.com/article/220949/great-forgotten-debate-paul-kengor.
Kennedy, Edward M. *True Compass: A Memoir*. New York: Twelve/Hatchette Book Group, 2009.
Kennedy, John F. "America's Stakes in Vietnam." Speech to the American Friends of Vietnam, June 1956. https://en.wikipedia.org/wiki/Vietnam_War#cite_note-133.
Kilgore, Ed. "The Ghost of Curtis LeMay." *Washington Monthly*, December 4, 2013. http://washingtonmonthly.com/2013/12/04/the-ghost-of-curtis-lemay/
King, Martin Luther, Jr. *The Autobiography of Martin Luther King, Jr.* (Chapter 15, Stanford University Libraries) https://swap.stanford.edu/20141218230019/http://mlk-kpp01.stanford.edu/kingweb/ publications/autobiography/chp_15.htm.
Kopelson, Gene. *Reagan's 1968 Dress Rehearsal: Ike, RFK, and Reagan's Emergence as a World Statesman*. Los Angeles: Figueroa Press, 2016.

Langer, Emily. "Robert L. Hardesty, Speechwriter for President Lyndon B. Johnson, Dies at 82." *Washington Post*, July 9, 2013. https://www.washingtonpost.com/national/robert-l-hardestyspeechwriter-for-president-lyndon-b-johnson-dies-at-82/2013/07/09/907f1834-e8b8-11e2-8f22de4bd2a2bd39_story.html.
Lardner, George Jr. "Chappaquiddick, 1989." *Washington Post*, July 16, 1989. https://www.washingtonpost.com/archive/opinions/1989/07/16/chappaquiddick-1989/28d50758-314b-49e190bd-78eb8fddf64f/.

Bibliography

Larner, Jeremy. *"Nobody Knows: Reflections on the McCarthy Campaign of 1968."* New York: Macmillan, 1970.

Lawrence Berkeley National Laboratories Image Library, Collection: Berkeley-Lab/Seaborg-Archive. "Breakfast at Owls Nest Camp, Bohemian Grove, July 23, 1967." http://imglib.lbl.gov/ImgLib/ COLLECTIONS/BERKELEY-LAB/SEABORG-ARCHIVE/index/96B05411.html.

LeMay, Curtis. Interview with the *Washington Post*, October 4, 1968.

Lesher, Stephen. *George Wallace: American Populist*. New York: Addison-Wesley Publishing Co., 1994.

Lewis, Joseph. *What Makes Reagan Run?* New York: McGraw-Hill 1968.

Life. "The Bomb Halt Decision." November 15, 1968

Mailer, Norman. *Miami and the Siege of Chicago*, New York: Random House, 1968 (2016 trade paperback edition).

Mankiewicz, Frank. "Nofziger: A Friend With Whom It Was A Pleasure To Disagree." *Washington Post*, March 29, 2006. http://www.washingtonpost.com/wp-dyn/content/article/2006/03/28/ AR2006032802142.html.

Marlin, George J. "Is Trump Repeating George Wallace's '68 Disaster?" *Newsmax*, November 7, 2016. http://www.newsmax.com/George-J-Marlin/george-marlin-george-wallace-1968-cautionarytale/2016/06/11/id/733409/.

McCarthy, Eugene J. *The Year of the People*. Garden City: Doubleday and Company, Inc., 1969.

McCarthy, Eugene J. *Up 'Til Now*. New York: Harcourt Brace Jovanovich, 1987.

McGowan, Tom. *The 1968 Democratic Convention*. New York: Children's Press, 2003.

Mears, Walter R. Associated Press. "McCarthy 4,000 Votes Behind Johnson." *Post Crescent*, Appleton, Wisconsin, March 13, 1968.

Mecham, E.L. Letter to the author, July 3, 1991.

Meese, Edwin III. *With Reagan: The Inside Story*. Washington: Regnery Gateway, 1992.

Moldea, Dan E. *The Killing of Robert F. Kennedy: An Investigation of Motive, Means, and Opportunity*. New York: W.W. Norton & Company, 1995.

Mondale, Walter F. *The Good Fight: A Life in Liberal Politics*. New York: Scribner, 2010.

Montgomery, Gayle B., and James W. Johnson. *One Step from the White House: The Rise and Fall of Senator William F. Knowland*. Los Angeles: University of California Press, 1998.

Morin, Relman. Associated Press. "Rocky Reverses—'In Race to Win.'" *Salt Lake Tribune*, May 1, 1968.

Morris, Edmund. *Dutch: A Memoir of Ronald Reagan*. New York: Random House, 1999.

Muskie, Edmund S. *Journeys*. New York: Doubleday & Co., 1972.

Narvaez, Alfonso. "Gen. Curtis LeMay, an Architect Of Strategic Air Power, Dies at 83." *New York Times*, October 2, 1990. http://www.nytimes.com/1990/10/02/obituaries/gen-curtis-lemay-anarchitect-of-strategic-air-power-dies-at-83.html.

New Hampshire Union Leader. "1968: McCarthy Stuns the President." May 3, 2011. http://www. unionleader.com/apps/pbcs.dll/article?AID=/99999999/NEWS0605/110509966.

Newsweek. "Ted Kennedy Car Accident in Chappaquiddick," August 3, 1969. http://www. newsweek.com/ted-kennedy-car-accident-chappaquiddick-207070.

Newsweek. "The Ronnie-Bobby Show." May 29, 1967.

Nixon, Richard. *RN: The Memoirs of Richard Nixon*. New York: Grosset & Dunlap, 1978.

Nixon, Richard. *RN: The Memoirs of Richard Nixon*. New York: Simon & Schuster, 1990.

Noah, Timothy. "The Legend of Strom's Remorse." *Slate*, December 16, 2002. http://www.slate. com/articles/news_and_politics/chatterbox/2002/12/the_legend_of_stroms_remorse.html.

Nofziger, Lyn. *Nofziger*. Washington: Regnery Gateway, 1992.

Bibliography

Noguchi, Dr. Thomas T. Los Angeles County Chief Medical Examiner-Coroner, Autopsy Report on Robert F. Kennedy, Case #68-5731, Second Rough Draft, September 20, 1968.

O'Brien, Lawrence F. *No Final Victories: A Life in Politics from John F. Kennedy to Watergate.* New York: Doubleday & Company, Inc., 1974.

O'Donnell, Kenneth P., and David F. Powers (with Joe McCarthy). *Johnny, We Hardly Knew Ye* Boston: Little, Brown and Co., 1972.

Official Program. The *Twenty-Ninth Republican National Convention.* New York: Wickersham Press, Inc., 1968.

Official Report of the Proceedings of the Twenty-Ninth Republican National Convention Held in Miami Beach, Florida. Republican National Committee, 1968.

O'Neill, Tip, and William Novak. *Man of the House.* New York: Random House, 1987.

Only in Our State. "These 8 Amazing Alabama Restaurants are Loaded with Local History." http://www. onlyinyourstate.com/alabama/historical-restaurants-al/.

Pearson, Drew, and Tyler Abell, ed. *Diaries 1949-1959.* New York: Holt, Rinehart and Winston, 1974.

Pearson, Drew, and Peter Hannaford, ed. *Washington Merry-Go-Round: The Drew Pearson Diaries, 1960-1969.* Lincoln: Potomac Books, 2015.

Persico, Joseph E. *The Imperial Rockefeller: A Biography of Nelson A. Rockefeller.* New York: Simon & Schuster, 1982.

Price, Raymond. *With Nixon.* New York: The Viking Press, 1977.

Public Broadcasting Service (PBS). "The American Experience: George Wallace—Settin' the Woods on Fire," Program Transcript. http://www.pbs.org/wgbh/amex/wallace/filmmore/transcript/ transcript1.html.

Public Broadcasting Service (PBS). "The American Experience: The 1964 Republican Campaign." http:// www.pbs.org/wgbh/americanexperience/features/general-article/rockefellers-campaign/.

Public Papers of the Presidents of the United States: Lyndon B. Johnson, 1968-69, Volume II. (Washington: Government Printing Office, 1970).

Roberts, Sam. "Curtis Gans, 77, is Dead; Worked to Defeat President Johnson." *New York Times*, March 16, 2015. http://www.nytimes.com/2015/03/17/us/curtis-gans-77-is-dead-worked-to-deposepresident-johnson.html.

Rogan, James E. *"And Then I Met… Stories of Growing Up, Meeting Famous People, and Annoying the Hell Out of Them."* Washington, DC: WND Books, 2014.

Rosenberg, Jonathan, and Zachary Karabell. *Kennedy, Johnson, and the Quest for Justice: The Civil Rights Tapes.* New York: WW Norton & Co., 2003.

Salinger, Pierre. *P.S. A Memoir.* New York: St. Martin's Press, 1995.

Schlesinger, Arthur M. Jr. *Journals 1952-2000.* New York: Penguin Books, 2007.

Schlesinger, Arthur M. Jr. *Robert Kennedy and His Times.* Boston: Houghton Mifflin Co., 1978.

Sherman, Norman. *From Nowhere to Somewhere—My Political Journey: A Memoir of Sorts.* Minneapolis: First Avenue Editions, 2016.

Shesol, Jeff. *Mutual Contempt: Lyndon Johnson, Robert Kennedy, and the Feud that Defined a Decade.* New York: W.W. Norton & Company, 1997.

Smith, Richard Norton. *On His Own Terms: A Life of Nelson Rockefeller.* New York: Random House, 2014.

Smith, Stephen, and Kate Ellis. "Campaign '68: Timeline of the 1968 Campaign." *American Radio Works*, American Public Media. http://americanradioworks.publicradio.org/features/campaign68/timeline.html.

Sorensen, Theodore C. *Counselor: A Life at the Edge of History*. New York: HarperCollins, 2008.

Sorensen, Theodore C. *The Kennedy Legacy*. New York: Macmillan, 1969.

Spectator. "Duty of a Prime Minister." February 19, 1942.

Stavis, Ben. *We Were the Campaign: New Hampshire to Chicago for McCarthy*. Boston: Beacon Press, 1969.

Steel, Ronald. *In Love with the Night: The American Romance with Robert Kennedy*. New York: Simon and Schuster, 2000.

Stepman, Jarrett. "Why We Use Electoral College, Not Popular Vote." *The Daily Signal*, November 7, 2016. http://dailysignal.com/2016/11/07/why-the-founders-created-the-electoral-college/.

Stone, Roger. *Nixon's Secrets*. New York: Skyhorse Publishing, 2014.

Sullivan, William C., and Bill Brown. *The Bureau: My Thirty Years in Hoover's FBI*. New York: W.W. Norton & Company, 1979.

Thomas, Evan. *Robert Kennedy: His Life*. New York: Simon & Schuster, 2000.

Thomas, Robert McG. Jr. John W. King, 79, Governor Who Instituted State Lottery. *New York Times*, August 14, 1996.

Time. "Anchors Aweigh," October 20, 1967.

Time. "General Nguyen Ngoc Loan," July 27, 1998.

Time. "In Unpath'd Waters," October 27, 1967.

Time. "Romney Rediyivus," January 26, 1968.

Time. "The Brainwashed Candidate," September 15, 1967.

Time. "The Tenacious Muckraker," September 12, 1969.

Torry, Jack. "Don't Blame Nixon for Scuttled Peace Overture." *Real Clear Politics*, August 9, 2015. http://www.realclearpolitics.com/articles/2015/08/09/dont_blame_nixon_for_scuttled_peace_ overture_127667.html

Town Meeting of the World. "The Image of America and the Youth of the World with Senator Robert F. Kennedy and Governor Ronald Reagan," as broadcast over the CBS television and radio network May 15, 1967, Charles Collingwood, moderator. http://reagan2020.us/speeches/reagan_kennedy_ debate.asp.

Tribe, Laurence H., and Thomas M. Rollins. "Deadlock," *Atlantic Monthly*, October 1980, http://www. theatlantic.com/past/docs/issues/80oct/deadlock.htm.

Trohan, Walter. "Final Campaigns are Opened for Nomination," *Chicago Tribune*, August 4, 1968.

Turner, Robert L. "Eugene McCarthy Confidently Predicts Victory at Fenway," *Boston Globe*, July 26, 1968.

United Press International. "Decision Hard Blow to Rocky Backers," *Cumberland News*, Cumberland, Maryland, March 22, 1968.

United Press International. "GOP Convention Opens Amid Fast and Furious Politicking," *Panama City News-Herald*, Panama City, Florida, August 6, 1968.

United Press International. "Kennedy 'Reconsidering' His Role in 1968 Election," *Bridgeport Post*, Bridgeport, Connecticut, March 13, 1968.

United Press International. "Nixon, Aides to Spend 10 Days in San Diego," *Chicago Tribune*, Chicago, Illinois, August 9, 1968.

United Press International. "Wallace Through? Nixon Points Up," *Kingsport Times-News*, Kingsport, Tennessee, June 2, 1968.

United States House of Representatives, Office of Art and Archives, Electoral College Fast Facts. http:// history.house.gov/Institution/Electoral-College/Electoral-College/.

Updegrove, Mark K. *Indomitable Will: LBJ in the Presidency*. New York: Skyhorse Publishing, 2014)

Bibliography

Valenti, Jack. *A Very Human President*. New York: W.W. Norton & Company, 1975.

Van Dyk, Ted. *Heroes, Hacks & Fools: Memoirs from the Political Inside*. Seattle and London: University of Washington Press, 2007.

Visitor: The Resort Magazine of South Florida, Souvenir Edition, 1968 Republican National Convention. Miami Beach: The Visitor Publishing Company, 1968.

Wainstock, Dennis D. *Election Year 1968: The Turning Point*. New York: Enigma Books, 2012.

Wallace-Wells, Benjamin. George Romney for President, 1968. *New York* magazine, May 20, 2012. http://nymag.com/news/features/george-romney-2012-5/.

Washington Merry-Go-Round. "History of the Column." http://washingtonmerrygoround.com/history-of-column/.

Washington-Williams, Essie Mae. *Dear Senator: A Memoir by the Daughter of Strom Thurmond*. New York: HarperCollins, 2005.

Welna, David. "Strom Thurmond at 100: Colorful South Carolinian Set Record as Oldest Living U.S. Senator," *National Public Radio*, December 5, 2002. http://www.npr.org/templates/story/story. php?storyId=865900.

Whalen, Richard J. *Catch the Falling Flag: A Republican's Challenge to His Party*. Boston: Houghton Mifflin Company, 1972.

White, F. Clifton, and Jerome Tuccille. *Politics as a Noble Calling: The Memoirs of F. Clifton White*. Ottawa: Jameson Books, 1994.

White, F. Clifton, and William J. Gill. *Why Reagan Won: The Conservative Movement 1964-1981*. Chicago: Regnery Gateway, 1981.

White, Theodore H. *The Making of the President 1968*. New York: Atheneum Publishers, 1969.

Wicker, Tom. "Nixon Makes a New Gain as Republicans Convene; Reagan Avows Candidacy; Drops Favorite Son Role," *New York Times*, August 6, 1968. https://partners.nytimes.com/library/politics/ camp/680806convention-gop-ra.html.

Wikipedia. "1968 in Television." https://en.wikipedia.org/wiki/1968_in_television.

Wikipedia. "Don Hewitt." https://en.wikipedia.org/wiki/Don_Hewitt/.

Wikipedia. "Federal Bureau of Investigation." https://en.wikipedia.org/wiki/Federal_Bureau_of_Investigation.

Wikipedia. "FBI Television Series." https://en.wikipedia.org/wiki/The_F.B.I._(TV_series).

Wikipedia. "Gridiron Club." https://en.wikipedia.org/wiki/Gridiron_Club.

Wikipedia. "Toots Shor's Restaurant." https://en.wikipedia.org/wiki/Toots_Shor%27s_Restaurant.

Wikipedia. "Wentworth by the Sea." https://en.wikipedia.org/wiki/Wentworth_by_the_Sea.

Wilkens, John. "RFK's Legacy Looms on the 50th Anniversary of His Assassination," the *San Diego Union-Tribune*, June 3, 2018, https://www.sandiegouniontribune.com/news/politics/sd-me-rfk-anniversary-20180531-story.html.

Witcover, Jules. *85 Days: The Last Campaign of Robert Kennedy*. New York: Putnam, 1969.

Witcover, Jules. *Very Strange Bedfellows: The Short and Unhappy Marriage of Richard Nixon and Spiro Agnew*. New York: Public Affairs, 2007.

Wolff, Natasha. "Room Request! Gurney's Montauk Resort & Seawater Spa, DuJour Newsletter." http:// dujour.com/lifestyle/room-request-gurneys-montauk-resort-seawater-spa/.

Zelizer, Barbie. *About to Die: How News Images Move the Public*. New York: Oxford University Press, 2010.

ACKNOWLEDGMENTS

The author's original notes that he made during lunch and on which he outlined his idea for writing *On to Chicago*, August 19, 2015.

Over my lunch hour on August 19, 2015, I sat alone at a small window table at the Stadium Tavern (now Fullerton Brew Co.) in Fullerton, California and ordered a burger. I looked forward to my upcoming vacation during which I planned to write the sequel to my third book, *And Then I Met… Stories of Growing Up, Meeting Famous People, and Annoying the Hell Out of Them.* Somewhere between the delivery of the food and my first bite, and from out of nowhere, came the inspiration for *On to Chicago: Rediscovering Robert F. Kennedy and the Lost Campaign of 1968.*

While my food grew cold, I sketched the entire outline for this story on the four note cards depicted on the previous page. Over the next 16 months, researching and writing *On to Chicago* became my mistress. As for my intended sequel to *And Then I Met*, that had to wait another five years. It released in December 2020 under the title, *Shaking Hands with History: My Encounters with the Famous, the Infamous, and the Once-Famous but Now-Forgotten.*

With this latest project now completed, I will resume work on my seventh book, tentatively titled *Look Mom, I'm a Congressman! (And Other Shames I Brought on My Family).* If the Lord tarries, watch for it sometime in 2022 or 2023—depending on my ability to grab snatches of quiet time for writing.

* * *

With *The Notes,* I am again reunited with two tremendous artists and friends. My deepest thanks to editorial director Geoff Stone and creative director Mark Karis. Thanks also to old friend and WND founder, Joseph Farah, for publishing *On to Chicago* in 2018 even though no other publisher wanted to gamble on my newly invented genre of fact-based "nonfiction fiction."

My wife, Christine, tolerates my writing clutter each time I embark on a new book. I remain *forever yors* [sic], which is the inscription on my wedding ring thanks to an illiterate Nordstrom jewelry engraver. Love and hugs to my daughters Dana and Claire, and to granddaughters Ellie Grace and Ava. I pray that all of you will keep Jesus in your hearts.

Lastly, my thanks to those of you who read *On to Chicago* and *The Notes*. Through your imagination, and after a half-century wait, Robert F. Kennedy completed his journey.

SENATOR ROBERT F. KENNEDY

Photograph signed during the 1968 California presidential primary

(Author's collection)

PRESIDENT AND MRS. LYNDON B. JOHNSON

Photograph signed for the author, 1969

VICE PRESIDENT HUBERT H. HUMPHREY

Photograph signed for the author, February 19, 1971

SENATOR EUGENE J. MCCARTHY

Photograph signed for the author, June 27, 1970

FORMER VICE PRESIDENT RICHARD M. NIXON

Photograph signed for the author, April 13, 1978

GOVERNOR RONALD REAGAN

Photograph signed for the author, July 30, 1970

GOVERNOR NELSON A. ROCKEFELLER

Photograph signed for the author, December 20, 1971

GOVERNOR GEORGE ROMNEY

Photograph signed for the author, December 22, 1972

GOVERNOR GEORGE WALLACE

Photograph signed for the author, January 3, 1972

www.ingramcontent.com/pod-product-compliance
Lightning Source LLC
Chambersburg PA
CBHW062111020426
42335CB00013B/927